The American West in Fiction

THE AMERICAN WEST IN FICTION

Edited and with a
General Introduction and Prefaces

BY

JON TUSKA

University of Nebraska Press
Lincoln and London

Manufactured in the United States of America

First Bison Book printing: 1988
Most recent printing indicated by the first digit below:
1 2 3 4 5 6 7 8 9 10

Library of Congress Cataloging-in-Publication Data

The American West in fiction / edited and with general introduction and prefaces by Jon Tuska.
p. cm.
"Bison."
Bibliography: p.
ISBN 0-8032-4417-7. ISBN 0-8032-9412-3 (pbk.)
1. Western stories. I. Tuska, Jon.
PS648.W4A53 1988
813'.0874'08—dc 19 88-11080 CIP

Reprinted by arrangement with Jon Tuska

ACKNOWLEDGMENTS

BELLAH, James Warner: "Massacre." Reprinted by permission of the estate of James Warner Bellah.

BRAND, Max: "Wine on the Desert," Reprinted by permission of Dodd, Mead & Company, Inc., from *Max Brand's Best Western Stories,* edited and with a Biographical Introduction by William F. Nolan. Copyright 1936 by Frederick Faust. Copyright renewed 1964 by Judith Faust, Jane F. Easton, and John Frederick Faust.

CAPPS, Benjamin: "The Slaughter." Reprinted by permission of the author. Copyright 1965 by Benjamin Capps.

CATHER, Willa: "The Wild Land" from *O Pioneers!* by Willa Cather. Reprinted by permission of Houghton Mifflin Company. Copyright 1913 and 1941 by Willa Sibert Cather.

CLARK, Walter Van Tilburg: "The Wind and Snow of Winter" from *The Watchful Gods and Other Stories*. Reprinted by permission of International Creative Management. Copyright 1944 by Walter Van Tilburg Clark. Copyright renewed 1972 by Robert M. Clark.

EVANS, Max: "Candles in the Bottom of the Pool," first published in the *South Dakota Review,* Autumn 1973. Reprinted by permission of the editor.

GREY, Zane: "The Desert Crucible" from *The Rainbow Trail*. Copyright 1915 by Harper & Brothers. Renewed 1943 in the name of Lina Elise Grey.

Contents

General Introduction

1

On a trip I made some time ago to Mexico, one of the books I took along for the journey was John R. Milton's *The Novel of the American West* (University of Nebraska Press, 1980). Now I must confess to the reader, as I have already to Professor Milton in the letters we have exchanged, that I find his definition of what constitutes legitimate Western American fiction too narrow and forbidding. Having surveyed the entire field of fiction set in the American West, he excluded many who I would insist made a definite and genuine literary contribution; indeed, with the exceptions of Walter Van Tilburg Clark and Max Evans, he excluded every author whose name appears in this anthology. Notwithstanding, I enjoyed Milton's book, primarily for what it does have to say about authors who I agree have enriched our American literature. Moreover, he raised a point which I feel is essential to any understanding of the nature and intention of Western fiction. "To continue reviving the past in order to maintain a belief that 'those were the good old days' is an act of nostalgia which is eventually self-defeating," he wrote in a chapter he titled "The Writer's West." "However, if we consider memory of the past to be spiritual as it conquers historical time, we then think not of a conserving memory, not of nostalgia, but of a creatively transfiguring memory, not static but dynamic, its purpose to keep what is alive for future generations." To this, I would add my own belief that there has to be a reason for setting a story or a novel in the American West. The land must be a character, and beyond that, the land must influence the characters, physically and spiritually.

For centuries the European has known what Professor Milton called the power of a creatively transfiguring memory. Just how much was brought home to me by another book I took along and which I read next, Heinrich Heine's *Die Götter im Exil* [The Gods in Exile], a book which Heine first published in 1836 and then had reissued in a new edition during the years of his own exile in Paris. There is a passage at the beginning of his book which portrays a German knight, a hero from the Northland on a pilgrimage to Italy, espying a statue from classical antiquity. In my own translation, it reads:

> It is perhaps the Goddess of Beauty, and he stands face to face across from her, and the heart of the young barbarian becomes secretly seized by the old magic. What is it? Such tapering limbs he has never seen before and in this marble he senses a vitalizing life, as he had found formerly in the red cheeks and lips and in the consummate physical sensuality of the peasant women of his own region. These white eyes regard him, seeming so filled with delight and yet at the same time so possessed by sadness that his breast fills with both love and compassion, compassion and love.

For Heine, as for a number of other Europeans, the gods and goddesses of antiquity, or at least their spirits, have never really died; they have only gone into hiding. Just how and where and what they were doing in 1836 is the subject of *Die Götter im Exil.* Heine rejected the traditional Judaism of his family and he could never embrace Christianity, but his soul found sustenance in the creatively transfiguring memory of antiquity. The last time he was still able to walk under his own motion, he went to the Louvre and he broke down weeping before the feet of *Venus de Milo*. The spirit of Venus had a special meaning, a reality of her own for Heine.

When the European is inclined to seek an alternative culture, he has the varied heritage of century upon century from which to draw. If he does not like one culture, he can readily choose another. The American is even more fortunate—he has the combined experiences of dozens of cultures transposed to the New World as well as the cultures of hundreds of tribes of native Americans. Yet, despite this embarrassment of riches, there are all too many Americans who are only able to look back toward Europe with love and yearning. In the words of an editor at a large New York publishing house who was shocked to learn that I lived in Oregon: "But doesn't civilization end at the Jersey border?" However, for me, and I would hope that I am not alone, culture, like civilization, is a nebulous word and should never be associated with a place, *any* place. It is, to the contrary, descriptive of an inner state.

The European was very early shaped by an urban culture. Elysium, the Islands of the Blest in the Western Ocean, along with the Garden of Eden of the Semites, was replaced quickly enough by the city state, the grandeur of Rome in the Augustan age, St. John's New Jerusalem, and St. Augustine's City of God. But Americans have still the option to have both, just as I can sit in my living room of a night and listen to a recording of a Mozart string quartet or go out and walk with my dog the short distance from my home to the shore of the Willamette River and listen to a beaver slap his tail against the current because he has heard our approach. The American has had an unique kind of love affair, one Willa Cather evoked in her story "The Wild Land" when she wrote of her character, Alexandra, that

> For the first time, perhaps, since that land emerged from the waters of geologic ages, a human face was set toward it with love and yearning. It seemed beautiful to her, rich and strong and glorious. Her eyes drank in the breadth of it, until her tears blinded her. Then the Genius of the Divide, the great, free spirit which breathes across it, must have bent lower than it ever bent to a human will before. The history of every country begins in the heart of a man or a woman.

And so, too, the history of a culture.

However divergent from each other they may have been or may continue to be, the multitudinous American cultures underwent a common fate, what historians call the American frontier experience. It did, of course, mean something different to almost every person who underwent it, as it has to virtually everyone who has come to write about it; but it is this unifying notion—the American frontier experience—which is at the heart of all the fiction I have assembled for this collection, the American frontier experience as it applies to the opening of the West and to the American West as it exists today and as it will exist tomorrow.

2

Before going farther, there is a distinction I should like to make regarding the *types* of Western fiction. I have found it convenient to divide Western novels and stories into two general categories, the formulary Western and the historical reconstruction. Between these two, there is a third, partial category, since it draws something from each: the romantic historical reconstruction. Because it is the most familiar, I should like to comment first on formulary Western fiction.

Frederick D. Glidden, who as Luke Short wrote some of the best formulary Westerns, once told author Brian Garfield that a good Western is first of all a good story and should be able to stand on its own merits no matter where it is set. Glidden wanted Garfield to know that a Western isn't all gunplay and horsemanship. However, what Glidden was saying has an even greater implication: in the formulary Western as Glidden wrote it, the Western setting is altogether irrelevant. This is borne out in the posthumous tribute Glidden paid Ernest Haycox in *The Call Number* (Fall 1963–Spring 1964). ". . . My favorite Haycox yarns don't lean on a known time or place," Glidden wrote. "In these stories, I suspect Haycox made his own geography, named his own towns and mountains and rivers; he peopled them with tough and abrasive characters whose only law was their self-will." The world of the formulary Western is, therefore, a world of total make-believe; what charm it has is derived from the fact that it can never intersect with the real world.

Once this premise is accepted, it then becomes possible to approach critically each formulary author and, by reading his (or in a few cases her) Western stories, to reconstruct and compare the various make-believe worlds uniquely true for each one of these authors. One is also free to speculate about innovations and who influenced whom, never forgetting that while the terrain may have a Western appearance the topography is imaginary and the characters components of a ritualized, conventionalized, and collective fantasy the sole function of which is to divert us from our lives and never to touch in any way the depths of the soul. As Hoot Gibson, a movie cowboy, once put it to me, "People like Westerns because they always know who's gonna win." Then he smiled, a bit sadly because he had had a bitter and hard time of it. "But," he added, "it ain't that way in life." The formulary Western has always been popular with a certain kind of reader, the reader who prefers always to know beforehand how the story must come out.

C. G. Jung developed a concept in his book *Zwei Schriften über Analytische Psychologie* [*Two Essays on Analytical Psychology*] (Rascher Verlag, 1967) that I think might be helpful in understanding the meaning of the formulary Western.

The concept is that of the *mana-personality*, an archetype of the collective unconscious, "a being filled with an occult, conjuring capacity, or mana, and endowed with magical skills and powers." In the chapter Jung devoted to this phenomenon, he felt compelled to warn:

> One can only alter his attitude in an effort to impede being naively possessed by an archetype that forces him to play a role at the cost of his humanity. Possession by an archetype makes a man into a purely collective figure, after the fashion of a mask, behind which his humanity can no longer develop, but rather increasingly atrophies. One must remain conscious of the danger of falling beneath the dominant of the mana-personality. The danger consists not merely in the fact that one person assumes the mask of a father figure but that that person can fall victim to the same mask when it's worn by another person. In this sense, master and pupil are one and the same.

Expressed in other words and applied to the subject at hand: if we allow ourselves to believe in the existence of Western heroes, we will attempt frequently to emulate in ourselves the values we have projected onto them; and when we do this, we become, as they, purely collective figures, and our humanity atrophies. Nothing serves as a better illustration of this process than the development of the formulary Western in the twentieth century.

The mana of the formulary Western has already been described in Glidden's encomium for Ernest Haycox. It is the Western hero's virtuous and triumphantly superior self-will. In the unfolding of the ritualized, violent competitiveness between the degrees of self-willedness, from Owen Wister's *The Virginian* (Macmillan, 1902) to the ultraviolent series Westerns today, the heroine must become as dehumanized and as convinced of the efficacy of violence as the only solution to social frustration as is the hero. Accepting the Virginian as a hero requires of heroine Molly Stark Wood that she condone the Virginian's placing property before friendship through his participation in the execution of his friend Steve and that, in order for the Virginian to maintain his status as a hero in the community, he must shoot and kill Trampas. The Virginian set the tone for the formulary Western hero. He might be a gunfighter like Lassiter in Zane Grey's *Riders of the Purple Sage* (Harper's, 1912) or an Easterner forced by necessity into violence like Jack Hare in Grey's *The Heritage of the Desert* (Harper's, 1910) or like

John Shefford in Grey's *The Rainbow Trail* (Harper's, 1915), but in any case the heroine is required finally to endorse the hero's violence as when Jane Withersteen in *Riders of the Purple Sage* exclaims: "*'Roll the stone! . . . Lassiter, I love you!'* "—when rolling the stone means that the principal villain and all his followers will be crushed beneath a rock slide.

In *The Range Boss* (A. C. McClurg, 1917), Charles Alden Seltzer had his hero inform the heroine, an Easterner who inherits a ranch, " 'You'll shape up real Western—give you time. . . . You'll be ready to take your own part, without depending on laws to do it for you—laws that don't reach far enough.' " Such a hero has to have some kind of motivation and in a later novel, *Square Deal Sanderson* (A. C. McClurg, 1922), Seltzer spelled it out rather succinctly when we learn that Sanderson "was deliberately and unwarrantedly going to the Double A to interfere, to throw himself into a fight with persons with whom he had no previous acquaintance, for no other reason than that his chivalrous instincts had prompted him." Engaging in such a contest means that Sanderson must and will vanquish the villain.

Seltzer drew Western heroes who were grim, quiet, powerful men, thus initiating a convention since embellished by dozens of other writers and perhaps most significantly by Ernest Haycox, Luke Short, Norman A. Fox, Wayne D. Overholser, and Louis L'Amour. Within the rigid boundaries allowed a formulary Western plot, there are nonetheless a wide assortment of acceptable variations. Max Brand, one of nineteen pen names used by Frederick Faust, made his first appearance as a Western writer with *The Untamed* (Putnam's, 1919). Faust was disgusted by the actual physical West and avoided, whenever possible, even driving through it; he made his heroes and locales mythological and, therefore, timeless. He preferred in his hundreds of novels to employ one basic plot structure—pursuit and capture—with one variation—delayed revelation. Within this structure he projected his two basic myths: the son in search of an illustrious father and a warrior who has an Achilles' heel. Faust's advice to beginning writers was to read a story halfway through and imagine how it comes out. Then come up with a new beginning for the new conclusion and you have a new story. He wanted to write better fiction, but when he tried to write a more sophisticated formulary Western as in *Destry Rides Again* (Dodd, Mead, 1930), his agent warned him that he was writing too well: he must concentrate less on characterization, more on story. In this context, more story meant more action.

Dane Coolidge in *Hidden Water* (A. C. McClurg, 1910) was in the vanguard among authors who used the theme of the two heroines in formulary Westerns, although, of course, James Fenimore Cooper had employed it in the previous century. In this plot the hero must choose between the two heroines at the end of the story. Ernest Haycox frequently used this theme, but no matter where you find it in Haycox' fiction, the reason behind the selection is nearly always identical. " 'We're exactly the same kind of people,' " heroine Diana Castle says in Haycox' *Alder Gulch* (Little, Brown, 1941), speaking about herself and hero Jeff Pierce. " 'It is all or nothing with each of us.' " In Luke Short's first published Western novel, *The Feud at Single Shot* (Farrar and Rinehart, 1936), hero Dave Turner tells heroine Dorsey Hammond that the only way the world gives a man what belongs to him is if he is willing to fight and die for it. By the end of the novel, after a number of villains have been dispatched by Turner, he remarks to Dorsey: " 'It was pretty bloody.' " Dorsey, however, has become a convert. " 'But,' " she responds, " 'if a man doesn't fight for what he has and loves, people will take them away from him.' " This same thralldom with property and violence in Short's *Ride the Man Down* (Doubleday, 1942) is combined with the theme of the two heroines. Heroine Celia Evarts is drawn to hero Will Ballard because she, as opposed to the other heroine, Lottie Priest, admires Ballard for the violence by which he must live to protect her property; she doesn't even object when Ballard must shoot and kill her fiancé. In contrast to Ballard and his ascendant mana, there is a weak man named Kennedy, with virtually no mana at all, and a corresponding difference in the kind of woman he has: "She was a plain drudge of a girl, Will saw, probably the only kind of woman Kennedy could attract." From this it is only a short step to Louis L'Amour's *Hondo* (Fawcett, 1953), in which Angie Lowe takes Hondo for her second husband and Johnny accepts Hondo as a second father despite the fact that it was Hondo who killed Angie's first husband and Johnny's real father. Hondo's mana is obviously the more powerful and the more desirable.

A novel nearly as influential as Wister's *The Virginian* in the development of the formulary Western was Dashiell Hammett's *Red Harvest* (Knopf, 1929), in which there is so much killing that the characters, in Hammett's words, become "blood simple." Eugene Cunningham, whom critic W. H. Hutchinson once described as "one of the greatest lapidaries who ever polished a 'horse opera' for public consumption . . ." transposed Hammett's plot into a Western setting in *Riders of the Night* (Houghton Mifflin, 1932), in which, in the course of the novel, some seventy villains are killed. In *Buckaroo* (Houghton Mifflin, 1933) Cunningham expanded this number of villains who "needed" killing to three hundred!

While in *Riders of the Night* Cunningham, too, resorted to the theme of the two heroines, he did something else slightly more original: he introduced a trio of gunfighters named Sandrock Tom, Three Rivers, and Happy Jack, to whom he gave the sobriquet the Three Mesquiteers. Cunningham employed another trio in *Buckaroo*, and so it was left to William Colt MacDonald to pick up on this idea and fashion a different trio which he also called the Three Mesquiteers, beginning with *Law of the Forty-fives* (Covici, Friede, 1933). MacDonald's trio of Tucson Smith, Stony Brooke, and Lullaby Joslin appeared in some ten novels and some fifty-two B Western films. MacDonald's pattern for his novels was identical with Cunningham's and he invariably had his trio riding into a community intimidated by a master villain and his minions, a situation which, in Tucson Smith's words in *Law of the Forty-fives,* called upon the Mesquiteers to invoke "the only law effective in this sort of case—gun law."

However indigenous violence may have been in formulary Westerns prior to Cunningham and MacDonald, never before had it been present in such abundance, nor had the death of a human being been treated with quite their attitude of casual indifference. They did their work well; so well, in fact, that it would be extremely unlikely these days for a formulary Western writer to treat the death of a human being in any other way. MacDonald's Mesquiteer novels consist of one chapter after another of bloodletting until the final chapter, in which the master villain is himself destroyed. This plot structure has become almost a subgenre within formulary Western fiction, but even when it isn't used, the moral posture embodied in it is all-pervasive. In Norman A. Fox's *Silent in the Saddle* (Dodd, Mead, 1945) Fox's hero Brad Seldon reflects after a shoot-out that he will never know "a moment's regret for that killing," and in Louis L'Amour's *To Tame a Land* (Fawcett, 1955) L'Amour's hero Rye Tyler observes that "for once I didn't feel bad about a shooting."

The idea of a Western story as an occasion for killing has become self-propagating. To echo a character from *Smoke of the Gun* (New American Library, 1958), written by Wayne D. Overholser under his John S. Daniels pseudonym, "Murder was a treadmill. Once you started it, you couldn't stop it, and you couldn't get off." A. Leslie Scott under his Bradford Scott pseudonym wrote nearly 125 entries in his Walt Slade, Texas Ranger series in which Slade is joined by his friends Estevàn (a Mexican knife-man whose dialogue is generally confined to "my blade thirsts") and Sheriff Gene Putnam. Together they battle it out with a master villain and his minions, killing and bloodletting. This tradition has currently been continued by British writers, among them J. T. Edson, whose American publishers guarantee the reader at least twelve major killings per book, and Terry Harknett. Harknett's career began with his novelization of Sergio Leone's *A Fistful of Dollars* (United Artists, 1967), after which, under the pen name George G. Gilman, he created the Edge series of *Blut und Boden* Western fiction as well as coauthoring the Apache series with Laurence James under the *nom de plume* William M. James. Gordon D. Shirreffs has promoted the tradition among American writers, particularly in his Lee Kershaw saga. Typically in a book of this kind the end of the story will find the hero alone because everyone else is dead.

All of which brings me to a further observation about the mana-personality. The stronger the hero's mana—and we can now expand this idea to encompass the hero's self-willedness, his ability to kill better than anyone else, his inhumanity reflected in his indifference to human life—the greater the dehumanization of the heroine. Once killing becomes wholesale, the traditional heroine must either vanish completely or be transformed herself into a bloodletter. Jack Slade's girlfriend in the Bradford Scott series is named Jerry Nolan. She operates the Deuces Up dance hall and Slade likes her best when she wears tights. He sees her only when driven by carnal desire; otherwise, she has no function and really no existence. For Shirreffs' Lee Kershaw, although Kershaw attracts a different female companion in each adventure, the woman is able to engage in cold-blooded killing right along with Kershaw. When in Shirreffs' *The Marauders* (Fawcett, 1977) the woman is smashed in the face with a rifle butt by the master villain and her thigh ripped into by a shark—when, in short, she is dying—all she can think of is having sexual congress with Kershaw one last time and all Kershaw can feel about her after he takes her and after she dies is that "she was only a woman and a half-breed Yaqui at that."

There is an inevitable progression from this to the porno Westerns, which, since 1979, have proven such a bonanza for publishers. In the porno Westerns—and nearly every major Western paperback-publishing house has one or is contemplating one—women are stripped of their clothing and their souls; they are reduced to nothing but physical objects capable of producing detumescence in the heroes following the heroes' bouts of incredible carnage and slaughter. These series are written by several different authors but published under house names like Jake Logan or Tabor Evans. To take but a single instance, in *Slocum's Revenge* (Playboy, 1979) by Jake Logan, Slocum (a play on words?) asks as his price for returning a deed to a property owned by a beautiful young Spanish virgin that they spend a night together. The ecstasy and repeated orgasms she experiences are recounted in graphic detail. Jake Logan is billed as "the hottest best-selling Western author since Louis L'Amour," but there is nothing Western about this series, or the other porno Westerns, save the manner of dress. All such series are merely pornography in a period setting and the logical consequence of all the lying about life in general and life in the American West in particular which has so long been a characteristic of the formulary Western. What the porno Westerns illustrate are stories completely under the dominant of the mana-personality. Men and women are denied all possibility of humanity. They are purely collective figures, indulging in orgies of sexuality and violence. Slocum and his brethren use women insensately and sometimes brutally before casually moving on to their next conquest. But let me remind the reader of Leo Tolstoy's warning in the scene from *War and Peace* (1862–1869) where Napoleon surveys the battlefield at Borodino: *Quos vult perdere—dementat* [whoso looks upon perdition—becomes insane]. If it is true that many young people enjoy reading Western fiction, I shudder to think what will be their impression—should they be males—of women after reading these books; and be they either male or female what will be their impression of the value of human life?

The tradition of the formulary Western hero as a loner was given much of its initial impetus by Owen Wister; but so also was the idea of the family Western. Wister was primarily a short-story writer, and from the beginning, he populated his West with characters who are bound together by common experiences and emotional ties, such as the Virginian, Lin McLean, and Scipio LeMoyne. Indeed, one of Wister's story collections bears the title *Members of the Family* (Macmillan, 1911). B. M. Bower was the first to follow Wister in this direction, beginning with her first novel, *Chip of the Flying U* (Dillingham, 1906). Although she would continue writing Western fiction for almost forty years, she included regularly among her output more adventures with Chip and other Flying U punchers, whom she referred to collectively as the Happy Family. Clarence E. Mulford similarly with *Bar 20* (Outing, 1907) began his saga of the Bar 20 outfit held together by ties of friendship and mutual commitment, including Hopalong Cassidy, Red Connors, Johnny Nelson, Buck Peters, Tex Ewalt, and, later, Mesquite Jenkins. The Bar 20 saga proved so popular that with *Corson of the JC* (Doubleday, 1927) Mulford launched a second saga with a different set of characters.

The groundwork was thus well laid for Janice Holt Giles when she began her own saga with *The Kentuckians* (Houghton Mifflin, 1953), tracing the settlement of the American frontier through four generations of a Kentucky family that eventually moves West. Although scarcely in a class with Giles, Louis L'Amour subsequently created three separate series of sagas having to do with large families who migrate West. What Giles and L'Amour and a number of others have most in common is that they have united the formerly loose conclaves of individuals in Wister, Bower, and Mulford into actual family units bound by blood ties. For example, in *Bar 20 Three* (A. C. McClurg, 1921), Mulford had Cassidy and Connors come to the aid of Johnny Nelson when he is beset by villains; at the conclusion of *Mojave Crossing* (Bantam, 1964), L'Amour had Tell Sackett saved from torture and death by Nolan Sackett, a distant relative and up until then in the employ of the villains.

The unifying spirit behind these family-oriented formulary Westerns is the same which Ralph Brauer discerned in his excellent book *The Horse, the Gun, and the Piece of Property: Changing Images of the TV Western* (Bowling Green Popular Press, 1975) in the plethora of family and community Westerns which figured so prominently on television in the sixties and seventies. "Seth Adams [of *Wagon Train*]," Brauer wrote, "and Gil Favor [of *Rawhide*] and John Kennedy ask not what you can do for truth, justice, and morality . . . but rather ask what you can do for the trail crew, the wagon train, the organization, the country"—or, in a word, the family. Although there is a degree of individual initiative permitted in the family-oriented Westerns, the fact remains that their major significance in the history of the formulary Western is the emphasis they place on collectivism as opposed to isolated individuals, their repudiation of individual freedom for cooperation within a community, their rejection of the native American notion that each man must seek his own vision and follow his own destiny, for which they substitute the overwhelming desire for social conformity, the search for that feeling of consensus which has so long preoccupied and eluded white America. If you look objectively at formulary Western fiction, I fear you cannot help but agree with La Rochefoucauld's observation in his *Reflections Morales* (1678): *"Nos vertus ne sont, le plus souvent, que des vices déguisés"* [Our virtues are most often nothing but our vices disguised].

3

An example of a romantic historical reconstruction is Zane Grey's *The Vanishing American* (Harper's, 1925), which first appeared in the *Ladies' Home Journal* in 1922, a Curtis publication as were *The Saturday Evening Post* and *The Country Gentleman.* The story tells of Nophaie, a full-blood Navajo brave, kidnapped when a child and educated by whites, returning to his reservation as a young man only to find it dominated by an unscrupulous Indian agent and, still worse, a vicious missionary who uses his dogmatic creed to get his way. In the romantic historical reconstruction, as opposed to the formulary Western, characters have greater depth; events are more complicated; and whatever occurs, occurs for *ideological* reasons. Ideologically Zane Grey was a social Darwinist, a man who believed that human existence and the survival of the races are guided by inflexible laws of an evolutionary scheme which endorses industrial progress and technology and which therefore endows white civilization with a self-evident and wholly natural superiority, provided, however, that what Grey meant by the "heritage of the desert"—the character developed as a result of subduing the elements of nature and the need for everyone to develop such a character—is always taken into account. In one of Grey's Indian stories, "Blue Feather," unpublished until long after his death when it appeared in *Blue Feather and Other Stories* (Harper's, 1961), Grey articulated his ideology of evolutionary social history, highest to lowest: "Human being, man, Indian, savage, primitive beast."

In *The Vanishing American,* Grey not only stripped Nophaie of his Nopah religion but also made him reject the missionary's Christianity, arriving instead at some nebulous pantheism in which the white Christ and nature become dual manifestations of God. "Indians," Grey summed up his view of the native American, "were merely closer to the original animal progenitor of human beings." Nophaie falls in love with the blonde-haired, blue-eyed schoolteacher, and so inspired by his love does he become that he is prompted to enforce among his own people Grey's personal prejudice regarding the supreme importance of sexual virginity prior to marriage. Morgan, the missionary, likes to seduce young Indian maidens at his mission school. One of them, Gekin Yasha, is taught by Nophaie that "when a white woman loves she holds herself sacred for the man who has won her." This moral exhortation doesn't do Gekin Yasha much good. She is seduced by Morgan, becomes pregnant, returns to the reservation, and marries an Indian, only to pay the price frequently paid in Zane Grey's West by those who indulge in sexual intercourse outside a single monogamous relationship: she dies.

" 'Let the Indians marry white women and Indian girls marry white men,' " Nophaie comments in the magazine version, betraying himself and his people. " 'It would make for a more virile race . . . absorbed by the race that has destroyed him. Red blood into white! It means the white race will gain and the Indian vanish. . . .' " And so Grey furthered a notion designed to replace James Fenimore Cooper's division of native Americans into either villains or noble savages; Nophaie is a *romantic* savage who wants to vanish for the betterment of the white race. " 'Example of the white man's better ways,' " he says, " 'would inevitably follow association.' " The magazine version concluded with Nophaie and the yellow hair in each other's arms, about to achieve Grey's synthesis of "red blood into white." But this ending—to say nothing of Grey's partially accurate portrayal of reservation missionaries—caused such a furor at the offices of the *Ladies' Home Journal,* what with thousands upon thousands of angry letters of protest, Harper's refused flatly to publish the magazine serial as a book until Grey changed the ending. Assimilation had been suggested in the previous century as a solution to what Anglo-Americans termed the "Indian problem"; it was rejected in favor of a policy of extermination. Fiction, retaining the romance, had to align itself with the latter ideology. In the book version Grey had Nophaie shot fatally; while dying, he murmurs, " 'Vanishing . . . vanishing . . . vanishing. . . .' "

Paramount Pictures frequently filmed Grey's books while they were still in magazine serial form because Grey, to earn more money, had stepped up his production. Harper's, willing to publish two a year while Grey was writing three and sometimes four, was building up a backlog of novels. For the motion-picture version of *The Vanishing American* (Paramount, 1925), Lucien Hubbard, who did the adaptation, borrowed a portion from the first chapter of *The Thundering Herd* (Harper's, 1925) and some of "Blue Feather." In this way the film could have a prologue in which it was shown how the Indians had preyed upon each other, one tribe wiping out another, albeit weaker, tribe, until at last the culmination of the evolutionary scheme had been reached, the white man had arrived, signaling with his coming to all native Americans who might have survived the struggle thus far that the time had now come for them to vanish.

Nor was this all of it. After the unhappy experience with *The Vanishing American,* all Curtis publications adopted an editorial policy prohibiting authors of Western stories and serials from characterizing native Americans in their fiction. Indians might be present, but only as renegades on the warpath or minor characters. The far-reaching psychological effects of this policy can be seen in a number of the serials which ran in *The Saturday Evening Post* and which were subsequently made into films: Ernest Haycox' *Bugles in the Afternoon* published in 1943 and his *Canyon Passage* in 1945; Luke Short's *Ambush* in 1948; Alan LeMay's *The Searchers* in 1954 and *The Unforgiven* in 1957; James Warner Bellah's stories about Fort Starke (four of which comprise film director John Ford's cavalry trilogy); Will Cook's *Comanche Captives* in 1959, which was filmed under the title *Two Rode Together* (Columbia, 1961). I could go on, but the point is it would be absurd to expect, when the Indians were not characterized in the original stories, that they should somehow come to be characterized in the films based on those stories. Editors were exhorting Western writers to tell romantic lies if they wanted to be published, and so Western writers were telling romantic lies.

I will admit that some of those writing Western fiction during these years probably didn't know anything about Western history; or, if they did, they held it in contempt. They probably comforted themselves with the notion that deceit had nothing to do with what they were writing; their only objective was to entertain, to spin a good yarn, to tell an interesting story that seemed more "historical" than a formulary Western. The moral issue that an artist has a responsibility to be the conscience of his or her society either didn't appeal or didn't occur to them. In the words of one of Will Cook's characters in *Comanche Captives* concerning the manner in which he deceives his feebleminded wife: " '. . . If I can give her comfort in a lie, then I guess God won't kick me out of heaven for it.' "

But for one of the writers whom I have named above it wasn't this way. When he died, Ernest Haycox' library was transferred to the Special Collections Division of the University of Oregon Library in Eugene. His widow, Jill Marie Haycox, made it a provision of the bequest that the books of her late husband be kept in a room apart, and so it was convenient for me some time ago to go through them volume by volume. Haycox once commented that he never read Western fiction. He didn't want to "borrow" something from what others had written. When he read about the American West, he read its history; and he assembled what still is an excellent library on a complex subject. In the forties, he abandoned formulary Western fiction for romantic historical reconstructions. He knew the story that in the most cursory fashion I am about to relate. It is recounted—much of it—in books to be found in his library.

In 1855 James Lupton, a self-proclaimed "major," marched into Jacksonville, Oregon, with a group of Yreka volunteers. These men called a public meeting to sound out Oregonians on adopting a policy of exterminating the Indians. Things went so well for Lupton that he convened a second meeting on October 7, which consisted of a recitation of complaints against the Indians, the crowd becoming increasingly worked up. Thinking the time for action had come, once the meeting broke up, Lupton led his company of volunteers to an old Indian village on Butte Creek, a short distance from the reservation. They found the village asleep and opened fire in the dark, killing without quarter everyone they could find. Eight men were shot, three of them aged, along with fifteen women and children. Charles Drew, quartermaster for the volunteers, declared the action "admirably executed" and only regretted that a larger number of Indians had not been killed.

"The Rogues struck back in reprisal," Stephen Dow Beckham explained in his history, *Requiem for a People: The Rogue Indians and the Frontiersmen* (University of Oklahoma Press, 1971), citing in his footnotes many of the sources Haycox had in his personal library.

> Too many memories of past wrongs and injustices, too many deaths from sickness, starvation, and murder had occurred for them to trust the white men again. . . . At dawn on October 9 the settlers living along the river between Gold Hill and Vannoy's Ferry near Grants Pass began another workday. The actions of Lupton's volunteers were unknown to them. The Rogues, pushing downriver toward the wilderness in the coast mountains, first struck the Jacob B. Wagner ranch, where they murdered Wagner's wife and daughter and left the body of Miss Sarah Pellett, a temperance lecturer on her way to Jacksonville, in the smoldering ruins.

And so the Rogue War of 1855–56 began. There were approximately 9,500 of these essentially peaceful Rogue country people in 1851; after the war and their removal to the Siletz reservation, there were only some 2,000. After less than a decade of reservation life, this number had dwindled to 600. Is it any wonder that officials from Nazi Germany came to Washington, D.C., in the thirties to study the records of the Bureau of Indian Affairs to see if the American reservation solution to the Indian problem could be applied as a solution for what they called the Jewish problem?

Many of the settlers didn't know about Lupton and his volunteers and there is no mention of anything like this in Haycox' *Canyon Passage.* Every time one of Haycox' white characters sees a Rogue, there is uneasiness; the Rogue War, which occupies the final chapters of the novel and brings all the dramatic situations to a climax, is in this sense wholly predictable. All the reader sees are the atrocities committed by the Rogues against characters he has come to know and some of whom he has even come to like. There is a motivation given for this uprising. Honey Bragg, one of Haycox' villains, sets off the hostilities when he attempts to rape, and then murders, two Indian squaws. There is, however, a very important difference between such an action—an isolated depredation—and the collective activities of Lupton and his volunteers to exterminate the Rogues; and, lest it be overlooked, Lupton did have the endorsement of the majority of Oregonians in Jacksonville. These warring Rogues in history were fighting for their very survival—they were not like Haycox' fictional Indians seeking revenge because of the behavior of a single stereotypical white villain.

Canyon Passage (Universal, 1946) appeared as a film after the novel had been serialized in the *Post* and had been published in book form. Jill Marie Haycox recalled in her Introduction to the Gregg Press reissue of the novel in 1979:

> The world première was to have national importance. The newspaper stories and radio announcements went to all parts of the U.S. There was a tie-in with the NBC radio show "People Are Funny" giving *Canyon Passage* additional publicity. Wayne Morse, colorful Senator from Oregon, lauded the picture from the floor of the Senate. The *Congressional Record* for that day bears his entire speech which was sent out over the wires and printed by hundreds of newspapers throughout the country. . . . Hollywood distributors arranged for a showing of the film in Washington, D.C., for Oregon members of Congress—Senators, Representatives, and their families.

The world premiere itself was held in Portland, Oregon, and a number of Universal stars attended the occasion. After receiving his honorary Doctor of Literature degree from Lewis & Clark College, Haycox rode in a parade in an open convertible. According to D'Arcy McNickle's *The Indian Tribes of the United States: Ethnic and Cultural Survival,* published by the London Institute of Race Relations in 1962, there were in 1946 approximately eighty-two Tututni and seventy-nine Umpqua descendants of the original Rogue tribes. The decision to film *Canyon Passage* in Oregon was made to add significantly to its authenticity, but the Indians playing Rogues were not Rogues. They were Yakimas from the Yakima reserve in the State of Washington. Many of them, in Jill Marie Haycox' words, "moved into Portland" for the premiere, "using the park blocks, close to the downtown area for their encampment. They added a lot of color with their tepees, spotted ponies, and baled hay."

Unfortunately the Rogue Indians did not live in tepees, but the idea of treating American history as a Wild West Show was already well established in the nineteenth century. Americans are so accustomed to being sold romantic lies in this fashion, it was no surprise to me that Robert Altman—who once told me that in all of his films he's just parodying the Greatest Show on Earth: the United States—should have titled one of his better pictures *Buffalo Bill and the Indians, or Sitting Bull's History Lesson* (United Artists, 1976). Or as George Orwell put it in *1984* (Harcourt, Brace, 1949):

> Day by day and almost minute by minute the past was brought up to date. In this way every prediction made by the Party could be shown by documentary evidence to have been correct; nor was any item of news, or any expression of opinion, which conflicted with the needs of the moment, ever allowed to remain on record. All history was a palimpsest, scraped clean and reinscribed exactly as often as was necessary.

Count Joseph de Maistre wrote in the nineteenth century: "*. . . le véritable vainqueur, comme le véritable vaincu, c'est celui qui croit l'être*" [The true conqueror, like the truly vanquished, is whoever believes himself to be the conqueror]. It is the same with historical personalities and the events of history in a romantic historical reconstruction: they are whatever we wish them to have been. To quote Oakley Hall in the Prefatory Note to his novel *Warlock* (Viking, 1958), "by combining what did happen with what might have happened, I have tried to show what should have happened." There is no ultimate historical reality. It is argued that we can never know the truth. All we can have is an *interpretation* of what happened. In socialist countries, we call this phenomenon propaganda; in the United States, we call it entertainment.

4

"You look at me," Sandoval (Old Man Buffalo Grass) told Aileen O'Bryan, who was acting as the Navajo chief's amanuensis in November 1928, recording the stories and myths of his people, "you look at me, and you see only an ugly old man, but within I am filled with great beauty. I sit as on a mountain top and I look into the future. I see my people and your people living together. In time to come my people will have forgotten their early way of life unless they learn it from white men's books. So you must write down what I tell you; and you must have it made into a book that coming generations may know this truth."

For the white man, too, it is necessary to go to the white

man's books to learn what happened in his past. But the truth isn't always concerned with purely physical events; sometimes, maybe even most of the time, it has to do with spiritual events. To reclaim this past, the spiritual past, to know what happened truly and why it happened, is the primary objective of sound historical fiction, of what I have called the historical reconstruction, and for this reason I do not hesitate for a moment in recognizing it as true art. The finest kind of Western fiction is set in the American West because it must be, because it has everything to do with the American West and couldn't really have happened elsewhere in quite the same way. This is the distance we have traveled from the advice Luke Short once gave to Brian Garfield.

Perhaps the best way in which to illustrate the difference between a romantic historical reconstruction and a historical reconstruction is to select a theme and contrast the varying ways it has been treated in the two respective modes. One such theme, surely, is that of the captivity novel, a narrative form which has exerted a fascination for the reading public since the apeparance of *A Narrative of the Captivity and Restoration of Mrs. Mary Rowlandson,* which dates from Colonial times and which deals with events during King Philip's War in 1675–76. To focus on novels which deal with the captivity of whites by—to take only one nation—the Comanches during the middle of the nineteenth century, Alan LeMay's *The Searchers* comes to mind as does Will Cook's *Comanche Captives,* both of which I have already mentioned, as well as Benjamin Capps' *A Woman of the People* (Duell, Sloan, and Pearce, 1966) and Matthew Braun's *Black Fox* (Fawcett, 1972). The first two are romantic historical reconstructions. It was a trend in the fifties to introduce antihero elements into even formulary Westerns, but generally this trend was more apparent in romantic historical reconstructions. It was usually accomplished, as in *The Searchers* and in *Comanche Captives,* by splitting the traditional formulary Western hero into two distinct characters. Alan LeMay did it by splitting his hero into Amos Edwards, a dark figure, and Mart Pauley, a young man adopted as a boy by the Edwards family; Will Cook did it by splitting his hero into Jim Gary, a lieutenant in the U.S. cavalry, and Guthrie McCabe, sheriff of Oldham County, Texas. In calling this a trend, I do not wish to imply that it originated in the fifties. It had been done with Indians as early as James Fenimore Cooper's *The Last of the Mohicans* (1826) with Chingachgook and Magua, and film director Delmer Daves preferred to resort to this splitting device in films like *Broken Arrow* (20th Century-Fox, 1950) between Cochise and Goklia—in this instance his source was Elliott Arnold's romantic historical reconstruction *Blood Brother* (Duell, Sloan, and Pearce, 1947)—and in *Drumbeat* (Warner's, 1954) between Captain Jack and Mannik, a film which Daves himself wrote. In the fifties the real novelty was the splitting of the leading white characters.

In *The Searchers,* Amos Edwards' two nieces are taken captive by the Comanches. One of them is raped and killed. The other, Debbie, is apparently still alive, and for nearly six years Amos and Mart search for her. LeMay's Comanches are savages and it is their unredeemably savage spirit which comes to influence the conduct of both Amos and Mart in their quest. LeMay did not find both sides in the conflict *equally* savage; nor was he the least sympathetic with the Comanches, whatever momentary lip service he gave to the fact that they were fighting to protect their sacred lands. The whites, Amos and Mart, become nearly superhuman during their heroic undertaking. Amos, however, is clearly intent on killing Debbie because of the humiliation she has experienced by being made the wife of a Comanche war chief. In this he is frustrated, and ironically, he dies at the hands of a Comanche squaw. Mart finds Debbie and, together, they find their once innocent love again—or at least the reader is led to believe that they do.

In *Comanche Captives,* McCabe is hired by the U.S. cavalry to bring back white captives from among the Comanches. He is accompanied on this mission by Jim Gary. All the white captives these two discover have been transformed into brutish animals as a result of their captivity and the one adolescent boy McCabe does bring back commits a vicious murder and is hanged by the outraged whites. Jim Gary rescues Janice Tremain, the niece of a U.S. senator, who for five years has been the captive wife of Stone Calf. Gary kills Stone Calf, but he finds he must reject Janice because "he was a prudish man who wanted all women pure, until they were married at least." This wasn't so much a consideration for Mart Pauley as for men in general on the real American frontier, where there were very few single women to be had, virgins or otherwise. McCabe for his part is saved from Amos Edwards' fate by being enslaved by the Comanches and only rescued by Jim Gary once he has learned the value of friendship and the virtue of community spirit.

Both of these novels appeared in *The Saturday Evening Post,* and so it is of course not to be expected that the Comanches would be humanly characterized. But it isn't this deficiency alone which makes them romantic historical reconstructions. This is the consequence chiefly of their reliance on heroes. A hero, like a villain, isn't really human, and never can be.

Let me return for a moment to Heine's *Die Götter im Exil.* The last scene in the book is that of Jupiter, a pitiable old man, isolated at the North Pole and bewailing his fate of being forgotten by humankind: "he of whom Homer sang and whom Phidias sculpted in gold and ivory; he who could make the world tremble with the blink of an eye; he, the lover of Leda, Alkmene, Semele, Danae, Callisto, Io, Leto, Europa, etc.—in the end he must conceal himself behind mountains of ice at the North Pole and to preserve his noble life must deal in rabbit pelts just like a shabby Savoyard." Yet, Heine insisted, this should not sadden us, since "hidden rodents gnaw at every great one who strides the earth and even the gods themselves must finally, shamefully be brought back to the earth." Tolstoy said it more pointedly yet, in *War and Peace,* the prototype of the historical reconstruction. "The ancients have left us examples of epic poems in which the heroes provide the entire interest of the story," he wrote, "and we are still unable to accustom ourselves to the fact that for our epoch history of that sort is meaningless."

In *The Works and Days,* Hesiod told of the five generations of creation; after the third . . .

> Zeus, son of Kronos, created yet another fourth generation on the fertile earth, and these were better and nobler, the wonderful generation of hero-men, who are also called half-gods, the generation before our own on this vast earth.
>
> (155–160)

This generation was removed to a place far from the immortals and from the mortals whom Zeus created next. For many writers of Western fiction—and many of them, as writers of English prose, very fine writers indeed—Zeus' actions were abrogated and the generation of heroes was brought back. "The pioneering past has now been diligently debunked," Harvey Fergusson wrote in his Foreword to *Followers of the Sun: A Trilogy of the Santa Fe Trail* (Knopf, 1936), an omnibus of three of his best romantic historical reconstructions, "but as surely as the flavor of reality has been recaptured the quality of the heroic has been lost. I sought to unite them because it seemed to me the heroism of the pioneer life was genuine and had its value." Similarly, Eugene Manlove Rhodes, another author of exceptional romantic historical reconstructions, wrote in his Prologue to *Stepsons of Light* (Houghton Mifflin, 1921) that the settlement of the West was "the greatest upbuilding of recorded time; and prime motive of that great migration was the motive of all migrations—the search for food and land. They went West for food. What they did there was to work; if you require a monument—take a good look!" Critics who particularly favor authors like Fergusson and Rhodes try to claim that they wrote of a place Rhodes once called "the West that was." I like Fergusson and Rhodes very much, but this does not interfere with my acknowledging that the West they wrote about, like the characters and events in Oakley Hall's *Warlock*, is a West that might have been or maybe should have been, but for all that—to express it in terms of Latin grammar—a West in the subjunctive mood of the imperfect tense or, in short, an idea of the West occurring in the historical past which was never brought to completion yet which has some kind of relevance for us today. Both the formulary Western and the romantic historical reconstruction can claim accordingly to be literary art of a kind because at no time are they completely irrelevant to humankind.

But what distinguishes the historical reconstruction, what sets it on a much higher literary plane is that in it the hero is replaced by a human being, a person of flesh and blood, while the structure is expanded to encompass an even greater complexity of character and incident than in the romantic historical reconstruction. "No longer confident of the inevitability of its own history, or the 'American way of life,'" Lawrence W. Towner wrote in his Introduction to the reissue of D'Arcy McNickle's splendid historical reconstruction, *The Surrounded* (1936; University of New Mexico Press, 1978), "the America of the 1970s may be more sympathetic to other peoples and their cultures than it was, or at least more understanding of other peoples who may seem to have lost their way."

When they came to write their respective novels, Capps and Braun knew a great deal more about Comanches than had LeMay and Cook. This may be because the history of the American West is being written more conscientiously today than it used to be, but it is probably also true that these authors cared enough about historical reality to discover it for themselves. Mircea Eliade observed in his book *Myth and Reality* (Harper's, 1963):

> This is one of the few encouraging syndromes of the modern world. Western cultural provincialism—which began history with Egypt, literature with Homer, and philosophy with Thales—is being rapidly outmoded. But this is not all: through this historiographic *anamnesis* man enters deep into himself. If we succeed in understanding a contemporary Australian, or his homologue, a paleolithic hunter, we have succeeded in "awakening" in the depths of our being the existential situation and the resultant behavior of a prehistoric humanity. It is not a matter of a mere "external" knowledge, as when we learn the name of the capital of a country or the date of the fall of Constantinople. A true historiographic *anamnesis* finds expression in the discovery of our solidarity with these vanished or peripheral peoples.

And this is what happens in a historical reconstruction. We come to recognize our solidarity with people from the past; we relive their lives, face the issues which confronted them, and, we hope, come to some deeper understanding of ourselves. The historical reconstruction demonstrates in the best instances that it is possible to write fiction that is stirring and entertaining and still be historically accurate, truthful to the time, the place, and the people.

In *A Woman of the People,* Helen Morrison and her younger sister, Katy, are made captives of the Mutsani Comanches in 1854. The entire story is told from Helen Morrison's point of view, and for all of it she remains living with the Comanches. We see her grow to womanhood among them, learn their customs and language, and marry Burning Hand and bear him a child; and we see the touching relationship between these two. Because the Comanches are thoughtfully characterized, because there is an absence of heroes and villains and therefore a corresponding presence of human beings, *everyone is humanized. A Woman of the People* transcends mere fiction to become literature.

Capps was not concerned with arguing racial superiorities or cultural supremacy; instead, he showed us how and why the Comanches were different and in such a fashion that we must respect them for their differences. The same is true of Braun's *Black Fox.* The Black Fox of the title is Britt Johnson, a freed black from the South. When the Comanches and Kiowas stage a joint raid in 1860 to drive the white-eyes from their sacred lands and take captives, Black Fox, regarded by the whites as an uppity nigger, volunteers to negotiate to get the hostages back, not least because his own family is among the captives. Braun deftly characterized Running Dog and Santana among the Kiowas, and Little Buffalo among the Comanches, showing us at the same time all the minute and quite distinct differences between these two Plains tribes. In the same way, he characterized Black Fox and his relations within his own family and among the whites, the whites among themselves and with members of other races, and the multitude of ways in which various individuals perceive themselves and others. Britt comes to realize that "the strong fight the strong for the right to harness the meek to the plow." His greatest inner conflict is induced by Running Dog, his friend among the Kiowas, who cannot understand why Black Fox prefers to live among the whites, where he is subjected to the most demeaning treatment, when he might live in freedom and dignity among the Kiowas. Each of the central characters is a human being, and so, from this perspective, we are better able to understand the suffering and personal travail in which each must live and somehow find his own way within the human community and within himself.

I began this introductory essay with a reference to classical mythology. But historiography, too, began in antiquity. Herodotus said that he wrote his *Histories* so that the deeds of men should not be lost to the passage of time. Other historians of antiquity had different reasons for writing history. Thucydides wanted to show the effects of the struggle for power, a drive he felt indigenous to human nature; Polybius began writing history with the intention of demonstrating that the Roman empire was the logical culmination of the forces of world history before his time, but he had second thoughts which only further reinforced his conviction that the experience one has while studying history is the best kind of education one can have in life; Livy, like Plutarch, studied history to find "models for ourselves and for our country." Tacitus went so far as to see all history peopled by heroes and villains. Would I replace the formulary and romantic West with the historical West in Western fiction? My answer is an unequivocal yes. However, in the tradition of Herodotus, I believe history *is* verifiable and I think we must learn enough Western American history to know what is romance, and what is not; just as I believe that the best literary criticism is cosmopolitan and international in scope.

Unlike the characters in Orwell's *1984*, we cannot persist in constantly rewriting our history to suit the fashion of the moment, as if history were nothing more than the handmaiden of wish-fulfillment. To fall victim to romantic illusions, to dehumanize ourselves through the dominant of the mana-personality, and therefore to become wholly uncritical in our acceptance of what amounts to self-serving lies can only assure us that, as a people, we will neither understand ourselves better nor be able to endure the spiritual state we will have created for ourselves and from which, left unattended, there may be no escape. I write this because I believe that the purpose of Western American fiction, as of all art, is—to paraphrase Dr. Samuel Johnson—to better prepare us to understand life, or when that proves impossible, at least to better endure it.

To the foregoing, I would add only one final suggestion, and one based on Mary Austin's essay "Regionalism in American Fiction," which first appeared in the *English Journal* (Vol. XXI, February 1932). Ms. Austin counseled that she would require two factors to be indispensable in a regional story. The first of these is that the region itself must be an integral part of the structure of the story, either as a character or as a prime mover of the plot. The second is that the story must be *of* the region, and not just about it. These factors, when combined with historical accuracy, are invariably to be found in the best examples of what I call the historical reconstruction.

It may strike the reader that I have singled out unfairly the work of Ernest Haycox in what I have written above. I did not do so without knowing at the same time that he was ultimately a champion of the historical reconstruction and that, had he lived, he may well have fulfilled the promise of the new direction he took in the last books he wrote. "I could not write some of the stories I wrote five years ago," he once confessed. "I wish I could, since I enjoyed them so much. But my fingers will not trace the same patterns—and it would be foolish for me to try to force them into the old patterns." There are writers of Western fiction—some of whom I have been able to include in this anthology; some of whom, given the limitations of space, I could not—who have recognized, as Haycox finally did, in the depths of their being that the past does have something to teach us, if we are willing to learn from it, and that the Western novel and story are the ideal literary form through which our American past can be evoked vividly and painfully—painfully because it was mostly painful. The story of the American West is not romance; it is very often tragedy. But even in tragedy, as writers since Aeschylus have known, there can be human nobility. Most of all fiction about the American West is about *man in nature*, not the denatured, mechanical, sterile world that increasingly has come to serve as a backdrop for human activity in other kinds of fiction. In this sense, the West is just what the Indians always thought it was, the land beyond the setting sun, the Spiritland.

5

It was not my intention in selecting the stories for this anthology to illustrate what I have had to say above about the origins, permutations, and development of Western fiction. I have chosen stories which I believe can be read with pleasure. I am also aware, however, that much of the fiction which follows is in the form of short stories. There was a time—especially during the first five decades of the present century—when the short story was very much in vogue with readers, and a good many of the stories in this collection date from that period. This is no longer the case. First, motion pictures and radio and now finally television appear to have dissipated the tremendous market which once existed for shorter fiction. Confronted with the present climate regarding short stories, I felt it advisable to organize the stories in this anthology in a particular way.

The first section is titled "The East Goes West" and is comprised of fiction written by authors who in the nineteenth century journeyed West and found themselves sufficiently inspired to transform their experiences into fiction. On the Contents page each title is followed by the date of composition, first publication, or first *book* appearance—whichever proved more convenient—and then the name of the author. I have pursued this practice throughout so that the reader intent on reading each story in more or less its order of appearance can do so by following these dates. In the first section I found in rereading the stories one after the other that they read best in chronological order. However, this did not prove to be the case in the other three sections, and I assembled the stories in these sections so that a chronology of another sort could be maintained. According to this arrangement, the inherent historical time-frame of each story creates its own sort of progression. If read consecutively in their assembled order, it should be possible for the reader to read more than one story at a sitting without experiencing the jarring contrast which sometimes results when reading collections of stories set in widely diverse locales and featuring quite different characters and situations.

The second section, "Where West Was West," is made up of stories by writers who were born in the West and who perhaps experienced the West at variance to the Easterners in the first section. Although it is always a dangerous practice to generalize, the stories in the first section appear to have been written primarily for an Eastern audience, and the image of the West implicit in them stresses the exotic and the violent. The stories in the second section focus more clearly on what might be termed community, or "Western," values. The fiction in the third section has little to do with the geographical West and makes use of the historical West only to embody a certain ideology; the ideology used varies, depending on who wrote the story, but there is always an ideology.

In the final section formulary and romantic elements recede and are replaced by a commensurately greater depth of perspective. There is also a significant change in tone. Collectively these stories constitute a promise for the future of Western fiction. It remains my hope that the reader, by passing from Mark Twain at the very beginning to Max Evans at the very end, will be able to see something of the totality of what the American West has meant to writers, and readers, from different generations; to find that there is a tremendous variety in Western American fiction; and to discover that some of the most compelling, dramatic, and imaginative contributions to American literature as a whole have come from its ranks.

PART ONE

THE EAST GOES WEST

MARK TWAIN

SAMUEL LANGHORNE CLEMENS (1835–1910) was born at Florida, Missouri, and when he was five, his family, which was always on the move, settled in Hannibal; there, in 1847, Clemens' father died. This brought to an end the young Clemens' limited schooling and he was at once apprenticed to his brother Orion, who ran a country newspaper, *The Missouri Courier*. In 1853 Clemens decided to head East as a journeyman printer, but presently he was back again with his brother, who was by this time publishing a newspaper in Keokuk, Iowa. After trying and failing to get to South America, in 1857 he became an apprentice pilot on a Mississippi riverboat.

He first went West after serving about two weeks as a second lieutenant in the Confederate army. He became an unsuccessful prospector in the Nevada Territory and finally a reporter for a newspaper in Carson City. By 1862 he was city editor for *The Enterprise* in Virginia City and it was here that Clemens officially adopted Mark Twain as his pseudonym, after a depth call of the Mississippi riverboat pilots. A ridiculous duel was the immediate cause of his sudden departure from Nevada and for his landing in San Francisco, where he met Bret Harte for the first time. In 1865 he published his famed short story, "The Celebrated Jumping Frog of Calaveras County," in a New York newspaper and was on his way to becoming nationally known as a frontier humorist.

Twain's contribution to Western American literature is varied, but a substantial part of it comes as a result of his nonfictional books such as *Roughing It* (1872) and *Life on the Mississippi* (1883), both of which are more contemporary in tone and more perceptive of frontier conditions than much

Western fiction which appeared after them, and yet both are written in a style that makes them seem almost like fiction.

It is very well documented that Jack Slade killed only one man, the horse thief, Jules Reni, who a year before their final showdown near Cold Springs, Colorado, had put five bullets into Slade in a street fight. Granted, Twain in narrating all the gossip he had heard about Slade was only indulging his readers' appetite for sensationalism and, after all, it does make for an amusing contrast with the man Jack Slade once Twain does meet him. I think we must always be careful when reading Twain's accounts of events and people to keep his literary purpose in mind. At any rate, the facts about Slade can be found in brief in the *Encyclopedia of Western Gunfighters* (University of Oklahoma Press, 1979) by Bill O'Neal, and Professor Thomas J. Dimsdale's book *The Vigilantes of Montana* (1866)—to which Twain made a reference in what follows—is also still in print from the University of Oklahoma Press in their remarkable Western Frontier Library series.

In my view Mark Twain is the most controversial literary figure in American letters in all of the nineteenth century, beloved as much today for what he didn't publish as he once was admired for what he did publish. He succeeded so well at making himself into a literary folk personality that he has been kept alive into the present by various actors who continue to portray him in stage and television shows. Twain was ambivalent about frontier freedom, feeling when in the midst of it—as he was during the days of *Roughing It*—that one could only be appalled by it. Yet when living in the East in the Gilded Age, he dreamed with Huck about heading back to the frontier.

Roughing It is one of the greatest firsthand accounts of life and letters ever written by an American. I do not shrink, however, from labeling the following episode fiction, and I think most readers will agree with me. Slade is very much a perfect example of how a man could pay a terrible penalty on the frontier, not for what he was or what he had really done, but for what people thought about him.

Jack Slade, Desperado

We passed Fort Laramie in the night, and on the seventh morning out we found ourselves in the Black Hills, with Laramie Peak at our elbow (apparently) looming vast and solitary—a deep, dark, rich indigo blue in hue, so portentously did the old colossus frown under his beetling brows of storm cloud. He was thirty or forty miles away, in reality, but he only seemed removed a little beyond the low ridge at our right. We breakfasted at Horse-Shoe Station, six hundred and seventy-six miles out from St. Joseph. We had now reached hostile Indian country, and during the afternoon we passed Laparelle Station, and enjoyed great discomfort all the time we were in the neighborhood, being aware that many of the trees we dashed by at arm's length concealed a lurking Indian or two. During the preceding night an ambushed savage had sent a bullet through the pony rider's jacket, but he had ridden on, just the same, because pony riders were not allowed to stop and inquire into such things except when killed. As long as they had life enough left in them they had to stick to the horse and ride, even if the Indians had been waiting for them a week, and were entirely out of patience. About two hours and a half before we arrived at Laparelle Station, the keeper in charge of it had fired four times at an Indian, but he said with an injured air that the Indian had "skipped around so's to spile everything—and ammunition's blamed skurse, too." The most natural inference conveyed by his manner of speaking was, that in "skipping around," the Indian had taken an unfair advantage. The coach we were in had a neat hole through its front—a reminiscence of its last trip through this region. The bullet that made it wounded the driver slightly, but he did not mind it much. He said the place to keep a man "huffy" was down on the Southern Overland, among the Apaches, before the company moved the stage line up on the northern route. He said the Apaches used to annoy him all the time down there, and that he came up as near as anything to starving to death in the midst of abundance, because they kept him so leaky with bullet holes that he "couldn't hold his vittles." This person's statements were not generally believed.

We shut the blinds down very tightly that first night in the hostile Indian country, and lay on our arms. We slept on them some, but most of the time we only lay on them. We did not talk much, but kept quiet and listened. It was an inky-black night, and occasionally rainy. We were among woods and rocks, hills and gorges—so shut in, in fact, that when we peeped through a chink in a curtain, we could discern nothing. The driver and conductor on top were still, too, or only spoke at long intervals, in low tones, as is the way of men in the midst of invisible dangers. We listened to raindrops pattering on the roof; and the grinding of the wheels through the muddy gravel; and the low wailing of the wind; and all the time we had that absurd sense upon us, inseparable from travel at night in a close-curtained vehicle, the sense of remaining perfectly still in one place, notwithstanding the jolting and swaying of the vehicle, the trampling of the horses, and the grinding of the wheels. We listened a long time, with intent faculties and bated breath; every time one of us would relax, and draw a long sigh of relief and start to say something, a comrade would be sure to utter a sudden "Hark!" and instantly the experimenter was rigid and listening again. So that the tiresome minutes and decades of minutes dragged away, until at last our tense forms filmed over with a dulled consciousness, and we slept, if one might call such a condition by so strong a name—for it was a sleep set with a hair trigger. It was a sleep seething and teeming with a weird and distressful confusion of shreds and fag ends of dreams—a sleep that was a chaos. Presently, dreams and sleep and the sullen hush of the night were startled by a ringing report, and cloven by *such* a long, wild, agonizing shriek! Then we heard—ten steps from the stage—

"Help! help! help!" [It was our driver's voice.]

"Kill him! Kill him like a dog!"

"I'm being murdered! Will no man lend me a pistol?"

"Look out! Head him off! Head him off!"

[Two pistol shots; a confusion of voices and the trampling of many feet, as if a crowd were closing and surging together around some object; several heavy, dull blows, as with a club; a voice that said appealingly, "Don't, gentlemen, please don't—I'm a dead man!" Then a fainter groan, and another blow, and away sped the stage into the darkness, and left the grisly mystery behind us.]

What a startle it was! Eight seconds would amply cover the time it occupied—maybe even five would do it. We only had time to plunge at a curtain and unbuckle and unbutton part of it in an awkward and hindering flurry, when our whip cracked sharply overhead, and we went rumbling and thundering away, down a mountain grade.

We fed on that mystery the rest of the night—what was left of it, for it was waning fast. It had to remain a present mystery, for all we could get from the conductor in answer to our hails was something that sounded, through the clatter of the wheels, like "Tell you in the morning!"

So we lit our pipes and opened the corner of a curtain for a chimney, and lay there in the dark, listening to each other's story of how he first felt and how many thousand Indians he first thought had hurled themselves upon us, and what his remembrance of the subsequent sounds was, and the order of their occurrence. And we theorized, too, but there was never a theory that would account for our driver's voice being out there, nor yet account for his Indian murderers talking such good English, if they *were* Indians.

So we chatted and smoked the rest of the night comfortably away, our boding anxiety being somehow marvelously dissipated by the real presence of something to be anxious *about.*

We never did get much satisfaction about that dark occurrence. All that we could make out of the odds and ends of the information we gathered in the morning was that the disturbance occurred at a station; that we changed drivers there, and that the driver that got off there had been talking roughly about some of the outlaws that infested the region ("for there wasn't a man around there but had a price on his head and didn't dare show himself in the settlements," the conductor said); he had talked roughly about these characters, and ought to have "drove up there with his pistol cocked and ready on the seat alongside of him, and begun business himself, because any softy would know they would be laying for him."

That was all we could gather, and we could see that neither the conductor nor the new driver was much concerned about the matter. They plainly had little respect for a man who would deliver offensive opinions of people and then be so simple as to come into their presence unprepared to "back his judgment," as they pleasantly phrased the killing of any fellow being who did not like said opinions. And likewise they plainly had a contempt for the man's poor discretion in venturing to rouse the wrath of such utterly reckless wild beasts as those outlaws—and the conductor added:

"I tell you it's as much as Slade himself wants to do!"

This remark created an entire revolution in my curiosity. I cared nothing now about the Indians, and even lost interest in the murdered driver. There was such magic in that name, SLADE! Day or night, now, I stood always ready to drop any subject in hand, to listen to something new about Slade and his ghastly exploits. Even before we got to Overland City, we had begun to hear about Slade and his division (for he was a division agent) on the Overland; and from the hour we had left Overland City we had heard drivers and conductors talk about only three things—"Californy," the Nevada silver mines, and this desperado Slade. And a deal the most of the talk was about Slade. We had gradually come to have a realizing sense of the fact that Slade was a man whose heart and hands and soul were steeped in the blood of offenders against his dignity; a man who awfully avenged all injuries, affronts, insults or slights, of whatever kind—on the spot if he could, years afterward if lack of earlier opportunity compelled it; a man whose hate tortured him day and night till vengeance appeased it—and not an ordinary vengeance either, but his enemy's absolute death—nothing less; a man whose face would light up with a terrible joy when he surprised a foe and had him at a disadvantage. A high and efficient servant of the Overland, an outlaw among outlaws and yet their relentless scourge, Slade was at once the most bloody, the most dangerous, and the most valuable citizen that inhabited the savage fastnesses of the mountains.

Really and truly, two-thirds of the talk of drivers and conductors had been about this man Slade, ever since the day before we reached Julesburg. In order that the Eastern reader may have a clear conception of what a Rocky Mountain desperado is, in his highest state of development, I will reduce all this mass of overland gossip to one straightforward narrative, and present it in the following shape:

Slade was born in Illinois, of good parentage. At about twenty-six years of age he killed a man in a quarrel and fled the country. At St. Joseph, Missouri, he joined one of the early California-bound emigrant trains, and was given the post of train master. One day on the plains he had an angry dispute with one of his wagon drivers, and both drew their revolvers. But the driver was the quicker artist, and had his weapon cocked first. So Slade said it was a pity to waste life on so small a matter, and proposed that the pistols be thrown on the ground and the quarrel settled by a fist fight. The unsuspecting driver agreed, and threw down his pistol—whereupon Slade laughed at his simplicity, and shot him dead!

He made his escape, and lived a wild life for a while, dividing his time between fighting Indians and avoiding an Illinois sheriff, who had been sent to arrest him for his first murder. It is said that in one Indian battle he killed three savages with his own hand, and afterward cut their ears off and sent them, with his compliments, to the chief of the tribe.

Slade soon gained a name for fearless resolution, and this was sufficient merit to procure for him the important post of overland division agent at Julesburg, in place of Mr. Jules, removed. For some time previously, the company's horses had been frequently stolen, and the coaches delayed, by gangs of outlaws, who were wont to laugh at the idea of any man's having the temerity to resent such outrages. Slade resented them promptly. The outlaws soon found that the new agent was a man who did not fear anything that breathed the breath of life. He made short work of all offenders. The result was that delays ceased, the company's property was let alone, and no matter what happened or who suffered, Slade's coaches went through, every time! True, in order to bring about this wholesome change, Slade had to kill several men—some say three, others say four, and others six—but the world was the richer for their loss. The first prominent difficulty he had was with the ex-agent Jules, who bore the reputation of being a reckless and desperate man himself. Jules hated Slade for supplanting him, and a good fair occasion for a fight was all he was waiting for. By and by Slade dared to employ a man whom Jules had once discharged. Next, Slade seized a team of stage horses which he accused Jules of having driven off and hidden somewhere for his own use. War was declared, and for a day or two the two men walked warily about the streets, seeking each other, Jules armed with a double-barreled shotgun, and Slade with his history-creating revolver. Finally, as Slade stepped into a store, Jules poured the contents of his gun into him from behind the door. Slade was plucky, and Jules got several bad pistol wounds in return. Then both men fell, and were carried to their respective lodgings, both swearing that better aim should do deadlier work next time. Both were bedridden a long time, but Jules got on his feet first, and gathering his possessions together, packed them on a couple of mules, and fled to the Rocky Mountains to gather strength in safety against the day of reckoning. For many months he was not seen or heard of, and was gradually dropped out of the remembrance of all save Slade himself. But Slade was not the man to forget him. On the contrary, common report said that Slade kept a reward standing for his capture, dead or alive!

After a while, seeing that Slade's energetic administration had restored peace and order to one of the worst divisions of the road, the Overland stage company transferred him to the Rocky Ridge division in the Rocky Mountains, to see if he could perform a like miracle there. It was the very paradise of outlaws and desperadoes. There was absolutely no semblance of law there. Violence was the rule. Force was the only recognized authority. The commonest misunderstandings were settled on the spot with the revolver or the knife. Murders were done in open day, and with sparkling frequency, and nobody thought of inquiring into them. It was considered that the parties who did the killing had their private reasons for it; for other people to meddle would have been looked upon as indelicate. After a murder, all that Rocky Mountain etiquette required of a spectator was, that he should help the gentleman bury his game—otherwise his churlishness would surely be remembered against him the first time he killed a man himself and needed a neighborly turn in interring him.

Slade took up his residence sweetly and peacefully in the midst of this hive of horse thieves and assassins, and the very first time one of them aired his insolent swaggerings in his presence he shot him dead! He began a raid on the outlaws, and in a singularly short space of time he had completely stopped their depredations on the stage stock, recovered a large number of stolen horses, killed several of the worst desperadoes of the district, and gained such a dread ascendancy over the rest that they respected him, admired him, feared him, obeyed him! He wrought the same marvelous change in the ways of the community that had marked his administration at Overland City. He captured two men who had stolen Overland stock, and with his own hands he hanged them. He was supreme judge in his district, and he was jury and executioner likewise—and not only in the case of offenses against his employers, but against passing emigrants as well. On one occasion some emigrants had their stock lost or stolen, and told Slade, who chanced to visit their camp. With a single companion he rode to a ranch, the owners of which he suspected, and opening the door, commenced firing, killing three, and wounding the fourth.

From a bloodthirstily interesting little Montana book* I took this paragraph:

> While on the road, Slade held absolute sway. He would ride down to a station, get into a quarrel, turn the house out of windows, and maltreat the occupants most cruelly. The unfortunates had no means of redress, and were compelled to recuperate as best they could. On one of these occasions, it is said he killed the father of the fine little half-breed boy Jemmy, whom he adopted, and who lived with his widow after his execution. Stories of Slade's hanging men, and of innumerable assaults, shootings, stabbings, and beatings, in which he was a principal actor, form part of the legends of the stage line. As for minor quarrels and shootings, it is absolutely certain that a minute history of Slade's life would be one long record of such practices.

Slade was a matchless marksman with a navy revolver. The legends say that one morning at Rocky Ridge, when he was feeling comfortable, he saw a man approaching who had offended him some days before—observe the fine memory he had for matters like that—and, "Gentlemen," said Slade, drawing, "it is a good twenty-yard shot—I'll clip the third button on his coat!" Which he did. The bystanders all admired it. And they all attended the funeral, too.

On one occasion a man who kept a little whiskey shelf at the station did something which angered Slade—and went and made his will. A day or two afterward Slade came in and called for some brandy. The man reached under the counter (ostensibly to get a bottle—possibly to get something else), but Slade smiled upon him that peculiarly bland and satisfied smile of his which the neighbors had long ago learned to recognize as a death warrant in disguise, and told him to "none of that!—pass out the high-priced article." So the poor barkeeper had to turn his back and get the high-priced brandy from the shelf; and when he faced around again he was looking into the muzzle of Slade's pistol. "And the next instant," added my informant, impressively, "he was one of the deadest men that ever lived."

The stage drivers and conductors told us that sometimes Slade would leave a hated enemy wholly unmolested, unno-

***The Vigilantes of Montana,* by Prof. Thos. J. Dimsdale.

ticed, and unmentioned, for weeks together—had done it once or twice at any rate. And some said they believed he did it in order to lull the victims into unwatchfulness, so that he could get the advantage of them, and others said they believed he saved up an enemy that way, just as a schoolboy saves up a cake, and made the pleasure go as far as it would by gloating over the anticipation. One of these cases was that of a Frenchman who had offended Slade. To the surprise of everybody Slade did not kill him on the spot, but let him alone for a considerable time. Finally, however, he went to the Frenchman's house very late one night, knocked, and when his enemy opened the door, shot him dead—pushed the corpse inside the door with his foot, set the house on fire, and burned up the dead man, his widow and three children! I heard this story from several different people, and they evidently believed what they were saying. It may be true, and it may not. "Give a dog a bad name," etc.

Slade was captured, once, by a party of men who intended to lynch him. They disarmed him, and shut him up in a strong log house, and placed a guard over him. He prevailed on his captors to send for his wife, so that he might have a last interview with her. She was a brave, loving, spirited woman. She jumped on a horse and rode for life and death. When she arrived they let her in without searching her, and before the door could be closed she whipped out a couple of revolvers, and she and her lord marched forth defying the party. And then, under a brisk fire, they mounted double and galloped away unharmed!

In the fullness of time Slade's myrmidons captured his ancient enemy Jules, whom they found in a well-chosen hiding-place in the remote fastnesses of the mountains, gaining a precarious livelihood with his rifle. They brought him to Rocky Ridge, bound hand and foot, and deposited him in the middle of the cattle yard with his back against a post. It is said that the pleasure that lit Slade's face when he heard of it was something fearful to contemplate. He examined his enemy to see that he was securely tied, and then went to bed, content to wait till morning before enjoying the luxury of killing him. Jules spent the night in the cattle yard, and it is a region where warm nights are never known. In the morning Slade practiced on him with his revolver, nipping the flesh here and there, and occasionally clipping off a finger, while Jules begged him to kill him outright and put him out of his misery. Finally Slade reloaded, and walking up close to his victim, made some characteristic remarks and then dispatched him. The body lay there half a day, nobody venturing to touch it without orders, and then Slade detailed a party and assisted at the burial himself. But he first cut off the dead man's ears and put them in his vest pocket, where he carried them for some time with great satisfaction. That is the story as I have frequently heard it told and seen it in print in California newspapers. It is doubtless correct in all essential particulars.

In due time we rattled up to a stage station, and sat down to breakfast with a half-savage, half-civilized company of armed and bearded mountaineers, ranchmen, and station employees. The most gentlemanly appearing, quiet, and affable officer we had yet found along the road in the Overland Company's service was the person who sat at the head of the table, at my elbow. Never youth stared and shivered as I did when I heard them call him SLADE!

Here was romance, and I sitting face to face with it!—looking upon it—touching it—hobnobbing with it, as it were! Here, right by my side, was the actual ogre who, in fights and brawls and various ways, *had taken the lives of twenty-six human beings*, or all men lied about him! I suppose I was the proudest stripling that ever traveled to see strange lands and wonderful people.

He was so friendly and so gentle-spoken that I warmed to him in spite of his awful history. It was hardly possible to realize that this pleasant person was the pitiless scourge of the outlaws, the raw-head-and-bloody-bones the nursing mothers of the mountains terrified their children with. And to this day I can remember nothing remarkable about Slade except that his face was rather broad across the cheekbones, and that the cheekbones were low and the lips peculiarly thin and straight. But that was enough to leave something of an effect upon me, for since then I seldom see a face possessing those characteristics without fancying that the owner of it is a dangerous man.

The coffee ran out. At least it was reduced to one tincupful, and Slade was about to take it when he saw that my cup was empty. He politely offered to fill it, but although I wanted it, I politely declined. I was afraid he had not killed anybody that morning, and might be needing diversion. But still with firm politeness he insisted on filling my cup, and said I had traveled all night and better deserved it than he—and while he talked he placidly poured the fluid, to the last drop. I thanked him and drank it, but it gave me no comfort, for I could not feel sure that he would not be sorry, presently, that he had given it away, and proceed to kill me to distract his thoughts from the loss. But nothing of the kind occurred. We left him with only twenty-six dead people to account for, and I felt a tranquil satisfaction in the thought that in so judiciously taking care of No. 1 at that breakfast table I had pleasantly escaped being No. 27. Slade came out to the coach and saw us off, first ordering certain rearrangements of the mailbags for our comfort, and then we took leave of him, satisfied that we should hear of him again, someday, and wondering in what connection.

And sure enough, two or three years afterward, we did hear of him again. News came to the Pacific coast that the Vigilance Committee in Montana (whither Slade had removed from Rocky Ridge) had hanged him. I find an account of the affair in the thrilling little book I quoted a paragraph from in the last chapter—*The Vigilantes of Montana, Being a Reliable Account of the Capture, Trial and Execution of Henry Plummer's Notorious Road Agent Band,* by Prof. Thos. J. Dimsdale, Virginia City, M. T. Mr. Dimsdale's chapter is well worth reading, as a specimen of how the people of the frontier deal with criminals when the courts of law prove inefficient. Mr. Dimsdale makes two remarks about Slade, both of which are accurately descriptive, and one of which is exceedingly picturesque: "Those who saw him in his natural state only, would pronounce him to be a kind husband, a most hospitable host and a courteous gentleman; on the contrary, those who met him when maddened with liquor and surrounded by a gang of armed roughs, would pronounce him a fiend incarnate." And this: "From Fort Kearney, west, he was feared *a great deal more than the Almighty.*" For compactness, simplicity, and vigor of expression, I will "back" that sentence against anything in literature. Mr. Dimsdale's narrative is as follows. In all places where italics occur, they are mine:

> After the execution of the five men on the 14th of January, the Vigilantes considered that their work was nearly ended. They had freed the country of highwaymen and murderers to a great extent, and they determined that in the absence of the regular civil authority they would establish a People's Court where all offenders should be tried by judge and jury. This was the nearest approach to social order that

the circumstances permitted, and, though strict legal authority was wanting, yet the people were firmly determined to maintain its efficiency, and to enforce its decrees. It may here be mentioned that the overt act which was the last round on the fatal ladder leading to the scaffold on which Slade perished, *was the tearing in pieces and stamping upon a writ of this court, followed by his arrest of the Judge, Alex. Davis, by authority of a presented Derringer, and with his own hands.*

J. A. Slade was himself, we have been informed, a Vigilante; he openly boasted of it, and said he knew all that they knew. He was never accused, or even suspected, of either murder or robbery, committed in this Territory (the latter crime was never laid to his charge, in any place); but that he had killed several men in other localities was notorious, and his bad reputation in this respect was a most powerful argument in determining his fate, when he was finally arrested for the offense above mentioned. On returning from Milk River he became more and more addicted to drinking, until at last it was a common feat for him and his friends to "take the town." He and a couple of his dependents might often be seen on one horse, galloping through the streets, shouting and yelling, firing revolvers, etc. On many occasions he would ride his horse into stores, break up bars, toss the scales out of doors and use most insulting language to parties present. Just previous to the day of his arrest, he had given a fearful beating to one of his followers; but such was his influence over them that the man wept bitterly at the gallows, and begged for his life with all his power. *It had become quite common, when Slade was on a spree, for the shop-keepers and citizens to close the stores and put out all the lights;* being fearful of some outrage at his hands. For his wanton destruction of goods and furniture, he was always ready to pay, when sober, if he had money; but there were not a few who regarded payment as small satisfaction for the outrage, and these men were his personal enemies.

From time to time Slade received warnings from men that he well knew would not deceive him, of the certain end of his conduct. There was not a moment, for weeks previous to his arrest, in which the public did not expect to hear of some bloody outrage. The dread of his very name, and the presence of the armed band of hangers-on who followed him alone prevented a resistance which must certainly have ended in the instant murder or multilation of the opposing party.

Slade was frequently arrested by order of the court whose organization we have described, and had treated it with respect by paying one or two fines and promising to pay the rest when he had money; but in the transaction that occurred at this crisis, he forgot even this caution, and goaded by passion and the hatred of restraint, he sprang into the embrace of death.

Slade had been drunk and "cutting up" all night. He and his companions had made the town a perfect hell. In the morning, J. M. Fox, the sheriff, met him, arrested him, took him into court and commenced reading a warrant that he had for his arrest, by way of arraignment. He became uncontrollably furious, and *seizing the writ, he tore it up, threw it on the ground and stamped on it.* The clicking of the locks of his companions' revolvers was instantly heard, and a crisis was expected. The sheriff did not attempt his retention; but being at least as prudent as he was valiant, he succumbed, leaving Slade the *master of the situation and the conqueror and the ruler of the courts, law and law-makers.* This was a declaration of war, and was so accepted. The Vigilance Committee now felt that the question of social order and the preponderance of the law-abiding citizens had then and there to be decided. They knew the character of Slade, and they were well aware that they must submit to his rule without murmur, or else that he must be dealt with in such fashion as would prevent his being able to wreak his vengeance on the committee, who could never have hoped to live in the Territory secure from outrage or death, and who could never leave it without encountering his friends, whom his victory would have emboldened and stimulated to a pitch that would have rendered them reckless of consequences. The day previous he had ridden into Dorris's store, and on being requested to leave, he drew his revolver and threatened to kill the gentleman who spoke to him. Another saloon he had led his horse into, and buying a bottle of wine, he tried to make the animal drink it. This was not considered an uncommon performance, as he had often entered saloons and commenced firing at the lamps, causing a wild stampede.

A leading member of the committee met Slade, and informed him in the quiet, earnest manner of one who feels the importance of what he is saying: "Slade, get your horse at once, and go home, or there will be ——— to pay." Slade started and took a long look, with his dark and piercing eyes, at the gentleman. "What do you mean?" said he. "You have no right to ask me what I mean," was the quiet reply, "get your horse at once, and remember what I tell you." After a short pause he promised to do so, and actually got into the saddle; but, being still intoxicated, he began calling aloud to one after another of his friends, and at last seemed to have forgotten the warning he had received and became again uproarious, shouting the name of a well-known courtesan in company with those of two men whom he considered heads of the committee, as a sort of challenge; perhaps, however, as a simple act of bravado. It seems probable that the intimation of personal danger he had received had not been forgotten entirely; though fatally for him, he took a foolish way of showing his remembrance of it. He sought out Alexander Davis, the Judge of the Court, and drawing a cocked Derringer, he presented it at his head, and told him that he should hold him as a hostage for his own safety. As the judge stood perfectly quiet, and offered no resistance to his captor, no further outrage followed on this score. Previous to this, on account of the critical state of affairs, the committee had met, and at last resolved to arrest him. His execution had not been agreed upon, and, at that time, would have been negatived, most assuredly. A messenger rode down to Nevada to inform the leading men of what was on hand, as it was desirable to show that there was a feeling of unanimity on the subject, all along the gulch.

The miners turned out almost *en masse*, leaving their work and forming in solid column. About six hundred strong, armed to the teeth, they marched up to Virginia. The leader of the body well knew the temper of his men on the subject. He spurred on ahead of them, and hastily calling a meeting of the executive, he told them plainly that the miners meant "business," and that, if they came up, they would not stand in the street to be shot down by Slade's friends; but that they would take him and hang him. The meeting was small, as the Virginia men were loath to act at all. This momentous announcement of the feeling of the Lower Town was made to a cluster of men, who were deliberating behind a wagon, at the rear of a store on Main Street.

The committee were most unwilling to proceed to extremities. All the duty they had ever performed seemed as nothing to the task before them; but they had to decide, and that quickly. It was finally agreed that if the whole body of the miners were of the opinion that he should be hanged, that the committee left it in their hands to deal with him. Off, at hot speed, rode the leader of the Nevada men to join his command.

Slade had found out what was intended, and the news sobered him instantly. He went into P. S. Pfout's store, where Davis was, and apologized for his conduct, saying that he would take it all back.

The head of the column now wheeled into Wallace Street and marched up at quick time. Halting in front of the store, the executive officer of the committee stepped forward and arrested Slade, who was at once informed of his doom, and inquiry was made as to whether he had any business to settle. Several parties spoke to him on the subject; but to all such inquiries he turned a deaf ear, being entirely absorbed in the terrifying reflections on his own awful position. He never ceased his entreaties for life, and to see his dear wife. The unfortunate lady referred to, between whom and Slade there existed a warm affection, was at this time living at their ranch on the Madison. She was possessed of considerable personal attractions; tall, well-formed, of graceful carriage, pleasing manners, and was, withal, an accomplished horsewoman.

A messenger from Slade rode at full speed to inform her of her husband's arrest. In an instant she was in the saddle, and with all the energy that love and despair could lend to an ardent temperament and a strong physique, she urged her fleet charger over the twelve miles of rough and rocky ground that intervened between her and the object of her passionate devotion.

Meanwhile a party of volunteers had made the necessary preparations for the execution, in the valley traversed by the branch. Beneath the site of Pfout's and Russell's stone building there was a corral, the gate-posts of which were strong and high. Across the top was laid a beam, to which the rope was fastened, and a dry-goods box served for the platform. To this place Slade was marched, surrounded by a guard, composed of the best armed and most numerous force that has ever appeared in Montana Territory.

The doomed man had so exhausted himself by tears, prayers and lamentations, that he had scarcely strength left to stand under the fatal beam. He repeatedly exclaimed, "My God! my God! must I die? Oh, my dear wife!"

On the return of the fatigue party, they encountered some friends of Slade, staunch and reliable citizens and members of the committee, but who were personally attached to the condemned. On hearing of his sentence, one of them, a stout-hearted man, pulled out his handkerchief and walked away, weeping like a child. Slade still begged to see his wife, most piteously, and it seemed hard to deny his request; but the bloody consequences that were sure to follow the inevitable attempt at a rescue, that her presence and entreaties would have certainly incited, forbade the granting of his request. Several gentlemen were sent for to see him, in his last moments, one of whom (Judge Davis) made a short address to the people; but in such low tones as to be inaudible, save to a few in his immediate vicinity. One of his friends, after exhausting his powers of entreaty, threw off his coat and declared that the prisoner could not be hanged until he himself was killed. A hundred guns were instantly leveled at him; whereupon he turned and fled; but, being brought back, he was compelled to resume his coat, and to give a promise of future peaceable demeanor.

> Scarcely a leading man in Virginia could be found, though numbers of the citizens joined the ranks of the guard when the arrest was made. All lamented the stern necessity which dictated the execution.
>
> Everything being ready, the command was given, "Men, do your duty," and the box being instantly slipped from beneath his feet, he died almost instantaneously.
>
> The body was cut down and carried to the Virginia Hotel, where, in a darkened room, it was scarcely laid out when the unfortunate and bereaved companion of the deceased arrived, at headlong speed, to find that all was over, and that she was a widow. Her grief and heart-piercing cries were terrible evidences of the depth of her attachment for her lost husband, and a considerable period elapsed before she could regain the command of her excited feelings.

There is something about the desperado nature that is wholly unaccountable—at least it looks unaccountable. It is this. The true desperado is gifted with splendid courage, and yet he will take the most infamous advantage of his enemy; armed and free, he will stand up before a host and fight until he is shot all to pieces, and yet when he is under the gallows and helpless he will cry and plead like a child. Words are cheap, and it is easy to call Slade a coward (all executed men who do not "die game" are promptly called cowards by unreflecting people), and when we read of Slade that he "had so exhausted himself by tears, prayers and lamentations, that he had scarcely strength left to stand under the fatal beam," the disgraceful word suggests itself in a moment—yet in frequently defying and inviting the vengeance of banded Rocky Mountain cutthroats by shooting down their comrades and leaders, and never offering to hide or fly, Slade showed that he was a man of peerless bravery. No coward would dare that. Many a notorious coward, many a chicken-livered poltroon, coarse, brutal, degraded, has made his dying speech without a quaver in his voice and been swung into eternity with what looked like the calmest fortitude, and so we are justified in believing, from the lowest intellect of such a creature, that it was not *moral* courage that enabled him to do it. Then, if moral courage is not the requisite quality, what could it have been that this stouthearted Slade lacked?—this bloody, desperate, kindly mannered, urbane gentleman, who never hesitated to warn his most ruffianly enemies that he would kill them whenever or wherever he came across them next! I think it is a conundrum worth investigating.

BRET HARTE

FRANCIS BRETT HARTE (1836–1902) was born in Albany, New York. He deserted the East at seventeen and went to California, where he worked variously as a printer, a schoolteacher, and in a mint. Presently he began publishing short sketches and poems in magazines, and in 1857 when he became a typesetter for *Golden Era* in San Francisco, he contributed several sketches to this publication under the name Bret Harte, as well as an early version of his short novel *M'liss: An Idyll of Red Mountain* (1863), based on his experiences as a schoolteacher in a mining district. *M'liss* was to be Harte's longest, most sustained inspiration and it vividly captures the people who had come West in pursuit of gold. By 1868 Harte had achieved local fame as a writer and was made editor of a new magazine, the *Overland Monthly*. It was in the pages of this magazine that Harte's most famous short stories first saw publication, "The Outcasts of Poker Flat," "The Luck of Roaring Camp," and "Tennessee's Partner." Because of the national circulation of the *Overland Monthly*, Harte's tales, so filled with new characters, new experiences, and new ways of looking at things, caused a sensation in the East and his reputation became such that his poem "The Heathen Chinee" (1870) was a national best-seller and on everyone's lips.

In his short fiction over the next three decades, Harte introduced a number of original characters who eventually were turned into stereotypes by his many imitators. Among the more memorable are his stage driver Yuba Bill, the gamblers John Oakhurst in four stories and Jack Hamlin in nineteen stories and Harte's novel *Gabriel Conroy* (1876), the garrulous Spanish-American Enrique Saltello, the lawyer and gentleman Colonel Culpepper Starbottle, the Chinese characters See Yup and Wan Lee, and the backwoods practitioner

Dr. Duchesne. Harte wrote sympathetically of children and animals and was ever the champion of the oppressed. Not only did he object to the way in which Chinese and blacks were made victims of racial intolerance, but he once lost a job as editor of a newspaper because of a diatribe aimed at the townspeople for massacring a village of peaceful Indians.

Harte's literary West was not the black-and-white stereotype of virtue versus vice typical of so many later writers; rather, it was an image of a harsh, hostile world where, quite literally, luck or even a change in the weather could mean the difference between life and death. "It *was* a very special world, that gold-rush world, with ways of living, thinking, feeling, and acting so particularly its own that there has never been anything quite like it anywhere, before or since," Walter Van Tilburg Clark wrote in his Foreword to the anthology *Bret Harte: Stories of the Early West* (Platt & Munk, 1964).

In 1871, at the behest of several Eastern editors, Harte went to New York City, and as it happened, never returned to the West. For a time he lived extravagantly and relished his stature as a literary idol, but soon fell into financial difficulties, trying lecture tours and collaborating with Mark Twain in 1877 on a play. In 1878 Harte accepted a position as a U.S. consular agent in Krefeld, Germany. Two years later he was transferred to Glasgow, eventually settling in London, where he continued to write short stories and was a welcome guest in literary circles. When he died in 1902, his reputation had been eclipsed by that of Mark Twain. Subsequently it has become fashionable to dismiss Harte's fiction. Wallace Stegner in his Introduction to the best available collection of Harte's work, *The Outcasts of Poker Flat and Other Tales* (New American Library, 1961), treated him almost with derision. This is unfair.

Harte wrote with economy. He could generate mood, tone, and a visually distinctive sense of place in a matter of a few words. He mastered the art *de façon entendue*, as the French term it. At times he was sentimental and in "Salomy Jane's Kiss" he saw the West as a place of new beginnings; but it was just that for thousands of people.

Paul Armstrong adapted "Salomy Jane's Kiss" for the stage and it opened in New York City on January 19, 1907; in due course he directed the first film version, *Salomy Jane* (Alco Films, 1914). It was later remade under the same title (Paramount, 1923), directed by George Melford. The play and both movie versions include characters from other Harte stories, Yuba Bill, Colonel Starbottle, and the prototypical Harte frontier gambler. Yet the short story does not diminish one jot for their absence. It is one of Harte's most enduring and interesting literary creations.

Salomy Jane's Kiss

Only one shot had been fired. It had gone wide of its mark—the ringleader of the vigilantes—and had left Red Pete, who had fired it, covered by their rifles and at their mercy. For his hand had been cramped by hard riding and his eyes distracted by their sudden onset, and so the inevitable end had come. He submitted sullenly to his captors; his companion fugitive and horse thief gave up the protracted struggle with a feeling not unlike relief. Even the hot and revengeful victors were content. They had taken their men alive. At any time during the long chase they could have brought them down by a rifle shot, but it would have been unsportsmanlike and have ended in a free fight instead of an example. Besides, their doom was already sealed. Their end, by a rope and a tree, although not sanctified by law, would have at least the deliberation of justice. It was the tribute paid by the vigilantes to that order which they had themselves disregarded in the pursuit and capture. Yet this strange logic of the frontier sufficed them and gave a certain dignity to the climax.

"Ef you've got anythin' to say to your folks, say it *now* and say it quick," said the ringleader.

Red Pete glanced around him. He had been run to earth at his own cabin in the clearing, whence a few relations and friends, mostly women and children, noncombatants, had outflowed, gazing vacantly at the twenty vigilantes who surrounded them. All were accustomed to scenes of violence, blood feud, chase and hardship; it was only the suddenness of the onset and its quick result that had surprised them. They looked on with dazed curiosity and some disappointment; there had been no fight to speak of—no spectacle! A boy, nephew of Red Pete, got upon the rain barrel to view the proceedings more comfortably; a tall handsome lazy Kentucky girl, a visiting neighbor, leaned against the doorpost, chewing gum. Only a yellow hound was actively perplexed. He could not make out if a hunt was just over or beginning, and ran eagerly backward and forward, leaping alternately upon the captives and the captors.

The ringleader repeated his challenge. Red Pete gave a reckless laugh and looked at his wife.

At which Mrs. Red Pete came forward. It seemed that she had much to say incoherently, furiously, vindictively to the ringleader. His soul would roast in hell for that day's work! He called himself a man, skunkin' in the open and afraid to show himself except with a crowd of other "Kiyi's" around a house of women and children. Heaping insult upon insult, inveighing against his low blood, his ancestors, his dubious origin, she at last flung out a wild taunt of his invalid wife, the insult of a woman to a woman, until his white face grew rigid and only that western American fetish of the sanctity of sex kept his twitching fingers from the lock of his rifle. Even her husband noticed it and with a half-authoritative "Let up on that, old gal," and a pat of his freed left hand on her back, took his last parting. The ringleader, still white under the lash of the woman's tongue, turned abruptly to the second captive. "And if *you've* got anybody to say good-by to, now's your chance."

The man looked up. Nobody stirred or spoke. He was a stranger there, being a chance confederate picked up by Red Pete and known to no one. Still young, but an outlaw from his abandoned boyhood of which father and mother were only a forgotten dream, he loved horses and stole them, fully accepting the frontier penalty of life for the interference with that animal on which a man's life so often depended. But he understood the good points of a horse as was shown by the one he bestrode, until a few days before the property of Judge Boompointer. This was his sole distinction.

The unexpected question stirred him for a moment out of the attitude of reckless indifference, for attitude it was, and a part of his profession. But it may have touched him that at that moment he was less than his companion and his virago wife. However, he only shook his head. As he did so his eye casually fell on the handsome girl by the doorpost, who was looking at him. The ringleader too may have been touched by his complete loneliness, for *he* hesitated. At the same moment he saw that the girl was looking at his friendless captive.

A grotesque idea struck him.

"Salomy Jane, ye might do worse than come yer and say good-by to a dyin' man, and him a stranger," he said.

There seemed to be a subtle stroke of poetry and irony in this that equally struck the apathetic crowd. It was well known that Salomy Jane Clay thought no small potatoes of herself and always held off the local swains with a lazy nymph-like scorn. Nevertheless she slowly disengaged herself from the doorpost, and to everybody's astonishment lounged with languid grace and outstretched hand toward the prisoner. The color came into the gray reckless mask which the doomed man wore as her right hand grasped his left, just loosed by his captors. Then she paused; her shy fawnlike eyes grew bold and fixed themselves upon him. She took the chewing gum from her mouth, wiped her red lips with the back of her hand, by a sudden lithe spring placed her foot on his stirrup, and bounding to the saddle, threw her arms about his neck and pressed a kiss upon his lips.

They remained thus for a hushed moment—the man on the threshold of death, the young woman in the fullness of youth and beauty—linked together. Then the crowd laughed; in the audacious effrontery of the girl's act the ultimate fate of the two men was forgotten. She slipped languidly to the ground; *she* was the focus of all eyes, she only! The ringleader saw it and his opportunity. He shouted: "Time's up! Forward!"—and urged his horse beside his captives. The next moment the whole cavalcade was sweeping over the clearing into the darkening woods.

Their destination was Sawyer's Crossing, the headquarters of the committee, where the council was still sitting and where both culprits were to expiate the offense of which that council had already found them guilty. They rode in great and breathless haste, a haste in which, strangely enough, even the captives seemed to join. That haste possibly prevented them from noticing the singular change which had taken place in the second captive since the episode of the kiss. His high color remained as if it had burned through his mask of indifference; his eyes were quick, alert and keen, his mouth half open as if the girl's kiss still lingered there. And that haste had made them careless, for the horse of the man who led him slipped in a gopher hole, rolled over, unseated his rider, and even dragged the bound and helpless second captive from Judge Boompointer's favorite mare. In an instant they were all on their feet again, but in that supreme moment the second captive felt the cords which bound his arms had slipped to his wrists. By keeping his elbows to his sides and obliging the others to help him mount it escaped their notice. By riding close to his captors and keeping in the crush of the throng he further concealed the accident, slowly working his hands downward out of his bonds.

Their way lay through a sylvan wilderness, mid-leg deep in ferns, whose tall fronds brushed their horses' sides in their furious gallop and concealed the flapping of the captive's loosened cords. The peaceful vista, more suggestive of the offerings of nymph and shepherd than of human sacrifice, was in a strange contrast to this whirlwind rush of stern armed men. The westering sun pierced the subdued light and the tremor of leaves with yellow lances; birds started into song on blue and dovelike wings, and on either side of the trail of this vengeful storm could be heard the murmur of hidden and tranquil waters. In a few moments they would be on the open ridge whence sloped the common turnpike to Sawyer's, a mile away. It was the custom of returning cavalcades to take this hill at headlong speed with shouts and cries that heralded their coming. They withheld the latter that day as inconsistent with their dignity; but emerging from the wood, swept silently like an avalanche down the slope. They were well under way, looking only to their horses, when the second captive slipped his right arm from the bonds and succeeded in grasping the reins that lay trailing on the horse's neck. A sudden vaquero jerk which the well-trained animal understood threw him on his haunches with his forelegs firmly planted on the slope. The rest of the cavalcade swept on; the man who was leading the captive's horse by the riata, thinking only of another accident, dropped the line to save himself from being dragged backward from his horse. The captive wheeled and the next moment was galloping furiously up the slope.

It was the work of a moment, a trained horse and an experienced hand. The cavalcade had covered nearly fifty yards before they could pull up; the freed captive had covered half that distance uphill. The road was so narrow that only two shots could be fired, and these broke dust two yards ahead of the fugitive. They had not dared to fire low; the horse was the more valuable animal. The fugitive knew this in his extremity also, and would have gladly taken a shot in his own leg to spare that of his horse. Five men were detached to recapture or kill him. The latter seemed inevitable. But he had calculated his chances; before they could reload he had reached the woods again; winding in and out between the pillared tree trunks, he offered no mark. They knew his horse was superior to their own; at the end of two hours they returned, for he had disappeared without track or trail. The end was briefly told in the *Sierra Record:*

> Red Pete, the notorious horse thief who had so long eluded justice, was captured and hung by the Sawyer's Crossing Vigilantes last week; his confederate unfortunately escaped on a valuable horse belonging to Judge Boompointer. The judge had refused one thousand dollars for the horse only a week before. As the thief who is still at large would find it difficult to dispose of so valuable an animal without detection the chances are against either of them turning up again.

Salomy Jane watched the cavalcade until it had disappeared. Then she became aware that her brief popularity had passed. Mrs. Red Pete in stormy hysterics had included her in a sweeping denunciation of the whole universe, possibly for simulating an emotion in which she herself was deficient. The other women hated her for her momentary exaltation above them; only the children still admired her as one who had undoubtedly "canoodled" with a man "a-goin' to be hung"—a daring flight beyond their wildest ambition. Salomy Jane accepted the charge with charming unconcern. She put on her yellow nankeen sunbonnet—a hideous affair that would have ruined any other woman but which only enhanced the piquancy of her fresh brunette skin—tied the strings letting her blue-black braids escape below its frilled curtain behind, jumped on her mustang with a casual display of agile ankles in shapely white stockings, whistled to the hound, and waving her hand with a "So long, sonny!" to the lately bereft but admiring nephew, flapped and fluttered away in her short brown holland gown.

Her father's house was four miles distant. Contrasted with the cabin she had just left it was a superior dwelling with a long lean-to at the rear, which brought the eaves almost to the ground and made it look like a low triangle. It had a long barn and cattlesheds, for Madison Clay was a great stock raiser and the owner of a quarter section. It had a sitting room and a parlor organ whose transportation thither had been a marvel of packing. These things were supposed to give Salomy Jane an undue importance, but the girl's reserve and inaccessibility to local advances were rather the result of a cool lazy temperament and the preoccupation of a large protecting admiration for her father, for some years a widower. For Mr. Madison Clay's life had been threatened in one or two feuds, not without cause, it was said, and it is possible that the pathetic spectacle of her father doing his visiting with a shotgun may have touched her closely and somewhat prejudiced her against the neighboring masculinity. The thought that cattle, horses and quarter section would one day be hers did not disturb her calm. As for Mr. Clay, he accepted her as housewifely though somewhat interfering, and being one of his own womankind, not without some degree of merit.

"Wot's this yer I'm hearin' of your doin's over at Red Pete's? Honeyfoglin' with a horse thief, eh?" said Mr. Clay two days later at breakfast.

"I reckon you heard about the straight thing, then," said Salomy Jane unconcernedly, without looking around.

"What do you calkilate Rube will say to it? What are you goin' to tell *him?*" said Mr. Clay sarcastically.

Rube, or Reuben Waters was a swain supposed to be favored particularly by Mr. Clay. Salomy Jane looked up.

"I'll tell him that when *he's* on his way to be hung, I'll kiss him—not till then," said the young lady brightly.

This delightful witticism suited the paternal humor, and Mr. Clay smiled; nevertheless he frowned a moment afterward.

"But this yer hoss thief got away arter all, and that's a hoss of a different color," he said grimly.

Salomy Jane put down her knife and fork. This was certainly a new and different phase of the situation. She had never thought of it before, and strangely enough, for the first time she became interested in the man. "Got away?" she repeated. "Did they let him off?"

"Not much," said her father briefly. "Slipped his cords and goin' down the grade pulled up short, just like a vaquero agin a lassoed bull, almost draggin' the man leadin' him off his hoss, and then skyuted up the grade. For that matter, on that hoss o' Judge Boompointer's he mout had dragged the whole posse of 'em down on their knees ef he liked! Sarved 'em right, too. Instead of stringin' him up afore the door or shootin' him on sight they must allow to take him down afore the hull committee 'for an example.' Example be blowed! Ther' 's example enough when some stranger comes unbeknownst slap onter a man hanged to a tree and plugged full of holes. *That's* an example, and *he* knows what it means. Wot more do ye want? But then those vigilantes is allus clingin' and hangin' onter some mere scrap o' the law they're pretendin' to despise. It makes me sick! Why, when Jake Myers shot your ole Aunt Viney's second husband, and I laid in wait for Jake afterwards in the Butternut Hollow, did *I* tie him to his hoss and fetch him down to your Aunt Viney's cabin 'for an example' before I plugged him? No!" in deep disgust. "No! Why, I just meandered through the woods, carelesslike, till he comes out, and I just rode up to him, and I said—"

But Salomy Jane had heard her father's story before. Even one's dearest relatives are apt to become tiresome in narration. "I know, dad," she interrupted; "but this yer man—this hoss thief—did *he* get clean away without gettin' hurt at all?"

"He did, and unless he's fool enough to sell the hoss, he kin keep away, too. So ye see ye can't ladle out purp stuff about a dyin' stranger to Rube. He won't swaller it."

"All the same, dad," returned the girl cheerfully, "I reckon to say it, and say more; I'll tell him that ef *he* manages to get away too, I'll marry him—there! But ye don't ketch Rube takin' any such risks in gettin' ketched, or in gettin' away arter!"

Madison Clay smiled grimly, pushed back his chair, rose, dropped a perfunctory kiss on his daughter's hair, and taking his shotgun from the corner, departed on a peaceful Samaritan mission to a cow who had dropped a calf in the far pasture. Inclined as he was to Reuben's wooing from his eligibility as to property, he was conscious that he was sadly deficient in certain qualities inherent in the Clay family. It certainly would be a kind of *mésalliance*.

Left to herself Salomy Jane stared a long while at the coffee pot, and then called the two squaws who assisted her in her household duties to clear away the things while she went up to her own room to make her bed. Here she was confronted with a possible prospect of that proverbial bed she might be making in her willfulness, and on which she must lie, in the photograph of a somewhat serious young man of refined features—Reuben Waters—stuck in her window frame. Salomy Jane smiled over her last witticism regarding him and enjoyed it like your true humorist, and then, catching sight of her own handsome face in the little mirror, smiled again. But wasn't it funny about that horse thief getting off after all? Good Lordy! Fancy Reuben hearing he was alive and going around with that kiss of hers set on his lips! She laughed again, a little more abstractedly. And he had returned it like a man, holding her tight and almost breathless, and he going to be hung the next minute! Salomy Jane had been kissed at other times by force, chance or stratagem. In a certain ingenuous forfeit game of the locality known as "I'm a-pinin'," many had "pined" for a "sweet kiss" from Salomy Jane, which she had yielded in a sense of honor and fair play. She had never been kissed like this before—she would never again—and yet the man was alive! And behold, she could see in the mirror that she was blushing!

She should hardly know him again. A young man with very bright eyes, a flushed and sunburnt cheek, a kind of fixed look in the face and no beard; no, none that she could feel. Yet he was not at all like Reuben, not a bit. She took Reuben's picture from the window and laid it on her work-box. And to think she did not even know this young man's name! That was queer. To be kissed by a man whom she might never know! Of course he knew hers. She wondered if he remembered it and her. But of course he was so glad to get off with his life that he never thought of anything else. Yet she did not give more than four or five minutes to these speculations, but like a sensible girl thought of something else. Once again, however, in opening the closet she found the brown holland gown she had worn on the day before; she thought it very unbecoming and regretted that she had not worn her best gown on her visit to Red Pete's cottage. On such an occasion she really might have been more impressive.

When her father came home that night she asked him the news. No, they had *not* captured the second horse thief, who was still at large. Judge Boompointer talked of invoking the aid of the despised law. It remained, then, to see whether the horse thief was fool enough to try to get rid of the animal. Red Pete's body had been delivered to his widow. Perhaps it would only be neighborly for Salomy Jane to ride over to the funeral. But Salomy Jane did not take to the suggestion kindly, nor yet did she explain to her father that as the other man was still living, she did not care to undergo a second disciplining at the widow's hands. Nevertheless she contrasted her situation with that of the widow with a new and singular satisfaction. It might have been Red Pete who had escaped. But he had not the grit of the nameless one. She had already settled his heroic quality.

"Ye ain't harkenin' to me, Salomy."

Salomy Jane started.

"Here I'm askin' ye if ye've see that hound Phil Larrabee sneakin' by yer today?"

Salomy Jane had not. But she became interested and self-reproachful, for she knew that Phil Larrabee was one of her father's enemies. "He wouldn't dare to go by here unless he knew you were out," she said quickly.

"That's what gets me," he said, scratching his grizzled head. "I've been kind o' thinkin' o' him all day, and one of them Chinese said he saw him at Sawyer's Crossing. He was a kind of friend o' Pete's wife. That's why I thought yer might find out ef he'd been there." Salomy Jane grew more self-reproachful at her father's self-interest in her neighborliness. "But that ain't all," continued Mr. Clay. "Thar was tracks over the far pasture that warn't mine. I followed 'em, and they went round and round the house two or three times, ez ef they mout hev bin prowlin', and then I lost 'em in the woods again. It's just like that sneakin' hound Larrabee to hev bin lyin' in wait for me and afraid to meet a man fair and square in the open."

"You just lie low, dad, for a day or two more and let me do a little prowlin'," said the girl with sympathetic indignation in her dark eyes. "Ef it's that skunk, I'll spot him soon enough and let you know whar he's hidin'."

"You'll just stay where ye are, Salomy," said her father decisively. "This ain't no woman's work—though I ain't sayin' you haven't got more head for it than some men I know."

Nevertheless, that night after her father had gone to bed, Salomy Jane sat by the open window of the sitting room in an apparent attitude of languid contemplation, but alert and intent of eye and ear. It was a fine moonlit night. Two pines near the door, solitary pickets of the serried ranks of distant forest, cast long shadows like paths to the cottage and sighed their spiced breath in the windows. For there was no frivolity of vine or flower around Salomy Jane's bower. The clearing was too recent, the life too practical for vanities like these. But the moon added a vague elusiveness to everything, softened the rigid outlines of the sheds, gave shadows to the lidless windows, and touched with merciful indirectness the hideous debris of refuse gravel and the gaunt scars of burnt vegetation before the door. Even Salomy Jane was affected by it and exhaled something between a sigh and a yawn with the breath of the pines. Then she suddenly sat upright.

Her quick ear had caught a faint "click, click" in the direction of the wood; her quicker instinct and rustic training enabled her to determine that it was the ring of a horse's shoe on flinty ground; her knowledge of the locality told her it came from the spot where the trail passed over an outcrop of flint, scarcely a quarter of a mile from where she sat, and within the clearing. It was no errant stock, for the foot was shod with iron; it was a mounted trespasser by night and boded no good to a man like Clay.

She rose, threw her shawl over her head more for disguise than shelter, and passed out of the door. A sudden impulse made her seize her father's shotgun from the corner where it stood—not that she feared any danger to herself but it gave her an excuse. She made directly for the wood, keeping in the shadow of the pines as long as she could. At the fringe she halted; whoever was there must pass her before reaching the house.

Then there seemed to be a suspense of all nature. Everything was deadly still; even the moonbeams appeared no longer tremulous. Soon there was a rustle as of some stealthy animal among the ferns, and then a dismounted man stepped into the moonlight. It was the horse thief—the man she had kissed!

For a wild moment a strange fancy seized her usually sane intellect and stirred her temperate blood. The news they had told her was *not* true; he had been hung and this was his ghost! He looked as white and spiritlike in the moonlight, and was dressed in the same clothes as when she saw him last. He had evidently seen her approaching and moved quickly to meet her. But in his haste he stumbled slightly; she reflected suddenly that ghosts did not stumble, and a feeling of relief came over her. It was no assassin of her father that had been prowling around—only this unhappy fugitive. A momentary color came into her cheek; her coolness and hardihood returned; it was with a tinge of sauciness in her voice that she said:

"I reckoned you were a ghost."

"I mout have been," he said, looking at her fixedly. "But I reckon I'd have come back here all the same."

"It's a little riskier comin' back alive," she said with a levity that died on her lips, for a singular nervousness, half fear and half expectation, was beginning to take the place of her relief of a moment ago. "Then it was *you* who was prowlin' round and makin' tracks in the far pasture?"

"Yes; I came straight here when I got away."

She felt his eyes were burning her but did not dare to raise her own. "Why," she began, hesitated, and ended vaguely. "*How* did you get here?"

"You helped me!"

"I?"

"Yes. That kiss you gave me put life into me, gave me strength to get away. I swore to myself I'd come back and thank you, alive or dead."

Every word he said she could have anticipated, so plain the situation seemed to her now. And every word he said she knew was the truth. Yet her cool common sense struggled against it.

"What's the use of your escapin' ef you're comin' back here to be ketched again?" she said pertly.

He drew a little nearer to her, but seemed to her the more awkward as she resumed her self-possession. His voice, too, was broken as if by exhaustion as he said, catching his breath at intervals:

"I'll tell you. You did more for me than you think. You made another man o' me. I never had a man, woman or child do to me what you did. I never had a friend—only a pal like Red Pete who picked me up on shares. I want to quit this yer—what I'm doin'. I want to begin by doin' the square thing to you." He stopped, breathed hard and then said brokenly, "My hoss is over thar, staked out. I want to give him to you. Judge Boompointer will give you a thousand dollars for him. I ain't lyin'; it's God's truth! I saw it on the handbill agin a tree. Take him and I'll get away afoot. Take him. It's the only thing I can do for you, and I know it don't half pay for what you did. Take it; your father can get the reward for you if you can't."

Such were the ethics of this strange locality that neither the man who made the offer nor the girl to whom it was made was struck by anything that seemed illogical or indelicate, or at all inconsistent with justice or the horse thief's real conversion. Salomy Jane nevertheless dissented, from another and weaker reason.

"I don't want your hoss, though I reckon dad might; but you're just starvin'. I'll get suthin'." She turned toward the house.

"Say you'll take the hoss first," he said, grasping her hand. At the touch she felt herself coloring and struggled, expecting perhaps another kiss. But he dropped her hand. She turned again with a saucy gesture, said, "Hol' on; I'll come right back," and slipped away, the mere shadow of a coy and flying nymph in the moonlight, until she reached the house.

Here she not only procured food and whiskey but added a long dust coat and hat of her father's to her burden. They would serve as a disguise for him and hide that heroic figure, which she thought everybody must now know as she did. Then she rejoined him breathlessly. But he put the food and whiskey aside.

"Listen," he said. "I've turned the hoss into your corral. You'll find him there in the morning, and no one will know but that he got lost and joined the other horses."

Then she burst out. "But you—*you*—what will become of you? You'll be ketched!"

"I'll manage to get away," he said in a low voice, "ef—ef—"

"Ef what?" she said tremblingly.

"Ef you'll put the heart in me agin, as you did!" he gasped.

She tried to laugh, to move away. She could do neither. Suddenly he caught her in his arms with a long kiss, which she returned again and again. Then they stood embraced as they had embraced two days before, but no longer the same. For the cool, lazy Salomy Jane had been transformed into another woman—a passionate clinging savage. Perhaps something of her father's blood had surged within her at that supreme moment. The man stood erect and determined.

"Wot's your name?" she whispered quickly. It was a woman's quickest way of defining her feelings.

"Dart."

"Yer first name?"

"Jack."

"Let me go now, Jack. Lie low in the woods till tomorrow sunup. I'll come again."

He released her. Yet she lingered a moment. "Put on those things," she said, with a sudden happy flash of eyes and teeth, "and lie close till I come." And then she sped away home.

But midway up the distance she felt her feet going slower, and something at her heartstrings seemed to be pulling her back. She stopped, turned and glanced to where he had been standing. Had she seen him then she might have returned. But he had disappeared. She gave her first sigh, and then ran quickly again. It must be nearly one o'clock! It was not very long to morning!

She was within a few steps of her own door when the sleeping woods and silent air appeared to suddenly awake with a sharp "crack!"

She stopped, paralyzed. Another "crack!" followed, that echoed over the far corral. She recalled herself instantly and dashed off wildly to the woods again.

As she ran she thought of one thing only. He had been dogged by one of his old pursuers and attacked. But there were two shots and he was unarmed. Suddenly she remembered that she had left her father's gun standing against the tree where they were talking. Thank God! She might again have saved him. She ran to the tree; the gun was gone. She ran hither and thither, dreading at every step to fall upon his lifeless body. A new thought struck her; she ran to the corral. The horse was not there! He must have been able to regain it and escape *after* the shots had been fired. She drew a long breath of relief, but it was caught up in an apprehension of alarm. Her father, awakened from his sleep by the shots, was hurriedly approaching her.

"What's up now, Salomy Jane?" he demanded excitedly.

"Nothin'," said the girl, with an effort. "Nothin', at least, that *I* can find." She was usually truthful because fearless, and a lie stuck in her throat; but she was no longer fearless, thinking of *him*. "I wasn't abed; so I ran out as soon as I heard the shots fired," she answered in return to his curious gaze.

"And you've hid my gun somewhere where it can't be found," he said reproachfully. "Ef it was that sneak Larrabee and he fired them shots to lure me out, he might have potted me without a show a dozen times in the last five minutes."

She had not thought since of her father's enemy! It might indeed have been he who had attacked Jack. But she made a quick point of the suggestion. "Run in, dad, run in and find the gun; you've got no show out here without it." She seized him by the shoulders from behind, shielding him from the woods and hurried him, half expostulating, half struggling, to the house.

But there no gun was to be found. It was strange; it must have been mislaid in some corner! Was he sure he had not left it in the barn? But no matter now. The danger was over; the Larrabee trick had failed. He must go to bed now and in the morning they would make a search together. At the same time she had inwardly resolved to rise before him and make another search of the wood, and perhaps—fearful joy as she recalled her promise!—find Jack alive and well, awaiting her!

Salomy Jane slept little that night, nor did her father. But toward morning he fell into a tired man's slumber until the sun was well up the horizon. Far different was it with his daughter; she lay with her face to the window, her head half lifted to catch every sound, from the creaking of the sun-warped shingles above her head to the far-off moan of the rising wind in the pine trees. Sometimes she fell into a breathless half-ecstatic trance, living over every moment of the stolen interview, feeling the fugitive's arm still around her, hearing his whispered voice in her ears—the birth of her new life! This was followed again by a period of agonizing the stolen interview, feeling the fugitive's arm still around dread—that he might even then be lying in the woods, his life ebbing away, with her name on his lips and she resting here inactive, until she half started from her bed to go to his succor. And this went on until a pale opal glow came into the sky, followed by a still paler pink on the summit of the white Sierras. Then she rose and hurriedly began to dress. Still so sanguine was her hope of meeting him that she lingered yet a moment to select the brown holland skirt and yellow sunbonnet she had worn when she first saw him. And she had only seen him twice! Only *twice!* It would be cruel, too cruel, not to see him again!

She crept softly down the stairs, listening to the long-drawn breathing of her father in his bedroom, and then by the light of a guttering candle scrawled a note to him, begging him not to trust himself out of the house until she returned from her search. Then leaving the note open on the table she swiftly ran out into the growing day.

Three hours afterward Mr. Madison Clay awoke to the sound of loud knocking. At first this forced itself upon his consciousness as his daughter's regular morning summons, and was responded to by a grunt of recognition and a nestling closer in the blankets. Then he awoke with a start and a muttered oath, remembered the events of last night and his intention to get up early, and rolled out of bed. Becoming aware by this time that the knocking was at the outer door and hearing the shout of a familiar voice he hastily pulled on his boots and his jean trousers, and fastened a single suspender over his shoulder as he clattered downstairs. The outside door was open, and waiting on the threshold was his kinsman, an old ally in many a blood feud—Breckenridge Clay!

"You *are* a cool one, Mad!" said the latter in half-admiring indignation.

"What's up?" said the bewildered Madison.

"*You* ought to be, and scootin' out o' this," said Breckenridge grimly. "It's all very well to know nothin', but here Phil Larrabee's friends hev just picked him up drilled through with slugs and deader nor a crow, and now they're lettin' loose Larrabee's two half-brothers on you. And you must go like a durned fool and leave these yer things behind you in the bresh," he went on querulously, lifting Madison Clay's dust coat, hat and shotgun from his horse, which stood saddled at the door. "Luckily I picked them up in the woods comin' here. Ye ain't got more than time to get over the state line and among your folks thar afore they'll be down on you. Hustle, old man! What are you gawkin' and starin' at?"

Madison Clay had stared amazed and bewildered—horror-stricken. The incidents of the past night for the first time flashed upon him clearly—hopelessly! The shots, his finding Salomy Jane alone in the woods, her confusion and anxiety to rid herself of him, the disappearance of the shotgun, and now this new discovery of the taking of his hat and coat for a disguise! *She* had killed Phil Larrabee in that disguise after provoking his first harmless shot! She, his own child, Salomy Jane, had disgraced herself by a man's crime, had disgraced him by usurping his right and taking a mean advantage, by deceit, of a foe!

"Gimme that gun," he said hoarsely.

Breckenridge handed him the gun in wonder and slowly gathering suspicion. Madison examined nipple and muzzle; one barrel had been discharged. It was true! The gun dropped from his hand.

"Look here, old man," said Breckenridge, with a darkening face, "there's bin no foul play here. Thar's bin no hiring of men, no deputy to do this job. *You* did it fair and square—yourself?"

"Yes, by God!" burst out Madison Clay in a hoarse voice. "Who says I didn't?"

Reassured, yet believing that Madison Clay had nerved himself for the act by an overdraught of whiskey which had affected his memory, Breckenridge said curtly, "Then wake up and lite out ef ye want me to stand by you."

"Go to the corral and pick me out a hoss," said Madison slowly yet not without a certain dignity of manner. "I've suthin' to say to Salomy Jane afore I go." He was holding her scribbled note, which he had just discovered, in his shaking hand.

Struck by his kinsman's manner and knowing the dependent relations of father and daughter, Breckenridge nodded and hurried away. Left to himself, Madison Clay ran his fingers through his hair and straightened out the paper on which Salomy Jane had scrawled her note, turned it over, and wrote on the back:

> You might have told me you did it, and not leave your ole father to find it out how you disgraced yourself with him, too, by a lowdown, underhanded woman's trick! I've said I done it and took the blame myself, and all the sneakiness of it that folks suspect. If I get away alive, and I don't care much which, you needn't foller. The house and stock are yours; but you ain't any longer the daughter of your disgraced father.
>
> MADISON CLAY

He had scarcely finished the note, when with a clatter of hoofs and a led horse, Breckenridge reappeared at the door, elated and triumphant. "You're in luck, Mad! I found that stole hoss of Judge Boompointer's had got away and strayed among your stock in the corral. Take him and you're safe; he can't be outrun this side of the state line."

"I ain't no hoss thief," said Madison grimly.

"Nobody sez ye are, but you'd be wuss—a fool—ef you didn't take him. I'm testimony that you found him among your hosses; I'll tell Judge Boompointer you've got him, and ye kin send him back when you're safe. The judge will be mighty glad to get him back and call it quits. So ef you've writ to Salomy Jane, come."

Madison Clay no longer hesitated. Salomy Jane might return at any moment—it would be part of her "fool womanishness"—and he was in no mood to see her before a third party. He laid the note on the table, gave a hurried glance around the house which he grimly believed he was leaving forever, and striding to the door, leaped on the stolen horse and swept away with his kinsman.

But that note lay for a week undisturbed on the table in full view of the open door. The house was invaded by leaves, pine cones, birds and squirrels during the hot, silent, empty days, and at night by shy, stealthy creatures, but never again, day or night, by any of the Clay family. It was known in the district that Clay had flown across the state line; his daughter was believed to have joined him the next day; and the house was supposed to be locked up. It lay off the main road and few passed that way. The starving cattle in the corral at last broke bounds and spread over the woods. And one night a stronger blast than usual swept through the house and carried the note from the table to the floor where, whirled into a crack in the flooring, it slowly rotted.

But though the sting of her father's reproach was spared her, Salomy Jane had no need of the letter to know what had happened. For as she entered the woods in the dim light of that morning she saw the figure of Dart gliding from the shadow of a pine toward her. The unaffected cry of joy that rose from her lips died there as she caught sight of his face in the open light.

"You are hurt," she said, clutching his arm passionately.

"No," he said. "But I wouldn't mind that if—"

"You're thinkin' I was afeared to come back last night when I heard the shootin', but I *did* come," she went on feverishly. "I ran back here when I heard the two shots, but you was gone. I went to the corral but your hoss wasn't there, and I thought you'd got away."

"I *did* get away," said Dart gloomily. "I killed the man, thinkin' he was huntin' *me* and forgettin' I was disguised. He thought I was your father."

"Yes," said the girl joyfully, "he was after dad and you—*you* killed him." She again caught his hand admiringly.

But he did not respond. Possibly there were points of honor which this horse thief felt vaguely with her father. "Listen," he said grimly. "Others think it was your father killed him. When *I* did it—for he fired at me first—I ran to the corral agin and took my hoss, thinkin' I might be follered. I made a clear circuit of the house, and when I found he was the only one and no one was follerin', I come back here and took off my disguise. Then I heard his friends find him in the woods and I know they suspected your father. And then another man come through the woods while I was hidin' and found the clothes and took 'em away." He stopped and stared at her gloomily.

But all this was unintelligible to the girl. "Dad would have got the better of him ef you hadn't," she said eagerly, "so what's the difference?"

"All the same," he said, "I must take his place."

She did not understand, but turned her head to her master.

"Then you'll go back with me and tell them *all?*" she said obediently.

"Yes," he said.

She put her hand in his and they crept out of the wood together. She foresaw a thousand difficulties, but chiefest of all, that he did not love as she did. *She* would not have taken these risks against their happiness.

But alas for ethics and heroism. As they were issuing from the wood they heard the sound of galloping hoofs and had barely time to hide themselves before Madison Clay, on the stolen horse of Judge Boompointer, swept past them with his kinsman.

Salomy Jane turned to her lover.

And here I might, as a moral romancer, pause, leaving the guilty, passionate girl eloped with her disreputable lover, destined to lifelong shame and misery, misunderstood to the last by a criminal fastidious parent. But I am confronted by certain facts, on which this romance is based. A month later a handbill was posted on one of the sentinel pines announcing that the property would be sold by auction to the highest bidder by Mrs. John Dart, daughter of Madison Clay, Esq., and it was sold accordingly. Still later, by ten years, the chronicler of these pages visited a certain stock or breeding farm in the Blue Grass Country, famous for the popular racers it has produced. He was told that the owner was the "best judge of horseflesh in the country." "Small wonder," added his informant, "for they say as a young man out in California he was a horse thief, and only saved himself by eloping with some rich farmer's daughter. But he's a straight-out and respectable man now, whose word about horses can't be bought; and as for his wife, *she's* a beauty! To see her at the Springs, rigged out in the latest fashion, you'd never think she had ever lived out of New York or wasn't the wife of a millionaire."

STEPHEN CRANE

STEPHEN CRANE (1871–1900) was born in Newark, New Jersey. He attended Lafayette College 1889–90 and then went to Syracuse University 1890–91, where he distinguished himself playing baseball. He was, however, an indifferent student, and after leaving Syracuse, he made a precarious living as a free-lance writer for newspapers. Already fascinated with New York City's Bowery while a student at Syracuse, Crane began work on his first novel, *Maggie: A Girl of the Streets,* which he published at his own expense in 1893. *The Red Badge of Courage* (1895), for which he is best remembered, was written with the help of reading history and Leo Tolstoy as well as interviewing Civil War veterans.

As early as August 1892, Crane proposed to the American Press Association that he submit sketches while taking a trip into the Far West. Once the Bacheller newspaper syndicate bought *The Red Badge of Courage* for syndication, Irving Bacheller agreed to finance such a trip. Early in 1895 Crane embarked on a journey that took him through Nebraska, to the Southwest, and to Mexico. ". . . What I contend for is the atmosphere of the West," Crane wrote back East in a letter, "which really is frank and honest and is bound to make eleven honest men for one pessimistic thief. More glory be with them." His first published Western story was "Horses—One Dash!" in 1895. Over the next three years, Crane continued to write stories set in the West, the best known among them "The Five White Mice" set in Mexico City, "The Bride Comes to Yellow Sky," and "A Man and Some Others." Fortunately all of these writings, sketches, and some letters have been brought together in a single collection titled *The Western Writings of Stephen Crane* (New American Library, 1979), edited with an Introduction by Frank Bergon. I feel that Crane's Western writings constitute his best work.

In the Preface to "Hank's Woman" by Owen Wister I mention how Wister altered a passage in his novel *The Virginian* (Macmillan, 1902) because Theodore Roosevelt objected to it. The same thing happened to Stephen Crane, but with somewhat different results. Crane sent a copy of "A Man and Some Others" to Roosevelt prior to its appearing in *Century Magazine*, one of the publications for which Roosevelt himself wrote. Roosevelt responded to Crane with a letter in which he expressed the sentiment that Crane should someday write "another story of the frontiersman and the Mexican Greaser in which the frontiersman shall come out on top; it is more normal that way!" Crane never did.

Crane's exceptional Western short novel *The Blue Hotel* (1899) introduced objective style into the Western story even more than had been true of Crane's previous stories of human confrontation with death and, at the same time, still managed to rival Bret Harte's stories for local color. It was vital to Crane's point of view that individual violence could often be, in the words used in *The Blue Hotel*, "the apex of a human movement." For this reason, Crane preferred surfaces to interiors in dealing with his characters. His long-range influence on Western writers like Luke Short, Walter Van Tilburg Clark, and Jack Schaefer was considerable, and they came to see him as one of the foremost literary experimentalists in the Western genre. It was only after Crane had reached Mexico City on his original trip into the West that his pessimism about life reasserted itself and he became convinced that it was only "the man who has not yet solved himself" who has not "discovered his own futility."

I regret that the most complete biography to appear so far, *Stephen Crane* (George Braziller, 1968) by R. W. Stallman, should have been written by a man of such quirky moods and tastes and, ultimately, lack of sympathy for his subject. As for "A Man and Some Others," Joseph Conrad praised it—rightly, I believe—and called it "immense" in a letter to Crane. A world tense, on the brink of bloodshed, where violence is meaningless but commonplace beneath an unblinking, savage sun—Crane was the first to give us this image of the American West; all else could be considered imitation.

A Man and Some Others

1

Dark mesquite spread from horizon to horizon. There was no house or horseman from which a mind could evolve a city or a crowd. The world was declared to be a desert and unpeopled. Sometimes, however, on days when no heat-mist arose, a blue shape, dim, of the substance of a specter's veil, appeared in the southwest, and a pondering sheep-herder might remember that there were mountains.

In the silence of these plains the sudden and childish banging of a tin pan could have made an iron-nerved man leap into the air. The sky was ever flawless; the manœuevring of clouds was an unknown pageant; but at times a sheep-herder could see, miles away, the long, white streamers of dust rising from the feet of another's flock, and the interest became intense.

Bill was arduously cooking his dinner, bending over the fire, and toiling like a blacksmith. A movement, a flash of strange color, perhaps, off in the bushes, caused him suddenly to turn his head. Presently he arose, and, shading his eyes with his hand, stood motionless and gazing. He perceived at last a Mexican sheep-herder winding through the brush toward his camp.

"Hello!" shouted Bill.

The Mexican made no answer, but came steadily forward until he was within some twenty yards. There he paused, and, folding his arms, drew himself up in the manner affected by the villain in the play. His serape muffled the lower part of his face, and his great sombrero shaded his brow. Being unexpected and also silent, he had something of the quality of an apparition; moreover, it was clearly his intention to be mysterious and devilish.

The American's pipe, sticking carelessly in the corner of his mouth, was twisted until the wrong side was uppermost, and he held his frying-pan poised in the air. He surveyed with evident surprise this apparition in the mesquite. "Hello, José!" he said; "what's the matter?"

The Mexican spoke with the solemnity of funeral tollings:

"Beel, you mus' geet off range. We want you geet off range. We no like. Un'erstan'? We no like."

"What you talking about?" said Bill. "No like what?"

"We no like you here. Un'erstan'? Too mooch. You mus' geet out. We no like. Un'erstan'?"

"Understand? No; I don't know what the blazes you're gittin' at." Bill's eyes wavered in bewilderment, and his jaw fell. "I must git out? I must git off the range? What you givin' us?"

The Mexican unfolded his serape with his small yellow hand. Upon his face was then to be seen a smile that was gently, almost caressingly murderous. "Beel," he said, "geet out!"

Bill's arm dropped until the frying-pan was at his knee. Finally he turned again toward the fire. "Go on, you dog-gone little yaller rat!" he said over his shoulder. "You fellers can't chase me off this range. I got as much right here as anybody."

"Beel," answered the other in a vibrant tone, thrusting his head forward and moving one foot, "you geet out or we keel you."

"Who will?" said Bill.

"I—and the others." The Mexican tapped his breast gracefully.

Bill reflected for a time, and then he said: "You ain't got no manner of license to warn me off'n this range, and I won't move a rod. Understand? I've got rights, and I suppose if I don't see 'em through, no one is likely to give me a good hand and help me lick you fellers, since I'm the only white man in half a day's ride. Now, look; if you fellers try to rush this camp, I'm goin' to plug about fifty per cent of the gentlemen present, sure. I'm goin' in for trouble, an' I'll git a lot of you. 'Nuther thing: if I was a fine valuable caballero like you, I'd stay in the rear till the shootin' was done, because I'm goin' to make a particular p'int of shootin' you through the chest." He grinned affably, and made a gesture of dismissal.

As for the Mexican, he waved his hands in a consummate expression of indifference. "Oh, all right," he said. Then, in a tone of deep menace and glee, he added: "We will keel you eef you no get. They have decide'."

"They have, have they?" said Bill. "Well, you tell them to go to the devil!"

2

Bill had been a mine-owner in Wyoming, a great man, an aristocrat, one who possessed unlimited credit in the saloons down the gulch. He had the social weight that could interrupt a lynching or advise a bad man of the particular merits of a remote geographical point. However, the fates exploded the toy balloon with which they had amused Bill, and on the evening of the same day he was a professional gambler with ill fortune dealing him unspeakable irritation in the shape of three big cards whenever another fellow stood pat. It is well here to inform the world that Bill considered his calamities of life all dwarfs in comparison with the excitement of one particular evening, when three kings came to him with criminal regularity against a man who always filled a straight. Later he became a cow-boy, more weirdly abandoned than if he had never been an aristocrat. By this time all that remained of his former splendor was his pride, or his vanity, which was one thing which need not have remained. He killed the foreman of the ranch over an inconsequent matter as to which of them was a liar, and the midnight train carried him eastward. He became a brakeman on the Union Pacific, and really gained high honors in the hobo war that for many years has devastated the beautiful railroads of our country. A creature of ill fortune himself, he practiced all the ordinary cruelties upon these other creatures of ill fortune. He was of so fierce a mien that tramps usually surrendered at once whatever coin or tobacco they had in their possession; and if afterward he kicked them from the train, it was only because this was a recognized treachery of the war upon the hoboes. In a famous battle fought in Nebraska in 1879, he would have achieved a lasting distinction if it had not been for a deserter from the United States army. He was at the head of a heroic and sweeping charge, which really broke the power of the hoboes in that county for three months; he had already worsted four tramps with his own coupling stick, when a stone thrown by the ex-third baseman of F Troop's nine laid him flat on the prairie, and later enforced a stay in the hospital in Omaha. After his recovery he engaged with other railroads, and shuffled cars in countless yards. An order to strike came upon him in Michigan, and afterward the vengeance of the railroad pursued him until he assumed a name. This mask is like the darkness in which the burglar chooses to move. It destroys many of the healthy fears. It is a small thing, but it eats that which we call our conscience. The conductor of No. 419 stood in the caboose within two feet of Bill's nose, and called him a liar. Bill requested him to use a milder term. He had not bored the foreman of Tin Can Ranch with any such request, but had killed him with expedition. The conductor seemed to insist, and so Bill let the matter drop.

He became the bouncer of a saloon on the Bowery in New York. Here most of his fights were as successful as had been his brushes with the hoboes in the West. He gained the complete admiration of the four clean bartenders who stood behind the great and glittering bar. He was an honored man. He nearly killed Bad Hennessy, who, as a matter of fact, had more reputation than ability, and his fame moved up the Bowery and down the Bowery.

But let a man adopt fighting as his business, and the thought grows constantly within him that it is his business to fight. These phrases became mixed in Bill's mind precisely as they are here mixed; and let a man get this idea in his mind, and defeat begins to move toward him over the unknown ways of circumstances. One summer night three sailors from the U.S.S. *Seattle* sat in the saloon drinking and attending to other people's affairs in an amiable fashion. Bill was a proud man since he had thrashed so many citizens, and it suddenly occurred to him that the loud talk of the sailors was very offensive. So he swaggered upon their attention, and warned them that the saloon was the flowery abode of peace and gentle silence. They glanced at him in surprise, and without a moment's pause consigned him to a worse place than any stoker of them knew. Whereupon he flung one of them through the side door before the others could prevent it. On the sidewalk there was a short struggle, with many hoarse epithets in the air, and then Bill slid into the saloon again. A frown of false rage was upon his brow, and he strutted like a savage king. He took a long yellow night-stick from behind the lunch-counter, and started importantly toward the main doors to see that the incensed seamen did not again enter.

The ways of sailormen are without speech, and, together in the street, the three sailors exchanged no word, but they moved at once. Landsmen would have required two years of discussion to gain such unanimity. In silence, and immediately, they seized a long piece of scantling that lay handily.

With one forward to guide the battering-ram, and with two behind him to furnish the power, they made a beautiful curve, and came down like the Assyrians on the front door of that saloon.

Strange and still strange are the laws of fate. Bill, with his kingly frown and his long night-stick, appeared at precisely that moment in the doorway. He stood like a statue of victory; his pride was at its zenith; and in the same second this atrocious piece of scantling punched him in the bulwarks of his stomach, and he vanished like a mist. Opinions differed as to where the end of the scantling landed him, but it was ultimately clear that it landed him in southwestern Texas, where he became a sheep-herder.

The sailors charged three times upon the plate-glass front of the saloon, and when they had finished, it looked as if it had been the victim of a rural fire company's success in saving it from the flames. As the proprietor of the place surveyed the ruins, he remarked that Bill was a very zealous guardian of property. As the ambulance surgeon surveyed Bill, he remarked that the wound was really an excavation.

3

As his Mexican friend tripped blithely away, Bill turned with a thoughtful face to his frying-pan and his fire. After dinner he drew his revolver from its scarred old holster, and examined every part of it. It was the revolver that had dealt death to the foreman, and it had also been in free fights in which it had dealt death to several or none. Bill loved it because its allegiance was more than that of man, horse, or dog. It questioned neither social or moral position; it obeyed alike the saint and assassin. It was the claw of the eagle, the tooth of the lion, the poison of the snake; and when he swept it from its holster, this minion smote where he listed, even to the battering of a far penny. Wherefore it was his dearest possession, and was not to be exchanged in southwestern Texas for a handful of rubies, nor even the shame and homage of the conductor of No. 419.

During the afternoon he moved through his monotony of work and leisure with the same air of deep meditation. The smoke of his supper-time fire was curling across the shadowy sea of mesquite when the instinct of the plainsman warned him that the stillness, the desolation, was again invaded. He saw a motionless horseman in black outline against the pallid sky. The silhouette displayed serape and sombrero, and even the Mexican spurs as large as pies. When this black figure began to move toward the camp, Bill's hand dropped to his revolver.

The horseman approached until Bill was enabled to see pronounced American features, and a skin too red to grow on a Mexican face. Bill released his grip on his revolver.

"Hello!" called the horseman.

"Hello!" answered Bill.

The horseman cantered forward. "Good evening," he said, as he again drew rein.

"Good evenin'," answered Bill, without committing himself by too much courtesy.

For a moment the two men scanned each other in a way that is not ill-mannered on the plains, where one is in danger of meeting horse-thieves or tourists.

Bill saw a type which did not belong in the mesquite. The young fellow had invested in some Mexican trappings of an expensive kind. Bill's eyes searched the outfit for some sign of craft, but there was none. Even with his local regalia, it was clear that the young man was of a far, black Northern city. He had discarded the enormous stirrups of his Mexican saddle; he used the small English stirrup, and his feet were thrust forward until the steel tightly gripped his ankles. As Bill's eyes traveled over the stranger, they lighted suddenly upon the stirrups and the thrust feet, and immediately he smiled in a friendly way. No dark purpose could dwell in the innocent heart of a man who rode thus on the plains.

As for the stranger, he saw a tattered individual with a tangle of hair and beard, and with a complexion turned brick-color from the sun and whisky. He saw a pair of eyes that at first looked at him as the wolf looks at the wolf, and then became childlike, almost timid, in their glance. Here was evidently a man who had often stormed the iron walls of the city of success, and who now sometimes valued himself as the rabbit values his prowess.

The stranger smiled genially, and sprang from his horse. "Well, sir, I suppose you will let me camp here with you to-night?"

"Eh?" said Bill.

"I suppose you will let me camp here with you to-night?"

Bill for a time seemed too astonished for words. "Well"—he answered, scowling in inhospitable annoyance—

"well, I don't believe this here is a good place to camp to-night, mister."

The stranger turned quickly from his saddle-girth.

"What?" he said in surprise. "You don't want me here? You don't want me to camp here?"

Bill's feet scuffled awkwardly, and he looked steadily at a cactus-plant. "Well, you see, mister," he said, "I'd like your company well enough, but—you see, some of these here greasers are goin' to chase me off the range to-night; and while I might like a man's company all right, I couldn't let him in for no such game when he ain't got nothin' to do with the trouble."

"Going to chase you off the range?" cried the stranger.

"Well, they said they were goin' to do it," said Bill.

"And—great heavens! will they kill you, do you think?"

"Don't know. Can't tell till afterwards. You see, they take some feller that's alone like me, and then they rush his camp when he ain't quite ready for 'em, and ginerally plug 'im with a sawed-off shot-gun load before he has a chance to get at 'em. They lay around and wait for their chance, and it comes soon enough. Of course a feller alone like me has got to let up watching some time. Maybe they ketch 'im asleep. Maybe the feller gits tired waiting, and goes out in broad day, and kills two or three just to make the whole crowd pile on him and settle the thing. I heard of a case like that once. It's awful hard on a man's mind—to git a gang after him."

"And so they're going to rush your camp to-night?" cried the stranger. "How do you know? Who told you?"

"Feller come and told me."

"And what are you going to do? Fight?"

"Don't see nothin' else to do," answered Bill, gloomily, still staring at the cactus-plant.

There was a silence. Finally the stranger burst out in an amazed cry. "Well, I never heard of such a thing in my life! How many of them are there?"

"Eight," answered Bill. "And now look-a-here; you ain't got no manner of business foolin' around here just now, and you might better lope off before dark. I don't ask no help in this here row. I know your happening along here just now don't give me no call on you, and you better hit the trail."

"Well, why in the name of wonder don't you go get the sheriff?" cried the stranger.

"Oh, h———!" said Bill.

4

Long, smoldering clouds spread in the western sky, and to the east silver mists lay on the purple gloom of the wilderness.

Finally, when the great moon climbed the heavens and cast its ghastly radiance upon the bushes, it made a new and more brilliant crimson of the camp-fire, where the flames capered merrily through its mesquite branches, filling the silence with the fire chorus, an ancient melody which surely bears a message of the inconsequence of individual tragedy—a message that is in the boom of the sea, the silver of the wind through the grassblades, the silken clash of hemlock boughs.

No figures moved in the rosy space of the camp, and the search of the moonbeams failed to disclose a living thing in the bushes. There was no owl-faced clock to chant the weariness of the long silence that brooded upon the plain.

The dew gave the darkness under the mesquite a velvet quality that made air seem nearer to water, and no eye could have seen through it the black things that moved like monster lizards toward the camp. The branches, the leaves, that are fain to cry out when death approaches in the wilds, were frustrated by these uncanny bodies gliding with the finesse of the escaping serpent. They crept forward to the last point where assuredly no frantic attempt of the fire could discover them, and there they paused to locate the prey. A romance relates the tale of the black cell hidden deep in the earth, where, upon entering, one sees only the little eyes of snakes fixing him in menaces. If a man could have approached a certain spot in the bushes, he would not have found it romantically necessary to have his hair rise. There would have been a sufficient expression of horror in the feeling of the death-hand at the nape of his neck and in his rubber knee-joints.

Two of these bodies finally moved toward each other until for each there grew out of the darkness a face placidly smiling with tender dreams of assassination. "The fool is asleep by the fire, God be praised!" The lips of the other widened in a grin of affectionate appreciation of the fool and his plight. There was some signaling in the gloom, and then began a series of subtle rustlings, interjected often with pauses, during which no sound arose but the sound of faint breathing.

A bush stood like a rock in the stream of firelight, sending its long shadow backward. With painful caution the little company traveled along this shadow, and finally arrived at the rear of the bush. Through its branches they surveyed for a moment of comfortable satisfaction a form in a gray blanket extended on the ground near the fire. The smile of joyful anticipation fled quickly, to give place to a quiet air of business. Two men lifted shot-guns with much of the barrels gone, and sighting these weapons through the branches, pulled trigger together.

The noise of the explosions roared over the lonely mesquite as if these guns wished to inform the entire world; and as the gray smoke fled, the dodging company back of the bush saw the blanketed form twitching. Whereupon they burst out in chorus in a laugh, and arose as merry as a lot of banqueters. They gleefully gestured congratulations, and strode bravely into the light of the fire.

Then suddenly a new laugh rang from some unknown spot in the darkness. It was a fearsome laugh of ridicule, hatred, ferocity. It might have been demoniac. It smote them motionless in their gleeful prowl, as the stern voice from the sky smites the legendary malefactor. They might have been a weird group in wax, the light of the dying fire on their yellow faces, and shining athwart their eyes turned toward the darkness whence might come the unknown and the terrible.

The thing in the gray blanket no longer twitched; but if the knives in their hands had been thrust toward it, each knife was now drawn back, and its owner's elbow was thrown upward, as if he expected death from the clouds.

This laugh had so chained their reason that for a moment they had no wit to flee. They were prisoners to their terror. Then suddenly the belated decision arrived, and with bubbling cries they turned to run; but at that instant there was a long flash of red in the darkness, and with the report one of the men shouted a bitter shout, spun once, and tumbled headlong. The thick bushes failed to impede the rout of the others.

The silence returned to the wilderness. The tired flames faintly illumined the blanketed thing and the flung corpse of the marauder, and sang the fire chorus, the ancient melody which bears the message of the inconsequence of human tragedy.

5

"Now you are worse off than ever," said the young man, dry-voiced and awed.

"No, I ain't," said Bill, rebelliously. "I'm one ahead."

After reflection, the stranger remarked, "Well, there's seven more."

They were cautiously and slowly approaching the camp. The sun was flaring its first warming rays over the gray wilderness. Upreared twigs, prominent branches, shone with golden light, while the shadows under the mesquite were heavily blue.

Suddenly the stranger uttered a frightened cry. He had arrived at a point whence he had, through openings in the thicket, a clear view of a dead face.

"Gosh!" said Bill, who at the next instant had seen the thing: "I thought at first it was that there José. That would have been queer, after what I told 'im yesterday."

They continued their way, the stranger wincing in his walk, and Bill exhibiting considerable curiosity.

The yellow beams of the new sun were touching the grim hues of the dead Mexican's face, and creating there an inhuman effect, which made his countenance more like a mask of dulled brass. One hand, grown curiously thinner, had been flung out regardlessly to a cactus bush.

Bill walked forward and stood looking respectfully at the body. "I know that feller; his name is Miguel. He—"

The stranger's nerves might have been in that condition when there is no backbone to the body, only a long groove. "Good heavens!" he exclaimed, much agitated; "don't speak that way!"

"What way?" said Bill. "I only said his name was Miguel."

After a pause the stranger said:

"Oh, I know; but—" He waved his hand. "Lower your voice, or something. I don't know. This part of the business rattles me, don't you see?"

"Oh, all right," replied Bill, bowing to the other's mysterious mood. But in a moment he burst out violently and loud in the most extraordinary profanity, the oaths winging from him as the sparks go from the funnel.

He had been examining the contents of the bundled gray blanket, and he had brought forth, among other things, his frying-pan. It was now only a rim with a handle; the Mexican volley had centered upon it. A Mexican shot-gun of the abbreviated description is ordinarily loaded with flat-irons, stove-lids, lead pipe, old horseshoes, sections of chain, window weights, railroad sleepers and spikes, dumb-bells, and any other junk which may be at hand. When one of these loads encounters a man vitally, it is likely to make an impression upon him, and a cooking-utensil may be supposed to subside before such an assault of curiosities.

Bill held high the desecrated frying-pan, turning it this way and that way. He swore until he happened to note the absence of the stranger. A moment later he saw him leading his horse from the bushes. In silence and sullenly the young man went about saddling the animal. Bill said, "Well, goin' to pull out?"

The stranger's hands fumbled uncertainly at the throat-latch. Once he exclaimed irritably, blaming the buckle for the trembling of his fingers. Once he turned to look at the dead face with the light of the morning sun upon it. At last he cried, "Oh, I know the whole thing was all square enough—couldn't be squarer—but—somehow or other, that man there takes the heart out of me." He turned his troubled face for another look. "He seems to be all the time calling me a—he makes me feel like a murderer."

"But," said Bill, puzzling, "you didn't shoot him, mister; I shot him."

"I know; but I feel that way, somehow. I can't get rid of it."

Bill considered for a time; then he said diffidently, "Mister, you're a' eddycated man, ain't you?"

"What?"

"You're what they call a'—a' eddycated man, ain't you?"

The young man, perplexed, evidently had a question upon his lips, when there was a roar of guns, bright flashes, and in the air such hooting and whistling as would come from a swift flock of steam-boilers. The stranger's horse gave a mighty, convulsive spring, snorting wildly in its sudden anguish, fell upon its knees, scrambled afoot again, and was away in the uncanny death run known to men who have seen the finish of brave horses.

"This comes from discussin' things," cried Bill, angrily.

He had thrown himself flat on the ground facing the thicket whence had come the firing. He could see the smoke weapon came slowly up from the ground and poised like the winding over the bush-tops. He lifted his revolver, and the glittering crest of a snake. Somewhere on his face there was a kind of smile, cynical, wicked, deadly, of a ferocity which at the same time had brought a deep flush to his face, and had caused two upright lines to glow in his eyes.

"Hello, José!" he called, amiable for satire's sake. "Got your old blunderbusses loaded up again yet?"

The stillness had returned to the plain. The sun's brilliant rays swept over the sea of mesquite, painting the far mists of the west with faint rosy light, and high in the air some great bird fled toward the south.

"You come out here," called Bill, again addressing the landscape, "and I'll give you some shootin' lessons. That ain't the way to shoot." Receiving no reply, he began to invent epithets and yell them at the thicket. He was something of a master of insult, and, moreover, he dived into his memory to bring forth imprecations tarnished with age, unused since fluent Bowery days. The occupation amused him, and sometimes he laughed so that it was uncomfortable for his chest to be against the ground.

Finally the stranger, prostrate near him, said wearily, "Oh, they've gone."

"Don't you believe it," replied Bill, sobering swiftly. "They're there yet—every man of 'em."

"How do you know?"

"Because I do. They won't shake us so soon. Don't put your head up, or they'll get you, sure."

Bill's eyes, meanwhile, had not wavered from their scrutiny of the thicket in front. "They're there, all right; don't you forget it. Now you listen." So he called out: "José! Ojo, José! Speak up, *hombre*! I want have talk. Speak up, you yaller cuss, you!"

Whereupon a mocking voice from off in the bushes said, "Señor?"

"There," said Bill to his ally; "didn't I tell you? The whole batch." Again he lifted his voice. "José—look—ain't you gittin' kinder tired? You better go home, you fellers, and git some rest."

The answer was a sudden furious chatter of Spanish, eloquent with hatred, calling down upon Bill all the calamities which life holds. It was as if some one had suddenly enraged a cageful of wildcats. The spirits of all the revenges which they had imagined were loosened at this time, and filled the air.

"They're in a holler," said Bill, chuckling, "or there'd be shootin'."

Presently he began to grow angry. His hidden enemies called him nine kinds of coward, a man who could fight only in the dark, a baby who would run from the shadows of such noble Mexican gentlemen, a dog that sneaked. They described the affair of the previous night, and informed him of the base advantage he had taken of their friend. In fact, they in all sincerity endowed him with every quality which he no less earnestly believed them to possess. One could have seen the phrases bite him as he lay there on the ground fingering his revolver.

6

It is sometimes taught that men do the furious and desperate thing from an emotion that is as even and placid as the thoughts of a village clergyman on Sunday afternoon. Usually, however, it is to be believed that a panther is at the time born in the heart, and that the subject does not resemble a man picking mulberries.

"B' G———!" said Bill, speaking as from a throat filled with dust, "I'll go after 'em in a minute."

"Don't you budge an inch!" cried the stranger, sternly. "Don't you budge!"

"Well," said Bill, glaring at the bushes—"well—"

"Put your head down!" suddenly screamed the stranger, in white alarm. As the guns roared, Bill uttered a loud grunt, and for a moment leaned panting on his elbow, while his arm shook like a twig. Then he upreared like a great and bloody spirit of vengeance, his face lighted with the blaze of his last passion. The Mexicans came swiftly and in silence.

The lightning action of the next few moments was of the fabric of dreams to the stranger. The muscular struggle may not be real to the drowning man. His mind may be fixed on the far, straight shadows back of the stars, and the terror of them. And so the fight, and his part in it, had to the stranger only the quality of a picture half drawn. The rush of feet, the spatter of shots, the cries, the swollen faces seen like masks on the smoke, resembled a happening of the night.

And yet afterward certain lines, forms, lived out so strongly from the incoherence that they were always in his memory.

He killed a man, and the thought went swiftly by him, like the feather on the gale, that it was easy to kill a man.

Moreover, he suddenly felt for Bill, this grimy sheep-herder, some deep form of idolatry. Bill was dying, and the dignity of last defeat, the superiority of him who stands in his grave, was in the pose of the lost sheep-herder.

The stranger sat on the ground idly mopping the sweat and powder-stain from his brow. He wore the gentle idiot smile of an aged beggar as he watched three Mexicans limping and staggering in the distance. He noted at this time that one who still possessed a serape had from it none of the grandeur of the cloaked Spaniard, but that against the sky the silhouette resembled a cornucopia of childhood's Christmas.

They turned to look at him, and he lifted his weary arm to menace them with his revolver. They stood for a moment banded together, and hooted curses at him.

Finally he arose, and, walking some paces, stooped to loosen Bill's gray hands from a throat. Swaying as if slightly drunk, he stood looking down into the still face.

Struck suddenly with a thought, he went about with dulled eyes on the ground, until he plucked his gaudy blanket from where it lay dirty from trampling feet. He dusted it carefully, and then returned and laid it over Bill's form. There he again stood motionless, his mouth just agape and the same stupid glance in his eyes, when all at once he made a gesture of fright and looked wildly about him.

He had almost reached the thicket when he stopped, smitten with alarm. A body contorted, with one arm stiff in the air, lay in his path. Slowly and warily he moved around it, and in a moment the bushes, nodding and whispering, their leaf-faces turned toward the scene behind him, swung and swung again into stillness and the peace of the wilderness.

FREDERIC REMINGTON

FREDERIC REMINGTON (1861–1909) was born in Canton, New York, and attended the Yale School of Fine Arts 1878–80 before he went to Kansas to take up sheep ranching. In the spring of 1884, Remington decided to sell his ranch, and became a wanderer. In the summer of 1885 while Remington was prospecting in the Pinal Range in Arizona Territory, Geronimo coincidentally broke loose from reservation captivity, and the Third Cavalry under General George Crook took up the pursuit. Remington used the situation to advantage, sketching several Apache Indians on the San Carlos reserve and three renegades who paid a hungry visit to his campsite one night. He never came within two hundred miles of Geronimo, but this didn't faze Easterners when, upon his return with a full portfolio of Indian portraits, Remington's sketches were instantly in demand with magazines to be used as illustrations for the conflict between the army and the Apaches. "The depth of Remington's understanding of the West and the degree to which his impressions of it approximated reality are certainly debatable issues," G. Edward White wrote in *The Eastern Establishment and the Western Experience* (Yale University Press, 1968). ". . . Remington's image of the West had both its complex and superficial, its 'realistic' and 'romantic' aspects and his understanding of Indian nature exhibited for the most part a considerable bias." Nothwithstanding, commencing in 1886 and for the next decade and a half, Remington was widely hailed as an expert on the West.

No less a one than Theodore Roosevelt, who had just begun to publish the sketches which would comprise his book *Ranch Life and the Hunting Trail* (1888), asked his publisher, *Century Magazine*, for Remington to be his illustrator.

Remington complied and he was commercially cynical enough, years later, to paint, on a commission directly from Roosevelt, the fantasy portrait of T.R. leading the Rough Riders in a charge up San Juan Hill. Along with his work as an illustrator, Remington himself turned to writing, often illustrating his own material, and in the nineties he collected his stories and sketches into a brace of volumes, *Pony Tracks* (1895) and *Crooked Trails* (1898).

For Remington, the meaning of the West was the confrontation between men and with a hostile environment. He was not quite the romantic that his friend Owen Wister was—whose stories he frequently illustrated; nor was he a believer, as was Roosevelt, in the rugged life for its own sake. In 1898 he purchased an island off Chippewa Bay, and in 1908 he retired to a fifty-acre farm in Ridgefield, Connecticut, where he literally ate and drank himself to death. In 1905, he summed up his disillusionment: "I knew the railroad was coming. I saw men already swarming into the land. I knew the derby hat, the smoking chimneys, the cord-binder, and the thirty-day note were upon us in a restless surge. I knew the wild riders and vacant land were about to vanish forever, and the more I considered the subject, the bigger the forever loomed." In 1907 he burned seventy-five of his Western canvases, retaining only his landscape studies; in 1908 he burned twenty-seven more of his best-known Western paintings.

"A Sergeant of the Orphan Troop" comes from the *Crooked Trails* collection. In the words of his ablest biographer to date, Ben Merchant Vorpahl in *Frederic Remington and the West* (University of Texas Press, 1978), "because of his preference for military subjects, his desire for war, and his wish to somehow formulate a scheme of things in which the present did not exist," Remington conceived of this story and set it during the Cheyenne ordeal of 1879 at Fort Robinson. Carter Johnson was a real person, a lieutenant in the Tenth Cavalry whom General Nelson Miles called "one of the most skilful and persistent cavalrymen of the young men in the army." Remington, who met him in the summer of 1896, made him his hero, and like that other hero whom he so often illustrated for his friend Wister, he called Johnson the "Virginian" more often than by his rightful name.

Remington believed in heroes, be they cowboys or soldiers. "Cowboys!" he cried when near death. "There are no cowboys any more." Yet he, along with Wister and Roosevelt, had helped create a fantasy West, and because what they created had such a powerful impact, others experienced their same feelings of loss. What was there to fill the void but the formulary Western and the cinema cowboy hero that, having absolutely nothing to do with the real West, were even more remote from the already romantic image of the West Remington bemoaned as having vanished?

A Sergeant of the Orphan Troop

While it is undisputed that Captain Dodd's troop of the Third Cavalry is not an orphan, and is, moreover, quite as far from it as any troop of cavalry in the world, all this occurred many years ago, when it was, at any rate, so called. There was nothing so very unfortunate about it, from what I gather, since it seems to have fought well on its own hook, quite up to all expectations, if not beyond. No officer at that time seemed to care to connect his name with such a rioting, nose-breaking band of desperado cavalrymen, unless it was temporarily, and that was always in the field, and never in garrison. However, in this case it did not have even an officer in the field. But let me go on to my sergeant.

This one was a Southern gentleman, or rather a boy, when he refugeed out of Fredericksburg with his family, before the Federal advance, in a wagon belonging to a Mississippi rifle regiment; but nevertheless some years later he got to be a gentleman, and passed through the Virginia Military Institute with honor. The desire to be a soldier consumed him, but the vicissitudes of the times compelled him, if he wanted to be a soldier, to be a private one, which he became by duly enlisting in the Third Cavalry. He struck the Orphan Troop.

Physically, Nature had slobbered all over Carter Johnson; she had lavished on him her very last charm. His skin was pink, albeit the years of Arizona sun had heightened it to a dangerous red; his mustache was yellow and ideally military; while his pure Virginia accent, fired in terse and jerky form at friend and enemy alike, relieved his natural force of character by a shade of humor. He was thumped and bucked and pounded into what was in the seventies considered a proper frontier soldier, for in those days the nursery idea had not been lugged into the army. If a sergeant bade a soldier "go" or "do," he instantly "went" and "did"—otherwise the sergeant belted him over the head with his six-shooter, and had him taken off in a cart. On pay-days, too, when men who did not care to get drunk went to bed in barracks, they slept under their bunks and not in them, which was conducive to longevity and a good night's rest. When buffalo were scarce they ate the army rations in those wild days; they had a fight often enough to earn thirteen dollars, and at times a good deal more. This was the way with all men at that time, but it was rough on recruits.

So my friend Carter Johnson wore through some years, rose to be a corporal, finally a sergeant, and did many daring deeds. An atavism from "the old border riders" of Scotland shone through the boy, and he took on quickly. He could act the others off the stage and sing them out of the theatre in his chosen profession.

There was fighting all day long around Fort Robinson, Nebraska—a bushwhacking with Dull-Knife's band of the Northern Cheyennes, the Spartans of the plains. It was January; the snow lay deep on the ground, and the cold was knifelike as it thrust at the fingers and toes of the Orphan Troop. Sergeant Johnson with a squad of twenty men, after having been in the saddle all night, was in at the post drawing rations for the troop. As they were packing them up for transport, a detachment of F Troop came galloping by, led by the sergeant's friend, Corporal Thornton. They pulled up.

"Come on, Carter—go with us. I have just heard that some troops have got a bunch of Injuns corralled out in the hills. They can't get 'em down. Let's go help 'em. It's a chance for the fight of your life. Come on."

Carter hesitated for a moment. He had drawn the rations for his troop, which was in sore need of them. It might mean a court-martial and the loss of his chevrons—but a fight! Carter struck his spurred heels, saying, "Come on, boys; get your horses; we will go."

The line of cavalry was half lost in the flying snow as it cantered away over the white flats. The dry powder crunched under the thudding hoofs, the carbines banged about, the overcoat capes blew and twisted in the rushing air, the horses grunted and threw up their heads as the spurs went into their bellies, while the men's faces were serious with the interest in store. Mile after mile rushed the little column, until it came to some bluffs, where it drew reign and stood gazing across the valley to the other hills.

Down in the bottoms they espied an officer and two men sitting quietly on their horses, and on riding up found a lieutenant gazing at the opposite bluffs through a glass. Far away behind the bluffs a sharp ear could detect the reports of guns.

"We have been fighting the Indians all day here," said the officer, putting down his glass and turning to the two "non-coms." "The command has gone around the bluffs. I have just seen Indians up there on the rim-rocks. I have sent for troops, in the hope that we might get up there. Sergeant, deploy as skirmishers, and we will try."

At a gallop the men fanned out, then forward at a sharp trot across the flats, over the little hills, and into the scrub pine. The valley gradually narrowed until it forced the skirmishers into a solid body, when the lieutenant took the lead, with the command tailing out in single file. The signs of the Indians grew thicker and thicker—a skirmisher's nest here behind a scrub-pine bush, and there by the side of a rock. Kettles and robes lay about in the snow, with three "bucks" and some women and children sprawling about, frozen as they had died; but all was silent except the crunch of the snow and the low whispers of the men as they pointed to the telltales of the morning's battle.

As the column approached the precipitous rim-rock the officer halted, had the horses assembled in a side cañon, putting Corporal Thornton in charge. He ordered Sergeant Johnson to again advance his skirmish-line, in which formation the men moved forward, taking cover behind the pine scrub and rocks, until they came to an open space of about sixty paces, while above it towered the cliff for twenty feet in the sheer. There the Indians had been last seen. The soldiers lay tight in the snow, and no man's valor impelled him on. To the casual glance the rim-rock was impassable. The men were discouraged and the officer nonplussed. A hundred rifles might be covering the rock fort for all they knew. On closer examination a cutting was found in the face of the rock which was a rude attempt at steps, doubtless made long ago by the Indians. Caught on a bush above, hanging down the steps, was a lariat, which, at the mottom, was twisted around the shoulders of a dead warrior. They had evidently tried to take him up while wounded, but he had died and had been abandoned.

After cogitating, the officer concluded not to order his men forward, but he himself stepped boldly out into the open and climbed up. Sergeant Johnson immediately followed, while an old Swedish soldier by the name of Otto Bordeson fell in behind them. They walked briskly up the hill, and placing their backs against the wall of rock, stood gazing at the Indian.

With a grin the officer directed the men to advance. The sergeant, seeing that he realized their serious predicament, said:

"I think, lieutenant, you had better leave them where they are; we are holding this rock up pretty hard."

They stood there and looked at each other. "We's in a fix," said Otto.

"I want volunteers to climb this rock," finally demanded the officer.

The sergeant looked up the steps, pulled at the lariat, and commented: "Only one man can go at a time; if there are Indians up there, an old squaw can kill this command with a hatchet; and if there are no Indians, we can all go up."

The impatient officer started up, but the sergeant grabbed him by the belt. He turned, saying, "If I haven't got men to go, I will climb myself."

"Stop, lieutenant. It wouldn't look right for the officer to go. I have noticed a pine-tree, the branches of which spread over the top of the rock," and the sergeant pointed to it. "If you will make the men cover the top of the rim-rock with their rifles, Bordeson and I will go up"; and turning to the Swede, "Will you go, Otto?"

"I will go anywhere the sergeant does," came his gallant reply.

"Take your choice, then, of the steps or the pine-tree," continued the Virginian; and after a rather short but sharp calculation the Swede declared for the tree, although both were death if the Indians were on the rim-rock. He immediately began sidling along the rock to the tree, and slowly commenced the ascent. The sergeant took a few steps up the cutting, holding on by the rope. The officer stood out and smiled quizzically. Jeers came from behind the soldiers' bushes—"Go it, Otto! Go it, Johnson! Your feet are loaded! If a snow-bird flies, you will drop dead! Do you need any help? You'll make a hell of a sailor!" and other gibes.

The gray clouds stretched away monotonously over the waste of snow, and it was cold. The two men climbed slowly, anon stopping to look at each other and smile. They were monkeying with death.

At last the sergeant drew himself up, slowly raised his head, and saw snow and broken rock. Otto lifted himself likewise, and he too saw nothing. Rifle-shots came clearly to their ears from far in front—many at one time, and scattering at others. Now the soldiers came briskly forward, dragging up the cliff in single file. The dull noises of the fight came through the wilderness. The skirmish-line drew quickly forward and passed into the pine woods, but the Indian trails scattered. Dividing into sets of four, they followed on the tracks of small parties, wandering on until night threatened. At length the main trail of the fugitive band ran across their front, bringing the command together. It was too late for the officer to get his horses before dark, nor could he follow with his exhausted men, so he turned to the sergeant and asked him to pick some men and follow on the trail. The sergeant picked Otto Bordeson, who still affirmed that he would go anywhere that Johnson went, and they started. They were old hunting companions, having confidence in each other's sense and shooting. They ploughed through the snow, deeper and deeper into the pines, then on down a cañon where the light was failing. The sergeant was sweating freely; he raised his hand to press his fur cap backward from his forehead. He drew it quickly away; he stopped and started, caught Otto by the sleeve, and drew a long breath. Still holding his companion, he put his glove again to his nose, sniffed at it again, and with a mighty tug brought the startled Swede to his knees, whispering, "I smell Indians; I can sure smell 'em, Otto—can you?"

Otto sniffed, and whispered back, "Yes, plain!"

"We are ambushed! Drop!" and the two soldiers sunk in the snow. A few feet in front of them lay a dark thing; crawling to it, they found a large calico rag, covered with blood.

"Let's do something, Carter; we's in a fix."

"If we go down, Otto, we are gone; if we go back, we are gone; let's go forward," hissed the sergeant.

Slowly they crawled from tree to tree.

"Don't you see the Injuns?" said the Swede, as he pointed to the rocks in front, where lay their dark forms. The still air gave no sound. The cathedral of nature, with its dark pine trunks starting from gray snow to support gray sky, was dead. Only human hearts raged, for the forms which held them lay like black bowlders.

"Egah—lelah washatah," yelled the sergeant.

Two rifle-shots rang and reverberated down the cañon; two more replied instantly from the soldiers. One Indian sunk, and his carbine went clanging down the rocks, burying itself in the snow. Another warrior rose slightly, took aim, but Johnson's six-shooter cracked again, and the Indian settled slowly down without firing. A squaw moved slowly in the half-light to where the buck lay. Bordeson drew a bead with his carbine.

"Don't shoot the woman, Otto. Keep that hole covered; the place is alive with Indians"; and both lay still.

A buck rose quickly, looked at the sergeant, and dropped back. The latter could see that he had him located, for he slowly poked his rifle up without showing his head. Johnson rolled swiftly to one side, aiming with his deadly revolver. Up popped the Indian's head, crack went the six-shooter; the head turned slowly, leaving the top exposed. Crack again went the alert gun of the soldier, the ball striking the head just below the scalp-lock and instantly jerking the body into a kneeling position.

Then all was quiet in the gloomy woods.

After a time the sergeant addressed his voice to the lonely place in Sioux, telling the women to come out and surrender—to leave the bucks, etc.

An old squaw rose sharply to her feet, slapped her breast, shouted "Lelah washatah," and gathering up a little girl and a bundle, she strode forward to the soldiers. Three other women followed, two of them in the same blanket.

"Are there any more bucks?" roared the sergeant, in Sioux.

"No more alive," said the old squaw, in the same tongue.

"Keep your rifle on the hole between the rocks; watch these people; I will go up," directed the sergeant, as he slowly mounted to the ledge, and with levelled six-shooter peered slowly over. He stepped in and stood looking down on the dead warriors.

A yelling in broken English smote the startled sergeant. "Tro up your hands, you d——— Injun! I'll blow the top off you!" came through the quiet. The sergeant sprang down to see the Swede standing with carbine levelled at a young buck confronting him with a drawn knife in his hands, while his blanket lay back on the snow.

"He's a buck—he ain't no squaw; he tried to creep on me with a knife. I'm going to kill him," shouted the excited Bordeson.

"No, no, don't kill him. Otto, don't you kill him," expostulated Johnson, as the Swede's finger clutched nervously at the trigger, and turning, he roared, "Throw away that knife, you d——— Indian!"

The detachment now came charging in through the snow, and gathered around excitedly. A late arrival came up, breathing heavily, dropped his gun, and springing up and down, yelled, "Be jabbers, I have got among om at last!" A general laugh went up, and the circle of men broke into a straggling line for the return. The sergeant took the little girl up in his arms. She grabbed him fiercely by the throat like a wild-cat, screaming. While nearly choking, he yet tried to mollify her, while her mother, seeing no harm was intended, pacified her in the soft gutturals of the race. She relaxed her grip, and the brave Virginian packed her down the mountain, wrapped in his soldier cloak. The horses were reached in time, and the prisoners put on double behind the soldiers, who fed them crackers as they marched. At two o'clock in the morning the little command rode into Fort Robinson and dismounted at the guard-house. The little girl, who was asleep and half frozen in Johnson's overcoat, would not go to her mother: poor little cat, she had found a nest. The sergeant took her into the guard-house, where it was warm. She soon fell asleep, and slowly he undid her, delivering her to her mother.

On the following morning he came early to the guard-house, loaded with trifles for his little Indian girl. He had expended all his credit at the post-trader's, but he could carry sentiment no further, for "To horse!" was sounding, and he joined the Orphan Troop to again ride on the Dull-Knife trail. The brave Cheyennes were running through the frosty hills, and the cavalry horses pressed hotly after. For ten days the troops surrounded the Indians by day, and stood guard in the snow by night, but coming day found the ghostly warriors gone and their rifle-pits empty. They were cut off and slaughtered daily, but the gallant warriors were fighting to their last nerve. Towards the end they were cooped in a gully on War-Bonnet Creek, where they fortified; but two six-pounders had been hauled out, and were turned on their works. The four troops of cavalry stood to horse on the plains all day, waiting for the poor wretches to come out, while the guns roared, ploughing the frozen dirt and snow over their little stronghold; but they did not come out. It was known that all the provisions they had was the dead horse of a corporal of E

Troop, which had been shot within twenty paces of their rifle-pits.

So, too, the soldiers were starving, and the poor Orphans had only crackers to eat. They were freezing also, and murmuring to be led to "the charge," that they might end it there, but they were an orphan troop, and must wait for others to say. The sergeant even asked an officer to let them go, but was peremptorily told to get back in the ranks.

The guns ceased at night, while the troops drew off to build fires, warm their rigid fingers, thaw out their buffalo moccasins, and munch crackers, leaving a strong guard around the Cheyennes. In the night there was a shooting—the Indians had charged through and had gone.

The day following they were again surrounded on some bluffs, and the battle waged until night. Next day there was a weak fire from the Indian position on the impregnable bluffs, and presently it ceased entirely. The place was approached with care and trepidation, but was empty. Two Indian boys, with their feet frozen, had been left as decoys, and after standing off four troops of cavalry for hours, they too had in some mysterious way departed.

But the pursuit was relentless; on, on over the rolling hills swept the famishing troopers, and again the Spartan band turned at bay, firmly intrenched on a bluff as before. This was the last stand—nature was exhausted. The soldiers surrounded them, and Major Wessells turned the handle of the human vise. The command gathered closer about the doomed pits—they crawled on their bellies from one stack of sage-brush to the next. They were freezing. The order to charge came to the Orphan Troop, and yelling his command, Sergeant Johnson ran forward. Up from the sage-brush floundered the stiffened troopers, following on. They ran over three Indians, who lay sheltered in a little cut, and these killed three soldiers together with an old frontier sergeant who wore long hair, but they were destroyed in turn. While the Orphans swarmed under the hill, a rattling discharge poured from the rifle-pits; but the troop had gotten under the fire, and it all passed over their heads. On they pressed, their blood now quickened by excitement, crawling up the steep, while volley on volley poured over them. Within nine feet of the pits was a rim-rock ledge over which the Indian bullets swept, and here the charge was stopped. It now became a duel. Every time a head showed on either side, it drew fire like a flue-hole. Suddenly our Virginian sprang on the ledge, and like a trill on a piano poured a six-shooter into the intrenchment, and dropped back.

Major Wessells, who was commanding the whole force, crawled to the position of the Orphan Troop, saying, "Doing fine work, boys. Sergeant, I would advise you to take off that red scarf"—when a bullet cut the major across the breast, whirling him around and throwing him. A soldier, one Lannon, sprang to him and pulled him down the bluff, the major protesting that he was not wounded, which proved to be true, the bullet having passed through his heavy clothes.

The troops had drawn up on the other sides, and a perfect storm of bullets whirled over the intrenchments. The powder blackened the faces of the men, and they took off their caps or had them shot off. To raise the head for more than a fraction of a second meant death.

Johnson had exchanged five shots with a fine-looking Cheyenne, and every time he raised his eye to a level with the rock White Antelope's gun winked at him.

"You will get killed directly," yelled Lannon to Johnson; "they have you spotted."

The smoke blew and eddied over them; again Johnson rose, and again White Antelope's pistol cracked an accompaniment to his own; but with movement like lightning the sergeant sprang through the smoke, and fairly shoving his carbine to White Antelope's breast, he pulled the trigger. A 50-calibre gun boomed in Johnson's face, and a volley roared from the pits, but he fell backward into cover. His comrades set him up to see if any red stains came through the grime, but he was unhurt.

The firing grew; a blue haze hung over the hill. Johnson again looked across the glacis, but again his eye met the savage glare of White Antelope.

"I haven't got him yet, Lannon, but I will"; and Sergeant Johnson again slowly reloaded his pistol and carbine.

"Now, men, give them a volley!" ordered the enraged man, and as volley answered volley through the smoke sprang the daring soldier, and standing over White Antelope as the smoke swirled and almost hid him, he poured his six balls into his enemy, and thus died one brave man at the hands of another in fair battle. The sergeant leaped back and lay down among the men, stunned by the concussions. He said he would do no more. His mercurial temperament had undergone a change, or, to put it better, he conceived it to be outrageous to fight these poor people, five against one. He characterized it as "a d——— infantry fight," and rising, talked in Sioux to the enemy—asked them to surrender, or they must otherwise die. A young girl answered him, and said they would like to. An old woman sprang on her and cut her throat with a dull knife, yelling meanwhile to the soldiers that "they would never surrender alive," and saying what she had done.

Many soldiers were being killed, and the fire from the pits grew weaker. The men were besides themselves with rage. "Charge!" rang through the now still air from some strong voice, and, with a volley, over the works poured the troops, with six-shooters going, and clubbed carbines. Yells, explosions, and amid a whirlwind of smoke the soldiers and Indians swayed about, now more slowly and quieter, until the smoke eddied away. Men stood still, peering about with wild open eyes through blackened faces. They held desperately to their weapons. An old bunch of buckskin rags rose slowly and fired a carbine aimlessly. Twenty bullets rolled and tumbled it along the ground, and again the smoke drifted off the mount. This time the air grew clear. Buffalo-robes lay all about, blood spotted everywhere. The dead bodies of thirty-two Cheyennes lay, writhed and twisted, on the packed snow, and among them many women and children, cut and furrowed with lead. In a corner was a pile of wounded squaws, half covered with dirt swept over them by the storm of bullets. One broken creature half raised herself from the bunch. A maddened trumpeter threw up his gun to shoot, but Sergeant Johnson leaped and kicked his gun out of his hands high into the air, saying, "This fight is over."

OWEN WISTER

OWEN WISTER (1860–1938) was born in Philadelphia, Pennsylvania, and was graduated from Harvard in 1882 with honors, having majored in music. In 1885, after suffering a nervous breakdown, Wister went to Wyoming for the first time. It was to be one of many trips West which Wister would make over the next several years, initially for his health and then to find more material for his fiction. Returning to the East in 1885, Wister attended Harvard Law School, from which he graduated in 1888, and went to work in a Philadelphia law office. In 1892, following his fifth trip to Wyoming, Wister's first two Western stories were published in *Harper's* magazine, "Hank's Woman" and "How Lin McLean Went East." The stories proved so popular that *Harper's* financed Wister on a trip throughout the West and hired Frederic Remington to illustrate the stories he wrote as a result of his experiences. It was through this collaboration that a friendship developed between the two men that is narrated in some detail in Ben Merchant Vorpahl's *My Dear Wister: The Frederic Remington-Owen Wister Letters* (American West Publishing, 1973).

In 1895 Wister published an essay titled "The Evolution of the Cow-Puncher," in which he articulated his vision of the cowboy as a modern incarnation of the medieval knight of romance. In retrospect, it would seem that Wister's personal values constantly interfered with his objective to describe the West and its people as they really were. Romance and marriage in his novels, as in some of his stories, served only to emasculate his cowboys, to make them docile Easterners concerned more with personal ambition, accumulation of wealth, and achieving what by Eastern standards could only be considered social standing, rather than luxuriating in their freedom, the openness and emptiness of the land, and the

West's utter disregard for family background. To make his cowboys acceptable heroes to *himself*, as well as to his Eastern readers, Wister felt compelled to provide them with distinctly Eastern values, and for this reason his stories always fail to depict truthfully the nature of the real clash between East and West.

In his political philosophy Wister was a progressive and what has come to be termed a social Darwinist, meaning that he believed in a natural aristocracy, a survival of the fittest—the fittest being those who measured up best to his Eastern values. In *The Virginian* (Macmillan, 1902), which became a best-seller the month it was published and has never been out of print since, he put this philosophy into the mouth of the Virginian, who remarks, "Now back East you can be middling and get along. But if you go to try a thing in this Western country, you've got to do it *well!*" Yet at the same time in his notebooks, later published as *Owen Wister Out West: His Journals and Letters* (University of Chicago Press, 1958), he lamented the sloth which he felt the West induced in people, and it was this lamentation that brought about his disillusionment with the West and his refusal, after 1911, ever to return there. Wister's only defense was through exalting his heroes, but as the late Mody C. Boatright observed in "The American Myth Rides the Range: Owen Wister's Man on Horseback" in the *Southwest Review* (Summer 1951), "Wister's pathetic search for a leader brought him to the conclusion that Theodore Roosevelt was 'the greatest benefactor we people have known since Lincoln.' " Wister ran an earlier version of a chapter from *The Virginian* in *Harper's* and told somewhat explicitly how a character named Balaam gouged out the eye of a horse. Theodore Roosevelt chided Wister for what he felt was a slip in good taste. Wister deleted the offensive passage from the book version, dedicated the novel to Roosevelt, and therefore, it ought come as little surprise that Wister's last book should have been *Roosevelt: The Story of a Friendship 1880–1919* (Macmillan, 1930).

Wister extensively revised "Hank's Woman" when he included it in his collection *The Jimmyjohn Boss and Other Stories* (Harper's, 1900). In *The Virginian* he made reference to this story in the chapter he titled "Through Two Snows." The narrator receives a letter from the Virginian proposing they go on a hunt together—which they do, the narrator commenting that "the expedition ended in an untravelled corner of the Yellowstone Park, near Pitchstone Cañon, where he [the Virginian] and young Lin McLean and others were witnesses of a sad and terrible drama that has been elsewhere chronicled." What follows is that chronicle.

Hank's Woman

1

Many fish were still in the pool; and though luck seemed to have left me, still I stood at the end of the point, casting and casting my vain line, while the Virginian lay and watched. Noonday's extreme brightness had left the river and the plain in cooling shadow, but spread and glowed over the yet undimmed mountains. Westward, the Tetons lifted their peaks pale and keen as steel through the high, radiant air. Deep down between the blue gashes of their cañons the sun sank long shafts of light, and the glazed laps of their snow-fields shone separate and white upon their lofty vastness, like handkerchiefs laid out to dry. Opposite, above the valley, rose that other range, the Continental Divide, not sharp, but long and ample. It was bare in some high places, and below these it stretched everywhere, high and low, in brown and yellow parks, or in purple miles of pine a world of serene undulations, a great sweet country of silence.

A passing band of antelope stood herded suddenly together at sight of us; then a little breeze blew for a moment from us to them, and they drifted like phantoms away, and were lost in the levels of the sage-brush.

"If humans could do like that," said the Virginian, watching them go.

"Run, you mean?" said I.

"Tell a foe by the smell of him," explained the cow-puncher; "at fifty yards—or a mile."

"Yes," I said; "men would be hard to catch."

"A woman needs it most," he murmured. He lay down again in his lounging sprawl, with his grave eyes intently fixed upon my fly-casting.

The gradual day mounted up the hills farther from the floor of earth. Warm airs eddied in its wake slowly, stirring the scents of the plain together. I looked at the Southerner;

and there was no guessing what his thoughts might be at work upon behind that drowsy glance. Then for a moment a trout rose, but only to look and whip down again into the pool that wedged its calm into the riffle from below.

"Second thoughts," mused the Virginian; and as the trout came no more, "Second thoughts," he repeated; "and even a fish will have them sooner than folks has them in this mighty hasty country." And he rolled over into a new position of ease.

At whom or what was he aiming these shafts of truth? Or did he moralize merely because health and the weather had steeped him in that serenity which lifts us among the spheres? Well, sometimes he went on from these beginnings and told me wonderful things.

"I reckon," said he, presently, "that knowing when to change your mind would be pretty near knowledge enough for plain people."

Since my acquaintance with him—this was the second summer of it—I had come to understand him enough to know that he was unfathomable. Still, for a moment it crossed my thoughts that perhaps now he was discoursing about himself. He had allowed a jealous foreman to fall out with him at Sunk Creek ranch in the spring, during Judge Henry's absence. The man, having a brief authority, parted with him. The Southerner had chosen that this should be the means of ultimately getting the foreman dismissed and himself recalled. It was strategic. As he put it to me: "When I am gone, it will be right easy for the Judge to see which of us two he wants. And I'll not have done any talking." All of which duly befell in the autumn as he had planned: the foreman was sent off, his assistant promoted, and the Virginian again hired. But this was meanwhile. He was indulging himself in a several months' drifting, and while thus drifting he had written to me. That is how we two came to be on our way from the railroad to hunt the elk and the mountain-sheep, and were pausing to fish where Buffalo Fork joins its waters with Snake River. In those days the antelope still ran there in hundreds, the Yellowstone Park was a new thing, and mankind lived very far away. Since meeting me with the horses in Idaho the Virginian had been silent, even for him. So now I stood casting my fly, and trusting that he was not troubled with second thoughts over his strategy.

"Have yu' studied much about marriage?" he now inquired. His serious eyes met mine as he lay stretched along the ground.

"Not much," I said; "not very much."

"Let's swim," he said. "They have changed their minds."

Forthwith we shook off our boots and dropped our few clothes, and heedless of what fish we might now drive away, we went into the cool, slow, deep breadth of backwater which the bend makes just there. As he came up near me, shaking his head of black hair, the cow-puncher was smiling a little.

"Not that any number of baths," he remarked, "would conceal a man's objectionableness from an antelope—not even a she-one."

Then he went under water, and came up again a long way off.

We dried before the fire, without haste. To need no clothes is better than purple and fine linen. Then he tossed the flap-jacks, and I served the trout, and after this we lay on our backs upon a buffalo-hide to smoke and watch the Tetons grow more solemn, as the large stars opened out over the sky.

"I don't care if I never go home," said I.

The Virginian nodded. "It gives all the peace o' being asleep with all the pleasure o' feeling the widest kind of awake," said he. "Yu' might say the whole year's strength flows hearty in every waggle of your thumb." We lay still for a while. "How many things surprise yu' any more?" he next asked.

I began considering; but his silence had at length worked round to speech.

"Inventions, of course," said he, "these hyeh telephones an' truck yu' see so much about in the papers—but I ain't speaking o' such things of the brain. It is just the common things I mean. The things that a livin', noticin' man is liable to see and maybe sample for himself. How many o' them kind can surprise yu' still?"

I still considered.

"Most everything surprised me onced," the cow-puncher continued, in his gentle Southern voice. "I must have been a mighty green boy. Till I was fourteen or fifteen I expect I was astonished by ten o'clock every morning. But a man begins to ketch on to folks and things after a while. I don't consideh that when—that afteh a man is, say twenty-five, it is creditable he should get astonished too easy. And so yu've not examined yourself that-a-way?"

I had not.

"Well, there's two things anyway—I know them for sure—that I expect will always get me—don't care if I live to thirty-five, or forty-five, or eighty. And one's the ways lightning can strike." He paused. Then he got up and kicked the fire, and stood by it, staring at me. "And the other is the people that other people will marry."

He stopped again; and I said nothing.

"The people that other people will marry," he repeated. "That will surprise me till I die."

"If my sympathy—" I began.

But the brief sound that he gave was answer enough, and more than enough cure for my levity.

"No," said he, reflectively; "not any such thing as a fam'ly for me, yet. Never, it may be. Not till I can't help it. And *that* woman has not come along so far. But I have been sorry for a woman lately. I keep thinking what she will do. For she will have to do something. Do yu' know Austrians? Are they quick in their feelings, like I-talians? Or are they apt to be sluggish, same as Norwegians and them other Dutch-speakin' races?"

I told him what little I knew about Austrians.

"This woman is the first I have ever saw of 'em," he continued. "Of course men will stampede into marriage in this hyeh Western country, where a woman is a scanty thing. It ain't what Hank has done that surprises me. And it is not on him that the sorrow will fall. For she is good. She is very good. Do yu' remember little black Hank? From Texas he claims he is. He was working on the main ditch over at Sunk Creek last summer when that Em'ly hen was around. Well, seh, yu' would not have pleasured in his company. And this year Hank is placer-mining on Galena Creek, where we'll likely go for sheep. There's Honey Wiggin and a young fello' named Lin McLean, and some others along with the outfit. But Hank's woman will not look at any of them, though the McLean boy is a likely hand. I have seen that; for I have done a right smart o' business that-a-way myself, here and there. She will mend their clothes for them, and she will cook lunches for them any time o' day, and her conduct gave them hopes at the start. But I reckon Austrians have good religion."

"No better than Americans," said I.

But the Virginian shook his head. "Better'n what I've saw any Americans have. Of course I am not judging a whole nation by one citizen, and especially her a woman. And of course in them big Austrian towns the folks has shook their virtuous sayin's loose from their daily doin's, same as we have. I expect selling yourself brings the quickest returns to man or woman all the world over. But I am speakin' not of towns, but of the back country, where folks don't just merely arrive on the cyars, but come into the world the natural way, and grow up slow. Onced a week anyway they see the bunch of old grave-stones that marks their fam'ly. Their blood and name are knowed about in the neighborhood, and it's not often one of such will sell themselves. But their religion ain't to them like this woman's. They can be rip-snortin' or'n'ary in ways. Now she is getting naught but hindrance and temptation and meanness from her husband and every livin' thing around her—yet she keeps right along, nor does she mostly bear any signs in her face. She was cert'nly come from where they are used to believing in God and a hereafter mighty hard, and all day long. She has got one o' them crucifixes, and Hank can't make her quit prayin' to it. But what is she going to do?"

"He will probably leave her," I said.

"Yes," said the Virginian—"leave her. Alone; her money all spent; knowin' maybe twenty words of English; and thousands of miles away from everything she can understand. For our words and ways is all alike strange to her."

"Then why did he want such a person?" I exclaimed.

There was surprise in the grave glance which the cow-puncher gave me. "Why, any man would," he answered. "I wanted her myself, till I found she was good."

I looked at this son of the wilderness, standing thoughtful and splendid by the fire, and unconscious of his own religion that had unexpectedly shone forth in these last words. But I said nothing; for words too intimate, especially words of esteem, put him invariably to silence.

"I had forgot to mention her looks to yu'," he pursued, simply. "She is fit for a man." He stopped again.

"Then there was her wages that Hank saw paid to her," he resumed. "And so marriage was but a little thing to Hank—agaynst such a heap of advantages. As for her idea in takin' such as him—maybe it was that he was small and she was big; tall and big. Or maybe it was just his white teeth. Them ridiculous reasons will bring a woman to a man, haven't yu' noticed? But maybe it was just her sorrowful, helpless state, left stranded as she was, and him keeping himself near her and sober for a week.

"I had been seein' this hyeh Yellowstone Park, takin' in its geysers, and this and that, for my enjoyment; and when I found what they claimed about its strange sights to be pretty near so, I landed up at Galena Creek to watch the boys prospectin'. Honey Wiggin, yu' know, and McLean, and the rest. And so they got me to go down with Hank to Gardner for flour and sugar and truck, which we had to wait for. We lay around the Mammoth Springs and Gardner for three days, playin' cyards with friends. And I got plumb inter-ested in them tourists. For I had partly forgot about Eastern people. And hyeh they come fresh every day to remind a man of the great size of his country. Most always they would talk to yu' if yu' gave 'em the chance; and I did. I have come mighty nigh regrettin' that I did not keep a tally of the questions them folks asked me. And as they seemed genu-winely anxious to believe anything at all, and the worser the thing the believinger they'd grow, why I—well, there's times when I have got to lie to keep in good health.

"So I fooled and I fooled. And one noon I was on the front poach of the big hotel they have opened at the Mammoth Springs for tourists, and the hotel kid, bein' on the watch-out, he sees the dust comin' up the hill, and he yells out, 'Stage!'

"Yu've not saw that hotel yet, seh? Well, when the kid says 'Stage,' the consequences is most sudden. About as con-spicuous, yu' may say, as when Old Faithful Geyser lets loose. Yu' see, one batch o' tourists pulls out right after breakfast for Norris Basin, leavin' things empty and yawnin'. By noon the whole hotel outfit has been slumberin' in its chairs steady for three hours. Maybe yu' might hear a fly buzz, but maybe not. Everything's liable to be restin', barrin' the kid. He's awatchin' out. Then he sees the dust, and he says 'Stage!' and it touches the folks off like a hot pokeh. The Syndicate manager he lopes to a lookin'-glass, and then organizes himself behind the book; and the young photograph chap bounces out o' his private door like one o' them cuckoo-clocks; and the fossil man claws his specimens and curiosities into shape, and the porters line up same as parade, and away goes the piano and fiddles up-stairs. It is mighty con-spicuous. So Hank he comes runnin' out from somewheres too, and the stage drives up.

"Then out gets a tall woman, and I noticed her yello' hair. She was kind o' dumb-eyed, yet fine to see. I reckon Hank noticed her too, right away. And right away her trouble begins. For she was a lady's maid, and her lady was out of the stage and roundin' her up quick. And it's 'Where have you put the keys, Willomene?' The lady was rich and stinkin'-lookin', and had come from New Yawk in her husband's private cyar.

"Well, Willomene fussed around in her pockets, and them keys was not there. So she started explaining in tanglefoot English to her lady how her lady must have took them from her before leavin' the cyar. But the lady seemed to relish hustlin' herself into a rage. She got tolerable con-spicuous, too. And after a heap o' words, 'You are discharged,' she says; and off she struts. Soon her husband came out to Willomene, still standin' like statuary, and he pays her a good sum of cash, and he goes way, and she keeps a standing yet for a spell. Then all of a sudden she says something I reckon was 'O, Jesus,' and sits down and starts a-cryin'.

"I would like to have given her comfort. But we all stood around on the hotel poach, and the right thing would not come into my haid. Then the baggage-wagon came in from Cinnabar, and they had picked the keys up on the road between Cinnabar and Gardner. So the lady and her toilet was rescued, but that did no good to Willomene. They stood her trunk down along with the rest—a brass-nailed little old concern—and there was Willomene out of a job and afoot a long, long ways from her own range; and so she kept sitting, and onced in a while she'd cry some more. We got her a room in the cheap hotel where the Park drivers sleeps when they're in at the Springs, and she acted grateful like, thanking the boys in her tanglefoot English. Next mawnin' her folks druv off in a private team to Norris Basin, and she seemed dazed. For I talked with her then, and questioned her as to her wishes, but she could not say what she wished, nor if it was East or West she would go; and I reckon she was too stricken to have wishes.

"Our stuff for Galena Creek delayed on the railroad, and I got to know her, and then I quit givin' Hank cause for jealousy. I kept myself with the boys, and I played more cyards, while Hank he sca'cely played at all. One night I came on them—Hank and Willomene—walkin' among the pines where the road goes down the hill. Yu' should have saw that pair o' lovers. Her big shape was plain and kind o' steadfast in the moon, and alongside of her little black Hank! And there it was. Of course it ain't nothing to be surprised at that a mean and triflin' man tries to seem what he is not when he wants to please a good woman. But why does she get fooled, when it's so plain to other folks that are not givin' it any special thought? All the rest of the men and women at the Mammoth understood Hank. They knowed he was a worthless proposition. And I cert'nly relied on his gettin' back to his whiskey and openin' her eyes that way. But he did not. I met them next evening again by the Liberty Cap. Supposin' I'd been her brother or her mother, what use was it me warning her? Brothers and mothers don't get believed.

"The railroad brought the stuff for Galena Creek, and Hank would not look at it on account of his courtin'. I took it alone myself by Yancey's and the second bridge and Miller Creek to the camp, nor I didn't tell Willomene good-bye, for I had got disgusted at her blindness."

The Virginian shifted his position, and jerked his overalls to a more comfortable fit. Then he continued:

"They was married the Tuesday after at Livingston, and Hank must have been pow'ful pleased at himself. For he gave Willomene a wedding present, with the balance of his cash, spending his last nickel on buying her a red-tailed parrot they had for sale at the First National Bank. The son-of-a-gun hollad so freely at the bank, the president awde'd the cashier to get shed of the out-ragious bird, or he would wring its neck.

"So Hank and Willomene stayed a week up in Livingston on her money, and then he fetched her back to Gardner, and bought their grub, and bride and groom came up to the camp we had on Galena Creek.

"She had never slep' out before. She had never been on a hawss, neither. And she mighty near rolled off down into Pitchstone Cañon, comin' up by the cut-off trail. Why, seh, I would not willingly take you through that place, except yu' promised me yu' would lead your hawss when I said to. But Hank takes the woman he had married, and he takes heavy-loaded pack-hawsses. 'Tis the first time such a thing has been known of in the country. Yu' remember them big tall grass-topped mountains over in the Hoodoo country, and how they descends slam down through the cross-timber that yu' can't sca'cely work through afoot, till they pitches over into lots an' lots o' little cañons, with maybe two inches of water runnin' in the bottom? All that is East Fork water, and over the divide is Clark's Fork, or Stinkin' Water, if yu' take the country yondeh to the southeast. But any place yu' go is them undesirable steep slopes, and the cut-off trail takes along about the worst in the business.

"Well, Hank he got his outfit over it somehow, and, gentlemen, hush! but yu'd ought t've seen him and that poor girl pull into our camp. Yu'd cert'nly never have conjectured them two was a weddin' journey. He was leadin', but skewed around in his saddle to jaw back at Willomene for riding so ignorant. Suppose it was a thing she was responsible for, yu'd not have talked to her that-a-way even in private; and hyeh was the camp a-lookin', and a-listenin', and some of us ashamed. She was setting straddleways like a mountain, and between him and her went the three pack-animals, plumb shiverin' played out, and the flour—they had two hundred pounds—tilted over hellwards, with the red-tailed parrot shoutin' landslides in his cage tied on top o' the leanin' sacks.

"It was that mean to see, that shameless and unkind, that even a thoughtless kid like the McLean boy felt offended, and favorable to some sort of remonstrance. 'The son-of-a———!' he said to me. 'The son-of-a———! If he don't stop, let's stop him.' And I reckon we might have.

"But Hank he quit. 'Twas plain to see he'd got a genuwine scare comin' through Pitchstone Cañon, and it turned him sour, so he'd hardly talk to us, but just mumbled 'How!' kind o' gruff, when the boys come up to congratulate him as to his marriage.

"But Willomene, she says when she saw me, 'Oh, I am so glad!' and we shook hands right friendly. And I wished I'd told her good-bye that day at the Mammoth. For she bore no spite, and maybe I had forgot her feelings in thinkin' of my own. I had talked to her down at the Mammoth at first, yu' know, and she said a word about old friends. Our friendship was three weeks old that day, but I expect her new experiences looked like years to her. And she told me how near she come to gettin' killed.

"Yu' ain't ever been over that trail, seh? Yu' cert'nly must see Pitchstone Cañon. But we'll not go there with packs. And we will get off our hawsses a good way back. For many animals feels that there's something the matter with that place, and they act very strange about it.

"The Grand Cañon is grand, and makes yu' feel good to look at it, and a geyser is grand and all right, too. But this hyeh Pitchstone hole, if Willomene had went down into that—well, I'll tell yu', that you may judge.

"She seen the trail a-drawin' nearer and nearer the aidge, between the timber and the jumpin'-off place, and she seen how them little loose stones and the crumble stuff would slide and slide away under the hawss's feet. She could hear the stuff rattlin' continually from his steps, and when she turned her haid to look, she seen it goin' down close beside her, but into what it went she could not see. Only, there was a queer steam would come up now and agayn, and her hawss trembled. So she tried to get off and walk without sayin' nothin' to Hank. He kep' on ahaid, and her hawss she had pulled up started to follo' as she was half off him, and that gave her a tumble, but there was an old crooked dead tree. It growed right out o' the aidge. There she hung.

"Down below is a little green water tricklin', green as the stuff that gets on brass, and tricklin' along over soft cream-colored formation, like pie. And it ain't so far to fall but what a man might not be too much hurt for crawlin' out. But there ain't no crawlin' out o' Pitchstone Cañon, they say. Down in there is caves that yu' cannot see. 'Tis them that coughs up the stream now and agayn. With the wind yu' can smell 'em a mile away, and in the night I have been layin' quiet and heard 'em. Not that it's a big noise, even when a man is close up. It's a fluffy kind of a sigh. But it sounds as if some awful thing was a-makin' it deep down in the guts of the world. They claim there's poison air comes out o' the caves and lays low along the water. They claim if a bear or an elk strays in from below, and the caves sets up their coughin', which they don't regular every day, the animals die. I have seen it come in two seconds. And when it comes that-a-way risin' upon yu' with that fluffy kind of a sigh, yu' feel mighty lonesome, seh.

"So Hank he happened to look back and see Willomene hangin' at the aidge o' them black rocks. And his scare made him mad. And his mad stayed with him till they come into camp. She looked around, and when she seen Hank's tent that him and her was to sleep in she showed surprise. And he showed surprise when he see the bread she cooked.

" 'What kind of a Dutch woman are yu',' says he, strainin' for a joke, 'if yu' can't use a Dutch-oven?'

" 'You say to me you have a house to live in,' says Willomene. 'Where is that house?'

" 'I did not figure on gettin' a woman when I left camp,' says Hank, grinnin', but not pleasant, 'or I'd have hurried up with the shack I'm a-buildin."

"He was buildin' one. When I left Galena Creek and come away from that country to meet you, the house was finished enough for the couple to move in. I hefted her brass-nailed trunk up the hill from their tent myself, and I watched her take out her crucifix. But she would not let me help her with that. She'd not let me touch it. She'd fixed it up agaynst the wall her own self her own way. But she accepted some flowers I picked, and set them in a can front of the crucifix. Then Hank he come in, and seein', says to me, 'Are you one of the kind that squats before them silly dolls?' 'I would tell yu', I answered him; 'but it would not inter-est yu'.' And I cleared out, and left him and Willomene to begin their housekeepin'.

"Already they had quit havin' much to say to each other down in their tent. The only steady talkin' done in that house was done by the parrot. I've never saw any go ahaid of that bird. I have told yu' about Hank, and how when he'd come home and see her prayin' to that crucifix he'd always get riled up. He would mention it freely to the boys. Not that she neglected him, yu' know. She done her part, workin' mighty hard, for she was a willin' woman. But he could not make her quit her religion; and Willomene she had got to bein' very silent before I come away. She used to talk to me some at first, but she dropped it. I don't know why. I expect maybe it was hard for her to have us that close in camp, witnessin' her troubles every day, and she a foreigner. I reckon if she got any comfort, it would be when we was off prospectin' or huntin', and she could shut the cabin door and be alone."

The Virginian stopped for a moment.

"It will soon be a month since I left Galena Creek," he resumed. "But I cannot get the business out o' my haid. I keep a studyin' over it."

His talk was done. He had unburdened his mind. Night lay deep and quiet around us, with no sound far or near, save Buffalo Fork plashing over its riffle.

2

We left Snake River. We went up Pacific Creek, and through Two Ocean Pass, and down among the watery willow-bottoms and beaver-dams of the Upper Yellowstone. We fished; we enjoyed existence along the lake. Then we went over Pelican Creek trail and came steeply down into the giant country of grass-topped mountains. At dawn and dusk the elk had begun to call across the stillness. And one morning in the Hoodoo country, where we were looking for sheep, we came round a jut of the strange, organ-pipe formation upon a long-legged boy of about nineteen, also hunting.

"Still hyeh?" said the Virginian, without emotion.

"I guess so," returned the boy, equally matter-of-fact. "Yu' seem to be around yourself," he added.

They might have been next-door neighbors, meeting in a town street for the second time in the same day.

The Virginian made me known to Mr. Lin McLean, who gave me a brief nod.

"Any luck?" he inquired, but not of me.

"Oh," drawled the Virginian, "luck enough."

Knowing the ways of the country, I said no word. It was bootless to interrupt their own methods of getting at what was really in both their minds.

The boy fixed his wide-open hazel eyes upon me. "Fine weather," he mentioned.

"Very fine," said I.

"I seen your horses a while ago," he said. "Camp far from here?" he asked the Virginian.

"Not specially. Stay and eat with us. We've got elk meat."

"That's what I'm after for camp," said McLean. "All of us is out on a hunt to-day—except him."

"How many are yu' now?"

"The whole six."

"Makin' money?"

"Oh, some days the gold washes out good in the pan, and others it's that fine it'll float off without settlin'."

"So Hank ain't huntin' to-day?"

"Huntin'! We left him layin' out in the clumb o' brush below their cabin. Been drinkin' all night."

The Virginian broke off a piece of the Hoodoo mud-rock from the weird eroded pillar that we stood beside. He threw it into a bank of last year's snow. We all watched it as if it were important. Up through the mountain silence pierced the long quivering whistle of a bull-elk. It was like an unearthly singer practicing an unearthly scale.

"First time she heard that," said McLean, "she was scared."

"Nothin' maybe to resemble it in Austria," said the Virginian.

"That's so," said McLean. "That's so, you bet! Nothin' just like Hank over there, neither."

"Well, flesh is mostly flesh in all lands, I reckon," said the Virginian. "I expect yu' can be drunk and disorderly in every language. But an Austrian Hank would be liable to respect her crucifix.

"That's so!"

"He 'ain't made her quit it yet?"

"Not him. But he's got meaner."

"Drunk this mawnin', yu' say?"

"That's his most harmless condition now."

"Nobody's in camp but them two? Her and him alone?"

"Oh, he dassent touch her."

"Who did he tell that to?"

"Oh, the camp is backin' her. The camp has explained that to him several times, you bet! And what's more, she has got the upper hand of him herself. She has him beat."

"How beat?"

"She has downed him with her eye. Just by endurin' him peacefully; and with her eye. I've saw it. Things changed some after yu' pulled out. We had a good crowd still, and it was pleasant, and not too lively nor yet too slow. And Willomene, she come more among us. She'd not stay shut in-doors, like she done at first. I'd have like to've showed her how to punish Hank."

"Afteh she had downed yu' with her eye?" inquired the Virginian.

Young McLean reddened, and threw a furtive look upon me, the stranger, the outsider. "Oh, well," he said, "I done nothing onusual. But that's all different now. All of us likes her and respects her, and makes allowances for her bein' Dutch. Yu' can't help but respect her. And she shows she knows."

"I reckon maybe she knows how to deal with Hank," said the Virginian.

"Shucks!" said McLean, scornfully. "And her so big and him so puny! She'd ought to lift him off the earth with one arm and lam him with a baste or two with the other, and he'd improve."

"Maybe that's why she don't," mused the Virginian, slowly; "because she is so big. Big in the spirit, I mean. She'd not stoop to his level. Don't yu' see she is kind o' way up above him and camp and everything—just her and her crucifix?"

"Her and her crucifix!" repeated young Lin McLean, staring at this interpretation, which was beyond his lively understanding. "Her and her crucifix. Turruble lonesome company! Well, them are things yu' don't know about. I kind o' laughed myself the first time I seen her at it. Hank, he says to me soft, 'Come here, Lin,' and I peeped in where she was a-prayin'. She seen us two, but she didn't quit. So I quit, and

Hank came with me, sayin' tough words about it. Yes, them are things yu' sure don't know about. What's the matter with you camping with us boys to-night?"

We had been going to visit them the next day. We made it to-day, instead. And Mr. McLean helped us with our packs, and we carried our welcome in the shape of elk meat. So we turned our faces down the grass-topped mountains toward Galena Creek. Once, far through an open gap away below us, we sighted the cabin with the help of our field-glasses.

"Pity we can't make out Hank sleepin' in that brush," said McLean.

"He has probably gone into the cabin by now," said I.

"Not him! He prefers the brush all day when he's that drunk, you bet!"

"Afraid of her?"

"Well—oneasy in her presence. Not that she's liable to be in there now. She don't stay inside nowadays so much. She's been comin' round the ditch, silent-like but friendly. And she'll watch us workin' for a spell, and then she's apt to move off alone into the woods, singin' them Dutch songs of hern that ain't got no toon. I've met her walkin' that way, tall and earnest, lots of times. But she don't want your company, though she'll patch your overalls and give yu' lunch always. Nor she won't take pay."

Thus we proceeded down from the open summits into the close pines; and while we made our way among the cross-timber and over the little streams, McLean told us of various days and nights at the camp, and how Hank had come to venting his cowardice upon his wife's faith.

"Why, he informed her one day when he was goin' to take his dust to town, that if he came back and found that thing in the house, he'd do it up for her. 'So yu' better pack off your wooden dummy somewheres,' says he. And she just looked at him kind o' stone-like and solemn. For she don't care for his words no more.

"And while he was away she'd have us all in to supper up at the shack, and look at us eatin' while she'd walk around puttin' grub on your plate. Day time she'd come around the ditch, watchin' for a while, and move off slow, singin' her Dutch songs. And when Hank comes back from spendin' his dust, he sees the crucifix same as always, and he says, 'Didn't I tell yu' to take that down?' 'You did,' says Willomene, lookin' at him very quiet. And he quit."

"And Honey Wiggin says to him, 'Hank, leave her alone.' And Hank, bein' all trembly from spreein' in town, he says, 'You're all agin me!' like as if he were a baby."

"I should think you would run him out of camp," said I.

"Well, we've studied over that some," McLean answered. "But what's to be done with Willomene?"

I did not know. None of us seemed to know.

"The boys got together night before last," continued McLean, "and after holdin' a unanimous meetin', we visited her and spoke to her about goin' back to her home. She was slow in corrallin' our idea on account of her bein' no English scholar. But when she did, after three of us takin' their turn at puttin' the proposition to her, she would not accept any of our dust. And though she started to thank us the handsomest she knowed how, it seemed to grieve her, for she cried. So we thought we'd better get out. She's tried to tell us the name of her home, but yu' can't pronounce such outlandishness."

As we went down the mountains, we talked of other things, but always came back to this; and we were turning it over still when the sun had departed from the narrow cleft that we were following, and shone only on the distant grassy tops which rose round us into an upper world of light.

"We'll all soon have to move out of this camp, anyway," said McLean, unstrapping his coat from his saddle and drawing it on. "It gets chill now in the afternoons. D'yu' see the quakin'-asps all turned yello', and the leaves keeps fallin' without no wind to blow 'em down? We're liable to get snowed in on short notice in this mountain country. If the water goes to freeze on us we'll have to quit workin'. There's camp."

We had rounded a corner, and once more sighted the cabin. I suppose it may have been still half a mile away, upon the further side of a ravine into which our little valley opened. But field-glasses were not needed now to make out the cabin clearly, windows and door. Smoke rose from it; for supper-time was nearing, and we stopped to survey the scene. As we were looking, another hunter joined us, coming from the deep woods to the edge of the pines where we were standing. This was Honey Wiggin. He had killed a deer, and he surmised that all the boys would be back soon. Others had met luck besides himself; he had left one dressing an elk over the next ridge. Nobody seemed to have got in yet, from appearances. Didn't the camp look lonesome?

"There's somebody, though," said McLean.

The Virginian took the glasses. "I reckon—yes, that's Hank. The cold has woke him up, and he's comin' in out o' the brush."

Each of us took the glasses in turn; and I watched the figure go up the hill to the door of the cabin. It seemed to pause and diverge to the window. At the window it stood still, head bent, looking in. Then it returned quickly to the door. It was too far to discern, even through the glasses, what the figure was doing. Whether the door was locked, whether he was knocking or fumbling with a key, or whether he spoke through the door to the person within—I cannot tell what it was that came through the glasses straight to my nerves, so that I jumped at a sudden sound; and it was only the distant shrill call of an elk. I was handing the glasses to the Virginian for him to see when the figure opened the door and disappeared in the dark interior. As I watched the square of darkness which the door's opening made, something seemed to happen there—or else it was a spark, a flash, in my own straining eyes.

But at that same instant the Virginian dashed forward upon his horse, leaving the glasses in my hand. And with the contagion of his act the rest of us followed him, leaving the pack animals to follow us as they should choose.

"Look!" cried McLean. "He's not shot her."

I saw the tall figure of a woman rush out of the door and pass quickly round the house.

"He's missed her!" cried McLean, again. "She's savin' herself."

But the man's figure did not appear in pursuit. Instead of this, the woman returned as quickly as she had gone, and entered the dark interior.

"She had something," said Wiggin. "What would that be?"

"Maybe it's all right, after all," said McLean. "She went out to get wood."

The rough steepness of our trail had brought us down to a walk, and as we continued to press forward at this pace as fast as we could, we compared a few notes. McLean did not think he saw any flash. Wiggin thought that he had heard a sound, but it was at the moment when the Virginian's horse had noisily started away.

Our trail had now taken us down where we could no longer look across and see the cabin. And the half-mile proved a long one over this ground. At length we reached and crossed the rocky ford, overtaking the Virginian there.

"These hawsses," said he, "are played out. We'll climb up to camp afoot. And just keep behind me for the present."

We obeyed our natural leader, and made ready for whatever we might be going into. We passed up the steep bank and came again in sight of the door. It was still wide open. We stood, and felt a sort of silence which the approach of two new-comers could not break. They joined us. They had been coming home from hunting, and had plainly heard a shot here. We stood for a moment more after learning this, and then one of the men called out the names of Hank and Willomene. Again we—or I at least—felt that same silence, which to my disturbed imagination seemed to be rising round us as mists rise from water.

"There's nobody in there," stated the Virginian. "Nobody that's alive," he added. And he crossed the cabin and walked into the door.

Though he made no gesture, I saw astonishment pass through his body, as he stopped still; and all of us came after him. There hung the crucifix, with a round hole through the middle of it. One of the men went to it and took it down; and behind it, sunk in the log, was the bullet. The cabin was but a single room, and every object that it contained could be seen at a glance; nor was there hiding-room for anything. On the floor lay the axe from the wood-pile; but I will not tell of its appearance. So he had shot her crucifix, her Rock of Ages, the thing which enabled her to bear her life, and that lifted her above life; and she—but there was the axe to show what she had done then. Was this cabin really empty? I looked more slowly about, half dreading to find that I had overlooked something. But it was as the Virginian had said; nobody was there.

As we were wondering, there was a noise above our heads, and I was not the only one who started and stared. It was the parrot; and we stood away in a circle, looking up at his cage. Crouching flat on the floor of the cage, his wings huddled tight to his body, he was swinging his head from side to side; and when he saw that we watched him, he began a low croaking and monotonous utterance, which never changed, but remained rapid and continuous. I heard McLean whisper to the Virginian, "You bet he knows."

The Virginian stepped to the door, and then he bent to the gravel and beckoned us to come and see. Among the recent footprints at the threshold the man's boot-heel was plain, as well as the woman's broad tread. But while the man's steps led into the cabin, they did not lead away from it. We tracked his course just as we had seen it through the glasses: up the hill from the brush to the window, and then to the door. But he had never walked out again. Yet in the cabin he was not; we tore up the half-floor that it had. There was no use to dig in the earth. And all the while that we were at this search the parrot remained crouched in the bottom of his cage, his black eye fixed upon our movements.

"She has carried him," said the Virginian. "We must follow up Willomene."

The latest heavy set of footprints led us from the door along the ditch, where they sank deep in the softer soil; then they turned off sharply into the mountains.

"This is the cut-off trail," said McLean to me. "The same he brought her in by."

The tracks were very clear, and evidently had been made by a person moving slowly. Whatever theories our various minds were now shaping, no one spoke a word to his neighbor, but we went along with a hush over us.

After some walking, Wiggin suddenly stopped and pointed.

We had come to the edge of the timber, where a narrow black cañon began, and ahead of us the trail drew near a slanting ledge, where the footing was of small loose stones. I recognize the odor, the volcanic whiffs, that so often prowls and meets one in the lonely woods of that region, but at first I failed to make out what had set us all running.

"Is he looking down into the hole himself?" some one asked; and then I did see a figure, the figure I had looked at through the glasses, leaning strangely over the edge of Pitchstone Cañon, as if indeed he was peering to watch what might be in the bottom.

We came near. But those eyes were sightless, and in the skull the story of the axe was carved. By a piece of his clothing he was hooked in the twisted roots of a dead tree, and hung there at the extreme verge. I went to look over, and Lin McLean caught me as I staggered at the sight I saw. He would have lost his own foothold in saving me had not one of the others held him from above.

She was there below; Hank's woman, brought from Austria to the New World. The vision of that brown bundle lying in the water will never leave me, I think. She had carried the body to this point; but had she intended this end? Or was some part of it an accident? Had she meant to take him with her? Had she meant to stay behind herself? No word came from these dead to answer us. But as we stood speaking there, a giant puff of breath rose up to us between the black walls.

"There's that fluffy sigh I told yu' about," said the Virginian.

"He's talkin' to her! I tell yu' he's talkin' to her!" burst out McLean, suddenly, in such a voice that we stared as he pointed at the man in the tree. "See him lean over! He's sayin', 'I have yu' beat after all.' " And McLean fell to whimpering.

Wiggin took the boy's arm kindly and walked him along the trail. He did not seem twenty yet. Life had not shown this side of itself to him so plainly before.

"Let's get out of here," said the Virginian.

It seemed one more pitiful straw that the lonely bundle should be left in such a vault of doom, with no last touches of care from its fellow-beings, and no heap of kind earth to hide it. But whether the place is deadly or not, man dares not venture into it. So they took Hank from the tree that night, and early next morning they buried him near camp on the top of a little mound.

But the thought of Willomene lying in Pitchstone Cañon had kept sleep from me through that whole night, nor did I wish to attend Hank's burial. I rose very early, while the sunshine had still a long way to come down to us from the mountain-tops, and I walked back along the cut-off trail. I was moved to look once more upon that frightful place. And as I came to the edge of the timber, there was the Virginian. He did not expect any one. He had set up the crucifix as near the dead tree as it could be firmly planted.

"It belongs to her, anyway," he explained.

Some lines of verse came into my memory, and with a change or two I wrote them as deep as I could with my pencil upon a small board that he smoothed for me.

"Call for the robin redbreast and the wren,
Since o'er shady groves they hover,
And with flowers and leaves do cover
The friendless bodies of unburied men.
Call to this funeral dole
The ant, the field-mouse, and the mole,
To rear her hillocks that shall keep her warm."

"That kind o' quaint language reminds me of a play I seen onced in Saynt Paul," said the Virginian. "About young Prince Henry."

I told him that another Poet was the author.

"They are both good writers," said the Virginian. And as he was finishing the monument that we had made, young Lin McLean joined us. He was a little ashamed of the feelings that he had shown yesterday, a little anxious to cover those feelings with brass.

"Well," he said, taking an offish, man-of-the-world tone, "all this fuss just because a woman believed in God."

"You have put it down wrong," said the Virginian; "it's just because a man didn't."

PART TWO

WHERE WEST WAS WEST

DOROTHY M. JOHNSON

DOROTHY MARIE JOHNSON (1905–) was born in McGregor, Iowa, grew up in Whitefish, Montana, and graduated with a bachelor's degree from the University of Montana at Missoula. She worked in various jobs as a stenographer before venturing to New York City in 1935, where she found employment in an editorial capacity with magazine publishers. During this period she turned to writing herself. Her first book was *Beulah Bunny Tells All* (Morrow, 1942), a collection of short stories about a fictitious schoolteacher published previously in *The Saturday Evening Post*. She became profoundly interested in the Plains Indians and began studying their culture, after having believed that all Indians are bad. She became an adopted member of the Crow tribe with the name Kills Both Places. In 1952 she moved back to Montana and has lived there ever since.

Her stature as an author of Western fiction is based chiefly on two collections of her short stories, *Indian Country* (1953; reissued by Gregg Press, 1979) and *The Hanging Tree* (1958; reissued by the Gregg Press, 1980). Like A. B. Guthrie, Jr., Jack Schaefer in his short stories, and Elmer Kelton in his more recent fiction, she readily broke away from Western stereotypes and instead wrote about ordinary people, some of whom are not particularly admirable, whose actions sometimes take on heroic dimensions in the face of frontier adversity. Her vast knowledge of frontier life makes her situations and characters credible.

"A Man Called Horse" is from the *Indian Country* collection. It was, of course, made into a film also titled *A Man Called Horse* (National General, 1970), directed by Elliott Silverstein.

"Rather than a tale of Indian life," Dan Georgakas

wrote in an essay contained in *The Pretend Indians: Images of Native Americans in the Movies* (Iowa State University Press, 1980), *A Man Called Horse* "is thus really about a white nobleman proving his superiority in the wilds. Almost every detail of Indian life is incorrect. An angry Sioux writing to the *Village Voice* complained . . . that the Sioux never abandoned widows, orphans, and old people to starve and freeze as shown in the film." I would amend this assertion. "Some old people, unwanted or without relatives, had no place to go," Royal B. Hassrick noted in his book *The Sioux* (University of Oklahoma Press, 1964). "These were forced to live alone at the edge of the encampment. Here they were given food and supplies by the generous young men who thereby gained prestige . . . but at best theirs was a tragic lot, too often filled with insecurity and despair." The same was true also for the Crows, in history as in Dorothy M. Johnson's story. But in our present-day culture—as in the film—it is worse. We have no generous young men, or an insufficient number of them, for I cannot count the times I have seen old people rummaging in garbage cans in our cities or buying dog food for their own consumption in our supermarkets. Caring for the poor carries no prestige at all.

There are two principal ways to end a captivity story: a captive might somehow secure freedom, or remain with the captors. "There was only one group lower in status than the women; that was the slave or captive group," Mildred P. Mayhall recorded in *The Kiowas* (University of Oklahoma Press, 1971). "This group held an impermanent status, for captives, showing fortitude and bravery, could be accepted into the tribe, usually by adoption into a family. For a girl, also, marriage with an important man might change captive status. *Many captives did not desire to return to their own people.*" (My italics.) Perhaps the most telling difference between last-century America and today is that there was *once* an alternative to the invaders' culture.

A Man Called Horse

He was a young man of good family, as the phrase went in the New England of a hundred-odd years ago, and the reasons for his bitter discontent were unclear, even to himself. He grew up in the gracious old Boston home under his grandmother's care, for his mother had died in giving him birth; and all his life he had known every comfort and privilege his father's wealth could provide.

But still there was the discontent, which puzzled him because he could not even define it. He wanted to live among his equals—people who were no better than he and no worse either. That was as close as he could come to describing the source of his unhappiness in Boston and his restless desire to go somewhere else.

In the year 1845, he left home and went out West, far beyond the country's creeping frontier, where he hoped to find his equals. He had the idea that in Indian country, where there was danger, all white men were kings, and he wanted to be one of them. But he found, in the West as in Boston, that the men he respected were still his superiors, even if they could not read, and those he did not respect weren't worth talking to.

He did have money, however, and he could hire the men he respected. He hired four of them, to cook and hunt and guide and be his companions, but he found them not friendly.

They were apart from him and he was still alone. He still brooded about his status in the world, longing for his equals.

On a day in June, he learned what it was to have no status at all. He became a captive of a small raiding party of Crow Indians.

He heard gunfire and the brief shouts of his companions around the bend of the creek just before they died, but he never saw their bodies. He had no chance to fight, because he was naked and unarmed, bathing in the creek, when a Crow warrior seized and held him.

His captor let him go at last, let him run. Then the lot of them rode him down for sport, striking him with their coup sticks. They carried the dripping scalps of his companions, and one had skinned off Baptiste's black beard as well, for a trophy.

They took him along in a matter-of-fact way, as they took the captured horses. He was unshod and naked as the horses were, and like them he had a rawhide thong around his neck. So long as he didn't fall down, the Crows ignored him.

On the second day they gave him his breeches. His feet were too swollen for his boots, but one of the Indians threw him a pair of moccasins that had belonged to the halfbreed, Henri, who was dead back at the creek. The captive wore the moccasins gratefully. The third day they let him ride one of the spare horses so the party could move faster, and on that day they came in sight of their camp.

He thought of trying to escape, hoping he might be killed in flight rather than by slow torture in the camp, but he never had a chance to try. They were more familiar with escape than he was and, knowing what to expect, they forestalled it. The only other time he had tried to escape from anyone, he had succeeded. When he had left his home in Boston, his father had raged and his grandmother had cried, but they could not talk him out of his intention.

The men of the Crow raiding party didn't bother with talk.

Before riding into camp they stopped and dressed in their regalia, and in parts of their victims' clothing; they painted their faces black. Then, leading the white man by the rawhide around his neck as though he were a horse, they rode down toward the tepee circle, shouting and singing, brandishing their weapons. He was unconscious when they got there; he fell and was dragged.

He lay dazed and battered near a tepee while the noisy, busy life of the camp swarmed around him and Indians came to stare. Thirst consumed him, and when it rained he lapped rain water from the ground like a dog. A scrawny, shrieking, eternally busy old woman with ragged graying hair threw a chunk of meat on the grass, and he fought the dogs for it.

When his head cleared, he was angry, although anger was an emotion he knew he could not afford.

It was better when I was a horse, he thought—when they led me by the rawhide around my neck. I won't be a dog, no matter what!

The hag gave him stinking, rancid grease and let him figure out what it was for. He applied it gingerly to his bruised and sun-seared body.

Now, he thought, I smell like the rest of them.

While he was healing, he considered coldly the advantages of being a horse. A man would be humiliated, and sooner or later he would strike back and that would be the end of him. But a horse had only to be docile. Very well, he would learn to do without pride.

He understood that he was the property of the screaming old woman, a fine gift from her son, one that she liked to show off. She did more yelling at him than at anyone else, probably to impress the neighbors so they would not forget what a great and generous man her son was. She was bossy and proud, a dreadful bag of skin and bones, and she was a devilish hard worker.

The white man, who now thought of himself as a horse, forgot sometimes to worry about his danger. He kept making mental notes of things to tell his own people in Boston about this hideous adventure. He would go back a hero, and he would say, "Grandmother, let me fetch your shawl. I've been accustomed to doing little errands for another lady about your age."

Two girls lived in the tepee with the old hag and her warrior son. One of them, the white man concluded, was his captor's wife and the other was his little sister. The daughter-in-law was smug and spoiled. Being beloved, she did not have to be useful. The younger girl had bright, wandering eyes. Often enough they wandered to the white man who was pretending to be a horse.

The two girls worked when the old woman put them at it, but they were always running off to do something they enjoyed more. There were games and noisy contests, and there was much laughter. But not for the white man. He was finding out what loneliness could be.

That was a rich summer on the plains, with plenty of buffalo for meat and clothing and the making of tepees. The Crows were wealthy in horses, prosperous and contented. If their men had not been so avid for glory, the white man thought, there would have been a lot more of them. But they went out of their way to court death, and when one of them met it, the whole camp mourned extravagantly and cried to their God for vengeance.

The captive was a horse all summer, a docile bearer of burdens, careful and patient. He kept reminding himself that he had to be better-natured than other horses, because he could not lash out with hoofs or teeth. Helping the old woman load up the horses for travel, he yanked at a pack and said, "Whoa, brother. It goes easier when you don't fight."

The horse gave him a big-eyed stare as if it understood his language—a comforting thought, because nobody else did. But even among the horses he felt unequal. They were able to look out for themselves if they escaped. He would simply starve. He was envious still, even among the horses.

Humbly he fetched and carried. Sometimes he even offered to help, but he had not the skill for the endless work of the women, and he was not trusted to hunt with the men, the providers.

When the camp moved, he carried a pack trudging with the women. Even the dogs worked then, pulling small burdens on travois of sticks.

The Indian who had captured him lived like a lord, as he had a right to do. He hunted with his peers, attended long ceremonial meetings with much chanting and dancing, and lounged in the shade with his smug bride. He had only two responsibilities: to kill buffalo and to gain glory. The white man was so far beneath him in status that the Indian did not even think of envy.

One day several things happened that made the captive think he might sometime become a man again. That was the day when he began to understand their language. For four months he had heard it, day and night, the joy and the mourning, the ritual chanting and sung prayers, the squabbles and the deliberations. None of it meant anything to him at all.

But on that important day in early fall the two young women set out for the river, and one of them called over her shoulder to the old woman. The white man was startled. She had said she was going to bathe. His understanding was so sudden that he felt as if his ears had come unstopped. Listening to the racket of the camp, he heard fragments of meaning instead of gabble.

On that same important day the old woman brought a pair of new moccasins out of the tepee and tossed them on the ground before him. He could not believe she would do anything for him because of kindness, but giving him moccasins was one way of looking after her property.

In thanking her, he dared greatly. He picked a little handful of fading fall flowers and took them to her as she squatted in front of her tepee, scraping a buffalo hide with a tool made from a piece of iron tied to a bone. Her hands were hideous—most of the fingers had the first joint missing. He bowed solemnly and offered the flowers.

She glared at him from beneath the short, ragged tangle of her hair. She stared at the flowers, knocked them out of his hand and went running to the next tepee, squalling the story. He heard her and the other women screaming with laughter.

The white man squared his shoulders and walked boldly over to watch three small boys shooting arrows at a target. He said in English, "Show me how to do that, will you?"

They frowned, but he held out his hand as if there could be no doubt. One of them gave him a bow and one arrow, and they snickered when he missed.

The people were easily amused, except when they were angry. They were amused, at him, playing with the little boys. A few days later he asked the hag, with gestures, for a bow that her son had just discarded, a man-size bow of horn. He scavenged for old arrows. The old woman cackled at his marksmanship and called her neighbors to enjoy the fun.

When he could understand words, he could identify his people by their names. The old woman was Greasy Hand, and her daughter was Pretty Calf. The other young woman's name was not clear to him, for the words were not in his vocabulary. The man who had captured him was Yellow Robe.

Once he could understand, he could begin to talk a little, and then he was less lonely. Nobody had been able to see any reason for talking to him, since he would not understand anyway. He asked the old woman, "What is my name?" Until he knew it, he was incomplete. She shrugged to let him know he had none.

He told her in the Crow language, "My name is Horse." He repeated it, and she nodded. After that they called him Horse when they called him anything. Nobody cared except the white man himself.

They trusted him enough to let him stray out of camp, so that he might have got away and, by unimaginable good luck, might have reached a trading post or a fort, but winter was too close. He did not dare leave without a horse; he needed clothing and a better hunting weapon than he had, and more certain skill in using it. He did not dare steal, for then they would surely have pursued him, and just as certainly they would have caught him. Remembering the warmth of the home that was waiting in Boston, he settled down for the winter.

On a cold night he crept into the tepee after the others had gone to bed. Even a horse might try to find shelter from the wind. The old woman grumbled, but without conviction. She did not put him out.

They tolerated him, back in the shadows, so long as he did not get in the way.

He began to understand how the family that owned him differed from the others. Fate had been cruel to them. In a short, sharp argument among the old women, one of them derided Greasy Hand by sneering. "You have no relatives!" and Greasy Hand raved for minutes of the deeds of her father and uncles and brothers. And she had had four sons, she reminded her detractor—who answered with scorn, "Where are they?"

Later the white man found her moaning and whimpering to herself, rocking back and forth on her haunches, staring at her mutilated hands. By that time he understood. A mourner often chopped off a finger joint. Old Greasy Hand had mourned often. For the first time he felt a twinge of pity, but he put it aside as another emotion, like anger, that he could not afford. He thought: What tales I will tell when I get home!

He wrinkled his nose in disdain. The camp stank of animals and meat and rancid grease. He looked down at his naked, shivering legs and was startled, remembering that he was still only a horse.

He could not trust the old woman. She fed him only because a starved slave would die and not be worth boasting about. Just how fitful her temper was he saw on the day when she got tired of stumbling over one of the hundred dogs that infested the camp. This was one of her own dogs, a large, strong one that pulled a baggage travois when the tribe moved camp.

Countless times he had seen her kick at the beast as it lay sleeping in front of the tepee, in her way. The dog always moved, with a yelp, but it always got in the way again. One day she gave the dog its usual kick and then stood scolding at it while the animal rolled its eyes sleepily. The old woman suddenly picked up her axe and cut the dog's head off with one blow. Looking well satisfied with herself, she beckoned her slave to remove the body.

It could have been me, he thought, if I were a dog. But I'm a horse.

His hope of life lay with the girl, Pretty Calf. He set about courting her, realizing how desperately poor he was both in property and honor. He owned no horse, no weapon but the old bow and the battered arrows. He had nothing to give away, and he needed gifts, because he did not dare seduce the girl.

One of the customs of courtship involved sending a gift of horses to a girl's older brother and bestowing much buffalo meat upon her mother. The white man could not wait for some far-off time when he might have either horses or meat to give away. And his courtship had to be secret. It was not for him to stroll past the groups of watchful girls, blowing a flute made of an eagle's wing bone, as the flirtatious young bucks did.

He could not ride past Pretty Calf's tepee, painted and bedizened; he had no horse, no finery.

Back home, he remembered, I could marry just about any girl I'd want to. But he wasted little time thinking about that. A future was something to be earned.

The most he dared do was wink at Pretty Calf now and then, or state his admiration while she giggled and hid her face. The least he dared do to win his bride was to elope with her, but he had to give her a horse to put the seal of tribal approval on that. And he had no horse until he killed a man to get one. . . .

His opportunity came in early spring. He was casually accepted by that time. He did not belong, but he was amusing to the Crows, like a strange pet, or they would not have fed him through the winter.

His chance came when he was hunting small game with three young boys who were his guards as well as his scornful companions. Rabbits and birds were of no account in a camp well fed on buffalo meat, but they made good targets.

His party walked far that day. All of them at once saw the two horses in a sheltered coulee. The boys and the man crawled forward on their bellies, and then they saw an Indian who lay on the ground, moaning, a lone traveler. From the way the boys inched forward, Horse knew the man was fair prey—a member of some enemy tribe.

This is the way the captive white man acquired wealth and honor to win a bride and save his life: He shot an arrow into the sick man, a split second ahead of one of his small companions, and dashed forward to strike the still-groaning man with his bow, to count first coup. Then he seized the hobbled horses.

By the time he had the horses secure, and with them his hope for freedom, the boys had followed, counting coup with gestures and shrieks they had practiced since boyhood, and one of them had the scalp. The white man was grimly amused to see the boy double up with sudden nausea when he had the thing in his hand. . . .

There was a hubbub in the camp when they rode in that evening, two of them on each horse. The captive was noticed. Indians who had ignored him as a slave stared at the brave man who had struck first coup and had stolen horses.

The hubbub lasted all night, as fathers boasted loudly of their young sons' exploits. The white man was called upon to settle an argument between two fierce boys as to which of them had struck second coup and which must be satisfied with third. After much talk that went over his head, he solemnly pointed at the nearest boy. He didn't know which boy it was and didn't care, but the boy did.

The white man had watched warriors in their triumph. He knew what to do. Modesty about achievements had no place among the Crow people. When a man did something big, he told about it.

The white man smeared his face with grease and charcoal. He walked inside the tepee circle, chanting and singing. He used his own language.

"You heathens, you savages," he shouted. "I'm going to get out of here someday! I am going to get away!" The Crow people listened respectfully. In the Crow tongue he shouted, "Horse! I am Horse!" and they nodded.

He had a right to boast, and he had two horses. Before dawn, the white man and his bride were sheltered beyond a far hill, and he was telling her, "I love you, little lady. I love you."

She looked at him with her great dark eyes, and he thought she understood his English words—or as much as she needed to understand.

"You are my treasure," he said, "more precious than jewels, better than fine gold. I am going to call you Freedom."

When they returned to camp two days later, he was bold but worried. His ace, he suspected, might not be high enough in the game he was playing without being sure of the rules. But it served.

Old Greasy Hand raged—but not at him. She complained

loudly that her daughter had let herself go too cheap. But the marriage was as good as any Crow marriage. He had paid a horse.

He learned the language faster after that, from Pretty Calf, whom he sometimes called Freedom. He learned that his attentive, adoring bride was fourteen years old.

One thing he had not guessed was the difference that being Pretty Calf's husband would make in his relationship to her mother and brother. He had hoped only to make his position a little safer, but he had not expected to be treated with dignity. Greasy Hand no longer spoke to him at all. When the white man spoke to her, his bride murmured in dismay, explaining at great length that he must never do that. There could be no conversation between a man and his mother-in-law. He could not even mention a word that was part of her name.

Having improved his status so magnificently, he felt no need for hurry in getting away. Now that he had a woman, he had as good a chance to be rich as any man. Pretty Calf waited on him; she seldom ran off to play games with other young girls, but took pride in learning from her mother the many women's skills of tanning hides and making clothing and preparing food.

He was no more a horse but a kind of man, a half-Indian, still poor and unskilled but laden with honors, clinging to the buckskin fringes of Crow society.

Escape could wait until he could manage it in comfort, with fit clothing and a good horse, with hunting weapons. Escape could wait until the camp moved near some trading post. He did not plan how he would get home. He dreamed of being there all at once, and of telling stories nobody would believe. There was no hurry.

Pretty Calf delighted in educating him. He began to understand tribal arrangements, customs and why things were as they were. They were that way because they had always been so. His young wife giggled when she told him, in his ignorance, things she had always known. But she did not laugh when her brother's wife was taken by another warrior. She explained that solemnly with words and signs.

Yellow Robe belonged to a society called the Big Dogs. The wife stealer, Cut Neck, belonged to the Foxes. They were fellow tribesmen; they hunted together and fought side by side, but men of one society could take away wives from the other society if they wished, subject to certain limitations.

When Cut Neck rode up to the tepee, laughing and singing, and called to Yellow Robe's wife, "Come out! Come out!" she did as ordered, looking smug as usual, meek and entirely willing. Thereafter she rode beside him in ceremonial processions and carried his coup stick, while his other wife pretended not to care.

"But why?" the white man demanded of his wife, his Freedom. "Why did our brother let his woman go? He sits and smokes and does not speak."

Pretty Calf was shocked at the suggestion. Her brother could not possibly reclaim his woman, she explained. He could not even let her come back if she wanted to—and she probably would want to when Cut Neck tired of her. Yellow Robe could not even admit that his heart was sick. That was the way things were. Deviation meant dishonor.

The woman could have hidden from Cut Neck, she said. She could even have refused to go with him if she had been *ba-wurokee*—a really virtuous woman. But she had been his woman before, for a little while on a berrying expedition, and he had a right to claim her.

There was no sense in it, the white man insisted. He glared at his young wife. "If you go, I will bring you back!" he promised.

She laughed and buried her head against his shoulder. "I will not have to go," she said. "Horse is my first man. There is no hole in my moccasin."

He stroked her hair and said, "*Ba-wurokee.*"

With great daring, she murmured, "*Hayha,*" and when he did not answer, because he did not know what she meant, she drew away, hurt.

"A woman calls her man that if she thinks he will not leave her. Am I wrong?"

The white man held her closer and lied, "Pretty Calf is not wrong. Horse will not leave her. Horse will not take another woman, either." No, he certainly would not. Parting from this one was going to be harder than getting her had been. "*Hayha,*" he murmured. "Freedom."

His conscience irked him, but not very much. Pretty Calf could get another man easily enough when he was gone, and a better provider. His hunting skill was improving, but he was still awkward.

There was no hurry about leaving. He was used to most of the Crow ways and could stand the rest. He was becoming prosperous. He owned five horses. His place in the life of the tribe was secure, such as it was. Three or four young women, including the one who had belonged to Yellow Robe, made advances to him. Pretty Calf took pride in the fact that her man was so attractive.

By the time he had what he needed for a secret journey, the grass grew yellow on the plains and the long cold was close. He was enslaved by the girl he called Freedom and, before the winter ended, by the knowledge that she was carrying his child. . . .

The Big Dog society held a long ceremony in the spring. The white man strolled with his woman along the creek bank, thinking: When I get home I will tell them about the chants and the drumming. Sometime. Sometime.

Pretty Calf would not go to bed when they went back to the tepee.

"Wait and find out about my brother," she urged. "Something may happen."

So far as Horse could figure out, the Big Dogs were having some kind of election. He pampered his wife by staying up with her by the fire. Even the old woman, who was a great one for getting sleep when she was not working, prowled around restlessly.

The white man was yawning by the time the noise of the ceremony died down. When Yellow Robe strode in, garish and heathen in his paint and feathers and furs, the women cried out. There was conversation, too fast for Horse to follow, and the old woman wailed once, but her son silenced her with a gruff command.

When the white man went to sleep, he thought his wife was weeping beside him.

The next morning she explained.

"He wears the bearskin belt. Now he can never retreat in battle. He will always be in danger. He will die."

Maybe he wouldn't, the white man tried to convince her. Pretty Calf recalled that some few men had been honored by the bearskin belt, vowed to the highest daring, and had not died. If they lived through the summer, then they were free of it.

"My brother wants to die," she mourned. "His heart is bitter."

Yellow Robe lived through half a dozen clashes with small parties of raiders from hostile tribes. His honors were many. He captured horses in an enemy camp, led two successful raids, counted first coup and snatched a gun from the hand of an enemy tribesman. He wore wolf tails on his moccasins and ermine skins on his shirt, and he fringed his leggings with scalps in token of his glory.

When his mother ventured to suggest, as she did many times, "My son should take a new wife, I need another woman to help me," he ignored her. He spent much time in prayer, alone in the hills or in conference with a medicine man. He fasted and made vows and kept them. And before he could be free of the heavy honor of the bearskin belt, he went on his last raid.

The warriors were returning from the north just as the white man and two other hunters approached from the south, with buffalo and elk meat dripping from the bloody hides tied on their restive ponies. One of the hunters grunted, and they stopped to watch a rider on the hill north of the teepee circle.

The rider dismounted, held up a blanket and dropped it. He repeated the gesture.

The hunters murmured dismay. "Two! Two men dead!" They rode fast into the camp, where there was already wailing.

A messenger came down from the war party on the hill. The rest of the party delayed to paint their faces for mourning and for victory. One of the two dead men was Yellow Robe. They had put his body in a cave and walled it in with rocks. The other man died later, and his body was in a tree.

There was blood on the ground before the tepee to which Yellow Robe would return no more. His mother, with her hair chopped short, sat in the doorway, rocking back and forth on her haunches, wailing her heartbreak. She cradled one mutilated hand in the other. She had cut off another finger joint.

Pretty Calf had cut off chunks of her long hair and was crying as she gashed her arms with a knife. The white man tried to take the knife away, but she protested so piteously that he let her do as she wished. He was sickened with the lot of them.

Savages! he thought. Now I will go back! I'll go hunting alone, and I'll keep on going.

But he did not go just yet, because he was the only hunter in the lodge of the two grieving women, one of them old and the other pregnant with his child.

In their mourning, they made him a pauper again. Everything that meant comfort, wealth and safety they sacrificed to the spirits because of the death of Yellow Robe. The tepee, made of seventeen fine buffalo hides, the furs that should have kept them warm, the white deerskin dress, trimmed with elk teeth, that Pretty Calf loved so well, even their tools and Yellow Robe's weapons—everything but his sacred medicine objects—they left there on the prairie, and the whole camp moved away. Two of his best horses were killed as a sacrifice, and the women gave away the rest.

They had no shelter. They would have no tepee of their own for two months at least of mourning, and then the women would have to tan hides to make it. Meanwhile they could live in temporary huts made of willows, covered with skins given them in pity by their friends. They could have lived with relatives, but Yellow Robe's women had no relatives.

The white man had not realized until then how terrible a thing it was for a Crow to have no kinfolk. No wonder old Greasy Hand had only stumps for fingers. She had mourned, from one year to the next, for everyone she had ever loved. She had no one left but her daughter, Pretty Calf.

Horse was furious at their foolishness. It had been bad enough for him, a captive, to be naked as a horse and poor as a slave, but that was because his captors had stripped him. These women had voluntarily given up everything they needed.

He was too angry at them to sleep in the willow hut. He lay under a sheltering tree. And on the third night of the mourning he made his plans. He had a knife and a bow. He would go after meat, taking two horses. And he would not come back. There were, he realized, many things he was not going to tell when he got back home.

In the willow hut, Pretty Calf cried out. He heard rustling there, and the old woman's querulous voice.

Some twenty hours later his son was born, two months early, in the tepee of a skilled medicine woman. The child was born without breath, and the mother died before the sun went down.

The white man was too shocked to think whether he should mourn, or how he should mourn. The old woman screamed until she was voiceless. Piteously she approached him, bent and trembling, blind with grief. She held out her knife and he took it.

She spread out her hands and shook her head. If she cut off any more finger joints, she could no more work. She could not afford any more lasting signs of grief.

The white man said, "All right! All right!" between his teeth. He hacked his arms with the knife and stood watching the blood run down. It was little enough to do for Pretty Calf, for little Freedom.

Now there is nothing to keep me, he realized. When I get home, I must not let them see the scars.

He looked at Greasy Hand, hideous in her grief-burdened age, and thought: I really am free now! When a wife dies, her husband has no more duty toward her family. Pretty Calf had told him so, long ago, when he wondered why a certain man moved out of one tepee and into another.

The old woman, of course, would be a scavenger. There was one other with the tribe, an ancient crone who had no relatives, toward whom no one felt any responsibility. She lived on food thrown away by the more fortunate. She slept in shelters that she built with her own knotted hands. She plodded wearily at the end of the procession when the camp moved. When she stumbled, nobody cared. When she died, nobody would miss her.

Tomorrow morning, the white man decided, I will go.

His mother-in-law's sunken mouth quivered. She said one word, questioningly. She said, *"Eero-oshay?"* She said, "Son?"

Blinking, he remembered. When a wife died, her husband was free. But her mother, who had ignored him with dignity, might if she wished ask him to stay. She invited him by calling him Son, and he accepted by answering Mother.

Greasy Hand stood before him, bowed with years, withered with unceasing labor, loveless and childless, scarred with grief. But with all her burdens, she still loved life enough to beg it from him, the only person she had any right to ask. She was stripping herself of all she had left, her pride.

He looked eastward across the prairie. Two thousand miles away was home. The old woman would not live forever. He could afford to wait, for he was young. He could afford to be magnanimous, for he knew he was a man. He gave her the answer. *"Eegya,"* he said. "Mother."

He went home three years later. He explained no more than to say, "I lived with Crows for a while. It was some time before I could leave. They called me Horse."

He did not find it necessary either to apologize or to boast, because he was the equal of any man on earth.

WILLA CATHER

WILLA CATHER (1873–1947) was born Wilella near Winchester, Virginia; she herself changed her first name, abbreviating it to Willa. In 1883 her family moved to Nebraska and the young Willa Cather, curious about her new and strange environment, spent many hours wandering about on the prairies. I do not doubt that she often felt as Alexandra does in "The Wild Land" when walking alone. Cather visited with foreign-born and second-generation settlers, many of whom she would someday use as models for characters in her pioneer stories. She was educated at home, by family and friends, studying English and the Greek and Latin classics, until her family settled permanently in Red Cloud, Nebraska. Red Cloud was a small railroad town—named after a great Sioux chieftain earlier removed from the area by the War Department—and Cather used it as a setting, although somewhat disguised, for several short stories and six of her thirteen novels.

Cather was very boyish as a youth and had plans to enter medicine. However, while attending the University of Nebraska, her ability to write became manifest and she decided instead to pursue a literary career. Shortly after graduating, she went to Pittsburgh, where she worked as a professional journalist until 1901, when she began teaching. In 1906 she was invited to New York City to join the staff of *McClure's* magazine, and she remained in New York the rest of her life. With the publication of her first novel, *Alexander's Bridge* (Houghton Mifflin, 1912), Cather both established herself in the literary world and felt a need to change her course which, until that time, had been greatly influenced in theme and style by Henry James. Sarah Orne Jewett, an author whom

Cather admired, told her in a letter that ". . . you must find your own quiet centre of life, and write from that to the world . . . in short, you must write to the human heart. . . ." Cather, who previously had had ambivalent feelings about small-town life and the years spent in Nebraska, finally found her "quiet centre" when she went back to her past and wrote about her childhood experiences and the people she had come to love on the Nebraska prairies.

O Pioneers! (Houghton Mifflin, 1913) heralded Cather's literary transition, followed by *My Ántonia* (Houghton Mifflin, 1918) and the stories collected in *Obscure Destinies* (Knopf, 1932). These are her great works about pioneers and pioneering, written in a nostalgic, elegaic tone, but filled with warmth, humanity, and the richness of life. Later authors like A. B. Guthrie, Jr., were to criticize her for dealing with only the positive aspects of pioneer life and omitting the brutality, the hardship, and the savagery. Of course, there is some justification in such a charge, but I don't believe it was ever Willa Cather's intention to present a complete portrait, but rather an impression, a mood, a moment of brightness in lives usually surrounded by shadows.

Among her books I particularly favor *The Professor's House* (Knopf, 1925) and *Death Comes for the Archbishop* (Knopf, 1927). The latter is set in New Mexico and has all the ingredients of a romantic fantasy; but it also has something else, something which makes it especially endearing, and that is its evocation of a lasting and meaningful friendship.

The final chapter in one of the best books about her—James Woodress's *Willa Cather: Her Life and Art* (1970; reissued by the University of Nebraska Press, 1975)—is titled "The Rest Is Silence: 1933–1947." It is apt, because Cather quit writing. She felt out of sorts with the changing world around her. During her last days, she listened over and over to recordings of Beethoven's Late Quartets. In her own best work she had found the profound harmony, the "quiet centre," of those quartets, and I suspect she found it, too, in the solitude of her own soul.

"The Wild Land" is from *O Pioneers!* It is set in Nebraska and it is an intimate glimpse into the lives of the Bergson family, Alexandra, her mother, and her brothers Oscar, Lou, and young Emil, who is like a son to his sister. When Alexandra's father dies, she becomes the head of the family. For women like Alexandra—and in the actual history of the American frontier there were many like her—the West was not by any means just a *masculine* experience.

The Wild Land

For the first three years after John Bergson's death, the affairs of his family prospered. Then came the hard times that brought every one on the Divide to the brink of despair; three years of drouth and failure, the last struggle of a wild soil against the encroaching plowshare. The first of these fruitless summers the Bergson boys bore courageously. The failure of the corn crop made labor cheap. Lou and Oscar hired two men and put in bigger crops than ever before. They lost everything they spent. The whole country was discouraged. Farmers who were already in debt had to give up their land. A few foreclosures demoralized the county. The settlers sat about on the wooden sidewalks in the little town and told each other that the country was never meant for men to live in; the thing to do was to get back to Iowa, to Illinois, to any place that had been proved habitable. The Bergson boys, certainly, would have been happier with their uncle Otto, in the bakery shop in Chicago. Like most of their neighbors, they were meant to follow in paths already marked out for them, not to break trails in a new country. A steady job, a few holidays, nothing to think about, and they would have been very happy. It was no fault of theirs that they had been dragged into the wilderness when they were little boys. A pioneer should have imagination, should be able to enjoy the idea of things more than the things themselves.

The second of these barren summers was passing. One September afternoon Alexandra had gone over to the garden across the draw to dig sweet potatoes—they had been thriving upon the weather that was fatal to everything else. But when Carl Linstrum came up the garden rows to find her, she was not working. She was standing lost in thought, leaning upon her pitchfork, her sunbonnet lying beside her on the ground. The dry garden patch smelled of drying vines and was strewn with yellow seed-cucumbers and pumpkins and citrons. At one end, next the rhubarb, grew feathery asparagus, with red berries. Down the middle of the garden was a row of gooseberry and currant bushes. A few tough zenias and marigolds and a row of scarlet sage bore witness to the buckets of water that Mrs. Bergson had carried there after sundown, against the prohibition of her sons. Carl came quietly and slowly up the garden path, looking intently at Alexandra. She did not hear him. She was standing perfectly still, with that serious ease so characteristic of her. Her thick, reddish braids, twisted about her head, fairly burned in the sunlight. The air was cool enough to make the warm sun pleasant on one's back and shoulders, and so clear that the eye could follow a hawk up and up, into the blazing blue depths of the sky. Even Carl, never a very cheerful boy, and considerably darkened by these last two bitter years, loved the country on days like this, felt something strong and young and wild come out of it, that laughed at care.

"Alexandra," he said as he approached her, "I want to talk to you. Let's sit down by the gooseberry bushes." He picked up her sack of potatoes and they crossed the garden. "Boys gone to town?" he asked as he sank down on the warm, sun-baked earth. "Well, we have made up our minds at last, Alexandra. We are really going away."

She looked at him as if she were a little frightened. "Really, Carl? Is it settled?"

"Yes, father has heard from St. Louis, and they will give him back his old job in the cigar factory. He must be there by the first of November. They are taking on new men then. We will sell the place for whatever we can get, and auction the stock. We haven't enough to ship. I am going to learn engraving with a German engraver there, and then try to get work in Chicago."

Alexandra's hands dropped in her lap. Her eyes became dreamy and filled with tears.

Carl's sensitive lower lip trembled. He scratched in the soft earth beside him with a stick. "That's all I hate about it, Alexandra," he said slowly. "You've stood by us through so much and helped father out so many times, and now it seems as if we were running off and leaving you to face the worst of it. But it isn't as if we could really ever be of any help to you. We are only one more drag, one more thing you look out for and feel responsible for. Father was never meant for a farmer, you know that. And I hate it. We'd only get in deeper and deeper."

"Yes, yes, Carl, I know. You are wasting your life here. You are able to do much better things. You are nearly nineteen now, and I wouldn't have you stay. I've always hoped you would get away. But I can't help feeling scared when I think how I will miss you—more than you will ever know." She brushed the tears from her cheeks, not trying to hide them.

"But, Alexandra," he said sadly and wistfully, "I've never been any real help to you, beyond sometimes trying to keep the boys in a good humor."

Alexandra smiled and shook her head. "Oh, it's not that. Nothing like that. It's by understanding me, and the boys, and mother, that you've helped me. I expect that is the only way one person ever really can help another. I think you are about the only one that ever helped me. Somehow it will take more courage to bear your going than everything that has happened before."

Carl looked at the ground. "You see, we've all depended so on you," he said, "even father. He makes me laugh. When anything comes up he always says, 'I wonder what the Bergsons are going to do about that? I guess I'll go and ask her.' I'll never forget that time, when we first came here, and our horse had the colic, and I ran over to your place—your father was away, and you came home with me and showed father how to let the wind out of the horse. You were only a little girl then, but you knew ever so much more about farm work than poor father. You remember how homesick I used to get, and what long talks we used to have coming from school? We've someway always felt alike about things."

"Yes, that's it; we've liked the same things and we've liked them together, without anybody else knowing. And we've had good times, hunting for Christmas trees and going for ducks and making our plum wine together every year. We've never either of us had any other close friend. And now—" Alexandra wiped her eyes with the corner of her apron, "and now I must remember that you are going where you will have many friends, and will find the work you were meant to do. But you'll write to me, Carl? That will mean a great deal to me here."

"I'll write as long as I live," cried the boy impetuously. "And I'll be working for you as much as for myself, Alexandra. I want to do something you'll like and be proud of. I'm a fool here, but I know I can do something!" He sat up and frowned at the red grass.

Alexandra sighed. "How discouraged the boys will be when they hear. They always come home from town discouraged, anyway. So many people are trying to leave the country, and they talk to our boys and make them low-spirited. I'm afraid they are beginning to feel hard toward me because I won't listen to any talk about going. Sometimes I feel like I'm getting tired of standing up for this country."

"I won't tell the boys yet, if you'd rather not."

"Oh, I'll tell them myself, to-night, when they come home. They'll be talking wild, anyway, and no good comes of keeping bad news. It's all harder on them than it is on me. Lou wants to get married, poor boy, and he can't until times are better. See, there goes the sun, Carl. I must be getting back. Mother will want her potatoes. It's chilly already, the moment the light goes."

Alexandra rose and looked about. A golden afterglow throbbed in the west, but the country already looked empty and mournful. A dark moving mass came over the western hill, the Lee boy was bringing in the herd from the other half-section. Emil ran from the windmill to open the corral gate. From the log house, on the little rise across the draw, the smoke was curling. The cattle lowed and bellowed. In the sky the pale half-moon was slowly silvering. Alexandra and Carl walked together down the potato rows. "I have to keep telling myself what is going to happen," she said softly. "Since you have been here, ten years now, I have never really been lonely. But I can remember what it was like before. Now I shall have nobody but Emil. But he is my boy, and he is tender-hearted."

That night, when the boys were called to supper, they sat down moodily. They had worn their coats to town, but they ate in their striped shirts and suspenders. They were grown men now, and, as Alexandra said, for the last few years they had been growing more and more like themselves. Lou was still the slighter of the two, the quicker and more intelligent, but apt to go off at half-cock. He had a lively blue eye, a thin, fair skin (always burned red to the neckband of his shirt in summer), stiff, yellow hair that would not lie down on his head, and a bristly little yellow mustache, of which he was very proud. Oscar could not grow a mustache; his pale face was as bare as an egg, and his white eyebrows gave it an empty look. He was a man of powerful body and unusual endurance; the sort of man you could attach to a corn-sheller as you would an engine. He would turn it all day, without hurrying, without slowing down. But he was as indolent of mind as he was unsparing of his body. His love of routine amounted to a vice. He worked like an insect, always doing the same thing over in the same way, regardless of whether it was best or no. He felt that there was a sovereign virtue in mere bodily toil, and he rather liked to do things in the hardest way. If a field had once been in corn, he couldn't bear to put it into wheat. He liked to begin his corn-planting at the same time every year, whether the season were backward or forward. He seemed to feel that by his own irreproachable regularity he would clear himself of blame and reprove the weather. When the wheat crop failed, he threshed the straw at a dead loss to demonstrate how little grain there was, and thus prove his case against Providence.

Lou, on the other hand, was funny and flighty; always planned to get through two days' work in one, and often got only the least important things done. He liked to keep the place up, but he never got round to doing odd jobs until he had to neglect more pressing work to attend to them. In the middle of the wheat harvest, when the grain was over-ripe and every hand was needed, he would stop to mend fences or to patch the harness; then dash down to the field and overwork and be laid up in bed for a week. The two boys balanced each other, and they pulled well together. They had been good friends since they were children. One seldom went anywhere, even to town, without the other.

To-night, after they sat down to supper, Oscar kept looking at Lou as if he expected him to say something, and Lou blinked his eyes and frowned at his plate. It was Alexandra herself who at last opened the discussion.

"The Linstrums," she said calmly, as she put another plate of hot biscuit on the table, "are going back to St. Louis. The old man is going to work in the cigar factory again."

At this Lou plunged in. "You see, Alexandra, everybody who can crawl out is going away. There's no use of us trying to stick it out, just to be stubborn. There's something in knowing when to quit."

"Where do you want to go, Lou?"

"Any place where things will grow," said Oscar grimly.

Lou reached for a potato. "Chris Arnson has traded his half-section for a place down on the river."

"Who did he trade with?"

"Charley Fuller, in town."

"Fuller the real estate man? You see, Lou, that Fuller has

a head on him. He's buying and trading for every bit of land he can get up here. It'll make him a rich man, some day."

"He's rich now, that's why he can take a chance."

"Why can't we? We'll live longer than he will. Some day the land itself will be worth more than all we can ever raise on it."

Lou laughed. "It could be worth that, and still not be worth much. Why, Alexandra, you don't know what you're talking about. Our place wouldn't bring now what it would six years ago. The fellows that settled up here just made a mistake. Now they're beginning to see this high land wasn't never meant to grow nothing on, and everybody who ain't fixed to graze cattle is trying to crawl out. It's too high to farm up here. All the Americans are skinning out. That man Percy Adams, north of town, told me that he was going to let Fuller take his land and stuff for four hundred dollars and a ticket to Chicago."

"There's Fuller again!" Alexandra exclaimed. "I wish that man would take me for a partner. He's feathering his nest! If only poor people could learn a little from rich people! But all these fellows who are running off are bad farmers, like poor Mr. Linstrum. They couldn't get ahead even in good years, and they all got into debt while father was getting out. I think we ought to hold on as long as we can on father's account. He was so set on keeping this land. He must have seen harder times than this, here. How was it in the early days, mother?"

Mrs. Bergson was weeping quietly. These family discussions always depressed her, and made her remember all that she had been torn away from. "I don't see why the boys are always taking on about going away," she said, wiping her eyes. "I don't want to move again; out to some raw place, maybe, where we'd be worse off than we are here, and all to do over again. I won't move! If the rest of you go, I will ask some of the neighbors to take me in, and stay and be buried by father. I'm not going to leave him by himself on the prairie, for cattle to run over." She began to cry more bitterly.

The boys looked angry. Alexandra put a soothing hand on her mother's shoulder. "There's no question of that, mother. You don't have to go if you don't want to. A third of the place belongs to you by American law, and we can't sell without your consent. We only want you to advise us. How did it use to be when you and father first came? Was it really as bad as this, or not?"

"Oh, worse! Much worse," moaned Mrs. Bergson. "Drouth, chince-bugs, hail, everything! My garden all cut to pieces like sauerkraut. No grapes on the creek, no nothing. The people all lived just like coyotes."

Oscar got up and tramped out of the kitchen. Lou followed him. They felt that Alexandra had taken an unfair advantage in turning their mother loose on them. The next morning they were silent and reserved. They did not offer to take the women to church, but went down to the barn immediately after breakfast and stayed there all day. When Carl Linstrum came over in the afternoon, Alexandra winked to him and pointed toward the barn. He understood her and went down to play cards with the boys. They believed that a very wicked thing to do on Sunday, and it relieved their feelings.

Alexandra stayed in the house. On Sunday afternoon Mrs. Bergson always took a nap, and Alexandra read. During the week she read only the newspaper, but on Sunday, and in the long evenings of winter, she read a good deal; read a few things over a great many times. She knew long portions of the "Frithjof Saga" by heart, and, like most Swedes who read at all, she was fond of Longfellow's verse—the ballads and the "Golden Legend" and "The Spanish Student." To-day she sat in the wooden rocking-chair with the Swedish Bible open on her knees, but she was not reading. She was looking thoughtfully away at the point where the upland road disappeared over the rim of the prairie. Her body was in an attitude of perfect repose, such as it was apt to take when she was thinking earnestly. Her mind was slow, truthful, steadfast. She had not the least spark of cleverness.

All afternoon the sitting-room was full of quiet and sunlight. Emil was making rabbit traps in the kitchen shed. The hens were clucking and scratching brown holes in the flower beds, and the wind was teasing the prince's feather by the door.

That evening Carl came in with the boys to supper.

"Emil," said Alexandra, when they were all seated at the table, "how would you like to go traveling? Because I am going to take a trip, and you can go with me if you want to."

The boys looked up in amazement; they were always afraid of Alexandra's schemes. Carl was interested.

"I've been thinking, boys," she went on, "that maybe I am too set against making a change. I'm going to take Brigham and the buckboard to-morrow and drive down to the river country and spend a few days looking over what they've got down there. If I find anything good, you boys can go down and make a trade."

"Nobody down there will trade for anything up here," said Oscar gloomily.

"That's just what I want to find out. Maybe they are just as discontented down there as we are up here. Things away from home often look better than they are. You know what your Hans Andersen book says, Carl, about the Swedes liking to buy Danish bread and the Danes liking to buy Swedish bread, because people always think the bread of another country is better than their own. Anyway, I've heard so much about the river farms, I won't be satisfied till I've seen for myself."

Lou fidgeted. "Look out! Don't agree to anything. Don't let them fool you."

Lou was apt to be fooled himself. He had not yet learned to keep away from the shell-game wagons that followed the circus.

After supper Lou put on a necktie and went across the fields to court Annie Lee, and Carl and Oscar sat down to a game of checkers, while Alexandra read "The Swiss Family Robinson" aloud to her mother and Emil. It was not long before the two boys at the table neglected their game to listen. They were all big children together, and they found the adventures of the family in the tree house so absorbing that they gave them their undivided attention.

Alexandra and Emil spent five days down among the river farms, driving up and down the valley. Alexandra talked to the men about their crops and to the women about their poultry. She spent a whole day with one young farmer who had been away at school, and who was experimenting with a new kind of clover hay. She learned a great deal. As they drove along, she and Emil talked and planned. At last, on the sixth day, Alexandra turned Brigham's head northward and left the river behind.

"There's nothing in it for us down there, Emil. There are a few fine farms, but they are owned by the rich men in town, and couldn't be bought. Most of the land is rough and hilly. They can always scrape along down there, but they can never do anything big. Down there they have a little certainty, but up with us there is a big chance. We must have faith in the high land, Emil. I want to hold on harder than ever, and when you're a man you'll thank me." She urged Brigham forward.

When the road began to climb the first long swells of the Divide, Alexandra hummed an old Swedish hymn, and Emil wondered why his sister looked so happy. Her face was so radiant that he felt shy about asking her. For the first time, perhaps, since that land emerged from the waters of geologic ages, a human face was set toward it with love and yearning. It seemed beautiful to her, rich and strong and glorious. Her eyes drank in the breadth of it, until her tears blinded her. Then the Genius of the Divide, the great, free spirit which breathes across it, must have bent lower than it ever bent to a human will before. The history of every country begins in the heart of a man or a woman.

Alexandra reached home in the afternoon. That evening she held a family council and told her brothers all that she had seen and heard.

"I want you boys to go down yourselves and look it over. Nothing will convince you like seeing with your own eyes. The river land was settled before this, and so they are a few years ahead of us, and have learned more about farming. The land sells for three times as much as this, but in five years we will double it. The rich men down there own all the best land, and they are buying all they can get. The thing to do is to sell our cattle and what little old corn we have, and buy the Linstrum place. Then the next thing to do is to take out two loans on our half-sections, and buy Peter Crow's place; raise every dollar we can, and buy every acre we can."

"Mortgage the homestead again?" Lou cried. He sprang up and began to wind the clock furiously. "I won't slave to pay off another mortgage. I'll never do it. You'd just as soon kill us all, Alexandra, to carry out some scheme!"

Oscar rubbed his high, pale forehead. "How do you propose to pay off your mortgages?"

Alexandra looked from one to the other and bit her lip. They had never seen her so nervous. "See here," she brought out at last. "We borrow the money for six years. Well, with the money we buy a half-section from Linstrum and a half from Crow, and a quarter from Struble, maybe. That will give us upwards of fourteen hundred acres, won't it? You won't have to pay off your mortgages for six years. By that time, any of this land will be worth thirty dollars an acre—it will be worth fifty, but we'll say thirty; then you can sell a garden patch anywhere, and pay off a debt of sixteen hundred dollars. It's not the principal I'm worried about, it's the interest and taxes. We'll have to strain to meet the payments. But as sure as we are sitting here to-night, we can sit down here ten years from now independent landowners, not struggling farmers any longer. The chance that father was always looking for has come."

Lou was pacing the floor. "But how do you *know* that land is going to go up enough to pay the mortgages and—"

"And make us rich besides?" Alexandra put in firmly. "I can't explain that, Lou. You'll have to take my word for it. I *know*, that's all. When you drive about over the country you can feel it coming."

Oscar had been sitting with his head lowered, his hands hanging between his knees. "But we can't work so much land," he said dully, as if he were talking to himself. "We can't even try. It would just lie there and we'd work ourselves to death." He sighed, and laid his calloused fist on the table.

Alexandra's eyes filled with tears. She put her hand on his shoulder. "You poor boy, you won't have to work it. The men in town who are buying up other people's land don't try to farm it. They are the men to watch, in a new country. Let's try to do like the shrewd ones, and not like these stupid fellows. I don't want you boys always to have to work like this. I want you to be independent, and Emil to go to school."

Lou held his head as if it were splitting. "Everybody will say we are crazy. It must be crazy, or everybody would be doing it."

"If they were, we wouldn't have much chance. No, Lou, I was talking about that with the smart young man who is raising the new kind of clover. He says the right thing is usually just what everybody don't do. Why are we better fixed than any of our neighbors? Because father had more brains. Our people were better people than these in the old country. We *ought* to do more than they do, and see further ahead. Yes, mother, I'm going to clear the table now."

Alexandra rose. The boys went to the stable to see to the stock, and they were gone a long while. When they came back Lou played on his *dragharmonika* and Oscar sat figuring at his father's secretary all evening. They said nothing more about Alexandra's project, but she felt sure now that they would consent to it. Just before bedtime Oscar went out for a pail of water. When he did not come back, Alexandra threw a shawl over her head and ran down the path to the windmill. She found him sitting there with his head in his hands, and she sat down beside him.

"Don't do anything you don't want to do, Oscar," she whispered. She waited a moment, but he did not stir. "I won't say any more about it, if you'd rather not. What makes you so discouraged?"

"I dread signing my name to them pieces of paper," he said slowly. "All the time I was a boy we had a mortgage hanging over us."

"Then don't sign one. I don't want you to, if you feel that way."

Oscar shook his head. "No, I can see there's a chance that way. I've thought a good while there might be. We're in so deep now, we might as well go deeper. But it's hard work pulling out of debt. Like pulling a threshing-machine out of the mud; breaks your back. Me and Lou's worked hard, and I can't see it's got us ahead much."

"Nobody knows about that as well as I do, Oscar. That's why I want to try an easier way. I don't want you to have to grub for every dollar."

"Yes, I know what you mean. Maybe it'll come out right. But signing papers is signing papers. There ain't no maybe about that." He took his pail and trudged up the path to the house.

Alexandra drew her shawl closer about her and stood leaning against the frame of the mill, looking at the stars which glittered so keenly through the frosty autumn air. She always loved to watch them, to think of their vastness and distance, and of their ordered march. It fortified her to reflect upon the great operations of nature, and when she thought of the law that lay behind them, she felt a sense of personal security. That night she had a new consciousness of the country, felt almost a new relation to it. Even her talk with the boys had not taken away the feeling that had overwhelmed her when she drove back to the Divide that afternoon. She had never known before how much the country meant to her. The chirping of the insects down in the long grass had been like the sweetest music. She had felt as if her heart were hiding down there, somewhere, with the quail and the plover and all the little wild things that crooned or buzzed in the sun. Under the long shaggy ridges, she felt the future stirring.

JOHN G. NEIHARDT

JOHN GNEISENAU NEIHARDT (1881–1973) was born near Sharpsburg, Illinois, but in 1886 he went with his family to live in his pioneer grandparents' sod house on the upper Solomon River in Kansas. In 1891 the family moved to Wayne, Nebraska, and it was here that Neihardt was graduated with a bachelor's degree at the age of sixteen from the Nebraska Normal College. Neihardt's first book was a volume of poetry, *The Divine Enchantment* (James T. White, 1900). In 1901 he became assistant to a trader working among the Omaha Indians on their reservation. For a time he edited a country weekly newspaper and in 1908 he married Mona Martinsen, a sculptress and a former student of Auguste Rodin. Although his wife came from a family of comfortable wealth, she willingly committed herself to sharing Neihardt's frugal life as a poet while he worked on what he felt was his masterpiece, the five American epic poems which began with *The Song of Hugh Glass* (Macmillan, 1915) and which were finally all brought out together in *A Cycle of the West* (Macmillan, 1949). In his old age, no longer able to read print, busloads of students would still regularly visit Neihardt and sit around his wheelchair as he would recite his poetry from memory.

For me, however, Neihardt's most significant contribution to American literature rests with his short-story collections, *The Lonesome Trail* (John Lane, 1907) and *Indian Tales and Others* (Macmillan, 1926), his novel *When the Tree Flowered: An Authentic Tale of the Old Sioux World* (Macmillan, 1951), and for his work as amanuensis for the aged Sioux medicine man, Black Elk. Black Elk himself felt that his vision, imparted to him when he was but nine, failed; but neither Neihardt nor many modern readers—myself among them—are so sure of this, since the vision was not limited to the present time. Neihardt recognized that the fulfillment of both the cultural and spiritual ideals of Americans could not be separated from the vision of man's role as a part of nature; that not until all subsequent Americans came to love and respect the land as much as native Americans always have would a truly spiritual and epical period be possible. This may strike some readers as ridiculous idealism. But it was accepted by the Sioux themselves, who, at Neihardt's funeral service in 1973, held their own sacred ceremony.

I recall when I was a young man in college I read André Malraux' *La Tentation de l'occident* [*The Temptation of the West*] (Paris, 1926). It is written in the form of letters exchanged between Ling, a Chinese traveling in Europe, and A.D., a Frenchman living in the Far East. I was extremely moved by Ling's observation in one of his letters that Christians, in attempting to picture their god and redeemer, do not show the stone thrust back at his grave, but rather most of the time depict his bleeding, lacerated body hanging on a crucifix.

I was reminded of that book when I first read the story which follows, taken from *The Lonesome Trail* collection. The native American at the time of first contact with the invading Europeans was religious in a far more profound fashion than the European has ever been. Yet the first thing the European set about doing, beyond physical exploitation of the New World and its peoples, was to attempt to destroy native American religion. Nor has this impulse completely vanished today. It is, I believe, an unforgivable sin of one people against another. Neihardt obviously felt the same way. It comes out in this story. And in those cases where the European, and later the Anglo-American, was successful, when belief in the Great Spirit was destroyed and replaced by the cross, what, then, was left? Neihardt's experiences on the Omaha reserve suggested the answer to him and he framed it dramatically in a form approaching parable.

If you haven't read *Black Elk Speaks* (Morrow, 1932; reissued by Pocket Books in 1972 and continuously since), I cannot recommend the book highly enough. Also, Lucile F. Aly has written an interesting, if brief, literary appraisal of Neihardt's poetry and fiction in her chapbook *John G. Neihardt* (Boise State University Press, 1976). Let Black Elk have the last word. He once told Neihardt:

I could see that the Wasichus [white people] did not care for each other the way our people did. . . . They would take everything from each other if they could, and so there were some who had more of everything than they could use, while crowds of people had nothing at all and maybe were starving. They had forgotten that the earth was their mother.

The Last Thunder Song

It is an ancient custom to paint tragedy in blood tints. This is because men were once merely animals, and have not as yet been able to live down their ancestry. Yet the stroke of a dagger is a caress beside the throb of hopeless days.

Life can ache; the living will tell you this. But the dead make no complaint.

There is no greater tragedy than the fall of a dream! Napoleon dreamed; so did a savage. It is the same. I know of the scene of a great tragedy. Very few have recognized it as such; there was so little noise along with it. It happened at the Omaha Agency, which is situated on the Missouri River some seventy miles above Omaha.

The summer of 1900 debilitated all thermal adjectives. It was not hot; it was *Saharical!* It would hardly have been hyperbole to have said that the Old Century lay dying of a fever. The untilled hills of the reservation thrust themselves up in the August sunshine like the emaciated joints of one bedridden. The land lay as yellow as the skin of a fever patient, except in those rare spots where the melancholy corn struggled heartlessly up a hillside, making a blotch like a bedsore!

The blood of the prairie was impoverished, and the sky would give no drink with which to fill the dwindling veins. When one wished to search the horizon for the cloud that was not there, he did it from beneath an arched hand. The small whirlwinds that awoke like sudden fits of madness in the sultry air, rearing yellow columns of dust into the sky—these alone relieved the monotony of dazzle.

Every evening the clouds rolled flashing about the horizon and thundered back into the night. They were merely taunts, like the holding of a cool cup just out of reach of a fevered mouth; and the clear nights passed, bringing dewless dawns, until the ground cracked like a parched lip!

The annual Indian powwow was to be ended prematurely that year, for the sun beat uninvitingly upon the flat bottom where the dances were held, and the Indians found much comfort in the shade of their summer tepees. But when it was noised about that, upon the next day, the old medicine-man Mahowari (Passing Cloud) would dance potent dances and sing a thunder song with which to awaken the lazy thunder spirits to their neglected duty of rain-making, then the argument of the heat became feeble.

So the next morning, the bronze head of every Indian tepeehold took his pony, his dogs, his squaw, and his papooses of indefinite number to the powwow ground. In addition to these, the old men carried with them long memories and an implicit faith. The young men, who had been away to Indian school, and had succeeded to some extent in stuffing their brown skins with white souls, carried with them curiosity and doubt, which, if properly united, beget derision.

The old men went to a shrine; the young men went to a show. When a shrine becomes a show, the World advances a step. And *that* is the benevolence of Natural Law!

About the open space in which the dances were held, an oval covering had been built with willow boughs, beneath which the Indians lounged in sweating groups. Slowly about the various small circles went the cumbersome stone pipes.

To one listening, drowsed with the intense sunlight, the buzzle and mutter and snarl of the gossiping Omahas seemed the grotesque echoes from a vanished age. Between the dazzle of the sun and the sharply contrasting blue shade, there was but a line of division; yet a thousand years lay between one gazing into the sun and those dozing in the shadow. It was as if God had flung down a bit of the Young World's twilight into the midst of the Old World's noon. Here lounged the masterpiece of the toiling centuries—a Yankee. There sat the remnant of a race as primitive as Israel. Yet the white man looked on with the contempt of superiority.

Before ten o'clock everybody had arrived and his family with him. A little group, composed of the Indian Agent, the Agency Physician, the Mission Preacher, and a newspaper man, down from the city for reportorial purposes, waited and chatted, sitting upon a ragged patch of available shadow.

"These Omahas are an exceptional race," the preacher was saying in his ministerial tone of voice; "an exceptional race!"

The newspaper man mopped his face, lit a cigarette and nodded assent with a hidden meaning twinkling in his eye.

"Quite exceptional!" he said, tossing his head in the direction of an unusually corpulent bunch of steaming, sweating, bronze men and women. "God, like some lesser master-musicians, has not confined himself to grand opera, it seems!"

He took a long pull at his cigarette, and his next words came out in a cloud of smoke.

"This particular creation savours somewhat of opera bouffe!"

With severe unconcern the preacher mended the broken thread of his discourse. "Quite an exceptional race in many ways. The Omaha is quite as honest as the white man."

"That is a truism!" The pencil-pusher drove this observation between the minister's words like a wedge.

"In his natural state he was much more so," uninterruptedly continued the preacher; he was used to continuous discourse. "I have been told by many of the old men that in the olden times an Indian could leave his tepee for months at a time, and on his return would find his most valuable possessions untouched. I tell you, gentlemen, the Indian is like a prairie flower that has been transplanted from the blue sky and the summer sun and the pure winds into the steaming, artificial atmosphere of the hothouse! A glass roof is not the blue sky! Man's talent is not God's genius! That is why you are looking at a perverted growth.

"Look into an Indian's face and observe the ruins of what was once manly dignity, indomitable energy, masterful prowess! When I look upon one of these faces, I have the same thought as, when travelling in Europe, I looked upon the ruins of Rome.

"Everywhere broken arches, fallen columns, tumbled walls! Yet through these as through a mist one can discern the magnificence of the living city. So in looking upon one of these faces, which are merely ruins in another sense. They were once as noble, as beautiful as—"

In his momentary search for an eloquent simile, the minister paused.

"As pumpkin pies!" added the newspaper man with a chuckle; and he whipped out his notebook and pencil to jot down his brilliant thought, for he had conceived a very witty "story" which he would pound out for the Sunday edition.

"Well," said the Agency Physician, finally sucked into the whirlpool of discussion, "it seems to me that there is no room for crowding on either side. Indians are pretty much like white men; liver and kidneys and lungs, and that sort of thing; slight difference in the pigment under the skin. I've looked into the machinery of both species and find just as much room in one as the other for a soul!"

"And both will go upward," added the minister.

"Like different grades of tobacco," observed the Indian Agent, "the smoke of each goes up in the same way."

"Just so," said the reporter; "but let us cut out the metaphysics. I wonder when this magical *cuggie* is going to begin his humid evolutions. Lamentable, isn't it, that such institutions as rain prayers should exist on the very threshold of the Twentieth Century?"

"I think," returned the minister, "that the Twentieth Century has no intention of eliminating God! This medicine-man's prayer, in my belief, is as sacred as the prayer of any churchman. The difference between Wakunda and God is merely orthographical."

"But," insisted the cynical young man from the city, "I had not been taught to think of God as of one who forgets! Do you know what I would do if I had no confidence in the executive ability of my God?"

Taking the subsequent silence as a question, the young man answered: "Why, I would take a day off and whittle one out of wood!"

"A youth's way is the wind's way," quoted the preacher, with a paternal air.

"And the thoughts of youth are long, long thoughts; but what is all this noise about?" returned the reporter.

A buzz of expectant voices had grown at one end of the oval, and had spread contagiously throughout the elliptical strip of shade. For with slow, majestic steps the medicine-man, Mahowari, entered the enclosure and walked towards the centre. The fierce sun emphasized the brilliancy of the old man's garments and glittered upon the profusion of trinkets, the magic heirlooms of the medicine-man. It was not the robe nor the dazzling trinkets that caught the eye of one acquainted with Mahowari. It was the erectness of his figure, for he had been bowed with years, and many vertical suns had shone upon the old man's back since his face had been turned toward the ground. But now with firm step and form rigidly erect he walked.

Any sympathetic eye could easily read the thoughts that passed through the old man's being like an elixir infusing youth. Now in his feeble years would come his greatest triumph! Today he would sing with greater power than ever he had sung. Wakunda would hear the cry. The rains would come! Then the white men would be stricken with belief!

Already his heart sang before his lips. In spite of the hideous painting of his face, the light of triumph shone there like the reflection of a great fire.

Slowly he approached the circle of drummers who sat in the glaring centre of the ellipse of sunlight. It was all as though the First Century had awakened like a ghost and stood in the very doorway of the Twentieth!

When Mahowari had approached within a yard of the drums, he stopped, and raising his arms and his eyes to the cloudless sky, uttered a low cry like a wail of supplication. Then the drums began to throb with that barbaric music as old as the world; a sound like the pounding of a fever temple, with a recurring snarl like the warning of a rattlesnake.

Every sound of the rejoicing and suffering prairie echoes in the Indian's drum.

With a slow, majestic bending of the knees and an alternate lifting of his feet, the medicine-man danced in a circle about the snarling drums. Then like a faint wail of winds toiling up a wooded bluff, his thunder song began.

The drone and whine of the mysterious, untranslatable words pierced the drowse of the day, lived for a moment with the echoes of the drums among the surrounding hills, and languished from a whisper into silence. At intervals the old man raised his face, radiant with fanatic ecstasy, to the meridian glare of the sun, and the song swelled to a supplicating shout.

Faster and faster the old man moved about the circle; louder and wilder grew the song. Those who watched from the shade were absorbed in an intense silence, which, with the drowse of the sultry day, made every sound a paradox! The old men forgot their pipes and sat motionless.

Suddenly, at one end of the covering, came the sound of laughter! At first an indefinite sound like the spirit of merriment entering a capricious dream of sacred things; then it grew and spread until it was no longer merriment, but a loud jeer of derision! It startled the old men from the intenseness of their watching. They looked up and were stricken with awe. The young men were jeering this, the holiest rite of their fathers!

Slower and slower the medicine-man danced; fainter and fainter grew the song and ceased abruptly. With one quick glance, Mahowari saw the shattering of his hopes. He glanced at the sky; but saw no swarm of black spirits to avenge such sacrilege. Only the blaze of the sun, the glitter of the arid zenith!

In that one moment, the temporary youth of the old man died out. His shoulders drooped to their wonted position. His limbs tottered. He was old again.

It was the Night stricken heart-sick with the laughter of the Dawn. It was the audacious Present jeering at the Past, tottering with years. At that moment, the impudent, cruel, brilliant youth called Civilisation snatched the halo from the grey hairs of patriarchal Ignorance. Light flouted the rags of Night. A clarion challenge shrilled across the years.

Never before in all the myriad moons had such a thing occurred. It was too great a cause to produce an effect of grief or anger. It stupefied. The old men and women sat motionless. They could not understand.

With uneven step and with eyes that saw nothing, Mahowari passed from among his kinsmen and tottered up the valley toward his lonesome shack and tepee upon the hillside. It was far past noon when the last of the older Omahas left the scene of the dance.

The greatest number of the white men who had witnessed the last thunder dance of the Omahas went homeward much pleased. The show had turned out quite funny indeed. "Ha, ha, ha! Did you see how surprised the old *cuggie* looked? He, he, he!" Life, being necessarily selfish, argues from its own standpoint.

But as the minister rode slowly toward his home there was no laughter in his heart. He was saying to himself: "If the whole fabric of my belief should suddenly be wrenched from me, what then?" Even this question was born of selfishness, but it brought pity.

In the cool of the evening the minister mounted his horse and rode to the home of Mahowari, which was a shack in the winter and a tepee in the summer. Dismounting, he threw the bridle reins upon the ground and raised the door flap of the tepee. Mahowari sat cross-legged upon the ground, staring steadily before him with unseeing eyes.

"How!" said the minister.

The old Indian did not answer. There was no expression of grief or anger or despair upon his face. He sat like a statue.

Yet, the irregularity of his breathing showed where the pain lay. An Indian suffers in his breast. His face is a mask.

The minister sat down in front of the silent old man and, after the immemorial manner of ministers, talked of a better world, of a pitying Christ, and of God, the Great Father. For the first time the Indian raised his face and spoke briefly in English:

"God? He dead, guess!"

Then he was silent again for some time.

Suddenly his eyes lit up with a light that was not the light of age. The heart of his youth had awakened. The old memories came back and he spoke fluently in his own tongue, which the minister understood.

"These times are not like the old times. The young men have caught some of the wisdom of the white man. Nothing is sure. It is not good. I cannot understand. Everything is young and new. All old things are dead. Many moons ago, the wisdom of Mahowari was great. I can remember how my father said to me one day when I was yet young and all things lay new before me: 'Let my son go to a high hill and dream a great dream'; and I went up in the evening and cried out to Wakunda and I slept and dreamed.

"I saw a great cloud sweeping up from under the horizon, and it was terrible with lightning and loud thunder. Then it passed over me and rumbled down the sky and disappeared. And when I awoke and told my people of my dream, they rejoiced and said: 'Great things are in store for this youth. We shall call him the Passing Cloud, and he shall be a thunder man, keen and quick of thought, with the keenness and quickness of the lightning; and his name shall be as thunder in the ears of men.' And I grew and believed in these sayings and I was strong. But now I can see the meaning of the dream—a great light and a great noise and a passing."

The old man sighed, and the light passed out of his eyes. Then he looked searchingly into the face of the minister and said, speaking in English:

"You white medicine-man. You pray?"

The minister nodded.

Mahowari turned his gaze to the ground and said wearily:

"White God dead too, guess."

EUGENE MANLOVE RHODES

EUGENE MANLOVE RHODES (1869–1934) was born in Tecumseh, Nebraska, but his father soon relocated the family to Cherokee, Kansas, and then in 1881 to the New Mexico Territory. Other than a brief stint at the University of the Pacific in Stockton, California, Rhodes spent most of his early manhood in New Mexico. He married May Davison, an Eastern woman, in 1899; she disliked New Mexico, finding it too "lonesome," and by and by returned to live with her parents in Apalachin, New York. Rhodes followed her four years later, in 1906, and there Rhodes worked until 1926 as a farm laborer to support his wife, her two children by a previous marriage, his own son with her and a daughter who died in infancy, and May's aging parents. It was while living in Apalachin that Rhodes wrote nearly all of his fiction of consequence, and all of it was set in New Mexico as he had come to fancy it out of sheer homesickness. "To write stories one needs some ease and *rest* when you are worn out," he confided to a friend. "I am very tired, and yet I can write only at night." Rhodes' enlargement of the heart, which ultimately killed him, is generally blamed on a bout with influenza, but surely the long hours he put in as a farmer, followed by the equally long hours writing, proved a severe strain. Finally, for reasons of health, Rhodes insisted on returning to New Mexico, but it wasn't the same and, finally, in 1931 he and May settled in Pacific Beach, California. Here Rhodes died on June 27, 1934. His widow had his body transported back to New Mexico to a remote spot in the shadow of the San Andres Mountains he loved. He rests there still, on land near what was once his homestead but which is now controlled by the Department of the Army for the White Sands Missile Range.

Rhodes was already an old-fashioned writer when he was contemporary, and so he is old-fashioned today. He wrote of a romantic New Mexico peopled with characters transformed by the warmth of longing memory into incredibly virtuous heroes and wooden, preposterous heroines. At his best, he left out women altogether and described an ideal masculine society. Notwithstanding, his villains were modeled on the real villains of the Old West: land-speculating capitalists, eastern bankers, exploiters of human and natural resources, crooked politicians, and corrupt sheriffs. When he liked a man, he liked him all the way, as in the case of Pat Garrett, whom he knew and idealized as a character in his finest short novel *Pasó por Aquí,* first published in 1927; or as in the case of Albert B. Fall, formerly senator from New Mexico and secretary of the interior under Warren G. Harding, swept from office for dishonesty but defended to the death by Rhodes. The ablest collection of Rhodes' fiction ever to appear was *The Best Novels and Stories of Eugene Manlove Rhodes* (Houghton Mifflin, 1949), now in reissue from the University of Nebraska Press. It contains *Pasó por Aquí,* as well as Rhodes' splendid *The Trusty Knaves* (1934). Although it is now out of print, still the best biography on Rhodes is W. H. Hutchinson's *A Bar Cross Man: The Life and Personal Writings of Eugene Manlove Rhodes* (University of Oklahoma Press, 1956).

"The Bird in the Bush" first appeared in *Redbook* in April 1917. Andrew Jackson Aforesaid Bates, the protagonist, appears again in "Aforesaid Bates," a story from 1928. Rhodes based Bates, at least in part, on Hiram Yost, who had once played an avuncular role in Rhodes' early life, and Tom Tucker, one who like Rhodes himself sided with Oliver Milton Lee, who historians now agree *was* involved in the murder of Colonel A. J. Fountain. Bates' homestead resembles rather closely Rhodes' own homestead in New Mexico. Rhodes in later years referred to this story as "ultra-whimsical," but whatever the case it is typical of Rhodes at his best and more readable than some of his fiction.

The Bird in the Bush

I liked the Big Sandy, and I liked the people. But I saw what was coming. Good rains—high grass—double your herds every washday—everything lovely! Then along comes old Mr. Drought. *Bing!* There you are, busted. It's like playing double or quits; if you don't pinch your bets, you're going home talking to yourself. It's got to be that way. So I sold out.

Then I went off alone and tried to establish communication with myself. "Look here, Andy," says I, "are you going to be a dern fool all your whole life? You're getting old, and you're getting bald, and those that know you best, they love you most—but they put up quarantine signs against you. It's time to quit your wild, fool ways and settle down.

"But, still, yet," I rejoins, "you can't never be satisfied in town, planted in rows, or packed in cans or stacked on shelves. And you'll never be anything more than a bald-headed boy so long as you stay on the free range. With that rep' you got, people wouldn't let you behave if you wanted to. Your poor old dad tried to hammer some farmin' into your head," says I. "Why not try that?"

"But, again, then," says I, "you got to jar loose from the cow-business gradual. A little bunch of bossies fenced safe from the depredations of unprincipled men—that's what you want, to tide you over till you get the hang of farming."

Good scheme, wasn't it? I thought so. I'd held onto some of my wisest cow-ponies. So now I picked out two and sold the rest. Deacon was experienced and observing and level-headed; Quaker didn't have near such good judgment, but he was Deacon's pardner. I fixed me up a pack, and we went projecting off, still-huntin' a home for our declining years.

We skipped Prescott. Prescott had forgiven me, all right, allowing I was as much sinned against as sinning; but they was likewise strong of the opinion that if I ever came back, they'd sin against me some more. They was mighty explicit about that.

We shunned Tonto Basin too, where cattle- and sheep-men was enjoyin' a war. I wasn't in any hurry. I reckon we put in three or four months on that search. But I hadn't found nothing quite to fit me.

I'd been climbing uphill two or three days—hadn't seen a man since I left Salt River, and mighty few sheep-herders—just a steady up, up, up, through a crooked, winding, wavy, hazy, cold, blue-black piny-woods country, and at last I came out on the big top. Oh, man!

The mountain dropped off in fifteen minutes all I'd climbed up in three days. Right under me was a mesa of low, red foothills; then came a great, round, gray-greenish-yellow basin, thirty or fifty miles across any which way, saucer-shaped, heaped high with sunshine. There was big mountains all around it; where I sat, on the south, they made a level black wall with one gate-way off to my left. The eastern curve was piny-black too, broken hills, round, rolling and low. Across in the southwest, maybe forty mile away, was a stretch of bare gray cliffs, straight upandicular, ending in a limestone elephant with one eye and a granite trunk six miles long. He looked mighty curious. He kept that one eye on me, and I felt little cold shivers playing up and down my backbone.

Running catawampus across the basin, like a crack in the saucer, was a cañon. It headed in a gap in the northeast and slipped off to the Pacific through a fold in the cliffs this side of that elephant. He had a mean eye.

It was wide and deep and crooked, that cañon. My side of the basin was wavy; north of the cañon-crack it rose in benches; and 'way beyond and above the last bench was a half-circle of misty, pinky granite knobs and spikes and spires, notched and jagged, domes and turrets and things. They took my eye. Seems like the nicest places to live are where you find that worn-down granite for soil. It's so clean and cheerful.

Down under us I saw a big white road striking across to the front gate at my left. Only for the road, I'd 'a' thought I was the first man on the job.

I'd been pursuing around at random, and there wasn't rightly any way to get down from where I was. But we made it sliding, somehow. It took us half a day. Down in the red feethills we found mines and things, all nailed up and abandoned. We found a little spring and made camp.

Soon in the morning we was out on the plain. Prettiest rolling mesa you ever see—black grama and crowfoot; plenty slick fat cattle, mostly branded J. B.; antelope, and too many bands of wild horses. Presently we hit an old wagon-track, rutted deep but grown up with grass. More old roads comes anglin' in, and at last we come to the big white road I'd seen from the summit.

It had been traveled a heap once, but not lately. It was ruler-straight across the mesa, till we pitched off into the breaks of a draw that led down to the main big cañon, getting deeper and deeper. Directly we come to the jump-off place, and the wagon-road took to the side-hill. It was dug out two or three thousand years ago and hadn't been repaired since—ribbed and gullied—rubble, with the soil all washed away. We twisted down and down and down some more, till at last we come out on the cañon-floor to orchards and ditches and a white town asleep in the sun.

Yessir! Every man I see was asleep, under the trees or on the porches; and they was all old, old men. I followed along between vineyards and open doors and alfalfa and cottonwood trees to a shady plaza with a *'cequia* tinklin' down beside, mighty pleasant. I let the horses drink. There was a 'dobe store squandering around under the oldest cottonwood in the world, and in front sets an old jasper with a long, gray beard, sound asleep. I woke him up.

"Good evening," says I. "Can you tell me where I can find *Allan Quatermain?*"

He didn't get me. He wasn't literary. "Never heard of him," says he.

I heard some one laugh behind me. It was a cool, ripply little laugh, tuned to a little waterfall in the *'cequia.* I looked around and saw a girl in a streak of dancing sun that smuggled through the branches.

"S-sh! *Allan Quatermain* escaped—three years ago—across the mountain—and the forest—and the desert—toward Zanzibar! Hush-sh!" She put her finger to her lip and tiptoed across to me. She gave the old geezer a side-look and held her hand up, palm out. "S-sh!" she says again. . . .

Sometimes I dream of going back. I ride along dim old roads that never were, to old houses that couldn't be—great, ramshackle old barracks, doors open and sagging, shutters that swing and squeak over broken windows—dim and dark inside, old moldy pictures on the wall, dust on the tables and chairs and drifted in the fireplace. And I can't remember—quite. So I follow the old road, windin' and windin' through a level, brushy country. There's no tracks turning off, but the road gets dimmer and dimmer, and at last it plays out. So I go on and on to look for ranches I can almost remember, and a little swift river that ought to be somewhere: but the mountains are wrong, and all the gaps are in the wrong places, and everything is changed—except Minnie. She is just the same; she isn't any older; her eyes are sunny; she comes dancing and laughing to meet me through a deep shade. And—this is curious—she brings the sunlight with her, always the warm, clear sunshine rippling about her as she comes. I wasn't expecting her: I try to tell her so—and then I wake up.

I hopped down as she came—the really time, I mean, not the dream. Deacon stretched out his nose, and she pets him. "It is the custom of the valley," she says, "for strangers from the outside world to stay at the—at the palace—until their fate is decided."

She was just a little trick. There was a dimple in her cheek that come and went as she spoke; her eyes were brown, and down in each one lived a little, merry, dancing gold devil—you could see him when she laughed at you. Quaker come up alongside and crowded old Deacon off—he wanted to be petted too. So I pushed his head away, just like he done to Deacon—and then she laughed again. "Got to keep pack-horses in their places," says I.

"They want their dinner," said the girl. "So do you. Come along."

"That's right," said the old geezer, settlin' back for another snooze. "Cow-men, they all stop with her dad—he owns the J. B. You go along with her."

So we walked on down the street; the *'cequia* sung along beside us, Deacon and Quaker looking around, mighty interested, sizing things up.

"Who, which, why, when, where, what, how?" says I. "Where am I? Why is everyone asleep? And why are the mines closed down? Why doesn't no one ever travel the roads? Why hasn't no one ever heard of this place before? Why did the elephant try to scare me back? Why everything?"

So she told me why. "We're waiting for the railroad. It's our sole occupation. That's the answer to all the questions. And now it's your turn, isn't it? Who, where, how? Explain! No wanderer has found his way here since—"

"*Allan Quatermain?*" says I. "For me, Miss—why, I guess I couldn't have stayed away if I'd tried. It was predestined and foreordained that I was comin' here—to wait for the railroad."

"Here's the J. B. house," she said. "Father isn't at home, but Anselmo will show you where to put your horses." She give both of 'em a little pat. "Then come on in. Mother and I will have dinner ready for you."

I turned the horses to an alfalfa stack and went in. Mrs. Briscoe was a nice, motherly old lady, but she acted kinder worn-out and road-weary. After I met old man Briscoe, I knew why. He was a mean old whelp—just naturally cussed. The house was fixed up nice.

That evenin' Minnie sat out on the gallery with me, explainin'. The basin was called the Butterbowl—'member the Butterbowl on Rainbow? I named that myself, after this place. The river was San Lucas; the big range I'd crossed was Black Mountain, and my nice pinky hills was Dream Mountain.

In and around Butterbowl was everything a man could want—grass, lumber-woods, mines, water and soil to grow anything: but it took three days' hard riding in that direction to reach a given point. The early settlers saw that a railroad was bound to tap this country—some time. So they made 'em a town, Central, built them wagon-roads out to the tributary mines and lumber, built orchards and ditches and set down to wait for the whistle. Meantime they raised cattle.

There was one big cattle-company, the J. B., and a lot of little outfits beside. Leastwise, they called it a company, though Minnie's dad, he owned most of it. They hadn't overstocked yet, but they was fixin' to; they hadn't got to stealin' much yet, but they was practicing; and old J. Briscoe allowed the little cow-men was all worthless and not fit company for his daughter: so they had all the makin's of trouble. I thought I'd stay.

In the morning I struck out for my pinky mountains. One of them nice little Southwest spring winds, like we got here, was beating in my face, mighty raw. Once I climbed the mesa, I quit the road and sidled off, so's to split the difference between the one-eyed elephant and the stage-road gap, Holbrook way. I was needin' a place where I wouldn't be in nobody's way, d'yuh see—an' likewise, where nobody'd be in my way. I passed all the cattle, and I passed all the cattle-tracks; I got up on the last bench, level as a billiard-table, right under them pinky mountains: I put in between two of them back-bones and run spang onto exactly what I wanted.

I heard the wind ravin' and howlin' up overhead, but in between them two spurs of hill it was still as a Monday meetin'-house. After facing that wind all day, it seemed like a box-seat in Paradise, complimentary. I named it Shelter, right off.

I guess Adam had the best time anybody ever did, namin' things. Ever notice what good names you find in a thin-settled country? That's cause they didn't have no prominent citizens to call things after.

There was a narrow box between the hills for about a quarter, and a big gravel wash. Then we came out in a wide open valley with a big granite fence about two thousand foot high all around it, and I knowed Andrew Jackson Bates had found him a home.

Come to find out afterward, the Butterbowl folks called the place Bottle Basin. That was the shape of it, maybe five miles across from rim-rock to rim-rock, and about six the long way. There was crowfoot, black grama and short, curly, yellow buffalo-grass, and mesquite beans; plenty cedar, juniper and live-oak on the ridges. Put a little fence across the mouth of the bottle, and there I was, snug, my cows fenced in and other people's fenced out. I made camp and went a-prospectin'.

There wasn't any living water, as I knowed before, by there being no fresh cow-tracks, but I could see by the wash that a heap of water come down the draw when it rained. My play was to build tanks and store flood-water—see? By sundown I had it all figured out. Here I was to build a little tank, to hold water for my teams, whilst I was weavin' a big one. Both was to be in a smooth side-draw, where there was first a wide place to hold a world of water, and then a narrow place to make a dam. I was going to put a wing-dam in on the main cañon, and carry flood-water to my tanks in a ditch through a little saddle—so too much heap flood would never break my dams; I was going to make my waste-ways first, make 'em twice as big as they'd ever need to be, and then make 'em bigger. I'd seen dams built before.

It was full moon, that night. I prowled around, a-plannin', proud as a pawn in the king-row. I reckon that was about the happiest one time I ever put in. "Andrew Jackson, I sure made a stake to-morrow," says I. Here I was to build my big dam, and here my spillway; here was to be my corrals, and here my orchard; I began farmin' by breaking in a little flat and edged a little further down every year.

Next day we ambled around looking for water. I followed the dim cow-trails till they got plain, and the plain ones till they got dusty, and we struck a spring, fifteen miles away, where a fellow named Hall held out—give the Bow-and-Arrow brand. Come dinner, I found this was the nearest place for me to haul water from to begin my work. Of course, I didn't tip my hand. Cow-men sure hate to be crowded.

That night I cached my pack and hiked to Holbrook for a surveyor. He ran out my section numbers for me, and made me plots and plans and estimates and specifications. I didn't want 'em: I built my dam by guess and by golly when I got at it; but the law calls for 'em.

Then I wandered over and broke the news gently to old man Hall and asked him if I could borrow some water to haul over to Shelter. He fought his head right smart at first, till he found out what my name was. Then he come to his feed. He'd heard of me. And he judged I'd come in handy to hold the J. B. outfit level. So I got him and his boy Bill to slip down to Globe with me as witnesses when I filed on my claim.

I got a wagon in Globe, a darky named Eph and a span of mules, a Mex boy and a span of big horses, a plow and two scrapers, water-barrels, tools and a tent and such. We took rounders on the Butterbowl and pussy-footed into Shelter unbeknownst.

Hall drawed me over a first load of water on his wagon, for a starter. I set Eph and Esteban to tanking while I broke Deacon and Quaker to the water-wagon. They was dead set against it. It was some comedown from bein' crack cow-horses. I reckon they thought I'd put 'em on the scraper next.

I see they wasn't going to be satisfied, and we hadn't brought much corn up from Globe; so after a few trips I put off down to Central. They was bound to find out about me and Shelter before long, anyway. I dickered for a span of spankin' black mares, Zip and Jezebel, and carried out a load of corn and supplies, with Deacon and Quaker at the tail-gate. They were sure tickled. I knew some one would be curious about me. And sure enough, the next day but one, here comes old John Briscoe, just a-snuffin'. I hadn't never seen him before, but I knowed him right off. He looked like a cartoon of himself.

"What's this? What's all this? What you doing here?" he sizzles.

"Just now I'm a-prizing long, wide, hard, heavy, thick, big rocks out o' my spillway with a crowbar," says I. "And directly I'm going to compound the finest dinner you ever flopped your lip over. Get down and look at your saddle a spell."

"Of all the gall!" says J. B. "We'll fix *your* clock! You'll be glad to get out o' here, quicker than you came—crowdin' yourself in where you ain't wanted. If you're hunting trouble, you've come to the right shop. You'll get it, and you'll get it good!"

Wasn't that a nice crack to make? That's what a man gets himself by going where he's not known.

"Did you ever chance to hear the honored name of Aforesaid Andrew Jackson Bates?" I asked him.

"The pleasure is mine," he says, mighty sneerin'. "I have not. Desperado, I reckon?'

"Worse than that," says I. "A heap worse. I'm a stayer. I've got a positive genius for bad luck—witness them opprobrious syllables, Aforesaid, wished onto me by acclamation of five States and Territories. Fair sir," says I, "you was mentionin' trouble to me. I've had all kinds of trouble a mere single man can have, and most generally got the worst of it; but let me tell you, beloved, none of my victorious and laurel-wreathed antagonists has ever bragged about it any, and that includes the sovereign State of California, the Republic of Mexico, the Espee Railroad, the Diamond-A Cattle Company, Yavapai County, Prescott, Bucky O'Neill and the Arizona House of Reprobates, besides Montana and some few other commonwealths whose memory is now fadin' in the mists that rise down the River of Time. So far, I've had no mix-up with the United States or the Daughters of the Revolution," says I, "but outside o' that, I've met everything in the shape of man or beast that the umpire could furnish and have never yet lowered my arm.

"Trouble?" says I. "Trouble? Before you come talking trouble to me, you'd better read the history of your country. Pending them investigations," says I, "don't you try to run any blazers on me, and likewise smooth your wrinkled front. You may not know it, but you're allowin' yourself to make horrid frowns at me, and I won't have it. I like smilin' faces and cheerful words and happy laughter around me, and I'm goin' to have 'em. I came here seekin' a quiet and peaceful spot to while away the Indian summer of my soul, and if you pester me any, I'm going to do you a great personal injury, forthwith, at once, *ahorita, immediatamente* and now! Declare yourself, Marmaduke Mortimer—a gold chain or a wooden leg?"

J. B. was some impressed by them remarks. He come back at me easy. "But it wouldn't be right for you to turn no cattle loose on this range," says he. "You ain't got no water-right. And you can't get no water by digging—not around here. I've drilled a well five hundred foot, right here in Bottom Basin."

"Shelter," I corrects him.

He was right on! "And this mizzable little tank you're making won't have a drop of water in it three months after the rains. You can't—I mean, it wouldn't be the square thing to turn a herd in the Butterbowl on the strength of that."

"The audience will kindly retain their rompers," says I. "I ain't goin' to turn any cattle loose on your range. This is only my family cistern, to water my horses whilst we collaborate on a big he-tank. I'm goin' to make the desert do that blossom thing; I'm goin' to be a bold yeomanry, my country's pride, and sit under my own vine and fig-tree. I'm going to raise Early Martyr potatoes; I'm going to walk abroad and view the fields where oats, peas, beans and barley grows. You cast your eagle eye down the hollow betwixt them two hills," says I. "Right there, in about ten months or two years, I'm goin' to have me a tame ten-acre lake."

"Huh! There ain't watershed enough, in this little draw," says he.

"Goin' to tap the main draw and lead it through yonder little saddle," I explains to him.

He looks kinder interested. "Why—I believe that would work," says he. "But if you want to farm, why don't you buy a place down on the San Lucas?"

"Me? Shucks, I never could see any good times herdin' with them sleep-walkin' nesters," says I. "Dern a granger, anyhow!"

"Why—why—why, you're going to be one yourself!" says Briscoe.

He had me there. I hadn't thought o' that. It struck me all in a heap.

"Well, not so's you can notice it. I may irritate the soil a little, as a gentlemanly relaxation—but do I look anyways like a splay-footed, sod-hopping, apple-grafting granger? I'm as good a cow-man as ever throwed a loop by moonlight," says I.

"But you said you wouldn't turn no cattle loose on my range," said Briscoe, stuttering.

"Ain't it the truth?" says I. "What's the matter with my range—*m–y, my?* Throw a little fence across that cañon, like a stopper in a bottle—"

I didn't finish, 'cause Briscoe, he was carryin' on something fierce. He was a natural-born hawg, that man was.

I let him rave a spell, till I see that I might as well stop him first as last. "See here, Aloysius," says I, "you're talking pretty brash. I wonder at myself that I ain't bent this crowbar over your old hard head."

He reined his horse around. "Where you goin'?" says I, and I grabbed up a rock. "I'm a patient man," says I, "but if you don't light off that cayuse and stay to dinner, I'm goin' to bounce a pebble off your medulla obligato. It isn't anywise neighborly to go off that way just as dinner's ready; it casts reflections on my cookin'. Welcome, little stranger!" I says, as he climbs off. "Welcome to Shelter!"

I tried to rib him up with a jolly whilst I was wrangling chuck. "I know what makes your sorrows grieve you so, Montmorency," says I. "You tot it up that because I've got a pasture I'm goin' to get implicated with your calves. I been all along that road, same as you have—we won't deny it, Epaminondas; but I wouldn't choose any more of the pie. Honesty is the best policy, as who should know better than me? You and the J. B. punchers is welcome to prowl around in here, auditing, any time, and there'll always be a meal's victuals for you and a nice level place to sleep."

But he wouldn't mellow up and he went away dissatisfied. That old man never did like me.

Next time I went to town, old J. B. had me over to the house and offered me five hundred to quit-claim Shelter to him. Seems like he'd set his heart on it, and he couldn't forgive me for him not thinkin' of buildin' a tank there first. That night I met Minnie's cousin Jane, who was the Central school-ma'am, and old man Duffy, Methodist preacher from St. Johns, and Dee Macfarlane. Dee had sunny hair, the rascal—wavy and sunny. He owned a nice little bunch of cattle, but he didn't 'tend to his business very close, *I* thought. He was settin' around up to Minnie's nearly every time I went near there. That's no way to run cattle. You got to be out amongst 'em.

Well, there come an early rain that year, along in April. That filled my cistern so I got shut of water-hauling. So long as I had a township for pasture, ready-made all but the gate, I thought we'd better fix the gate. So we strung up the wire fence across the box. After that we could turn our work-horses loose at night, instead of hobbling, and they done better. I got another scraper down to Central, and another Mexican—Eusebio. He wasn't much force, not sized up with Eph and Esteban. He had a Candelaria girl in Central. Candy, she worked for Mamma Briscoe. I didn't mind him going down Sundays so much, though he was lonesome to ride with—but he did sing such long-drawn and mournful despair around the camp-fire after supper:

> *"Tal vez, mi amada, en brazos de otro amor,*
> *Duerme y descansa—ay! sin pensar en mi!"*

We began makin' dirt fly on this new dam. Beat all, what a difference it made not havin' to draw water fifteen mile for six horses and a camp. I tied up Deacon or Quaker, turn about, for night-horse. Every morning I was out wranglin' work-stock before day, while the boys rustled breakfast. I did the rest o' the cookin' and all the pot-walloping and black-smithing. I hauled corn and chuck, and kep' camp in venison, and rustled wood: I jumped in to hold the plow or whatever was needed quick and most, and we inched right along. I hadn't never worked so steady since I was a boy on Staten Island. The plowed dirt smelled good, and the green grass it smelled good, and the chuck tasted good. I felt virtuouser and virtuouser every day. I'd put away childish things: I looked back with pain to them ranikiboo plays I'd hitherto promulgated.

The neighbors took to droppin' in to see me. Nice lot of two-handed punchers, they was—Hall and Billy Hall, Spike and Doc and Squatty Robinson and San Simon—he was a prospector, San Simon was.

J. Briscoe, he mostly flocked by his only, but he come out twice more, raising his offer to fifteen hundred. He sure wanted the Shelter place. Joe Only, the J. B. wagon boss, he happened in pretty frequent, and Chuck Barefoot.

For I began to have other company too. Minnie Briscoe and her cousin Jane, they took to comin' out Saturday nights and stayin over Sunday. I got a new tent for 'em, soon as I see they was formin' the habit. I'd go deer-hunting with Minnie at first—or just go browsing around with both of 'em. Jane was an easy keeper, but she wasn't exciting. Sometimes they brought Minnie's ma along for chaperon, sometimes not. It didn't make no difference. Them girls didn't need no chaperon—not much, anyway.

Did I say that the boys had quit visiting each other and made Shelter the reg'lar Sunday headquarters since the girls took to comin' out? Well, they did. It was bound to be that way. So I wasn't obliged to go huntin' with 'em any more. Somehow I wasn't near as glad as I might 'a' been. But I was the host, and also I wasn't much young any more. The play come for me to take a back seat.

Minnie thought there wasn't no place like Shelter, and she kept coaxin' me to sell out to her father. "If you will, I'll get Poppa to let me homestead it," she says, "and I'll have it for my very own. Poppa has used his homestead right. I think you might, Andrew J."

This was about the thirteenth time she'd named it to me. "Why, yes, so I might, but then will I?" says I. "There ain't another place just like this in the whole dinky world, I don't believe. I've done used my homestead right, too. Your little scheme would mean forfeiting my desert claim—and where would Aforesaid A. J. Bates be then, poor thing?"

"You might buy a place," says Minnie, pouting.

"I want to tell you, Miss Minnie," says I, "that there can't no man buy a place—not if it cost him a million dollars—and get so much solid comfort from it as he can where he was the very first man that ever nested there since the world began, and where he has cut every post and built in every stone and set out every tree with his own fair hands. So I go along with Shelter as an encumbrance. If you're dead set to make your home here—take a chance! A bird in the bush is the noblest work of God," says I. "I'm old and I'm stove-up and I'm unlucky, but I'll do my da——— I'll do my best to make it a safe shelter, Minnie," says I.

She flushed all rosy red, and she dropped her eyes, but she shook her head. "I can't," she whispers. "You'd make it a safe shelter, Andy, and maybe it would be better if I could. But I can't."

"Why?" says I. "Don't you like me at all, Minnie, not the least little bit?"

"Oh, I do!" says she. "I do like you, ever so much—but not that way."

"How do you know?" says I.

"I know!" says Minnie.

"Who is it, Minnie? Dee, I reckon?"

"*Don't!* You mustn't!" she says, catchin' her breath short. She let me see her face—my pretty! And there were tears in her eyes. I knowed when she let me see them tears that no matter how much she liked Dee, she might have liked me pretty well too, if the play had come different.

Then she gave me a straight look. "And you don't really want me, Andy—not really! Oh, you think you do—just now! But it's partly because you want to be neighborly, and maybe because you know that I don't have a very good time at home. And you'd always be good and kind to me, I guess. But after a while, you'd be sorry. For there's just two kinds of people in this world," says Minnie. "The kind that thinks a bird in the hand is worth two in the bush—and your kind, Mr. Aforesaid Andrew Jackson Bates! Wherever you are, the soil of that place will be burning your foot-soles. You'll always be wondering what is on the other side of the hill, and you'll always be wondering what is on the other side of the world, and wanting to go see: and you'll always be wearyin' for the bird in the bush!"

"Well, then, don't you grieve your pretty head about me, honey," says I. "I'm old, and I'm tough, and I'll winter through some way. Maybe there's a good deal in what you say. But just you remember Shelter, if ever the world don't use you well. I'll be here, waiting."

"I'll remember," says Minnie. "But don't you put on such a long face. You can't fool me much, Andrew Jackson! You're one-half sorry and disappointed, and the other half is glad you've done your duty and no harm come of it. You'll be good as new in no time, and dreamin' about the bird in the bush. Good-by, and good luck!" she says, and turns her pony's head to town.

"You ain't going to let this make no difference about comin' out, when you feel like it?" says I.

"Oh, no! I'll be out, same as usual—after a little." Her face was kind of smily and teary and cheery all at once, and part mischievous, and kind of poutish too. "I know you only want what's best for me," she threw back over her shoulder, "and that's why I know you don't really-truly like me—that way," she says. "If you did, you wouldn't know you was old or unlucky or anything—and you'd be insisting on havin' your own way, whether 'twas best for me or not!"

I spurred up, but she hit her pony a lick and held up her open hand. So I stopped. "It's too late to insist now, Andy J.—after what I just said," says Minnie, reinin' up. "You go on back to your dam-work that you're so all wrapped up in. And say, Andy—" Her pretty face was all mischief now.

"Orders!" says I, touching my hat.

"Don't let your kind heart coax you to ask Jane! If you do, Andrew Jackson, I sha'n't like it one little bit!" And she was gone.

I think of her a heap, sometimes. . . . Say, it's hell to be old! 'Specially when you're not really a little bit old, inside. I've had a lot of fun; sometimes I think I've had more fun than anyone. But I've missed a heap, too.

Minnie come back, after a few weeks, but it wasn't ever quite the same. She kept Dee or Jane right with her, and she didn't call me Andy J. any more. I was Mr. Bates. So I built dam.

We kep' things rockin' along as per usual, Eph and Esteban and me just a-humpin', and Eusebio trifling along, only a little above the average. Lordie, there's a heap of difference in men! My the'ry is that if a man don't earn more than you give him, no matter how much that is, he ain't worth having around. Half the time Eusebio was plumb in our way.

Along late in September, when it was likely there wouldn't be any more rains, I saw a big storm coming up. "Maybe the last of the season," thinks I. So I called the boys out.

"Vacation!" says I. "We'll just fix our ditch to fill up this hole-in-the-ground and see if she'll hold. The teams is pretty well jaded out. Steve, you and 'Sebio take a week's lay-off—more, if you want it."

"You theenk thees tank not break, Meester Bates?" says Esteban.

"I hope not, Steve, old socks," says I. "For if she goes, we're sure a-going with it. It's no more than the square thing for us to put on our slickers and set on the dam—just as a bet that we been doin' good work."

Well, we done so, and she didn't break. My recipe for perpetratin' dams is to make 'em twice-and-a-half as strong and long and deep and wide and high as there is any use of, 'special the spillway, and then to say a little prayer.

The sun come out warm and pleasant, and we all took a big swim. The Mexican men, they went to rustle their horses so's they could pull their freight after supper, and I set there on the dam, seein' things.

Next mornin' Eph and me slep' till the horses woke us up beggin' for corn. Eph, he went off to pluck a venison, and I stayed in camp.

I reckon there was where I made a mistake—quittin' work sudden in the middle of the week. If it had been Sunday, now, and folks around, maybe things might 'a' come different. All of a sudden, I felt tired out and old and blue and bald and all-alonesome; and I couldn't get seein' things any more. I couldn't see myself makin' *'cequias* and settin' our fruit-trees; I just knowed that soil wouldn't grow alfalfa; my cows would climb out over them pinnacles; I couldn't think of no decent brand for 'em, and I couldn't think of no name for my cussed lake; and as for rip-rappin' that dam when the water got low, it made me fair sick to think of it.

No sir, all I could do was to study about how sad it would be if anything was to happen to Minnie's little boy-doll. I hadn't a thing against Dee, you understand—square and white a kid as ever rode leather. It just broke my heart to think of that hazardous occupation he was following, and nothing ever goin' wrong. He might fall off a horse, or down a shaft, or in my new lake: a steer might butt him, or somebody might shoot him. There was a new man, Petey Simmons, breakin' bronc's for the J. B.; six or seven feet high, no eyebrows or hair on his face, 'count of having had smallpox—mighty ugly man; I wondered if maybe Petey wouldn't do it. Then Dee might get snake-bit or quick consumption. Railroads, too, they was mighty dangerous. I did wish that railroad would hurry up and come.

Before noon I'd about compromised by havin' Dee run off with Jane. But I see that wouldn't do.

"You're getting morbid, Andy," says I. "I know what's the matter with you. You want to take a little horse-ride."

So I caught up old Quaker and went for a *pasear*—not anywhere particular, you know—just riding the curse off. I felt better right straight. Pretty soon I was singing about how once in the saddle I used to be a gay old bird.

About the middle of the evenin' I was 'way up on a pinnacle, when I saw some one chasing a bunch of cattle in the hills just under me. I took a small peep through my field-glasses.

It was old Squatty Robinson on a blue bronco. He caught

a big yearlin' and tied it to a saplin'; then he took in after the bunch and fought 'em on up the draw. I knew what he was up to. He'd drive the mammy-cow off up in the hills three or four miles; then he'd hurry back and adopt that yearlin'.

Quaker was prancing; I began to feel frisky, like I was only a big grown-up boy. Quaker was a flighty, hoity-toity horse, anyway—no fit company for a serious-minded man.

"Andrew Jackson," says I, "this is plumb dishonest, and it ought to be discouraged. Be you goin' to allow such goin's-on, or be you not?"

I went down there. I set that calf loose, and I took the rope that was on her and flung it over a limb, so the noose hung down just about high enough to hang a short man, and I tied the other end around the tree-trunk. Squatty was a short man.

I knowed Squatty would be back soon to drive home his foundling. I hid out to watch him. Just as I got myself spotted, here come a bunch of wild mares up the cañon, forty or fifty, and went on up the way Squatty did. They was burnin' the breeze; and behind them, here comes Esteban and Eusebio. That was funny too, because they told me the night before they was goin' to Holbrook. I lay right still.

They come pretty near up to where I was. I had to pinch Quaker's nose to keep him from whinnyin'. They turned out of the cañon opposite me and rode up the hill to a big slick piece of granite below a cliff. They climbed up that afoot, and they hid something in a hole under the cliff. Then they rode back down the cañon.

"I go look-see!" says I, soon as they was out of sight. When I come to the tracks, they was barefoot tracks; yet them horses was fresh shod only yesterday: curious thing! I took away the stones and felt in that hidey-hole. What do you think I found? Two slickers with eye-holes cut in the backs of 'em just below the collar! I tried again and fished out a package. It was little: it had the express-company's seal on it, broken; it had been tied up again. Inside was a bunch of yellow-backs. Them triflin' boys of mine had robbed the stage!

"I'm plumb surprised at Steve," I says. "This ain't honest!" I counted the money. There was twenty-five bills, each for one hundred perfectly good dollars. "Sufferin' Moses!" says I. "I didn't think the stage carried as much as that, all told, in a year." I turned the package over. 'Twas addressed to *J. Briscoe, Central, Arizona.*

"Twenty-five hundred is a heap of cash for the Butterbowl," I thinks. I tucked it away in my shirt-bosom. "Whatever did J. B. want of that much in cold cash? And when did my enterprisin' young friends know so pat when to get busy? And I thought that triflin' Steve was a pretty good *hombre*, dern him. Say! By Jings, I bet that Candy girl of his has been snoopin' through the letters on Poppa Briscoe's desk—and that's how they knew when the money was comin'! They started up them mares to account for themselves if they run onto anybody—and so they didn't see Squatty's trail, or mine, 'cause the mares had done run over 'em. That part is nearly right. But what I don't see, is what J. B. wanted of all that wad."

I was so absorbed I didn't see that same bunch of mares sky-hootin' back down the hill to my horse that I'd left with his bridle-reins dangling. But I was too late. That ornery Quaker up with his tail and threw in with 'em. They went on down to the plain—and I was afoot!

I was pretty sore. I judged Squatty had met them broomtails and turned 'em as he was coming back. So I got behind a boulder and waited. I didn't want to walk home—not if I could get Squatty's horse.

Squatty come directly. He was real surprised at not finding no yearling, and he said so. When he got down to get his rope, I cut loose a few shots, puffin' up dust between him and his horse. Squatty, he went to the wild bunch.

I kept foggin' away till I saw him come out of the timber two or three hundred yards up and cross a little glade to the main woods. Then I knowed Squatty had gone to waterin' at night.

I climbed his blue bronc'. I turned across toward home, studying up something real severe to say to Steve. But I never got to Shelter. I looked up, and there was that same bunch of mares quartering along in front of me. Some one had headed 'em off again and turned 'em back. They was almost beat out; they was strung along like a snake, rockin' up and down, noses to the ground, like one of them dream-gallops we have, where we don't get any forwarder. Some of 'em could hardly navigate. That old gray fool of a Quaker was hanging on behind. I could see his saddle shine.

I made a circle and fell in beside, sorter headin' 'em toward the stage-road. I closed in, riding easy, took after old Quaker and hurled my twine. The loop drawed up pretty deep on Quaker's shoulders—and just then my blue stumbled, and down we went!

I kep' out from under, but my foot hung in the stirrup. The blue horse scrambled up before I could kick loose: I grabbed for my gun, but it was jarred out where we fell—and away we went, kicking and bucking and squealing, with Andrew J. Bates, Baron Shelter, Lord of the Lake, dragging by one hind leg, on his back or belly as the case might be, grubbing up cactus and soapweed with himself.

One end of the rope bein' fast to my saddle-horn and the other end on Quaker's neck, Blue Beelzebub had to go round and round like a circus-horse doing tricks, hurdling mesquite bushes and the like.

As luck would have it, little Andrew was dragging on the inside. That was what saved him. When Beezy kicked, he missed my face more'n two inches. Old Quaker gave a little to keep from chokin', so the little geometrical design I was inscribing with my carcass was a free-hand spiral, like the writing-teacher used to show us to develop the whole-arm movement, only more so.

I kep' trying to climb up my leg far enough to grab that rope, but 'twas only as a matter of principle—I really didn't expect to do it. Then—bang! went a gun. Poor old Beelzebub come down on his side and lay there, with only his legs a-quivering.

I could 'a' had a real lovely time, just layin' still a week or two, but I judged it best not. I got my foot out pretty brisk and rolled over on my hands and knees. Beelzebub was shot right through the brainpan. He was mighty dead.

I boosted myself up by the saddle-horn and cantle and set down on the defunct: I poured the sand out o' my mouth and nose and ears and eyes, and looked round. I was considerable dizzy.

We was right beside the wagon-road: Beelzebub had stumbled crossing it. Quaker had got some slack and was getting his breath—head hanging down, legs braced. Then I see a man. It was Petey Simmons, the J. B. bronco-buster. His mouth was open; his eyes was buggin' out, and he had a gun in his hand; he sat there on his horse looking at me, and he was whispering to himself. "Well, *I'll* be damned!" he says. "I will be *damned!*"

I looked at Petey a spell, and Petey looked at me. After a bit things steadied down some, and I remembers my manners.

"Thank you!" says I.

"Oh, I *will* be damned!" whispers Petey again, as if his soul in them few words he would outpour.

I felt considerable nettled. It didn't seem to me that Petey was showin' the proper sort of spirit.

"Doubtless," says I. "But why so confidential about it? And what makes you think it's interesting to me? If you've fully made up your mind, all right—but *I* don't care, I'll tell you those!"

Petey took off his hat. The sweat was starting on his face. He seemed stunned and grieved and discouraged; he hadn't the joyful look a man ought to wear that had just saved a valuable life. It didn't seem much of a compliment to me.

"Petey, that was a pretty fair shot you made," says I.

"Well, I will—" he began again, but I cut him off short at the pockets.

"Petey, I'll give you just one more chance," says I in a firm yet trembling voice. "You hunt around and pick up my gun and my hat and any pieces of my hide you think can be used again," says I. "And compose your mind good' for if you say any more about your future fate, I'm going to shoot you five times in the middle West. You plumb displease me. But first of all, you look in the road and see if there ain't a lot of fresh tracks headin' for the Holbrook Gap."

He done so and nodded his head.

"I thought as much," says I. "Petey, some one robbed the stage out there this morning—two men named Doe and Roe. Central has done waked up and gone to see how about it."

"Hell's bells!" said Petey in a cracked and horrified voice. "Just the one time it's ever carried any money since Heck was a pup! Curse that black-hearted, liver-lipped, whip-sawin' old J.B., I believe he done it himself!"

"How'd you happen along so appropriate?" says I—wondering to myself how Petey knew there was any money on that stage.

"I been out to your place," says Petey, lickin' his dry lips. "You've gone; greasers gone; nigger gone. Comin' back, I see a saddled horse in a bunch of mares. I tried to cut him out, but they outrun me. So I shacked along on their trail, thinking maybe I'd aidge 'em along toward a corral and find some one to help pen 'em. Next I know, I saw a man clearin' off a place with himself for a three-ring circus. I tore off down here to keep him from being dragged to death—and it's *you!* Think of it!" says Petey, exceedin' bitter. "I run hellity-larrup through two miles of dog-holes, sixty miles an hour, hop, skip and jump, till each separate hair on my head stood up like feathers on the fretful concubine—and it's *you!* I'm ha'nted!" says Petey. "That's what is it—I'm ha'nted!"

Any way you look at it, Petey was showin' up mighty ungrateful. He stared at me some more and rode off, muttering, to look for my gun and things.

"Andrew Jackson!" thinks I to myself, "what call has this long, lean, lank son of Satan to show such deep and abiding chagrin because he has been the humble instrument, under Providence, for prolonging your days in the land? Why does he think J. B. had the stage robbed? If he did, wan't it his own money? Who would J. B. be whipsawing by stealing his own money, and why should it stir up Petey's bile? But if so, why? What lot or part did Petey have in that lost and vanished wad?" Here I felt in my shirt-bosom for the money, thinkin' it might have got lost durin' the late exhibition, but it was still there.

"You can't deny it, Mister Bates—you've never been quite reconciled to J.B. sending for that amount of cash. Cash is for people that ain't satisfied with checks. Who ain't satisfied with checks? People that ain't stayin' to have 'em cashed. Pretty big sum, ain't it? About the price of what? Of erasing somebody? Who ain't satisfied? Petey. How else could Petey earn that much so slick? Erasing who? Hey? Who's J. B. got it in for? Answer: Andrew Jackson Bates, of Naboth's vineyard.

"When did this money come? To-day, September 30th. When did Petey Simmons make his first and only visit to Shelter? To-day, September 30th. Was he displeased at the stage being robbed? He was. Why? Was he pleased at me not staying home? He was not. Why should a gentleman stay at home, if he didn't choose to wish to do so? Was Petey Simmons grateful to have saved a valued life? He was not. Last and most convincing of all, who was it you picked for to be poor Dee Macfarlane's murderer? Petey Simmons!

"Andrew Jackson, you ought to be thankful to J. Doe and R. Roe and Squatty. Only for their thoughtfulness there'd be a singin' soon at Shelter—and you'd be there, but you wouldn't hear it. Petey would just about have killed a J. B. beef beside your cold, unconscious clay, and said he caught you stealin' it. . . . I wonder if Minnie would 'a' believed that?" thinks I.

Of course I didn't think it out in words, like that. I just thought it in thoughts, all at once and good deal clearer.

Words is mighty poor, slow tools, and they never did a good job in this world.

That wasn't all I sensed, either. There was impressions, little sidewise glances, things like this: Joe Only was boss; it was his to hire and fire. He didn't hire Petey; old Briscoe hired him. 'Twasn't usual, and 'twasn't liked. Nobody's been real pleasant to Petey. The J. B. boys felt they was pretty adequate to break their own broncos.

All this grand and lofty thinkin' took place simultaneous like a sewing-bee. Petey brought me my things. I cleaned the sand out of my good old gun, shoved her in the scabbard and give her a loving pat. Then I cocks one eye at my noble benefactor.

"Petey," says I, "not to be pryin' into your personal affairs, but was the old man to give you all that twenty-five hundred for expurgatin' me?"

Petey just stared at me, choking the horn of the saddle with both hands. I guess he felt that I was kinder vaccinated against him, after him savin' my life; he doesn't make any break for his gun.

"And you figure that he framed up a fake stage-robbin', to saw off the blame on you?" says I. "So you'd either get rubbed out or scared out?"

"Say, I hadn't thought of that!" says Petey, some startled. He give a pretty accurate description of the old man. He was a real powerful talker. "I'll go kill him right now—the old double-crossin' hypocrite!" he says to wind up.

"Now, now, Petey!" says I, soothin' him. "You don't want to do nothing like that. People would talk. The old man has been dealin' 'em to you from the bottom, I can see that. But I wouldn't kill him, exactly. Say, Petey, if I show you how to get that twenty-five hundred to-night, honest and aboveboard, will you come to Squatty's place by sun-up and give me half?"

"Will I?" says Petey. "I'll give you all of it! But how? How? The money's gone."

"I don't know yet," says I. "You just keep your mind off your thoughts whilst I study a spell."

I unsaddled Quaker and felt in the saddle-bags to see if my fieldglass was broke, and it wasn't.

"First off, Petey," says I, "them bold bandit-chasers are going to be back along here about sundown, ain't they?"

He allowed they was, some of 'em, anyway.

"Bueno! Pues," says I, "they're going to see that dead

horse, shot by a master hand. Everyone knows my saddle—and you're going to help me put it on the dead horse, right now."

He done so. It was hard to make the change, but we rolled old Beelzebub into my saddle and cinched it on. Then I put the other outfit on Quaker.

"There!" says I. "What with that and the robbery and Squatty missing too, Central will be one wild and nervous uproar. And who so agitated as J. Briscoe? I grieve to think how scared that man will be!" said I. "Too scared to use any daylight judgment at all. So if you drop in and tell him you had the misfortune to kill me and would like to collect, I reckon he'd give you the wealth without asking for no receipt."

"How in blazes," said Petey, "is he going to give me any money, when the money's gone?"

"I meant, if they happen to find the money anywhere," says I. "If they don't get the money, you don't say anything to J. B. But I think maybe they'll find it. So you trot along and come out there to Squatty's soon as you can. Squatty, he ain't there. We'll divide even—you for doing the bloody deed and me for concealin' the body," says I. "You tell the old man the play didn't come out just right, as there wasn't any beef-critter handy, and that you've hid out the corpse. Offer to lead him to me, if he holds back. But he won't. I've took a snubbing-postgratuate-course in psychology, Petey," says I, "and I tell you that J. Briscoe will be scared."

Petey took a long look at me. "I believe you are the devil!" he said. He was sweating again. "Lord, I'd like to! But I'll tell you honest, I lost my nerve when I found out whose life I'd saved. A man can't stand but just so much. Suppose the boys suspect me of killing you and find that money on me? They'll put me to bed with a shovel; they'll hang me and old man Briscoe with one rope."

"It ain't likely," says I. "It seems a pity. But I can't take chances of losing my share of that money. I'll fix you out. Is Dee Macfarlane in town?"

Petey nodded, and I dug up my tally-book. I wrote a note to Dee, dating it September 30, six P.M., telling him not to be alarmed at any reports he might hear about me that night, that I was just having a little innocent relaxation after my arjous toils; and for him to tell Minnie—I wasn't going to have my pretty frightened—but on no account to tell anybody else except to save life. "Please return this note to bearer, who doesn't want to be hung," I adds as a post-script. Petey read it, he grinned and started. He turned around and hollered back at me mighty earnest, "Don't you let anything happen to you, Andrew Jackson Bates!"

Me and Quaker terrapinned up the road a stretch, till I come to a rise that I could watch from a long ways off. Here I built up a little stone monument in the road and put that money on top, still in the original package, address-side up. I tacked off east two or three miles, to a bench where I could keep cases on that money with my fieldglass.

After a while the push fell off down the slope, six or eight of the boys loping along in front. I see them stop at my monument. Then I dug it up a draw for Squatty's. Got in about half-past dark, mighty tired. I drove up a bunch of Squatty's saddle-stock with me, and I caught his sorrel Gold Dollar horse. Then I turned Quaker loose with the bunch, opened up a lot of canned stuff and slept a few lines.

About sun-up Petey shook me. "Get up!" he says. "We got to get out of this!"

"Breakfast first," says I.

"Breakfast, nothing!" says Petey. "You come look at the Butterbowl!"

I took one look, and I see Petey was right. The sun was just peepin' over the hills, and the valley looked cool and pleasant. There was bunches of men scurryin' around everywhere, like drunk ants. I guess about the whole he-population was present. The nearest was eight or ten miles.

Some was following Petey's trail, some on mine, but most of 'em was spreadin' out for general results. They got 'em. Every mess of wile horses they scared up stampeded three more batches, and those bands scared more, and all of 'em stampeded every bunch of cattle they passed, and those cattle scared the next lot, and so on—and on—and on: just like politics. 'Twas a stirrin' scene.

My bosom swelled with pride. "Petey," says I, "did you get it?"

"That's what I went after," said Petey. "Here's yours. You keep the odd hundred."

"Let this be a lesson to you, Petey," says I, pretty severe.

"We'd better take to the hills," says Petey.

"We will not," said I, saddlin' the sorrel horse. "I always wished I was a musician, so I could fiddle at a fight. And this is the day when all my dreams come true. You and me, Petey, will go out on the flat." Then I stopped short and slapped my leg. "Chickens!" says I. "Chickens!"

"What's the matter with you now, you old hag?" said Petey, edgin' off.

"Chickens! I never once thought of keepin' chickens at Shelter till this very now! Come on, Petey," says I. "Let's us go play hare and hounds."

Petey came on, but he didn't like it. "You red hellion," says that interesting beast, "I dassent leave you get an inch away from me till all the Butterbowl knows you're alive. Joe Only suspected me and J. B. right off. Otherwise I'd see you rot first. May my right hand cleave to the roof of my mouth if I don't think you're part fiend!"

We had to go a couple of miles toward the man-hunt to get down out of the hills. They seen us. Then we turned east across the big flat, heading for the big pass, where progress and the railroad was to come in—some time—and the Butterbowl fanned along after us. I reckon the cattle thought it was the Day of Judgment.

We let the boys gain on us, to encourage them—that is, I did. Petey, he was in favor of going on, but I held him back. "I never knowed how popular I was," said I. "Them boys are sure aimin' to avenge the deep damnation of my taking-off. And oh, Petey!" says I, "if you and me could only meet up with J. B. face to face, what a joyful reunion we would have!"

By the time we got in the foothills by the pass, they was pretty close—two of 'em 'way ahead of the others.

"That's Barefoot and Joe Only," says Petey. "They've got the best horses in the works."

And here I got my great surprise. We come out on a ridge above the wagon-road, and there I saw two numbers that wasn't down on my program at all. Right below us, outward bound, was Minnie and Dee, joggin' happily along dead to the world. They'd just climbed out of the San Lucas where the wagon-road quit the Narrows, so missing the glorious and inspirin' panorama being presented on the flats.

I got the idee. Reasonin' from my note that I wasn't dead enough to grieve about, they was makin' the best possible use of the chance the excitement gave 'em.

If so, it was providential; for a little ahead, around a turn, I saw Parson Duffy coming in from St. Johns. I knew his white horses and his little old buckboard.

I called to them, and they jumped their horses apart like I'd thrown a bomb. Then they saw who it was, and they waited.

"Walkin' away to be married, children?" says I. Minnie drooped her head and blushed, and Dee looked foolish. And then I knew that old Andy Jackson was leaving Butterbowl. " 'Cause, if you are," says I, "you'd better get to running."

I waved my hand down the pass. The hardy pursuers were just pouring into the scenery. One look was enough. The eloping party began hittin' the high places. There didn't seem to be any call to tell 'em that wasn't the angry father, but just a few friends desiring to lynch me for causing my own death.

"Easy!" I says. "You needn't ride so fast, for you won't have to ride far. You're both of age, and Parson Duffy is coming, Johnny-on-the-spot, up the road a stretch. If you'd like to be married while you are still in peaceful Butterbowl, Petey and I'll be witnesses, and you can be man and wife before you turn over the divide. Does it go?"

They said it went. We slowed down till we met the preacher. I did the explaining.

"Mr. Duffy," says, I, "if you'll turn right around, we'd like to have you perform the marriage ceremony for this young couple, short but binding. You know them; they're of age and otherwise unmarried."

The Parson saw the avengers coming, and there's a twinkle in his eye. "You are in some haste, perhaps?" says he as he turns back.

"Oh, no hurry, no hurry at all; just lope right along," says I, as a couple of bullets whanged over our heads. Then we turned a curve out o' range. And by thunder, that old sport stood up in that rocking old buckboard and married them on the run!

I kissed the bride. "Be a good girl, honey," says I. "Lots of happiness to you both. I'm leaving here for keeps, and I'm giving Shelter to you two for a wedding-present—Mr. Duffy bein' witness. Good luck, Dee!" says I. "Be good to Deacon and Quaker—yes, and to Minnie too. Here's the summit. I'll stay here to check the maddened parent. No, there won't be any violence, Minnie. I'll give you my word. Just moral suasion. I got a heap of influence with the Butterbowl. Good-by!"

"Good-by!" said Dee, and "Good-by, Andy Jackson," said Minnie. "We'll not forget you. If you ever find the bird in the bush—or if you don't—come back to Shelter. It is always yours. We'll look for you. Good-by!"

We waited, sky-lighted on the summit.

The pass opened up wide; across in the east it framed off a big country I'd never seen. Petey and I got off our horses and let 'em puff and blow: the parson fixed up his tally of the marriage for us to sign. I laid one of my blood-money bills in the buckboard seat, for his fee.

"I'm going to stay just long enough for Joe to see us together," Petey snapped at me. "Then you pick one side of the world and I'll take the other."

"All right, Petey," says I. "I'll sorter fade away over into New Mexico. I have always liked that country."

Then the committee of unsafety arrived. Joe Only set his horse up and looked at me a long time, real sad.

"What in the name of the seven deadly sins have you been up to?" says he. "I made sure Simmons had murdered you. Why didn't he?"

"It's a pretty note," I says to him, real peevish and bitter. "When a couple of white, male, free American citizens can't attend a wedding without such a hullabaloo as this!"

"Weddin'!" says Chuck. "Weddin'?"

"Sure—Miss Minnie Briscoe and Mr. Dee Macfarlane. Didn't you get an invite? Petey and I we rode over to be witnesses. Didn't we, Petey?"

"Don't ask me," said Petey. "I have went!" And he did so.

"But what—why—where's Squatty? Who robbed the stage? How'd that money get back?" says Joe.

Outraged citizens was a-burnin' around the bend. I wished I might have seen Poppa once more, but I see this was no place for Andrew J. Bates. "You go back, Joe," says I. "You go back and explain to 'em."

Joe Only was much of a man, but he let his voice go up to a screech. "Explain? Explain! What'll I tell 'em?"

"How should I know?" says I, giving him a little push. "Just explain!" And I came away.

ERNEST HAYCOX

ERNEST HAYCOX (1899–1950) was born in Portland, Oregon. He spent his boyhood in logging camps, shingle mills, on ranches, and in small towns. He served with the National Guard on the Mexican border in 1916 and went to France for fourteen months with the American Expeditionary Force during World War I. After the war, he attended Reed College and was graduated from the University of Oregon in 1923 with a bachelor's degree. While still an undergraduate, Haycox started writing fiction, living in an abandoned chicken coop where he literally papered three walls with rejection slips before his stories began to sell. His early fiction was mostly sea stories, but by 1924 he was specializing in Western fiction and it was as a Western writer that he won his literary reputation.

What made a difference in Haycox' life was his leaving Oregon, after graduation and a short stint as a reporter for *The Oregonian,* and going to New York. There he met Jill Marie Chord, an artist from Oregon. They were married and moved back to Oregon, where Haycox lived for the rest of his life, raising a family—a son and a daughter—and renting an office in downtown Portland where he would go every day to write just as if it were a regular office job. "It seemed reasonable," Haycox once told his son, ". . . that a fellow who writes about the West ought to be able to live in it." For Haycox, the West symbolized not only a way of life, but a spiritual freedom, an antidote to disillusionment, no matter how fraught with hardship it might be. His relationship with Jill Marie deepened and matured his innate romanticism, and although he would scarcely have thought it possible for a woman to function *without* need of a man, conversely he did not think it was possible for a man to function adequately without a woman.

When he was starting out, Haycox' stories and serials ran in pulps like *West,* better-than-pulps like *Short Stories,* and by the middle thirties he was a constant contributor to *Collier's.* In the forties he was the leading Western writer for *The Saturday Evening Post.* He had to adhere to slick-magazine editorial policy in what he wrote, but even this does not prevent novels like *The Border Trumpet* (1939; reissued by the Gregg Press, 1978) and *Bugles in the Afternoon* (1944; reissued by the Gregg Press, 1978) from being fine romantic historical reconstructions. I must confess even to having enjoyed some of Haycox' more formulary efforts, such as *Sundown Jim* (Little, Brown, 1938), *Saddle and Ride* (Little, Brown, 1940) and *Rim of the Desert* (Little, Brown, 1941).

Yet, I believe Haycox was a far better short-story writer than he was a novelist. He came to rely on too many repetitive formulae in his novels for me to feel that he was completely comfortable with the form. In his short stories, he experimented; he introduced a wide variety of very real and sympathetic characters; he developed a wide number of unusual, but historically accurate, situations, and he probed into the inner workings of both the economics and social structures of the communities he created. His cavalry stories are very nearly as fine as those of James Warner Bellah at his best; his first-person narratives of a youth growing up in New Hope, Nebraska, are reminiscent of Ernest Hemingway's Nick Adams stories—and I do not think it accidental that Hemingway took pleasure in reading Haycox' fiction. *The Best Western Stories of Ernest Haycox* (New American Library, 1975) contains the complete collections *Rough Justice* (Little, Brown, 1950) and *Murder on the Frontier* (Little, Brown, 1953). Vicki Piekarski has introduced a hardbound reissue edition titled *Stagecoach and Other Stories* (Gregg Press, 1982), which contains *Rough Justice* and the stories from *By Rope and Lead* (Little, Brown, 1951). But the collections *Prairie Guns* and *Pioneer Loves* (Little, Brown, 1952) are as fine as any of the above, and *Powersmoke and Other Stories* (Avon, 1966), also out-of-print and even more difficult to find, shows how carefully designed and well executed were Haycox' early short stories for pulp magazines. The current neglect of the short story is nowhere more apparent than in the way so much of Haycox' best fiction languishes in undeserved obscurity—as do, to name only a very few examples, the short stories of Jack Schaefer, Dorothy M. Johnson, and Walter Van Tilburg Clark.

McQuestion Rides

When Matt McQuestion came through the throat of the low pass and paused to regard the ranch below he already had made a thorough and unobserved survey of the roundabout hills; and there was in him a rising belief that the man he wanted—a legal John Doe whose face he never had seen—was at present sheltered down there.

Proceeding down the slope, Matt McQuestion observed all things with the senses of an old hunter. A sodden, cloud-congested sky lent an uneasy dimness to the day, and the wind ripped wildly against higher trees to create the fury of some vast cataract pouring into a chasm. Faintly through this sounded the beating of the ranch triangle, announcing noon; a pair of riders cantered homeward from an opposite slope. House and outbuildings seemed to crouch beneath the tempest and in a distant hillside corral a bunch of horses stood passively dejected, backs humped and tails driven between their legs. As McQuestion drew beside the house porch a stout and florid man emerged.

"Light an' come in!" he bellowed. "Judas, what a day to fare forth! Lonny—come, take this horse to the barn!"

But the rider kept his place until he had observed the necessary amenities. "My name," said he, "is Matt McQuestion, sheriff of the county."

"Heard of you and mighty pleased to have you drum your knuckles against my door!" shouted the ranchman. "I'm French Broadrick! You're just in time to eat! Get down, sir, get down! We're too condemned polite for good health! Lonny, take the horse!"

McQuestion dismounted then, surrendered his pony to an appearing puncher and, at Broadrick's continued gesture, moved inside. Crossing to the bright maw of a fireplace, he stripped off slicker and hat while Broadrick kicked the door shut. The boom of the storm diminished to an endless muttering groan about the eaves, a table lamp thrust lanes of topaz light against the false shadows, and from some other part of the house rose a clatter of dishes. Broadrick rubbed his hands in front of him with a gusty, growling satisfaction and though there was now no need to raise his voice against the storm it had an unruly manner of smacking into the silence. "Mighty pleased to have you as a guest, Sheriff. Our trails have often crossed but this is my first pleasure of meetin' you in the flesh. Right ahead of you, sir, is the dinin'-room door."

The sheriff went through it and paused, at once becoming the target of a sudden scrutiny from eight men and a girl seated around the table; and as he stood there he seemed very little like a law officer who had spent the major part of his life in an exceedingly rough country. Dressed in neat black, he made a distinctly genteel, clerk-like appearance. Though tall, there was a worn fragility about him and the slight stoop of age. His wrists were thin, the hollows of neck and cheek considerably accented and a gaunt Adam's apple terminated a series of thoughtful features rendered almost melancholy by the presence of a drooping, silver-streaked mustache. A pair of mild blue eyes met the general stare diffidently and fell without seeming to have observed much of the scene.

"My crew," said Broadrick. "And my daughter, Marybelle. Boys, the sheriff. Be good now, blast you. Sheriff, the chair at my right."

McQuestion bowed slightly and sat down, observing the sharper interest of those at the table when his profession was mentioned. The girl sitting opposite him smiled and as this sudden light broke across her candid, boyish face there was a flash of spirit that at once commanded McQuestion's instant adherence. She was no more than twenty, unmarked as yet by the sadness of the sheriff's world. Pale gold hair ran softly above fair temples; and in the firm, fresh lines of shoulder and breast was the hint of a vital fire that would one day burst from its prison. She spoke with a lilting, melody-making voice: "Who could be bad enough to bring you out in weather like this, Sheriff?"

"Outlaws," said the sheriff, "always pick poor weather."

"You're on that kind of business?" asked French Broadrick.

McQuestion marked the pause of sound at the table. And because he was by inclination a poker player on an errand requiring the finesse of poker strategy, he let his words fall distinctly into the calm: "I'm lookin' for a man who passed this way about a week ago, wearin' butternut britches and ridin' a stockin'-legged strawberry."

The deep silence held. There was no reaction from the men although Matt McQuestion's mild glance unexpectedly ranged down the table, no longer diffident. French Broadrick offered a platter of beef to the sheriff, still casually jovial. "What crime?"

"Murder," said the sheriff bluntly.

"Murder?" grunted Broadrick, easy humor vanishing. "Murder, you say?" His big shoulders advanced on the sheriff. "Or justifiable homicide? There's a difference between the two things."

It was on the sheriff's tongue to explain the case but he checked the impulse. For he knew at that moment logic and instinct had made one of their infrequent unions. His man was on the ranch; more, his man was within the room. The knowledge came not from any overt signal or from the faces of the punchers who sat dull and stiff around him. It came from Marybelle Broadrick. At the word "murder" she flinched visibly. Her head came up and turned toward the crew, to be the next instant drawn back as if warned by an inner voice that this was betrayal. She stared now at McQuestion, plastic features losing color, rigidly still, and a mutely agitated query moving in her widening eyes. But this too was betrayal and she looked into her plate, hands withdrawn from the table.

French Broadrick spoke again, ruddy cheeks broken by concentric, scowling lines. "Murder or justifiable homicide, Sheriff?"

"Might be an argument in that," replied McQuestion, lying gravely. The girl's eyes lifted and touched him once more. He saw hope faintly replace bewilderment.

"What's his name?" pressed Broadrick.

"On the warrant it appears as John Doe."

"You don't know him?" said Broadrick, surprised.

"Never met the man. It's a blind chase after a stranger in the county. But the circumstantial evidence against him is mighty strong and there's a couple men who saw him from a distance when he was on the run."

"How in thunder do you expect to find him?" Broadrick wanted to know.

"One item is the horse."

"Which he could soon swap for another," countered Broadrick.

"The butternut pants," mused McQuestion.

"He's probably thrown 'em away," said Broadrick. "What's left? Nothing, it seems to me. I'd hate to start after a man on information as slim as that."

"One detail yet to mention," said the sheriff in a slowly casual manner that instantly tightened the interest of the room. "When we got to the scene there was the dead man, past tellin'. No witnesses and no messages. But a few feet from this dead man a dribble of blood ran along the rocks—no rain that day. The dribble went as far as some hoofprints. The hoofprints led away. You see? The dead man got in his shot before he fell and wherever this John Doe may be, he's packin' a hole in him that won't wash off."

There was a brief, awkward silence. The girl ventured another straight, momentary glance toward Matt McQuestion and he detected a stiffening antagonism in her which at once strengthened his estimate of her character. She was partisan by nature and her loyalty, once fixed, would never waver. She would close her eyes and go unflinchingly the whole distance, to hell or to heaven.

So, at least, the sheriff guessed—and felt a more profound admiration for her. French Broadrick cleared his throat, staring above the heads of his men. "Well, that's enough to hook him up with the shootin'. But if nobody saw this affair, then nobody knows what brought it about or the justice of it. And you ain't caught your man yet, Sheriff."

"The trail," said McQuestion, quietly, "leads this way." His coffee was cold from stirring. All the while he had been exploring the table and at each successive glance he discarded one puncher and another from his mind. It took a certain toughness of fiber and a certain mental make-up to run with the wild bunch. Most of these fellows were middle-aged, plainly old retainers and lacking the impulses of a gun-toter. But a pair of younger men at the foot of the table increasingly interested him. One was a tall, slim character with deep red hair and a remarkably rippling coördination of muscle and nerve that expressed itself in each restless shift of his body. The other sat stolidly silent, dark and rugged and a fighter in every observable fiber. Contrasting the two, he heard French Broadrick bring the dinner to a curt close. "We'll go on with the work in the sheds this afternoon."

Rising with the rest, McQuestion let his eyes follow the crew out of a dining-room door as they filed into a rain-soaked yard. The red-haired man walked slowly and he took the descending steps with a faint stiffening of his carriage. The more rugged man brought up the rear; looking back, he caught the sheriff's glance and closed the door swiftly as he passed through. Somehow the gesture seemed almost protective of the red-head. McQuestion preceded his host into the living-room and put his back to the cheerful flames. The girl had disappeared. Broadrick moved aimlessly about the room, mind obviously struggling with a difficult thought. Presently he came to a stand in front of the sheriff, bluntly speaking: "You've told mighty little of the story. What's the rest of it?"

The blue glance of the sheriff narrowed against the firelight; still holding his place, he answered Broadrick: "In my life I've frequently had the disposition of some fellow's future at my command. It's no easy thing to play the part of judge and I'll not say I always decided right. It weighs on me sometimes—the mistakes I made. I'm slower to act than I used to be. Any sucker can make an arrest. The difficult thing is to know when not to."

Broadrick's face was increasingly somber. "If this John Doe's what you say, where's the problem?"

"Unless I'm wrong he's not the only one to consider now," said the sheriff.

There was a quickening light in French Broadrick's eyes and a sudden ridging of face muscles. "I understand how you get your reputation. You're a lone old wolf, McQuestion."

McQuestion nodded, knowing then Broadrick grasped the situation. He knew, too, that whatever the final issue, Broadrick would never reveal the hunted man. It was one of the oldest laws of the range—sanctuary of a sort. If there was trouble, Broadrick was prepared to settle it in his own way, within the confines of the ranch. Comprehending this, McQuestion reached for his slicker and hat. "I'll be lookin' after my horse," he explained and passed back through the dining-room. When he stepped into the sheeting, tempestuous descent of rain he heard the girl's voice rising from another part of the house, troubled and high-pitched. The barn was straight ahead; left of it stood the bunkhouse in which the crew idled through noon. To the right of the barn and past the last outlying corrals he saw again that hillside compound where the loose stock was held; but, though his attention straightened on that area, the dull gloom of the day defeated his search for a stocking-legged strawberry. He entered the gray alley of the stable, found a section of clean burlap and proceeded to rub down his pony.

His chore was not done when he abandoned it, left the barn and walked toward the bunkhouse, through the windows of which glimmered a fogged, crystal lamplight. Opening the door with a preliminary rattle—he wanted no surprises yet—he went into quarters similar to a thousand others throughout the land.

A solid, rugged young man reared up from one of the lower bunks, bawling gravely: "Have a chair, sir."

"Thanks, but I'll stand," was McQuestion's courteous answer. "Been sittin' in leather all day long."

"And a poor day to travel," said the rugged one in the manner of a man making talk to be agreeable.

"Can't pick and choose," replied the sheriff, letting his glance stray. All the lower bunks were filled, but only one upper. That was occupied by the red-head, who lay sprawled on his back. The red-head stared above him, cigarette drooping from a lip corner, and without turning to the sheriff he spoke with a lazy, sardonic drawl:

"Outlaws should be more considerate of the constituted authorities."

"Well, Red," said the sheriff, "as long as they're considerate enough to leave tracks behind, I'm not carin' about the weather."

"Did this one?" queried Red, making no comment on the sheriff's application of a nickname.

"Yes."

"Mighty careless of him," mused Red. "Must of been a greenhorn."

"I'll know more about that later," said McQuestion, and then silence again descended upon the room—silence of men guarding their tongues.

"Time," said the rugged one, "to get back on the job."

He opened the door and went out, other punchers rising to follow slowly. Red rolled, put his feet over the edge of the bunk frame and let himself to the floor carefully, knees springing when he landed; and for a moment he faced the sheriff, grinning out of a wide, thin mouth. He was not handsome. The conformation of his face was too angular and his eyes a too definite and unblinking green. But beneath the surface was a personality not to be mistaken, one at once restless, dominating, utterly self-certain. McQuestion caught the hard, unruffled competence behind that grin, and a lurking mockery.

"Was he a bad man at heart, Sheriff? Real bad?"

"I'm wonderin', Red," said the sheriff. "And I hope to find out."

Red turned casually and left the bunkhouse, a shadow of stiffness in his gait. McQuestion wheeled slowly where he stood, making a complete circle and taking in once more all that the room had to offer him. But it was an unnecessary move, for he knew then the identity of John Doe. "It's Red, for a certainty," he muttered. "The heavy boy with the good face is out of it."

But, strangely enough, the more or less definite end of his quest left him without the usual elation, without the hardening impulses preliminary to a capture. And as he paused in the open doorway another incident appeared through the weaving screen of rain to sway the even balance of his mind. Yonder on a side porch at the house Marybelle Broadrick stood beside Red, looking up to him and talking with swift gestures of her hands. Red was smiling. The smile broadened and he shook his head; one hand touched the girl's shoulder in a manner that seemed to the sheriff possessive and confident. The girl's body swayed back slightly and Red, turning, crossed the yard to an open shed. McQuestion, bent on having an answer to the increasing problem in his mind, ambled likewise to the shed and loitered there. An added hour or day didn't matter. There was such a thing as charity, even above justice, and that did matter. So, idling in the shed, he watched the working men with a patient interest.

In a kind of orderly confusion they were overhauling the ranch gear. At the forge one of the punchers bent livid iron over the anvil with swift, ringing strokes of his hammer. Another filed mower blades. The carpenter of the outfit ripped a board, saw whining into the anvil echoes. Meanwhile, the foreman had attacked a heavier chore. Pressing his back to a wagon frame, he began to lift, all his broad muscles swelling with the pressure. A helper stood by, attempting to slide a jack beneath the rising axle; but the weight was unwieldy and difficult to manage. Releasing his grip, the foreman looked about to find an unoccupied hand. His eyes touched the red-head slouching indolently at the forge and the sheriff saw the level features of the rugged one tighten up with a cool speculation. But it was only for a moment; the foreman called to another: "Bill, give me a hand here."

The red-head was aware of the fact that he had been passed by. The smiling irony of his face increased to a grin and he spoke to the crew generally: "Mighty muscles of our straw boss seem to grow weary."

"But not my tongue," observed the foreman, softly.

"Meanin' mine wags too much, uh?" murmured Red, grin widening. "Old son, you ought to be learnin' by now that muscle is cheap and brain rare. Anybody can sweat but blamed few can scheme well."

The appointed Bill came forward to help at the wagon, but the foreman stood still, features frowning on Red with an even-tempered concentration. "That may well be," he drawled. "But I'm inclined to wonder where the schemin' led. Consider it," he added gently, "as an idle question."

McQuestion turned from the shed and walked to the house, head bent against the rain and his blue glance kindling. "He could of asked Red to put a shoulder against that wagon. He could of made Red suffer with that game leg and let me catch on to the fact Red packed the injury. But he didn't because he's a dead sound sport. And how does Red pay back the compliment? By goadin' the foreman. He understands he's safe on these premises and so he uses his sharp tongue to hurt. Reckless—and a mite of a fool. There's one crooked play to his credit but the chance is still open to him to go straight, if he wanted. Hard to tell how this girl, if he got her, would affect him. She might pull him right, but if she didn't he'd force her to his own sad level. He's got a glitter—and that attracts her now."

The living-room, when he reached it, was empty. Saddle-weary, he sank into a leather arm chair, and fell into a doze. When he woke the room was darker and the pound of the storm had increased. Out on the front porch voices rose, suppressed but still near enough for him to hear. The girl was talking swiftly: "I know you wouldn't give him away. You're not that kind, Lee. I only asked what you thought of him, now that the sheriff has told us the story."

"Why ask me?" countered the foreman's voice, blunt and angry. "What difference does it make to me? I'm not his keeper, and not yours."

"Lee, it means nothing to you? Look at me and say that!"

"One of us is a fool, Marybelle. I can look at you and say this much. I have played faithful Rover around here a long time. I seemed to get along fine until he came here. Not beefin' about it, either. If you like him it's your business. And you brought this up. Don't expect me to tattle on him."

The girl said: "I'm not fickle! I like him—but I want to

know what men think of him. Lee, can't you understand a girl doubts her heart sometimes?"

"Better make up your mind. I'm not stayin' on the ranch if he does. We don't mix."

"Lee—you'd go! Would it be that easy for you?"

"Easy or hard, I'm not playin' faithful Rover any more. If you want him I'll not complain. But I ride—as soon as the sheriff leaves."

There was a prolonged silence, ended at last by the girl. "I never knew you cared that much, till now. Or that you cared at all. You have never spoken, Lee."

"Good lord, Marybelle! Where's your eyes?"

"Looking for something they couldn't find till this minute, Lee."

They moved away. McQuestion looked at his watch and found it beyond three. Rising, he picked up his hat and walked out into the gloom, adding fresh fuel to his thoughts. "The foreman was high card until Red came. The girl's troubled by his han'some manners. There's a little of the gambler in her and she catches the same thing in Red. But she ain't quite gone on him yet."

He came to an interested halt. A pair of men filed across the yard with a wagon tongue between them. The red-head held the front end of it, now limping obviously. Once he turned and called back to the other man, who twisted the tongue about to a different angle. The red-head slipped to his knees, dropped the tongue and ran back. There was a set rage on his cheeks, visible even through the murk, and his mouth framed some round, violent word. Deliberately he slapped the other man with both his palms and strode away. McQuestion withdrew, grumbling under his breath:

"So, he'll never soften up. That's the part the girl don't see. He'd destroy her, break her. What good's a bright mind if the heart's rotten?"

French Broadrick entered from the front, water cascading down his slicker. Marybelle came in from the kitchen, slim and graceful against the lamplight. Seeing her, Matt McQuestion's mind closed vault-like on all that he had learned this dismal afternoon. "I'm ridin'," said he, and moved toward his slicker.

"In this weather?" queried Broadrick. "Wait it out. Till mornin' anyhow."

"Spent too much time on a cold trail," said McQuestion. "Should be back in Sun Ford this minute tendin' more necessary business. I'm grateful for your hospitality."

Broadrick's round face was strictured by inquisitive lines and he stood there surveying McQuestion like a man listening beyond the spoken words. Marybelle rested silent in the background.

"You asked me if it was justifiable homicide or murder," proceeded the sheriff. "I'll tell you. This John Doe was out in the hills tamperin' with somebody else's beef. A line rider heaves over the rim. John Doe does a natural thing—slings lead. He takes a bullet in reply but his first shot lands the line rider in the dirt. The line rider lies there, alive. John Doe does what only a natural and cold killer would do. Steppin' up close, he puts a second bullet into the back of the man's skull. Personally, I consider that murder. I bid you good day."

The girl's fists slowly tightened; a small sigh escaped her. McQuestion bowed and moved toward the dining-room, Broadrick following. Together they walked to the barn where McQuestion saddled. When the sheriff swung up and turned to leave the barn, Broadrick broke the long silence:

"You're a wolf, a gray old wolf. I don't get all this and I ain't goin' to try. But my next chore is to get your picture and hang it on my wall. So long, and the Lord bless you."

"See you sometime," said McQuestion, and rode into the yard. The foreman was at that minute leaving the shed and McQuestion swerved to intercept the man and to lean down.

"My boy," he said, "forty-one years ago I lost a girl because I was mighty proud and stiff. Along came another man who had the grace to speak his piece. And I've been a little lonesome ever since. You've got to tell the ladies what they want to hear. Adiós."

Well away from the house, he turned from his due northern course, broke into a steady run and cut about the little valley, through heavy timber and across rugged defiles. Half an hour later, he arrived at a road coursing to the south—the exit from Broadrick's as well as the exit from the county. There was, a few rods above the road, a tumbled confusion of rocks. He placed his horse behind them, dismounted and crawled to an uncomfortable station beside the road.

"Man never knows," he grumbled, "whether his monkeyin' with the course of fated events is wise or not. And—"

He raised his rifle, training it on a figure suddenly coming around a near bend from the Broadrick ranch. Fifty yards closer the rider became Red, who advanced slackly on a stocking-legged strawberry horse. McQuestion turned the safety of his rifle and cast a metallic, thin order through the wind:

"Hands up—and sudden!"

Red reined in, made a confused move toward his gun, saw nothing for a target, and reached to the leaking heavens.

"Get down—put your back to me—lift your gun gently and throw it behind!"

Again Red obeyed. McQuestion rose and walked forward. The red-head twisted his head, recognized the sheriff then, and wrenched his whole body about. The reckless face broke into long lines of passion. "Sheriff! How'd you figger this?"

McQuestion paused, all adrip. Nothing showed clear between hat brim and slicker collar but two blue eyes. "I've done this for thirty years, Red. I ought to know. Broadrick wouldn't betray you. But after what I told him, I was pretty sure, he'd never tolerate you another minute on the ranch. He'd give you your horse and tell you to lope. Which way would you travel? South, because that's out of the county and opposite the direction you saw me go."

The red-head shook with greater fury; the blaze of his eyes grew hotter, brighter, half crazed. "Damn you—damn you forever! You lied about me! I never put a second shot in that line rider's skull! That's what stuck in Broadrick's craw! He believed it and he couldn't stand it! And the girl stared at me like I was a monster! I'll kill you for that lie—before God I will!"

"Yeah," said the sheriff, "I lied. But I gave you an even break—until you belted that puncher in the face for twistin' your bad leg. Then I knew what you'd do to the girl if you ever got her. There's a better man left behind to take care of Marybelle. So I lied. Still, I think the ample folds of justice will cover it. Say adiós to the land, Red. Say adiós. You'll see it no more."

PART THREE

THE WEST OF THE STORYTELLERS

ZANE GREY

ZANE GREY (1872–1939) was born Pearl Zane Gray at Zanesville, Ohio, and was graduated from the University of Pennsylvania in 1896 with a degree in dentistry. He conducted a practice in New York City from 1898 to 1904, meanwhile striving to become a writer. He met Lina Elise Roth in 1900 and in 1905 they were married. With Lina Grey's help, Grey published his first novel himself, *Betty Zane* (Charles Francis Press, 1903). Closing his dental office shortly after his marriage, the Greys moved into a cottage on the Delaware River, near Lackawaxen, Pennsylvania.

Although it took most of her savings, it was Lina Grey who insisted that Grey take his first trip to Arizona in 1907 with C. J ."Buffalo" Jones, a retired buffalo hunter. In point of fact, Grey couldn't have been more fortunate in his choice of a mate. Lina Grey assisted him in every way he desired and yet left him alone when he demanded solitude; trained in English at Hunter College, she proofread every manuscript he wrote and polished his prose; she managed all financial affairs and permitted Grey, once he began earning a good income, to indulge himself at will in his favorite recreations, hunting and fishing.

After his return to the East, Grey wrote *The Heritage of the Desert* (Harper's, 1910), which remains one of his finest novels. The profound effect that the desert had had on him was vibrantly captured so that, after all these years, it still comes alive for the reader. In a way, too, it established the pattern Grey would use in much of his subsequent Western fiction. Ann Ronald summed it up in her chapbook *Zane Grey* (Idaho State University Press, 1975):

> An Easterner—that is, an innocent—arrives in the West. He, or she, has been a failure in the past and seems unprepared to meet the challenges ahead. The land at first seems harsh and unforgiving—the sun is too hot, the canyons too deep, the peaks too rugged, the rivers too swift. Problems are compounded by the appearance of evil, of men who live by their guns and who care nothing for the rights of others. Gradually, however, the neophyte becomes a man. Rather than be beaten by the environment, he learns to conquer the elements, and in doing so he acquires a deep appreciation for the land. Rather than see innocent people tormented by evil, he learns to fight and to protect those he has come to love. The West, seeming almost a Garden of Eden, becomes a proving ground for man. Here he loses his innocence and gains knowledge. In Grey's words, the hero learns "the heritage of the desert" exactly as the author did on his first trip with Buffalo Jones, and exactly as he hopes the reader will do while reading his novels.

Even more than with Bret Harte, the modern tendency is to dismiss Grey; and, unlike Harte, Grey was never a favorite to begin with among literary critics. It is, of course, all a matter of inclination and I, for one, as much as I prefer reading Western history to much of the fiction written about it, somehow always find time in the course of a year to read a book or two by Zane Grey. His can be the sheerest and richest fantasy, and it is nowhere more resplendent than in *Riders of the Purple Sage* (Harper's, 1912) and its sequel, *The Rainbow Trail* (Harper's, 1915).

Nas Ta Bega, a Navajo, is a character who overshadows *The Rainbow Trail* and I think you are more likely to remember him after you have closed the book than any other aspect of the novel. Grey drew him from life. His real name was Nasjha Be Gay, and he was a Piute Indian guide who led the first white men—the Cummings Weatherill expedition—to the Rainbow Bridge in 1908, and he led Zane Grey there in 1913. Nasjha Be Gay died in the influenza epidemic which hit the Navajo reservation in 1918, but his spirit has been perpetuated by Grey in the novel he wrote.

"The Desert Crucible," which follows, is actually a section of the serialized version of *The Rainbow Trail* that appeared under this former title in *Argosy* in 1915. Loren Grey, youngest son of Zane Grey and executor of the Grey literary estate, included a longer version of it in *Yaqui and Other Great Indian Stories* (Belmont Tower, 1976). In the section I have included, John Shefford narrates events which are familiar to whoever has read *Riders of the Purple Sage*; later Shefford and Nas Ta Bega become friends. The native American has always regarded friendship differently than many white Americans. As cynical as I have often been, those occasions when a native American has addressed me as a friend—and treated me as a friend—have had about them for me a quality approaching the sacred. Maybe that is one of the reasons I so like this story.

The Desert Crucible

Shefford at first saw nothing except the monotonous gray valley reaching far to the strange, grotesque monuments of yellow cliff. Then, close under the foot of the slope, he espied two squat stone houses with red roofs, and a corral with a pool of water shining in the sun.

The trail leading down was steep and sandy, but it was not long. Shefford's sweeping eyes appeared to take in everything at once—the crude stone structures with their earthen roofs, the piles of dirty wool, the Indians lolling around, the tents, and wagons, and horses, little lazy burrows and dogs, and scattered everywhere, saddles, blankets, guns, and packs.

Then a white man came out of the door. He waved a hand and shouted. Dust and wool and flour were thick upon him. He was muscular and weatherbeaten, and appeared young in activity rather than face. A gun swung at his hip and a row of brass-tipped cartridges showed in his belt. Shefford looked into a face that he thought he had seen before, until he realized the similarity was only the bronze and hard line and rugged cast common to desert men. The gray searching eyes went right through him.

"Glad to see you. Get down and come in. I'm the trader Withers," he said to Shefford. His voice was welcoming and the grip of his hand made Shefford's ache.

Shefford told his name and said he was as glad as he was lucky to arrive at Kayenta.

Withers led Shefford by the first stone house, which evidently was the trading-store, into the second. The room Shefford entered was large, with logs smouldering in a huge open fireplace, blankets covering every foot of floor space, Indian baskets and silver ornaments everywhere, and strange Indian designs painted upon the whitewashed walls. Withers called his wife and made her acquainted with Shefford. She was a slight, comely little woman, with keen, earnest, dark eyes. She seemed to be serious and quiet, but she made Shefford feel at home immediately. He refused, however, to accept the room offered him, saying that he meant to sleep out under the open sky. Withers laughed at this and said he understood.

"Sure am glad you rode in," said Withers, for the fourth time. "Now you make yourself at home. Stay here—come over to the store—do what you like. I've got to work. Tonight we'll talk."

That night after supper, when Withers and Shefford sat alone before the blazing logs in the huge fireplace, the trader laid his hand on Shefford's and said, with directness and force:

"I've lived my life in the desert. I've met many men and have been a friend to most. . . . You're no prospector or trader or missionary?"

"No," replied Shefford.

"You've had trouble?"

"Perhaps I wronged myself, but no one else," replied Shefford, steadily.

"I reckoned so. Well, tell me, or keep your secret—it's all one to me."

Shefford felt a desire to unburden himself. This man was strong, persuasive, kindly. He drew Shefford.

"You're welcome in Kayenta," went on Withers. "Stay as long as you like. I take no pay from a white man. If you want work I have it plenty."

"Thank you. That is good. I need to work. We'll talk of it later. . . . But just yet I can't tell you why I came to Kayenta, what I want to do, how long I shall stay. My thoughts put in words would seem so like dreams. Maybe they are dreams. Perhaps I'm only chasing a phantom—perhaps I'm only hunting the treasure at the foot of the rainbow."

"Well, this is the country for rainbows," laughed Withers. "In summer from June to August when it storms we have rainbows that'll make you think you're in another world. The Navajos have rainbow mountains, rainbow canyons, rainbow bridges of stone, rainbow trails. It sure is rainbow country."

That deep and mystic chord in Shefford thrilled. Here it was again—something tangible at the bottom of his dream.

Withers did not wait for Shefford to say any more, and almost as if he read his visitor's mind he began to talk about the wild country he called home.

He had lived at Kayenta for several years—hard and profitless years by reason of marauding outlaws. He could not have lived there at all but for the protection of the Indians. His father-in-law had been friendly with the Navajos and Piutes for many years, and his wife had been brought up among them. She was held in peculiar reverence and affection by both tribes in that part of the country. Probably she knew more of the Indians' habits, religion, and life than any white person in the West. Both tribes were friendly and peaceable, but there were bad Indians, half-breeds, and outlaws that made the trading-post a venture Withers had long considered precarious, and he wanted to move and intended to some day. His nearest white neighbors in New Mexico and Colorado were a hundred miles distant and at some seasons the roads were impassable. To the north, however, twenty miles or so, was situated a Mormon village named Stonebridge. It lay across the Utah line. Withers did some business with this village, but scarcely enough to warrant the risks he had to run. During the last year he had lost several pack-trains, one of which he had never heard of after it left Stonebridge.

"Stonebridge!" exclaimed Shefford, and he trembled. He had heard that name. In his memory it had a place beside the name of another village Shefford longed to speak of to this trader.

"Yes—Stonebridge," replied Withers. "Ever heard the name?"

"I think so. Are there other villages in—in that part of the country?"

"A few, but not close. Glaze is now only a water-hole. Bluff and Monticello are far north across the San Juan. . . . There used to be another village—but that wouldn't interest you."

"Withers, pardon an impertinence—I am deeply serious. . . . Are you a Mormon?"

"Indeed I'm not," replied the trader, instantly.

"Are you for the Mormons or against them?"

"Neither. I get along with them. I know them. I believe they are a misunderstood people."

"That's for them."

"No. I'm only fair-minded."

Shefford paused, trying to curb his thrilling impulse, but it was too strong.

"You said there used to be another village. . . . Was the name of it—Cottonwoods?"

Withers gave a start and faced round to stare at Shefford in blank astonishment.

"You're no spy on the lookout for sealed wives?"

"Absolutely not. I don't even know what you mean by sealed wives."

"Well, it's damn strange that you'd know the name Cottonwoods. . . . Yes, that's the name of the village I meant—the one that used to be. It's gone now, all except a few stone walls."

"What became of it?"

"Torn down by Mormons years ago. They destroyed it and moved away. I've heard Indians talk about a grand spring that was there once. It's gone, too. Its name was—let me see—"

"Amber Spring," interrupted Shefford.

"By George, you're right!" rejoined the trader, again amazed. "Shefford, this beats me. I haven't heard that name for ten years. I can't help seeing what a tenderfoot—stranger—you are to the desert. Yet, here you are—speaking of what you should know nothing of . . . And there's more behind this."

Shefford rose, unable to conceal his agitation.

"Did you ever hear of a rider named Venters?"

"Rider? You mean a cowboy? Venters. No, I never heard that name."

"Did you ever hear of a gunman named Lassiter?" queried Shefford, with increasing emotion.

"No."

"Did you ever hear of a Mormon woman named—Jane Withersteen?"

"No."

Shefford drew his breath sharply. He had followed a gleam—he had caught a fleeting glimpse of it.

"Did you ever hear of a child—a girl—a woman—called Fay Larkin?"

Withers rose slowly with a paling face.

"If you're a spy it'll go hard with you—though I'm no Mormon," he said, grimly.

Shefford lifted a shaking hand.

"I *was* a clergyman. Now I'm nothing—a wanderer—least of all a spy."

Withers leaned closer to see into the other man's eyes; he looked long and then appeared satisfied.

"I've heard the name Fay Larkin," he said slowly. "I reckon that's all I'll say till you tell your story."

Shefford stood with his back to the fire and he turned the palms of his hands to catch the warmth. He felt cold. Withers had affected him strangely. What was the meaning of the trader's sombre gravity? Why was the very mention of Mormons attended by something austere and secret?

"My name is John Shefford. I am twenty-four," began Shefford. "My family—"

Here a knock on the door interrupted Shefford.

"Come in," called Withers.

The door opened and like a shadow Nas Ta Bega slipped in. He said something in Navajo to the trader.

"How," he said to Shefford, and extended his hand. He was stately, but there was no mistaking his friendliness. Then he sat down before the fire, doubled his legs under him after the Indian fashion, and with dark eyes on the blazing logs seemed to lose himself in meditation.

"He likes the fire," explained Withers. "Whenever he comes to Kayenta he always visits me like this. . . . Don't mind him. Go on with your story."

"My family were plain people, well-to-do, and very religious," went on Shefford. "When I was a boy we moved from the country to a town called Beaumont, Illinois. There was a college in Beaumont and eventually I was sent to it to study for the ministry. I wanted to be— But never mind that. . . . By the time I was twenty-two I was ready for my career as a clergyman. I preached for a year around at different places and then got a church in my home town of Beaumont. I became exceedingly good friends of a man named Venters, who had recently come to Beaumont. He was a singular man. His wife was a strange, beautiful woman, very reserved, and she had wonderful dark eyes. They had money and were devoted to each other, and perfectly happy. They owned the finest horses ever seen in Illinois, and their particular enjoyment seemed to be riding. They were always taking long rides. It was something worth going far for to see Mrs. Venters on a horse.

"It was through my own love of horses that I became friendly with Venters. He and his wife attended my church.

and as I got to see more of them, gradually we grew intimate. And it was not until I did get intimate with them that I realized that both seemed to be haunted by the past. They were sometimes sad even in their happiness. They drifted off into dreams. They lived back in another world. They seemed to be listening. Indeed, they were a singularly interesting couple, and I grew genuinely fond of them. By and by they had a little girl whom they named Jane. The coming of the baby made a change in my friends. They were happier, and I observed that the haunting shadow did not so often return.

"Venters had spoken of a journey West that he and his wife meant to take some time. But after the baby came he never mentioned his wife in connection with the trip. I gathered that he felt compelled to go to clear up a mystery or to find something—I did not make out just what. But eventually, and it was about a year ago, he told me his story—the strangest, wildest, and most tragic I ever heard.

"I can't tell it all now. It is enough to say that fifteen years before he had been a rider for a rich Mormon woman named Jane Withersteen, of this village Cottonwoods. She had adopted a beautiful Gentile child named Fay Larkin. Her interest in Gentiles earned the displeasure of her churchmen, and as she was proud there came a breach. Venters and a gunman named Lassiter became involved in her quarrel. Finally Venters took to the canyons. Here in the wilds he found the strange girl he eventually married. For a long time they lived in a wonderful hidden valley, the entrance to which was guarded by a huge balancing rock. Venters got away with the girl. But Lassiter and Jane Withersteen and the child Fay Larkin were driven into the canyon. They escaped to the valley where Venters had lived. Lassiter rolled the balancing rock, and, crashing down the narrow trail, it loosened the weathered walls and closed the narrow outlet forever."

Shefford ended his narrative out of breath, pale and dripping with sweat. Withers sat leaning forward with an expression of intense interest. Nas Ta Bega's easy, graceful pose had succeeded to one of strained rigidity. He seemed a statue of bronze. Could a few intelligible words, Shefford wondered, have created that strange, listening posture?

"Venters got out of Utah, of course, as you know," went on Shefford. "He got out, knowing—as I feel I would have known—that Jane, Lassiter, and little Fay Larkin were shut up, walled up in Surprise Valley. For years Venters considered it would not have been safe for him to venture to rescue them. He had no fears for their lives. They could live in Surprise Valley. But Venters always intended to come back with Bess and find the valley and his friends. No wonder he and Bess were haunted. However, when his wife had the baby that made a difference. It meant he had to go alone. And he was thinking seriously of starting when I—when there were developments that made it desirable for me to leave Beaumont. Venters' story haunted me as he had been haunted. I dreamed of that wild valley—of little Fay Larkin grown to womanhood—such a woman as Bess Venters was. And the longing to come was great. . . . And, Withers—here I am."

The trader reached out and gave Shefford the grip of a man in whom emotion was powerful, but deep and difficult to express.

"Listen to this . . . I wish I could help you. Life is a queer deal . . . Shefford, I've got to trust you. Over here in the wild canyon country there's a village of Mormons' sealed wives. It's in Arizona, perhaps twenty miles from here, and near the Utah line. When the United States government began to persecute, or prosecute, the Mormons for polygamy, the Mormons over in Stonebridge took their sealed wives and moved them out of Utah, just across the line. They built houses, established a village there. I'm the only Gentile who knows about it. And I pack supplies every few weeks in to these women. There are perhaps fifty women, mostly young—second or third or fourth wives of Mormons—sealed wives. And I want you to understand that sealed means *sealed* in all that religion or loyalty can get out of the word. There are also some old women and old men in the village, but they hardly count. And there's a flock of the finest children you ever saw in your life.

"The idea of the Mormons must have been to escape prosecution. The law of the government is one wife for each man—no more. All over Utah polygamists have been arrested. The Mormons are deeply concerned. I believe they are a good, law-abiding people. But this law is a direct blow at their religion. In my opinion they can't obey both. And therefore they have not altogether given up plural wives. Perhaps they will some day. I have no proof, but I believe the Mormons of Stonebridge pay secret night visits to their sealed wives across the line in the lonely, hidden village.

"Now once over in Stonebridge I overheard some Mormons talking about a girl who was named Fay Larkin. I never forgot the name. Later I heard the name in this sealed-wife village. But, as I told you, I never heard of Lassiter or Jane Withersteen. Still, if Mormons had found them I would never have heard of it . . . I'm not surprised at your rainbow-chasing adventure. It's a great story . . . This Fay Larkin I've heard of *might* be your Fay Larkin—I almost believe so. Shefford, I'll help you find out."

"Yes, yes—I must know," replied Shefford. "Oh, I hope, I pray we can find her! But—I'd rather she was dead—if she's not still hidden in the valley."

"Naturally. You've dreamed yourself into rescuing this lost Fay Larkin . . . But, Shefford, you're old enough to know life doesn't work out as you want it to. One way or another I fear you're in for a bitter disappointment."

"Withers, take me to the village."

"Shefford, you're liable to get in bad out here," said the trader gravely.

"I couldn't be any more ruined than I am now," replied Shefford, passionately.

"But there's risk in this—risk such as you never had," persisted Withers.

"I'll risk anything."

"Reckon this's a funny deal for a sheep-trader to have on his hands," continued Withers. "Shefford, I like you. I've a mind to see you through this. It's a damn strange story . . . I'll tell you what—I will help you. I'll give you a job packing supplies into the village. I meant to turn that over to a Mormon cowboy—Joe Lake. The job shall be yours, and I'll go with you first trip. Here's my hand on it . . . Now, Shefford, I'm more curious about you than I was before you told your story. What ruined you? As we're to be partners, you can tell me now. I'll keep your secret. Maybe I can do you good."

Shefford wanted to confess, yet it was hard. Perhaps, had he not been so agitated, he would not have answered to impulse. But this trader was a man—a man of the desert—he would understand.

"I told you I was a clergyman," said Shefford in low voice. "I didn't want to be one, but they made me one. I did my best. I failed. . . . I had doubts of religion—of the Bible—of God, as my church believed in them. As I grew older thought and study convinced me of the narrowness of religion as my congregation lived it. I preached what I believed. I alienated them. They put me out, took my calling from me, disgraced me, ruined me."

"So that's all!" exclaimed Withers, slowly. "You didn't believe in the God of the Bible. . . . Well, I've been in the desert long enough to know there *is* a God, but probably not the one your church worships. . . . Shefford, go to the Navajo for a faith!"

Shefford had forgotten the presence of Nas Ta Bega, and perhaps Withers had likewise. At this juncture the Indian rose to his full height, and he folded his arms to stand with the sombre pride of a chieftain while his dark, inscrutable eyes were riveted upon Shefford. At that moment he seemed magnificent. The difference was obscure to Shefford. But he felt that it was there in the Navajo's mind. Nas Ta Bega's strange look was not to be interpreted. Presently he turned and passed from the room.

"By George!" cried Withers, suddenly, and he pounded his knee with his fist. "I'd forgotten."

"What?" ejaculated Shefford.

"Why, that Indian understood every word we said. He knows English. He's educated. Well, if this doesn't beat me. . . . Let me tell you about Nas Ta Bega."

Withers appeared to be recalling something half forgotten.

"Years ago, in fifty-seven, I think, Kit Carson with his soldiers chased the Navajo tribes and rounded them up to be put on reservations. But he failed to catch all the members of one tribe. They escaped up into wild canyons like the Sagi. The descendants of these fugitives live there now and are the finest Indians on earth—the finest because they're unspoiled by the white man. Well, as I got the story, years after Carson's round-up one of his soldiers guided some interested travellers in there. When they left they took an Indian boy with them to educate. From what I know of Navajos I'm inclined to think the boy was taken against his parents' wish. Anyway, he was taken. That boy was Nas Ta Bega. The story goes that he was educated somewhere. Years afterward, and perhaps not long before I came in here, he returned to his people. There have been missionaries and other interested fools who have given Indians a white man's education. In all the instances I know of, these educated Indians returned to their tribes, repudiating the white man's knowledge, habits, life, and religion. I have heard that Nas Ta Bega came back, laid down the white man's clothes along with the education, and never again showed that he had known either.

"You have just seen how strangely he acted. It's almost certain he heard our conversation. Well, it doesn't matter. He won't tell. He can hardly be made to use an English word.

Besides, he's a noble red man, if there ever was one. He has been a friend in need to me. If you stay long out here you'll learn something from the Indians."

Later Shefford went outdoors to walk and think. There was no moon, but the stars made light enough to cast his shadow on the ground. The dark, illimitable expanse of blue sky seemed to be glittering with numberless points of fire. The air was cold and still. A dreaming silence lay over the land. Shefford saw and felt all these things, and their effect was continuous and remained with him and helped calm him. He was conscious of a burden removed from his mind. Confession of his secret had been like tearing a thorn from his flesh, but, once done, it afforded him relief and a singular realization that out here it did not matter much. In a crowd of men all looking at him and judging him by their standards he had been made to suffer. Here, if he were judged at all, it would be by what he could do, how he sustained himself and helped others.

He walked far across the valley toward the low bluffs, but they did not seem to get any closer. And, finally, he stopped beside a stone and looked around at the strange horizon and up at the heavens. He did not feel utterly aloof from them, nor alone in a waste, nor a useless atom amid incomprehensible forces. Something like a loosened mantle fell from about him, dropping down at his feet; and all at once he was conscious of freedom. He did not understand in the least why abasement left him, but it was so. He had come a long way, in bitterness, in despair, believing himself to be what men had called him. The desert and the stars and the wind, the silence of the night, the loneliness of this vast country where there was room for a thousand cities—these somehow vaguely, yet surely, bade him lift his head. They withheld their secret, but they made a promise. The thing which he had been feeling every day and every night was a strange enveloping comfort. And it was at this moment that Shefford, divining whence his help was to come, embraced all that wild and speaking Nature around and above and surrendered himself utterly.

"I am young. I am free. I have my life to live," he said. "I'll be a man. I'll take what comes. Let me learn here!"

When he had spoken out, settled once and for ever his attitude toward his future, he seemed to be born again, wonderfully alive to the influences around him, ready to trust what yet remained a mystery.

Then his thoughts reverted to Fay Larkin. Could this girl

be known to the Mormons? It was possible. Fay Larkin was an unusual name. Deep into Shefford's heart had sunk the story Venters had told. Shefford found that he had unconsciously created a like romance—he had been loving a wild and strange and lonely girl, like beautiful Bess Venters. It was a shock to learn the truth, but, as it had been only a dream, it could hardly be vital.

Shefford retraced his steps toward the post. Half-way back he espied a tall, dark figure moving toward him, and presently the shape and the step seemed familiar. Then he recognized Nas Ta Bega. Soon they were face to face. Shefford felt that the Indian had been trailing him over the sand, and that this was to be a significant meeting. Remembering Withers' revelation about the Navajo, Shefford scarcely knew how to approach him now. There was no difference to be made out in Nas Ta Bega's dark face and inscrutable eyes, yet there was a difference to be felt in his presence. But the Indian did not speak, and turned to walk by Shefford's side. Shefford could not long be silent.

"Nas Ta Bega, were you looking for me?" he asked.

"You have no gun," replied the Indian.

But for his very low voice, his slow speaking of the words, Shefford would have thought him a white man. For Shefford there was indeed instinct in this meeting, and he turned to face the Navajo.

"Withers told me you had been educated, that you came back to the desert, that you never showed your training. . . . Nas Ta Bega, did you understand all I told Withers?"

"Yes," replied the Indian.

"You won't betray me?"

"I am a Navajo."

"Nas Ta Bega, you trail me—you say I have no gun." Shefford wanted to ask this Indian if he cared to be the white man's friend, but the question was not easy to put, and, besides, seemed unnecessary. "I am alone and strange in this wild country. I must learn."

"Nas Ta Bega will show you the trails and the water-holes."

"For money—for silver you will do this?" inquired Shefford.

Shefford felt that the Indian's silence was a rebuke. He remembered Withers' singular praise of this red man. He realized he must change his idea of Indians.

"Nas Ta Bega, I know nothing. I feel like a child in the wilderness. When I speak it is out of the mouths of those who have taught me. I must find a new voice and a new life. . . . You heard my story to Withers. I am an outcast from my own people. If you will be my friend—be so."

The Indian clasped Shefford's hand and held it in a response that was more beautiful for its silence. So they stood for a moment in the starlight.

"Nas Ta Bega, what did Withers mean when he said go to the Navajo for a faith?" asked Shefford.

"He meant the desert is my mother. . . . Will you go with Nas Ta Bega into the canyons and the mountains?"

"Indeed I will."

They unclasped hands and turned toward the trading-post.

"Nas Ta Bega, have you spoken my tongue to any other white man since you returned to your home?" asked Shefford.

"No."

"Why do you—why are you different for me?"

"Bi Nai! The Navajo will call his white friend Bi Nai—brother," said Nas Ta Bega, and he spoke haltingly, not as if words were hard to find, but strange to speak. "I was stolen from my mother's hogan and taken to California. They kept me ten years in a mission at San Bernardino and four years in a school. They said my color and my hair were all that was left of the Indian in me. But they could not see my heart. They took fourteen years of my life. They wanted to make me a missionary among my own people. But the white man's ways and his life and his God are not the Indian's. They never can be."

How strangely productive of thought for Shefford to hear the Indian talk! What fatality in this meeting and friendship! Upon Nas Ta Bega had been forced education, training, religion, and that had made him something more and something less than an Indian. It was something assimilated from the white man which made the Indian unhappy and alien in his own home—something meant to be good for him and his kind that had ruined him. For Shefford felt the passion and the tragedy of this Navajo.

"Bi Nai, the Indian is dying!" Nas Ta Bega's low voice was deep and wonderful with its intensity of feeling. "The white man robbed the Indian of lands and homes, drove him into the deserts, made him a gaunt and sleepless spiller of blood. . . . The blood is all spilled now, for the Indian is broken. But the white man sells him rum and seduces his daughters. . . . He will not leave the Indian in peace with his own God! . . . Bi Nai, the Indian is dying!"

The heat of midsummer came, when the blistering sun shone, and a hot blast blew across the sand, and the furious storms made floods in the washes. Day and night Shefford was always in the open, and any one who had ever known him in the past would have failed to recognize him now.

In the early fall, with Nas Ta Bega as companion, he set out to the south of Kayenta upon long-neglected business of the trader. They visited Red Lake, Blue Canyon, Keams Canyon, Oribi, the Moki villages, Tuba, Moencopie, and Moen Ave. This trip took many weeks and gave Shefford all the opportunity he wanted to study the Indians, and the conditions near to the border of civilization. He learned the truth about the Indians and the missionaries. But he knew he must plunge on and on until he fulfilled his mission—to find Fay Larkin and make her his wife.

MAX BRAND

FREDERICK SCHILLER FAUST (1892–1944) was born in Seattle, Washington. He wrote over three hundred novels under nineteen different pseudonyms, but Max Brand—the Jewish cowboy, as he once dubbed it—has become the most familiar. Faust was convinced very early that to die in battle was the most heroic of deaths, and so, when World War I began, he tried to get overseas. All of his efforts came to nothing, and in 1917, working at manual labor in New York City, he wrote a letter that appeared in *The New York Times* protesting this social injustice. Mark Twain's sister came to his rescue, arranging for him to meet Robert H. Davis, an editor with the Munsey publications. Faust wanted to write—poetry. The story is probably apocryphal, but Davis is reputed to have given the would-be poet a brief plot idea, told him to go down the hall to a room where there was a typewriter, only to have Faust return some six hours later with a completed story suitable for publication. However it happened, it was Davis' idea that, having lost Zane Grey to the slick-magazine markets, Faust should try to duplicate his success and write Western stories and novels. When Davis left the Munsey group, Faust expanded his scope, writing for several magazines and especially for *Western Story Magazine*, to which he contributed a million words a year for thirteen years' running.

In 1921 Faust made the tragic discovery that he had an incurable heart condition from which he might die at any moment. Faust's son-in-law, Robert Easton, who in *Max Brand: The Big "Westerner"* (University of Oklahoma Press, 1970) has written the best book to appear on Faust, suggested that Faust's condition may have been in part emotional. At any rate, Faust eventually sought analysis with H. G. Baynes in

England, a Jungian analyst, and finally went to Zurich, where he consulted C. G. Jung. Jung refused to take him as a patient, but he did advise Faust that his best hope was to live a simple life. This advice Faust rejected. He went to Italy, where he rented a villa, lived extravagantly, and was perpetually in debt. Faust needed his speed in writing merely to keep afloat financially.

By the mid thirties he was spending more and more time in the United States, and toward the end of the decade, when he was writing increasingly for slick magazines, he moved his family to Hollywood and found work as a screenwriter. He had missed one war; he refused to miss World War II. He pulled strings to become a war correspondent and he sailed to Europe and the Italian front, where he lived in foxholes with men involved in some of the bloodiest fighting of the entire war, men who had grown up reading his stories with their superhuman heroes and their grand deeds, and that is where he died, on a dark night in 1944, from a shrapnel wound.

Faust's Western fiction has nothing to do intrinsically with the American West, but some of it is very engaging, and even gripping, to read. *The Untamed* (Putnam's, 1919), surely, and *The White Wolf* (Putnam's, 1926)—an excellent dog story—and *Mystery Ranch* (Dodd, Mead, 1930) as well as *Destry Rides Again* (Dodd, Mead, 1930) from his later period when he was making an effort to write better fiction, all can still provide a modern reader with pleasure. "Wine on the Desert" is a short story that shows its author to be every bit the master of plotting that O. Henry was, and I think the style in which it is written superior to O. Henry's superciliousness. One can carp—being a realist—and declare that men dying of thirst, as men in general when dying, have no look whatsoever on their dead faces, and scarcely a "screaming look" as claimed in this story. Realism wasn't Faust's long suit. Instead, he was a purveyor of moods; his best fiction, for this reason, remains with you even after you've forgotten the characters and the plot.

Until recently, "Wine in the Desert" was the one Max Brand story usually chosen by anthologists. William F. Nolan may have changed this in editing *The Best Western Stories of Max Brand* (Dodd, Mead, 1981). A reader of Nolan's collection might find a story preferable to this one. It is somewhat arbitrary and strictly personal, yet for me "Wine on the Desert" is still Brand's best.

Wine on the Desert

There was no hurry, except for the thirst, like clotted salt, in the back of his throat, and Durante rode on slowly, rather enjoying the last moments of dryness before he reached the cold water in Tony's house. There was really no hurry at all. He had almost twenty-four hours' head start, for they would not find his dead man until this morning. After that, there would be perhaps several hours of delay before the sheriff gathered a sufficient posse and started on his trail. Or perhaps the sheriff would be fool enough to come alone.

Durante had been able to see the wheel and fan of Tony's windmill for more than an hour, but he could not make out the ten acres of the vineyard until he had topped the last rise, for the vines had been planted in a hollow. The lowness of the ground, Tony used to say, accounted for the water that gathered in the well during the wet season. The rains sank through the desert sand, through the gravels beneath, and gathered in a bowl of clay hardpan far below.

In the middle of the rainless season the well ran dry but, long before that, Tony had every drop of the water pumped up into a score of tanks made of cheap corrugated iron. Slender pipe lines carried the water from the tanks to the vines and from time to time let them sip enough life to keep them until the winter darkened overhead suddenly, one November day, and the rain came down, and all the earth made a great hushing sound as it drank. Durante had heard that whisper of drinking when he was here before; but he never had seen the place in the middle of the long drought.

The windmill looked like a sacred emblem to Durante, and the twenty stodgy, tar-painted tanks blessed his eyes; but a heavy sweat broke out at once from his body. For the air of the hollow, unstirred by wind, was hot and still as a bowl of soup. A reddish soup. The vines were powdered with thin red dust, also. They were wretched, dying things to look at, for the grapes had been gathered, the new wine had been made, and now the leaves hung in ragged tatters.

Durante rode up to the squat adobe house and right

through the entrance into the patio. A flowering vine clothed three sides of the little court. Durante did not know the name of the plant, but it had large white blossoms with golden hearts that poured sweetness on the air. Durante hated the sweetness. It made him more thirsty.

He threw the reins off his mule and strode into the house. The water cooler stood in the hall outside the kitchen. There were two jars made of a porous stone, very ancient things, and the liquid which distilled through the pores kept the contents cool. The jar on the left held water; that on the right contained wine. There was a big tin dipper hanging on a peg beside each jar. Durante tossed off the cover of the vase on the left and plunged it in until the delicious coolness closed well above his wrist.

"Hey, Tony," he called. Out of his dusty throat the cry was throw some water into that mule of mine, would you, Tony?"

A voice pealed from the distance.

Durante, pouring down the second dipper of water, smelled the alkali dust which had shaken off his own clothes. It seemed to him that heat was radiating like light from his clothes, from his body, and the cool dimness of the house was soaking it up. He heard the wooden leg of Tony bumping on the ground, and Durante grinned; then Tony came in with that hitch and sideswing with which he accommodated the stiffness of his artificial leg. His brown face shone with sweat as though a special ray of light were focused on it.

"Ah, Dick!" he said. "Good old Dick! . . . How long since you came last! . . . Wouldn't Julia be glad! Wouldn't she be glad!"

"Ain't she here?" asked Durante, jerking his head suddenly away from the dripping dipper.

"She's away at Nogalez," said Tony. "It gets so hot. I said, 'You go up to Nogalez, Julia, where the wind don't forget to blow.' She cried, but I made her go."

"Did she cry?" asked Durante.

"Julia . . . that's a good girl," said Tony.

"Yeah. You bet she's good," said Durante. He put the dipper quickly to his lips but did not swallow for a moment; he was grinning too widely. Afterward he said: "You wouldn't throw some water into that mule of mine, would you, Tony?"

Tony went out with his wooden leg clumping loud on the wooden floor, softly in the patio dust. Durante found the hammock in the corner of the patio. He lay down in it and watched the color of sunset flush the mists of desert dust that rose to the zenith. The water was soaking through his body; hunger began, and then the rattling of pans in the kitchen and the cheerful cry of Tony's voice:

"What you want, Dick? I got some pork. You don't want pork. I'll make you some good Mexican beans. Hot. Ah ha, I know that old Dick. I have plenty of good wine for you, Dick. Tortillas. Even Julia can't make tortillas like me . . . And what about a nice young rabbit?"

"All blowed full of buckshot?" growled Durante.

"No, no. I kill them with the rifle."

"You kill rabbits with a rifle?" repeated Durante, with a quick interest.

"It's the only gun I have," said Tony. "If I catch them in the sights, they are dead . . . A wooden leg cannot walk very far. . . . I must kill them quick. You see? They come close to the house about sunrise and flop their ears. I shoot through the head."

"Yeah? Yeah?" muttered Durante. "Through the head?" He relaxed, scowling. He passed his hand over his face, over his head.

Then Tony began to bring the food out into the patio and lay it on a small wooden table; a lantern hanging against the wall of the house included the table in a dim half circle of light. They sat there and ate. Tony had scrubbed himself for the meal. His hair was soaked in water and sleeked back over his round skull. A man in the desert might be willing to pay five dollars for as much water as went to the soaking of that hair.

Everything was good. Tony knew how to cook, and he knew how to keep the glasses filled with his wine.

"This is old wine. This is my father's wine. Eleven years old," said Tony. "You look at the light through it. You see that brown in the red? That's the soft that time puts in good wine, my father always said."

"What killed your father?" asked Durante.

Tony lifted his hand as though he were listening or as though he were pointing out a thought.

"The desert killed him. I found his mule. It was dead, too. There was a leak in the canteen. My father was only five miles away when the buzzards showed him to me."

"Five miles? Just an hour . . . Good Lord!" said Durante. He stared with big eyes. "Just dropped down and died?" he asked.

"No," said Tony. "When you die of thirst, you always die just one way. . . . First you tear off your shirt, then your undershirt. That's to be cooler. . . . And the sun comes and cooks your bare skin. . . . And then you think . . . there is water everywhere, if you dig down far enough. You begin to dig. The dust comes up your nose. You start screaming. You break your nails in the sand. You wear the flesh off the tips of your fingers, to the bone." He took a quick swallow of wine.

"Without you seen a man die of thirst, how d'you know they start to screaming?" asked Durante.

"They got a screaming look when you find them," said Tony. "Take some more wine. The desert never can get to you here. My father showed me the way to keep the desert away from the hollow. We live pretty good here? No?"

"Yeah," said Durante, loosening his shirt collar. "Yeah, pretty good."

Afterward he slept well in the hammock until the report of a rifle waked him and he saw the color of dawn in the sky. It was such a great, round bowl that for a moment he felt as though he were above, looking down into it.

He got up and saw Tony coming in holding a rabbit by the ears, the rifle in his other hand.

"You see?" said Tony. "Breakfast came and called on us!" He laughed.

Durante examined the rabbit with care. It was nice and fat and it had been shot through the head. Through the middle of the head. Such a shudder went down the back of Durante that he washed gingerly before breakfast; he felt that his blood was cooled for the entire day.

It was a good breakfast, too, with flapjacks and stewed rabbit with green peppers, and a quart of strong coffee. Before they had finished, the sun struck through the east window and started them sweating.

"Gimme a look at that rifle of yours, Tony, will you?" Durante asked.

"You take a look at my rifle, but don't you steal the luck that's in it," laughed Tony. He brought the fifteen-shot Winchester.

"Loaded right to the brim?" asked Durante.

"I always load it full the minute I get back home," said Tony.

"Tony, come outside with me," commanded Durante.

They went out from the house. The sun turned the sweat of Durante to hot water and then dried his skin so that his clothes felt transparent.

"Tony, I gotta be damn mean," said Durante. "Stand right there where I can see you. Don't try to get close. . . . Now listen. . . . The sheriff's gunna be along this trail some time to-day, looking for me. He'll load up himself and all his gang with water out of your tanks. Then he'll follow my sign across the desert. Get me? He'll follow if he finds water on the place. But he's not gunna find water."

"What you done, poor Dick?" said Tony. "Now look. . . . I could hide you in the old wine cellar where nobody . . ."

"The sheriff's not gunna find any water," said Durante. "It's gunna be like this."

He put the rifle to his shoulder, aimed, fired. The shot struck the base of the nearest tank, ranging down through the bottom. A semicircle of darkness began to stain the soil near the edge of the iron wall.

Tony fell on his knees. "No, no, Dick! Good Dick!" he said. "Look! All the vineyard. It will die. It will turn into old, dead wood, Dick . . ."

"Shut your face," said Durante. "Now I've started, I kinda like the job."

Tony fell on his face and put his hands over his ears. Durante drilled a bullet hole through the tanks, one after another. Afterward, he leaned on the rifle.

"Take my canteen and go in and fill it with water out of the cooling jar," he said. "Snap into it, Tony!"

Tony got up. He raised the canteen, and looked around him, not at the tanks from which the water was pouring so that the noise of the earth drinking was audible, but at the rows of his vineyard. Then he went into the house.

Durante mounted his mule. He shifted the rifle to his left hand and drew out the heavy Colt from its holster. Tony came dragging back to him, his head down. Durante watched Tony with a careful revolver but he gave up the canteen without lifting his eyes.

"The trouble with you, Tony," said Durante, "is you're yellow. I'd of fought a tribe of wildcats with my bare hands, before I'd let 'em do what I'm doin' to you. But you sit back and take it."

Tony did not seem to hear. He stretched out his hands to the vines.

"Ah, my God," said Tony. "Will you let them all die?"

Durante shrugged his shoulders. He shook the canteen to make sure that it was full. It was so brimming that there was hardly room for the liquid to make a sloshing sound. Then he turned the mule and kicked it into a dog-trot.

Half a mile from the house of Tony, he threw the empty rifle to the ground. There was no sense packing that useless weight, and Tony with his peg leg would hardly come this far.

Durante looked back, a mile or so later, and saw the little image of Tony picking up the rifle from the dust, then staring earnestly after his guest. Durante remembered the neat little hole clipped through the head of the rabbit. Wherever he went, his trail never could return again to the vineyard in the desert. But then, commencing to picture to himself the arrival of the sweating sheriff and his posse at the house of Tony, Durante laughed heartily.

The sheriff's posse could get plenty of wine, of course, but without water a man could not hope to make the desert voyage, even with a mule or a horse to help him on the way. Durante patted the full, rounding side of his canteen. He might even now begin with the first sip but it was a luxury to postpone pleasure until desire became greater.

He raised his eyes along the trail. Close by, it was merely dotted with occasional bones, but distance joined the dots into an unbroken chalk line which wavered with a strange leisure across the Apache Desert, pointing toward the cool blue promise of the mountains. The next morning he would be among them.

A coyote whisked out of a gully and ran like a gray puff of dust on the wind. His tongue hung out like a little red rag from the side of his mouth; and suddenly Durante was dry to the marrow. He uncorked and lifted his canteen. It had a slightly sour smell; perhaps the sacking which covered it had grown a trifle old. And then he poured a great mouthful of lukewarm liquid. He had swallowed it before his senses could give him warning.

It was wine!

He looked first of all toward the mountains. They were as calmly blue, as distant as when he had started that morning. Twenty-four hours not on water, but on wine!

"I deserve it," said Durante. "I trusted him to fill the canteen. . . . I deserve it. Curse him!" With a mighty resolution, he quieted the panic in his soul. He would not touch the stuff until noon. Then he would take one discreet sip. He would win through.

Hours went by. He looked at his watch and found it was only ten o'clock. And he had thought that it was on the verge of noon! He uncorked the wine and drank freely and, corking the canteen, felt almost as though he needed a drink of water more than before. He sloshed the contents of the canteen. Already it was horribly light.

Once, he turned the mule and considered the return trip; but he could remember the head of the rabbit too clearly, drilled right through the center. The vineyard, the rows of old twisted, gnarled little trunks with the bark peeling off . . . every vine was to Tony like a human life. And Durante had condemned them all to death!

He faced the blue of the mountains again. His heart raced in his breast with terror. Perhaps it was fear and not the suction of that dry and deadly air that made his tongue cleave to the roof of his mouth.

The day grew old. Nausea began to work in his stomach, nausea alternating with sharp pains. When he looked down, he saw that there was blood on his boots. He had been spurring the mule until the red ran down from it flanks. It went with a curious stagger, like a rocking horse with a broken rocker; and Durante grew aware that he had been keeping the mule at a gallop for a long time. He pulled it to a halt. It stood with wide-braced legs. Its head was down. When he leaned from the saddle, he saw that its mouth was open.

"It's gunna die," said Durante. "It's gunna die . . . what a fool I been. . . ."

The mule did not die until after sunset. Durante left everything except his revolver. He packed the weight of that for an hour and discarded it in turn. His knees were growing weak. When he looked up at the stars they shone white and clear for a moment only, and then whirled into little racing circles and scrawls of red.

He lay down. He kept his eyes closed and waited for the shaking to go out of his body, but it would not stop. And every breath of darkness was like an inhalation of black dust.

He got up and went on, staggering. Sometimes he found himself running.

Before you die of thirst, you go mad. He kept remembering that. His tongue had swollen big. Before it choked him, if he lanced it with his knife the blood would help him; he would be able to swallow. Then he remembered that the taste of blood is salty.

Once, in his boyhood, he had ridden through a pass with his father and they had looked down on the sapphire of a mountain lake, a hundred thousand million tons of water as cold as snow. . . .

When he looked up, now, there were no stars; and this frightened him terribly. He never had seen a desert night so dark. His eyes were failing, he was being blinded. When the morning came, he would not be able to see the mountains, and he would walk around and around in a circle until he dropped and died.

No stars, no wind; the air as still as the waters of a stale pool, and he in the dregs at the bottom. . . .

He seized his shirt at the throat and tore it away so that it hung in two rags from his hips.

He could see the earth only well enough to stumble on the rocks. But there were no stars in the heavens. He was blind: he had no more hope than a rat in a well. Ah, but Italian devils know how to put poison in wine that will steal all the senses or any one of them: and Tony had chosen to blind Durante.

He heard a sound like water. It was the swishing of the soft deep sand through which he was treading; sand so soft that a man could dig it away with his bare hands. . . .

Afterward, after many hours, out of the blind face of that sky the rain began to fall. It made first a whispering and then a delicate murmur like voices conversing, but after that, just at the dawn, it roared like the hoofs of ten thousand charging horses. Even through that thundering confusion the big birds with naked heads and red, raw necks found their way down to one place in the Apache Desert.

LOUIS L'AMOUR

LOUIS L'AMOUR (1908–) was born in Jamestown, North Dakota. He apparently left home at fifteen and subsequently held a wide variety of jobs including ranch hand, merchant seaman, roustabout for a traveling circus, fruit picker, ship loader, and lumberjack. He began his writing career with book reviews. His first book was a volume of poems published in England, *Smoke from This Altar* (Lusk Publishers, 1939). During World War II he served with the U.S. Army Tank Destroyer Corps and the Transportation Corps. It was not until some years after the war that he launched himself as a writer of pulp Western fiction, contributing to magazines like *West* and *Giant Western.* Many of his early short stories were written under the pseudonym Jim Mayo, as for example the sixth Louis L'Amour novel, *Guns of the Timberlands* (Jason Press, 1955), which first appeared in *West* in 1950 under the name Jim Mayo. *Showdown at Yellow Butte* (Ace, 1953) and *Utah Blaine* (Ace, 1954), now in print as Louis L'Amour titles, were also originally Jim Mayo novels. Although he would rather not have it mentioned, L'Amour also wrote four Hopalong Cassidy novels for Doubleday & Company, which were published in 1951 under the house name Tex Burns. Clarence E. Mulford was no longer interested in writing any new novels about the characters he had created and L'Amour was expected to use as the hero, not Mulford's original Hopalong, but the debonair altruist with white hair portrayed by William Boyd in the theatrical films and the NBC television series.

L'Amour's early novels—with the exception of the Tex Burns titles—are his best. *Hondo* (Fawcett, 1953) can be read with enjoyment, with its self-sufficient, taciturn, capable protagonist and its evocation of the desert lands of Arizona, as can *Last Stand at Papago Wells* (Fawcett, 1957). In both novels the Apaches are used strictly for dramatic purposes; L'Amour has never used Indians in any other way. But this isn't an important consideration in terms of L'Amour's approach to Western fiction, where situation is always preeminent and no character or group of characters is ever really introduced except to move along the plot.

Like Zane Grey, L'Amour has had a consistent, albeit highly romantic, view of the American West which he has managed to embody in everything he has written; and like Max Brand, he has an amazing facility for rudimentary action plotting and usually introduces a new plot ingredient every thousand words. His paperback publishers have kept all of his titles in print and they are constantly being racked in Western fiction sections—as opposed to the usual mass-merchandise paperback cycle of reissuing a title every two or three years—and L'Amour has helped the cause by writing at least three and sometimes four new books a year. He writes rapidly, composing at the typewriter, and he never rewrites—a circumstance which accounts for many of the curious incongruities in characterization and formal plotting which can be found in his novels. I once mentioned to him that in *Last Stand at Papago Wells* only five characters are killed during an Apache attack but one character counts six corpses. "I'll have to go back and count them again," L'Amour said, and smiled. It really doesn't matter to the majority of his readers and, therefore, it doesn't matter to him or to his publishers. Most of all L'Amour is adept at the art of self-promotion, dressing himself in traditional, although Sunday-go-to-meetin', Western garb, traveling about the country in a motor home, visiting bookstores, talking on the radio, anywhere and everywhere a charming, engaging human being.

"War Party" first appeared in *The Saturday Evening Post* in June 1959. It has about it several of the characteristics that have served L'Amour so well: the young male narrator who is in the process of growing into manhood and who is evaluating other human beings and his own experiences; a resourceful frontier female character who has beauty as well as fortitude; a strong male character who is single and hence marriageable; and the powerful, romantic, strangely compelling vision of the American West which often makes L'Amour's fiction such a delightful escape from the cares of the day—

where one enters instead, in L'Amour's words in this story, "a big country needing big men and women to live in it" and where there is no place for "the frightened or the mean."

War Party

We buried pa on a sidehill out west of camp, buried him high up so his ghost could look down the trail he'd planned to travel.

We piled the grave high with rocks because of the coyotes, and we dug the grave deep, and some of it I dug myself, and Mr. Sampson helped, and some others.

Folks in the wagon train figured ma would turn back, but they hadn't known ma so long as I had. Once she set her mind to something she wasn't about to quit.

She was a young woman and pretty, but there was strength in her. She was a lone woman with two children, but she was of no mind to turn back. She'd come through the Little Crow massacre in Minnesota and she knew what trouble was. Yet it was like her that she put it up to me.

"Bud," she said, when we were alone, "we can turn back, but we've nobody there who cares about us, and it's of you and Jeanie that I'm thinking. If we go west you will have to be the man of the house, and you'll have to work hard to make up for pa."

"We'll go west," I said. A boy those days took it for granted that he had work to do, and the men couldn't do it all. No boy ever thought of himself as only twelve or thirteen or whatever he was, being anxious to prove himself a man, and take a man's place and responsibilities.

Ryerson and his wife were going back. She was a complaining woman and he was a man who was always ailing when there was work to be done. Four or five wagons were turning back, folks with their tails betwixt their legs running for the shelter of towns where their own littleness wouldn't stand out so plain.

When a body crossed the Mississippi and left the settlements behind, something happened to him. The world seemed to bust wide open, and suddenly the horizons spread out and a man wasn't cramped any more. The pinched-up villages and the narrowness of towns, all that was gone. The horizons simply exploded and rolled back into enormous distance, with nothing around but prairie and sky.

Some folks couldn't stand it. They'd cringe into themselves and start hunting excuses to go back where they came from. This was a big country needing big men and women to live in it, and there was no place out here for the frightened or the mean.

The prairie and sky had a way of trimming folks down to size, or changing them to giants to whom nothing seemed impossible. Men who had cut a wide swath back in the States found themselves nothing out here. They were folks who were used to doing a lot of talking who suddenly found that no one was listening any more, and things that seemed mighty important back home, like family and money, they amounted to nothing alongside character and courage.

There was John Sampson from our town. He was a man used to being told to do things, used to looking up to wealth and power, but when he crossed the Mississippi he began to lift his head and look around. He squared his shoulders, put more crack to his whip and began to make his own tracks in the land.

Pa was always strong, an independent man given to reading at night from one of the four or five books we had, to speaking up on matters of principle and to straight shooting with a rifle. Pa had fought the Comanche and lived with the Sioux, but he wasn't strong enough to last more than two days with a Kiowa arrow through his lung. But he died knowing ma had stood by the rear wheel and shot the Kiowa whose arrow it was.

Right then I knew that neither Indians nor country was going to get the better of ma. Shooting that Kiowa was the first time ma had shot anything but some chicken-killing varmint—which she'd done time to time when pa was away from home.

Only ma wouldn't let Jeanie and me call it home. "We came here from Illinois," she said, "but we're going home now."

"But ma," I protested, "I thought home was where we came from?"

"Home is where we're going now," ma said, "and we'll know it when we find it. Now that pa is gone we'll have to build that home ourselves."

She had a way of saying "home" so it sounded like a rare and wonderful place and kept Jeanie and me looking always at the horizon, just knowing it was over there, waiting for us to see it. She had given us the dream, and even Jeanie, who was only six, she had it too.

She might tell us that home was where we were going, but I knew home was where ma was, a warm and friendly place with biscuits on the table and fresh-made butter. We wouldn't have a real home until ma was there and we had a fire going. Only I'd build the fire.

Mr. Buchanan, who was captain of the wagon train, came to us with Tryon Burt, who was guide. "We'll help you," Mr. Buchanan said. "I know you'll be wanting to go back, and—"

"But we are not going back." Ma smiled at them. "And don't be afraid we'll be a burden. I know you have troubles of your own, and we will manage very well."

Mr. Buchanan looked uncomfortable, like he was trying to think of the right thing to say. "Now, see here," he protested, "we started this trip with a rule. There has to be a man with every wagon."

Ma put her hand on my shoulder. "I have my man. Bud is almost thirteen and accepts responsibility. I could ask for no better man."

Ryerson came up. He was thin, stooped in the shoulder, and whenever he looked at ma there was a greasy look to his eyes that I didn't like. He was a man who looked dirty even when he'd just washed in the creek. "You come along with me, ma'am," he said. "I'll take good care of you."

"Mr. Ryerson"—ma looked him right in the eye—"you have a wife who can use better care than she's getting, and I have my son."

"He's nothin' but a boy."

"You are turning back, are you not? My son is going on. I believe that should indicate who is more the man. It is neither size nor age that makes a man, Mr. Ryerson, but something he has inside. My son has it."

Ryerson might have said something unpleasant only Tryon Burt was standing there wishing he would, so he just looked ugly and hustled off.

"I'd like to say you could come," Mr. Buchanan said, "but the boy couldn't stand up to a man's work."

Ma smiled at him, chin up, the way she had. "I do not believe in gambling, Mr. Buchanan, but I'll wager a good Ballard rifle there isn't a man in camp who could follow a child all day, running when it runs, squatting when it squats, bending when it bends and wrestling when it wrestles and not be played out long before the child is."

"You may be right, ma'am, but a rule is a rule."

"We are in Indian country, Mr. Buchanan. If you are killed a week from now, I suppose your wife must return to the States?"

"That's different! Nobody could turn back from there!"

"Then," ma said sweetly, "it seems a rule is only a rule within certain limits, and if I recall correctly no such limit was designated in the articles of travel. Whatever limits there were, Mr. Buchanan, must have been passed sometime before the Indian attack that killed my husband."

"I can drive the wagon, and so can ma," I said. "For the past two days I've been driving, and nobody said anything until pa died."

Mr. Buchanan didn't know what to say, but a body could see he didn't like it. Nor did he like a woman who talked up to him the way ma did.

Tryon Burt spoke up. "Let the boy drive. I've watched this youngster, and he'll do. He has better judgment than most men in the outfit, and he stands up to his work. If need be, I'll help."

Mr. Buchanan turned around and walked off with his back stiff the way it is when he's mad. Ma looked at Burt, and she said, "Thank you, Mr. Burt. That was nice of you."

Try Burt, he got all red around the gills and took off like somebody had put a bur under his saddle.

Come morning our wagon was the second one ready to take its place in line, with both horses saddled and tied behind the wagon, and me standing beside the off ox.

Any direction a man wanted to look there was nothing but grass and sky, only sometimes there'd be a buffalo wallow or a gopher hole. We made eleven miles the first day after pa was buried, sixteen the next, then nineteen, thirteen and twenty-one. At no time did the country change. On the sixth day after pa died I killed a buffalo.

It was a young bull, but a big one, and I spotted him coming up out of a draw and was off my horse and bellied down in the grass before Try Burt realized there was game in sight. That bull came up from the draw and stopped there, staring at the wagon train, which was a half-mile off. Setting a sight behind his left shoulder I took a long breath, took in the trigger slack, then squeezed off my shot so gentle-like the gun jumped in my hands before I was ready for it.

The bull took a step back like something had surprised him, and I jacked another shell into the chamber and was sighting on him again when he went down on his knees and rolled over on his side.

"You got him, Bud!" Burt was more excited than me. "That was shootin'!"

Try got down and showed me how to skin the bull, and lent me a hand. Then we cut out a lot of fresh meat and toted it back to the wagons.

Ma was at the fire when we came up, a wisp of brown hair alongside her cheek and her face flushed from the heat of the fire, looking as pretty as a bay pony.

"Bud killed his first buffalo," Burt told her, looking at ma like he could eat her with a spoon.

"Why, Bud! That's wonderful!" Her eyes started to dance with a kind of mischief in them, and she said, "Bud, why don't you take a piece of that meat along to Mr. Buchanan and the others?"

With Burt to help, we cut the meat into eighteen pieces and distributed it around the wagons. It wasn't much, but it was the first fresh meat in a couple of weeks.

John Sampson squeezed my shoulder and said, "Seems to me you and your ma are folks to travel with. This outfit needs some hunters."

Each night I staked out that buffalo hide, and each day I worked at curing it before rolling it up to pack on the wagon. Believe you me, I was some proud of that buffalo hide. Biggest thing I'd shot until then was a cottontail rabbit back in Illinois, where we lived when I was born. Try Burt told folks about that shot. "Two hundred yards," he'd say, "right through the heart."

Only it wasn't more than a hundred and fifty yards the way I figured, and pa used to make me pace off distances, so I'd learn to judge right. But I was nobody to argue with Try Burt telling a story—besides, two hundred yards makes an awful lot better sound than one hundred and fifty.

After supper the menfolks would gather to talk plans. The season was late, and we weren't making the time we ought if we hoped to beat the snow through the passes of the Sierras. When they talked I was there because I was the man of my wagon, but nobody paid me no mind. Mr. Buchanan, he acted like he didn't see me, but John Sampson would not, and Try Burt always smiled at me.

Several spoke up for turning back, but Mr. Buchanan said he knew of an outfit that made it through later than this. One thing was sure. Our wagon wasn't turning back. Like ma said, home was somewhere ahead of us, and back in the States we'd have no money and nobody to turn to, nor any relatives, anywhere. It was the three of us.

"We're going on," I said at one of these talks. "We don't figure to turn back for anything."

Webb gave me a glance full of contempt. "You'll go where the rest of us go. You an' your ma would play hob gettin' by on your own."

Next day it rained, dawn to dark it fairly poured, and we were lucky to make six miles. Day after that, with the wagon wheels sinking into the prairie and the rain still falling, we camped just two miles from where we started in the morning.

Nobody talked much around the fires, and what was said was apt to be short and irritable. Most of these folks had put all they owned into the outfits they had, and if they turned back now they'd have nothing to live on and nothing left to make a fresh start. Except a few like Mr. Buchanan, who was well off.

"It doesn't have to be California," ma said once. "What most of us want is land, not gold."

"This here is Indian country," John Sampson said, "and a sight too open for me. I'd like a valley in the hills, with running water close by."

"There will be valleys and meadows," ma replied, stirring the stew she was making, "and tall trees near running streams, and tall grass growing in the meadows, and there will be game in the forest and on the grassy plains, and places for homes."

"And where will we find all that?" Webb's tone was slighting.

"West," ma said, "over against the mountains."

"I suppose you've been there?" Webb scoffed.

"No, Mr. Webb, I haven't been there, but I've been told of it. The land is there, and we will have some of it, my children and I, and we will stay through the winter, and in the spring we will plant our crops."

"Easy to say."

"This is Sioux country to the north," Burt said. "We'll be

lucky to get through without a fight. There was a war party of thirty or thirty-five passed this way a couple of days ago."

"Sioux?"

"Uh-huh—no women or children along, and I found where some war paint rubbed off on the brush."

"Maybe," Mr. Buchanan suggested, "we'd better turn south a mite."

"It is late in the season," ma replied, "and the straightest way is the best way now."

"No use to worry," White interrupted; "those Indians went on by. They won't likely know we're around."

"They were riding southeast," ma said, "and their home is in the north, so when they return they'll be riding northwest. There is no way they can miss our trail."

"Then we'd best turn back," White said.

"Don't look like we'd make it this year, anyway," a woman said; "the season is late."

That started the argument, and some were for turning back and some wanted to push on, and finally White said they should push on, but travel fast.

"Fast?" Webb asked disparagingly. "An Indian can ride in one day the distance we'd travel in four."

That started the wrangling again and ma continued with her cooking. Sitting there watching her I figured I never did see anybody so graceful or quick on her feet as ma, and when we used to walk in the woods back home I never knew her to stumble or step on a fallen twig or branch.

The group broke up and returned to their own fires with nothing settled, only there at the end Mr. Buchanan looked to Burt. "Do you know the Sioux?"

"Only the Utes and Shoshonis, and I spent a winter on the Snake with the Nez Perces one time. But I've had no truck with the Sioux. Only they tell me they're bad medicine. Fightin' men from way back and they don't cotton to white folks in their country. If we run into Sioux, we're in trouble."

After Mr. Buchanan had gone Tryon Burt accepted a plate and cup from ma and settled down to eating. After a while he looked up at her and said, "Beggin' your pardon, ma'am, but it struck me you knew a sight about trackin' for an Eastern woman. You'd spotted those Sioux your own self, an' you figured it right that they'd pick up our trail on the way back."

She smiled at him. "It was simply an observation, Mr.

Burt. I would believe anyone would notice it. I simply put it into words."

Burt went on eating, but he was mighty thoughtful, and it didn't seem to me he was satisfied with ma's answer. Ma said finally, "It seems to be raining west of here. Isn't it likely to be snowing in the mountains?"

Burt looked up uneasily. "Not necessarily so, ma'am. It could be raining here and not snowing there, but I'd say there was a chance of snow." He got up and came around the fire to the coffeepot. "What are you gettin' at, ma'am?"

"Some of them are ready to turn back or change their plans. What will you do then?"

He frowned, placing his cup on the grass and starting to fill his pipe. "No idea—might head south for Santa Fe. Why do you ask?"

"Because we're going on," ma said. "We're going to the mountains, and I am hoping some of the others decide to come with us."

"You'd go alone?" He was amazed.

"If necessary."

We started on at daybreak, but folks were more scary than before, and they kept looking at the great distances stretching away on either side, and muttering. There was an autumn coolness in the air, and we were still short of South Pass by several days with the memory of the Donner party being talked up around us.

There was another kind of talk in the wagons, and some of it I heard. The nightly gatherings around ma's fire had started talk, and some of it pointed to Tryon Burt, and some were saying other things.

We made seventeen miles that day, and at night Mr. Buchanan didn't come to our fire; and when White stopped by, his wife came and got him. Ma looked at her and smiled, and Mrs. White sniffed and went away beside her husband.

"Mr. Burt"—ma wasn't one to beat around a bush—"is there talk about me?"

Try Burt got red around the ears and he opened his mouth, but couldn't find the words he wanted. "Maybe—well, maybe I shouldn't eat here all the time. Only—well, ma'am, you're the best cook in camp."

Ma smiled at him. "I hope that isn't the only reason you come to see us, Mr. Burt."

He got redder than ever then and gulped his coffee and took off in a hurry.

Time to time the men had stopped by to help a little, but next morning nobody came by. We got lined out about as soon as ever, and ma said to me as we sat on the wagon seat, "Pay no attention, Bud. You've no call to take up anything if you don't notice it. There will always be folks who will talk, and the better you do in the world the more bad things they will say of you. Back there in the settlement you remember how the dogs used to run out and bark at our wagons?"

"Yes, ma."

"Did the wagons stop?"

"No, ma."

"Remember that, son. The dogs bark, but the wagons go on their way, and if you're going some place you haven't time to bother with barking dogs."

We made eighteen miles that day, and the grass was better, but there was a rumble of distant thunder, whimpering and muttering off in the canyons, promising rain.

Webb stopped by, dropped an armful of wood beside the fire, then started off.

"Thank you, Mr. Webb," ma said, "but aren't you afraid you'll be talked about?"

He looked angry and started to reply something angry, and then he grinned and said, "I reckon I'd be flattered, Mrs. Miles."

Ma said, "No matter what is decided by the rest of them, Mr. Webb, we are going on, but there is no need to go to California for what we want."

Webb took out his pipe and tamped it. He had a dark, devil's face on him with eyebrows like you see on pictures of the devil. I was afraid of Mr. Webb.

"We want land," ma said, "and there is land around us. In the mountains ahead there will be streams and forests, there will be fish and game, logs for houses and meadows for grazing."

Mr. Buchanan had joined us. "That's fool talk," he declared. "What could anyone do in these hills? You'd be cut off from the world. Left out of it."

"A man wouldn't be so crowded as in California," John Sampson remarked. "I've seen so many go that I've been wondering what they all do there."

"For a woman," Webb replied, ignoring the others, "you've a head on you, ma'am."

"What about the Sioux?" Mr. Buchanan asked dryly.

"We'd not be encroaching on their land. They live to the

north," ma said. She gestured toward the mountains. "There is land to be had just a few days further on, and that is where our wagon will stop."

A few days! Everybody looked at everybody else. Not months, but days only. Those who stopped then would have enough of their supplies left to help them through the winter, and with what game they could kill—and time for cutting wood and even building cabins before the cold set in.

Oh, there was an argument, such argument as you've never heard, and the upshot of it was that all agreed it was fool talk and the thing to do was keep going. And there was talk I overheard about ma being no better than she should be, and why was that guide always hanging around her? And all those men? No decent woman— I hurried away.

At break of day our wagons rolled down a long valley with a small stream alongside the trail, and the Indians came over the ridge to the south of us and started our way—tall, fine-looking men with feathers in their hair.

There was barely time for a circle, but I was riding off in front with Tryon Burt, and he said, "A man can always try to talk first, and Injuns like a palaver. You get back to the wagons."

Only I rode along beside him, my rifle over my saddle and ready to hand. My mouth was dry and my heart was beating so's I thought Try could hear it, I was that scared. But behind us the wagons were making their circle, and every second was important.

Their chief was a big man with splendid muscles, and there was a scalp not many days old hanging from his lance. It looked like Ryerson's hair, but Ryerson's wagons should have been miles away to the east by now.

Burt tried them in Shoshoni, but it was the language of their enemies and they merely stared at him, understanding well enough, but of no mind to talk. One young buck kept staring at Burt with a taunt in his eye, daring Burt to make a move; then suddenly the chief spoke, and they all turned their eyes toward the wagons.

There was a rider coming, and it was a woman. It was ma.

She rode right up beside us, and when she drew up she started to talk, and she was speaking their language. She was talking Sioux. We both knew what it was because those Indians sat up and paid attention. Suddenly she directed a question at the chief.

"Red Horse," he said, in English.

Ma shifted to English. "My husband was blood brother to Gall, the greatest warrior of the Sioux nation. It was my husband who found Gall dying in the brush with a bayonet wound in his chest, who took Gall to his home and treated the wound until it was well."

"Your husband was a medicine man?" Red Horse asked.

"My husband was a warrior," ma replied proudly, "but he made war only against strong men, not women or children or the wounded."

She put her hand on my shoulder. "This is my son. As my husband was blood brother to Gall, his son is by blood brotherhood the son of Gall, also."

Red Horse stared at ma for a long time, and I was getting even more scared. I could feel a drop of sweat start at my collar and crawl slowly down my spine. Red Horse looked at me. "Is this one a fit son for Gall?"

"He is a fit son. He has killed his first buffalo."

Red Horse turned his mount and spoke to the others. One of the young braves shouted angrily at him, and Red Horse replied sharply. Reluctantly, the warriors trailed off after their chief.

"Ma'am," Burt said, "you just about saved our bacon. They were just spoilin' for a fight."

"We should be moving," ma said.

Mr. Buchanan was waiting for us. "What happened out there? I tried to keep her back, but she's a difficult woman."

"She's worth any three men in the outfit," Burt replied.

That day we made eighteen miles, and by the time the wagons circled there was talk. The fact that ma had saved them was less important now than other things. It didn't seem right that a decent woman could talk Sioux or mix in the affairs of men.

Nobody came to our fire, but while picketing the saddle horses I heard someone say, "Must be part Injun. Else why would they pay attention to a woman?"

"Maybe she's part Injun and leadin' us into a trap."

"Hadn't been for her," Burt said, "you'd all be dead now."

"How do you know what she said to 'em? Who savvies that lingo?"

"I never did trust that woman," Mrs. White said; "too high and mighty. Nor that husband of hers, either, comes to that. Kept to himself too much."

The air was cool after a brief shower when we started in the morning, and no Indians in sight. All day long we moved over grass made fresh by new rain, and all the ridges were pineclad now, and the growth along the streams heavier. Short of sundown I killed an antelope with a running shot, dropped him mighty neat—and looked up to see an Indian watching from a hill. At the distance I couldn't tell, but it could have been Red Horse.

Time to time I'd passed along the train, but nobody waved or said anything. Webb watched me go by, his face stolid as one of the Sioux, yet I could see there was a deal of talk going on.

"Why are they mad at us?" I asked Burt.

"Folks hate something they don't understand, or anything seems different. Your ma goes her own way, speaks her mind, and of an evening she doesn't set by and gossip."

He topped out on a rise and drew up to study the country, and me beside him. "You got to figure most of these folks come from small towns where they never knew much aside from their families, their gossip and their church. It doesn't seem right to them that a decent woman would find time to learn Sioux."

Burt studied the country. "Time was, any stranger was an enemy, and if anybody came around who wasn't one of yours, you killed him. I've seen wolves jump on a wolf that was white or different somehow—seems like folks and animals fear anything that's unusual."

We circled, and I staked out my horses and took the oxen to the herd. By the time ma had her grub-box lid down, I was fixing at a fire when here come Mr. Buchanan, Mr. and Mrs. White and some other folks, including that Webb.

"Ma'am"—Mr. Buchanan was mighty abrupt—"we figure we ought to know what you said to those Sioux. We want to know why they turned off just because you went out there."

"Does it matter?"

Mr. Buchanan's face stiffened up. "We think it does. There's some think you might be an Indian your own self."

"And if I am?" Ma was amused. "Just what is it you have in mind, Mr. Buchanan?"

"We don't want no Injuns in this outfit!" Mr. White shouted.

"How does it come you can talk that language?" Mrs. White demanded. "Even Tryon Burt can't talk it."

"I figure maybe you want us to keep goin' because there's a trap up ahead!" White declared.

I never realized folks could be so mean, but there they

were facing ma like they hated her, like those witch-hunters ma told me about back in Salem. It didn't seem right that ma, who they didn't like, had saved them from an Indian attack, and the fact that she talked Sioux like any Indian bothered them.

"As it happens," ma said, "I am not an Indian, although I should not be ashamed of it if I were. They have many admirable qualities. However, you need worry yourselves no longer, as we part company in the morning. I have no desire to travel further with you—*gentlemen.*"

Mr. Buchanan's face got all angry, and he started up to say something mean. Nobody was about to speak rough to ma with me standing by, so I just picked up that ol' rifle and jacked a shell into the chamber. "Mr. Buchanan, this here's my ma, and she's a lady, so you just be careful what words you use."

"Put down that rifle, you young fool!" he shouted at me.

"Mr. Buchanan, I may be little and may be a fool, but this here rifle doesn't care who pulls its trigger."

He looked like he was going to have a stroke, but he just turned sharp around and walked away, all stiff in the back.

"Ma'am," Webb said, "you've no cause to like me much, but you've shown more brains than that passel o' fools. If you'll be so kind, me and my boy would like to trail along with you."

"I like a man who speaks his mind, Mr. Webb. I would consider it an honor to have your company."

Tryon Burt looked quizzically at ma. "Why, now, seems to me this is a time for a man to make up his mind, and I'd like to be included along with Webb."

"Mr. Burt," ma said, "for your own information, I grew up among Sioux children in Minnesota. They were my playmates."

Come daylight our wagon pulled off to one side, pointing northwest at the mountains, and Mr. Buchanan led off to the west. Webb followed ma's wagon, and I sat watching Mr. Buchanan's eyes get angrier as John Sampson, Neely Stuart, the two Shafter wagons and Tom Croft all fell in behind us.

Tryon Burt had been talking to Mr. Buchanan, but he left off and trotted his horse over to where I sat my horse. Mr. Buchanan looked mighty sullen when he saw half his wagon train gone and with it a lot of his importance as captain.

Two days and nearly forty miles further and we topped out on a rise and paused to let the oxen take a blow. A long valley lay across our route, with mountains beyond it, and tall grass wet with rain, and a flat bench on the mountainside seen through a gray veil of a light shower falling. There was that bench, with the white trunks of aspen on the mountainside beyond it looking like ranks of slim soldiers guarding the bench against the storms.

"Ma," I said.

"All right, Bud," she said quietly, "we've come home."

And I started up the oxen and drove down into the valley where I was to become a man.

JAMES WARNER BELLAH

JAMES WARNER BELLAH (1899–1976) was born in New York City and graduated from Columbia University in 1923 with a bachelor's degree. He was a second lieutenant during World War I in the 117th Squadron of the Royal Air Force and, after the armistice, served with the rank of captain in General Haller's Expedition for the Relief of Poland. Bellah worked in advertising in New York City 1923–25 and simultaneously taught English at Columbia. He served as a special correspondent in China in 1927–28 and in Europe in 1928 for *Aero Digest*; in 1929 he went to the West Indies and Central America as a correspondent for *The Saturday Evening Post*. During World War II, Bellah served in the 1st and 80th Infantry Divisions and as an American officer on the staff of Admiral Lord Louis Mountbatten at the headquarters of the Southeast Asia command. He saw combat service under General Stilwell, General Wingate, and Colonel Philip Cochran in Burma, emerging from the war with the rank of colonel and honored with the Legion of Merit, the Bronze Star, the Air Medal, and the Commendation Medal.

Bellah's first novel, *Sketch Book of a Cadet from Glascony* (Knopf, 1923), indicated the preoccupation with military subjects which would inform all of his subsequent fiction. It wasn't until after World War II that he began writing his memorable stories about Fort Starke during the Indian Wars. Unfortunately these stories were published in *The Saturday Evening Post* and the Indian point of view could never be shown, had Bellah been inclined to show it; but, on the contrary, Bellah's object seems to have been to glorify the role of the American military, and this he did well and yet with general accuracy. I recommend Don Rickey, Jr.'s *Forty Miles a Day on Beans and Hay: The Enlisted Soldier Fighting the*

Indian Wars (University of Oklahoma Press, 1963) as an accompaniment to Bellah's fiction, because it provides the necessary historical and social background while at the same time it will place Bellah's literary accomplishment in perspective, especially if augmented by reading Arrell Morgan Gibson's *The American Indian: Prehistory to the Present* (D. C. Heath, 1980).

Many of Bellah's stories and magazine serials were never collected in book form, although several, such as the story collection *Reveille* (Fawcett, 1962) and the short novel *Ordeal at Blood River* (Ballantine, 1959)—both of which I particularly recommend—were issued as paperback originals. John Ford, the film director, shared Bellah's ambivalence toward native Americans and I recall Mr. Ford telling me on more than one occasion that no one knew more about the history of the West than James Warner Bellah. Ford's *Sergeant Rutledge* (Warner's, 1960) was based on Bellah's *Post* serial of the same title and Bellah received credit for his work on the screenplay. Bellah was also credited for co-script on Ford's *The Man Who Shot Liberty Valance* (Paramount, 1962), based on a short story by Dorothy M. Johnson. On his own Bellah wrote *A Thunder of Drums* (Bantam Books, 1961) and adapted it for the screen, filmed under this title by M-G-M in 1961, directed by Joseph M. Newman, and recipient of *Time* magazine's Best Western of the Year award.

Bellah's most memorable association with John Ford was on what is called Ford's cavalry trilogy. *Fort Apache* (RKO, 1948) was based on "Massacre" (1947), the story I have included below. *She Wore a Yellow Ribbon* (RKO, 1949) was based on Bellah's stories "Big Hunt" (1947) and "Command" (1946)—"Command" was a short story later requested by the State Department for translation into Thai for the *This Is America* program. *Rio Grande* (Republic, 1950) was based on "Mission with No Record" (1947). Bellah also wrote the dialogue for the U.S. navy documentary *This Is Korea* (Republic, 1951), directed by John Ford.

Obviously, Major Thursday is based loosely on General George Armstrong Custer and "Massacre" is told from the career officer's point of view through the eyes of Lieutenant Flintridge Cohill, who was often Bellah's point-of-view character. Perhaps, too, on its most basic level, this story is about—in Bellah's words—"the overpowering knowledge of life's inevitable defeat." The Indians in this story are given no tribe, which is just as well, since they are present merely for the purpose of dramatizing a conflict between white men.

Massacre

The wind was out of the east, and there can be a great restlessness of soul in the east wind—a ghost shuffle of unfulfilled promise. Flintridge Cohill awakened quickly all over, and lay quite still from long habit, until it came back to him that he was safe in his own quarters at Fort Starke. He snaked out a hand to his repeater and pressed the ring-back release. The watch struck three quarters of an hour past three o'clock. And as the soft bell sang in the darkness, Flint was a little boy again, watching his father, the captain, come angrily up the path to their quarters at Sackets Harbor, seven years before Sumter, push open the door and fling his cap to the rosewood table in the hall. "Molly, they've finally got Grant. He's resigned . . . for the good of the service!" Why should those things come back years later? Some friend of his father's. Some captain out at Fort Humboldt. A brother officer who had fought at Contreras and Chapultepec with his father.

Flint sat upright in bed. "Good God, I'll bet that was General Grant!" he said out loud, and he snorted. "And at a quarter before four in the morning twenty years later, what difference does it make if it was?" Then he heard the distant staccato of feet running.

Someone's boots pounding the headquarters' duckboards. The sound bounced clearly across the parade ground to the row, on the east wind. In a moment, Fire Call would sound or someone would bawl for the corporal of the guard. Cohill flung out of bed and went out on his lean-to veranda. There was a carriage standing across the parade ground in the darkness by headquarters. A carriage with restless horses and dry axles.

It'll be twenty years more before I get within shooting distance of general officer's stars—like Grant and the Old Man—and by that time I won't care. It won't be nearly as important as making captain, in a few more years. But I'd like to be a general before I die—the best damned general in the world at the right time and the right place! It's only the middle of the month and that's a paymaster's wagon over there. I can see the glass glint silver in the starlight like a sheet of bucket-flung water.

Cohill was pulling on cold breeches and stiff boots, and his teeth were chattering in the east wind; he was running fast and silently through the living darkness of the parade ground, with somewhere in the cellars of his mind the nasty-sounding name of Custis Meacham, Indian agent at White River. What are those tricks of association?

Feet raced toward him. He pivoted with flung arms, bending down to silhouette whoever it was against the lighter darkness of the sky. "Brailey?"

Brailey came toward him. "Mr. Cohill, sir, I got orders to call you and Mr. Sitterding and Mr. Topliff. You're wanted at post headquarters, sir."

And Cohill said. "What's the paymaster's wagon got to do with it, Brailey?"

Brailey said, "The new post commander arrived in the wagon. Drove all night from Indian Wells."

Owen Thursday was a tall man, dried out to leather and bone and sinew. Whatever he was doing, he moved about incessantly, not with nerves, but with primeval restlessness; not with impatience, but with an echo of lost destiny. Brevet Major General Thursday, of Clarke's Corps—Thursday of Cumberland Station and of Sudler's Mountain, at twenty-six. Now a major of cavalry at thirty-eight, back in the slow Army runway again, with the flame of glory burning low on his horizon ("I don't know what you were in the habit of doing under similar circumstances when you commanded your division, major, but as long as you have a battalion in my regiment, you will—") for it is far worse to go up and come back again than it ever is not to go up at all. And the cities of the world should always be a vision. For few men can walk their streets and come back to live at peace with their souls in the quietude of their own villages.

"Lieutenant Cohill, sir"—the dark was alive and prowling, like a large cat. There was cool dampness in it, and the faint whisper of threat. A horse whinnied in screaming soprano. Close to, when the team moved the paymaster's wagon, its glass windows flashed black, like polished ebony in the starlight.

"You got here damned fast, Cohill. Where's the acting post

commander? Do you all sleep with the covers over your heads at Fort Starke?"

There were booted feet on the veranda boards of headquarters. Inside, someone cursed persistently over the lighting of a lamp. Bitter wood smoke fanned low from a chimney lip and stained the smell of the white dawn air to gray. "Your father, General Cohill, asked me to convey his affection to you, Cohill, when I left Washington."

"Thank you, general."

"Not 'general,' " Thursday said sharply. "A man is what he's paid for. I'm paid in the rank of major."

"Yes, sir. I remembered you as General Thursday."

Then Joplyn came sprinting down the duckboards and braked himself to a quick stop. "Captain Joplyn, sir, acting in command."

"Joplyn," Thursday said, "I've come all the way in from Indian Wells on the whip and two wheels. Mr. Meacham, the agent at White River, wants a show of strength up there at once. He's afraid Stone Buffalo will get out of hand without it."

"Stone Buffalo has been out of hand for months. He is trying to see how far Meacham's religious sentiment will let him go, sir. And Meacham is the biggest fool west of Kansas City and the biggest liar. I'll get a half company off by reveille. I'll take it up myself."

"I call it to your attention that Mr. Meacham is an agent of the United States Government. You will get two companies and an escort wagon train off before reveille, Captain Joplyn. And I'll take them up to White River myself. I've had the officer of the guard send a runner to knock out Mr. Sitterding and Mr. Topliff. Mr. Cohill has already reported in. I'd like all three of them with me, for I know their names and records from department files. And I suggest you keep an officer at headquarters in future—on night duty—until I get back to take over command formally. I don't like daylight soldiers."

"Yes, sir." Joplyn turned sharp about to Flint Cohill with no change of voice, no strain in his manner. "Mr. Cohill, pass the word at once to A and B. Turn them to. Full field equipment, and three hundred rounds of carbine ammunition per man. You will take eight escort wagons, rations and forage for fifteen days, and half of C as mounted wagon guards."

"That is a lot of ammunition . . . for men who are supposed to be trained to shoot," Major Thursday said. "One hundred rounds per man should be ample for any emergency."

"One hundred rounds of carbine ammunition per man, Mr. Cohill. Fifty rounds for revolving pistols per pistol. Sitterding commands A. Topliff, B. You command the escort train. It is twenty minutes after four. How soon can you move out, Mr. Cohill?"

"Reveille is five-forty-five. We can pass the head of the column through the main gate at five-thirty, sir. When Topliff and Sitterding get here, will you tell them I shall be forming the train in the area in front of the cavalry stables? They can find me there. Their first sergeants will know everything you've told me . . . Brailey, follow me on the double as runner." Flint Cohill then turned sharp about to Thursday. "Have you anything additional, sir?"

"Yes, I've several things. I've a few ideas of my own on how Indians should be dealt with. I shall want colors and a proper color guard, guidons and trumpeters. Have the men bring their polishing kits and button sticks and boot blacking. A little more military dignity and decorum out here, and a little less cowboy manners and dress, will engender a lot more respect for the Army. I'll meet you here to take over command, Cohill, as the column passes. You will act as adjutant, in addition to your other duties. Officers' Call in the saddle on the march for further orders as soon as the tail clears the post. Questions?"

"Nothing, sir."

"Move out."

The sun in August is a molten saber blade. It will burn the neckline and the back of a hand to blistered uselessness as you watch it. It sears the lower lip into stiff scar tissue and sweats up shirts and beltlines into noisome sogginess while you stand still. The column was headed due north to make a crossing of the upper reaches of the Paradise, girths frothed white, saddles hot damp, hat brims low, and the blue of trousers and shirts faded out to Southern gray with the dust silt that blanketed everything except eyeballs and the undersides of tongues.

Owen Thursday rode alone, off to the right of the leading files, where he could turn and look down the strung-out length with the faint echo in his eyes of larger columns he had commanded—of regiments of infantry with colors and field music; of artillery rolling inexorably in its heavy dust, hames taut and chains growling, wheels slithering in ruts with the protesting sound of cracking balk ends; of cavalry flank guards flung far out on his right and left by battalion.

All of which dissolved into a hundred and nine officers and men and eight escort wagons—as big a detachment as Mr. Cohill or Mr. Topliff or Mr. Sitterding had ever taken on the warpath in all their service.

"Mr. Cohill!"

Flint kneed out of column and put his horse to the gallop and rode in on Major Thursday's near side.

Thursday said, "Move down the column and have every man crease his hat fore and aft as a fedora. The front of the brim may be snapped downward as eye protection, but all the rest of the brim will be turned up. The hat will sit squarely on the head. Look at them, Mr. Cohill! They look like scratch farmers on market day! The hat is a uniform, not a subject for individual whimsical expression!"

Thursday had a point ahead and flankers out on either side and a tiny rear guard with a warning mission only, but somehow it seemed more like a maneuver—a problem—than it did a march into hostile territory. D'Arcy Topliff, heading up B, never knew where the thought came from. But it was there suddenly from something he'd read years before or heard someone say: The major has fewer years left to live than he has lived already, and when that knowledge hits a man's mind, he can break easily. He must hurry then, for his time is shortening. He must seek short cuts. And, seeking them, he may destroy the worth of his decisions, the power of his judgment. Only a solid character with a fine sense of balance can face the fewer years as they shrink ahead, and go on into them with complacent courage, all the way to the Door.

Flint Cohill, with the wagons and head down to the dust, thought, *Damn it, this isn't a ceremonial detail of the First City Troop turned out for a governor's funeral. He's got the men disliking him from the start, deliberately, for picayune cause.*

And then Flint remembered a name brought into conversation at a reception once, and he likewise remembered old Gen. Malcolm Hamilton's grave bow.

"Madame, only four officers in the Army know the facts of that incident, but none of them will talk as long as the colonel's widow lives."

Three days north of Fort Starke, the detachment went into bivouac on the high ground above the headwaters of Crazy

Man Creek, which is the south branch of White River, and a little under thirty miles from the agency. The commanding officer sent Clay Sitterding on ahead to scout and contact Custis Meacham, the agent.

Clay rode back in, about sundown. "Stone Buffalo is camped at the junction of White River and Crazy Man, sir, in the chevron the fork makes. His camp is about a week old. From three hundred to three hundred and fifty people, all told. Most of them warriors and dog soldiers. No women and children. It's a war camp. There are scouting parties all the way along between us."

"You contacted Meacham, Mr. Sitterding?"

"I did, sir. He professes to have Stone Buffalo's complete confidence. Stone Buffalo has attempted to have himself accepted as medicine chief as well as war chief of all his nation. Running Calf contested the claim and took the Red Hill people and left the reservation. Stone Buffalo followed him to force him back into the fold. Mr. Meacham sent for us to stop the two factions from warring, but the last four days seem to have settled the argument peaceably."

Major Thursday's lip thinned. "In other words, as soon as the Indians knew troops were on the way, they decided to behave."

"That could be it, sir. Stone Buffalo would like to smoke with you. Mr. Meacham requests it. I strongly advise against letting Indians into our camp. It will not be advisable to let them know any more about our strength than they do now."

"When I want advice from my officers, Mr. Sitterding, I ask for it. Will you remember that, please?"

The smell of an Indian is resinous and salty and rancid. It is the wood smoke of his tepee and the fetidity of his breath that comes of eating body-hot animal entrails. It is his uncured tobacco and the sweat of his unwashed body. It is animal grease in his hair and old leather and fur, tanned with bird lime and handed down unclean from ancestral bodies long since gathered to the Happy Lands.

Major Thursday saw their impassive Judaic faces, their dignity, their reserve. He felt the quiet impact of their silence, but being new to the game, he had no way of knowing that they drew all of it on as they drew on their trade-goods blankets—to cover a childish curiosity and the excitability of terriers. Stone Buffalo. Black Dog. Pony that Runs. Running Calf. Eagle Claw. Chiefs of tribes in the sovereign nation of Stone Buffalo—a nation under treaty of peace with the

United States. A nation, in effect, held as prisoners of war, so that it would keep that peace.

Custis Meacham was painfully nearsighted and frighteningly short of breath. It was necessary for him to gasp wide-mouthed when he spoke. His hands were damp in the palms and restless. His fingernails were concave, like the bowls of small blue spoons. He sat with the skirts of his greasy Prince Albert draped across his pendulous abdomen.

The pipe went solemnly around to the left, each man pulling it red until his cheeks, ached, drawing in its raw smoke until his lungs were stifled.

Custis Meacham coughed himself red-eyed and completely breathless. "Oh, dear," he said. "I can't stand to be near them when they smoke. I trust that you don't indulge in the vice for pleasure, Mr. Thursday?"

"I do, constantly," Thursday said. "And I am Major Thursday, Mr. Meacham, not Mr. Thursday."

"God bless you, I pay no attention whatever to military titles. I don't believe in titles of any kind. You can see from their faces and actions, as they pass the pipe, that they have settled all their troubles peaceably among themselves. Thanks be to God. You can take all your soldiers straight back tomorrow. What is your church, please?"

Owen Thursday looked long at Custis Meacham. He said, "You put in a request for this detachment, but that does not put you in command of it. Any further action on your part will be made through the same channel you used for the original request—direct to departmental headquarters. I am a back-slidden Presbyterian, Mr. Meacham. I intend to remain one."

"You cannot tell me what to do." Custis Meacham's voice was shrill. "I am quite used to the way the Army does things! When I was secretary of the International Bible Association, I once told General Scott—"

Flint Cohill touched the major's arm. "Stone Buffalo is going to speak, sir," and, after a moment, Stone Buffalo rose. He talked and for a great many minutes Cohill said nothing.

Then he said, "All he has said so far is that he is a very, very brave man." Thursday nodded, and Stone Buffalo talked on for many more minutes. Cohill said, "He says now that he is also a very great hunter—he and his whole tribe." Again Thursday nodded, and Stone Buffalo told how the railroads and the white hunters had killed off the buffalo, and how he alone, as medicine chief, could bring them back again.

Suddenly Cohill whispered, "I don't like any of it, sir. He's covering up for time. This is an insolent attempt at reconnaissance, I believe."

"Stop it then." Thursday's voice was hard.

"It will have to run out—protocol requires it—you cannot stop him now until he is finished. That would be a grave insult."

"Is there anyone at Fort Starke who recognizes an order when it is given?"

Cohill rose to his feet. Stone Buffalo stopped talking in vibrant anger. Major Thursday leaned forward. "Cohill, no preliminary nonsense with him, no ceremonial phrasing. Straight from the shoulder as I tell you, do you hear me? They are recalcitrant swine. They must feel it."

Cohill stood there, white-faced. He said, "I hear you, sir. What shall I tell them?"

"Tell them I find them without honor or manhood. Tell them it is written on sacred paper that they will remain on their reservation. That they have broken this promise puts them beneath fighting men's contempt, makes them turkey-eating women. Tell them they are not talking to me, but to the United States. Tell them the United States orders them to leave here at once. They will break camp at dawn and return to the reservation, for I move in to their camp site at daylight," and Major Thursday turned his back and stalked off into the darkness, calling sharply for the officer of the guard.

Clay Sitterding, D'Arcy Topliff and Flint Cohill squatted in the white mists, gulping their steaming coffee. The morning was a gaunt old woman in the shadows, standing there wrapped in a shawl, seeing what she would not see again. A thin old woman with sadness in her face, and courage and the overpowering knowledge of life's inevitable defeat.

Ten years and better had passed under the bridges of Sitterding, Topliff and Cohill. Ten knowledgeable years of hard and bitter learning. They could have talked. "I told him not to receive them, not to smoke with them last night, and he shut me up." They could have said, "One hundred rounds of ammunition instead of three!" But you learn not to talk before you can ever learn other things. Behind them in the mists there was the movement of many men, but not enough men now, because the shock action of cavalry at one to three is suicidal madness without surprise. Who cares what you have commanded before, or what people think of you, or what other wars you have fought in? In war it is always what happens now! What happens next! Who commands here . . . now!

Sitterding finished his bitter coffee and for one brief instant he could feel the harsh winds of March on his face—the winds that howl up the Hudson River Valley and cut across the parade ground at the Academy like canister fired at zero elevation. There had been a time when the melting heat of Starke had made him forget the chilled wine of those Eastern winds.

D'Arcy Topliff said, "I wish I'd married the one rich woman I ever met! I'd be a banker in St. Louis this morning, and still in bed."

Cohill tried to laugh, but some ancient instinct within him had dried up the wells of his laughter. The curtain was down across the back of his mind, shutting him off from all he had been, so that he could only move forward. Some men are fortunate that way.

"Here we go," he said quietly, and with both hands he pressed briefly on the shoulders of the other two. "Just remember that the escort train is in mobile reserve, and if you get a fight, save me a piece."

You have seen it so often in the Jonathan Redfield print. The powder-blue trace of Crazy Man Creek against the burnt yellow grass on the rising ground behind. The dead of Company A stripped naked and scalped, their heads looking like faces screaming in beards. Major Thursday, empty gun in hand, dying gloriously with what is left of Company B, in an attempt to rally and save the colors, but this is how it happened. *This is how it happened:*

The column moved out with the mists of the morning still cold, moved out in a long breath of saddle soap on still-stiffened leather, rough wool, not yet sweat-damp, and the thin brown of gun oil. Dog-faced cavalry, the like of which has passed from the knowledge of the world. Up the gently sloping rise from the bivouac to the ridge line above Crazy Man Creek. Across the hogback ridge, outlined against the spreading yellow light that rimmed the eastern horizon. Guidons, booted carbine butts, hats creased fore and aft, backs arched and colors flying. There are cowpokes who will tell you solemnly that sometimes when a murderous thunderstorm howls down the valley, you can see them again crossing that ridge. That you can hear the brass scream of the charge echoing. But that is not so, for soldiers pass once only, and all that they ever leave behind is memory. "Close up the intervals! Close up!"

The point crossed the ridge first and wound on down the slope where the trail weaves onto high and rock-strewn ground before it reaches the ford. The point went on through and forded Crazy Man and signaled back from the other side to Lieutenant Sitterding at the head of A. All clear.

Sitterding gave the word, and A crossed the ridge and started down, with B, under D'Arcy Topliff, three hundred yards behind and echeloned three hundred yards to the left, west, rear. Which was by explicit order of Owen Thursday. So much for the creek side of the ridge. On the bivouac side, there was still Flintridge Cohill and the wagon train and the mounted guards from C. Flintridge Cohill was held up as soon as he started . . . by a broken linchpin.

Owen Thursday, sitting his horse high on the sky line, was the only man who could see the entire command. He sat there against the whitening dawn as if he had chosen that position to sit on and wait for it.

Company A rode on slowly down into the defile, breakfasts still warm in stomachs, saddles softening to the butt, muscles limbering up to the new day's work. Then unbelievably there was a sudden ring of fire in their faces and on both flanks. One hundred and eighty degrees of fire—half the horizon around—splintered around them like dry and rotted timber, tearing around them like grommets ripped from heavy cloth. Clay Sitterding and forty-two men were down. Half their mounts, reeling, galloping, were thrashing back over them, trying to get out and up the slope again.

Flint Cohill, blind to the sight of it because the ridge line masked it, knew it desperately for what it might be. He stared into his farrier sergeant's face.

He said, "Sergeant Magee, fix that pin and hold the train here on my order!"

And he spurred furiously toward the ridge top. Almost it was as if Owen Thursday were trying to escape facing him. He seemed to wait until he could wait no longer, until Cohill was almost to him, then he sank his rowels into his horse and plunged him headlong down the opposite side toward the Valley of the Shadow. But not soon enough, for Cohill saw what he was going to do. Cohill saw it. With no further reconnaissance and no clear idea of what he was up against, with no brief withdrawal to reform, with all of A lying dead now in the defile for everyone to see, Thursday screamed to Topliff to deploy B and to hit the sides of the defile at the gallop as foragers.

Cohill turned his back. "Magee," he shouted through cupped hands, "get the wagons up here fast!"

Then Cohill turned again, and this time he saw that murderous ring of fire from the rocks, half a full circle round, and there were tears within him that would never, as long as he lived, quite leave him again. In that moment he knew that the train and the mounted guards were all that there was left; that he alone on an open ridge line was all that remained of the sovereign dignity of the United States for hundreds of miles around. But he way saying it this way—he was saying it out loud, "D'Arcy's gone . . . and Clay's gone . . . but no man gets off this ridge line . . . no man!"

"Sergeant Magee, take the wagon boxes from the beds! Put one here! . . . Put one twenty full paces to the left! . . . One down there where you're standing, and one here to the right! All hands turn to, to dig rifle pits between the boxes! Turn in all canteens! Corral all animals on the rope, down the back-slope!"

It's not always in the book. It's a hundred thousand years. It's a heritage and a curse and the white man's burden. It's Cannae and Agincourt and Wagram and Princeton, and it's the shambles of Shiloh. With Flint Cohill it was thirty-one men on a hog-back ridge and the thought in his angry mind that he'd never live now to be a general officer, but he'd die the best damned first lieutenant of cavalry that the world could find to do the job that morning!

Lying on the ridge top, searching the ghastly valley below with his glasses, Flint saw the last of it—an officer and three men and the colors on their broken staff. He couldn't swear to it, but it looked like Clay Sitterding and old Sergeant Shattuck and Aiken and Sergeant Ershick. Only for a minute before they went down under the final rush. Then Stone Buffalo's warriors were overrunning the dead of both A and B, pincushioning the bodies with arrows. Scalping. Lopping off a foot and the right hand, so that the spirits, too, would suffer mutilation and never fight again. Then the Indians withdrew to consider the ridge top, and, by the dust presently, they were commencing to ring it, to cut it off from water, to wither it for the kill.

Cohill called young Brailey over and squatted down with him. "Brailey, you're a show-off and a braggart, and I never thought I'd have the right job for you. But I have. Take the best horse on the picket line. Make Fort Starke. Tell 'em where we are, and tell 'em we may still be alive if they hurry. I'm making you corporal, but you'll never draw a dime of pay if we're dead when you get back. Move out and make it so."

Shortly after that, Cohill saw the tiny group far below, struggling painfully up the draw. Six men, crawling, dragging two, stumbling. Hatless and bleeding. Stopping exhausted, faces downward; starting up the slow way once again. Cohill finally got down to them. D'Arcy Topliff, hit four times and barely breathing. Glastonby of the red hair, from A. "Sir, we didn't have a chance!"—crying every time he tried to speak. Pointing back helplessly. Cursing, with the tears greasing the filth of his cheeks. "Get Mr. Topliff to the ridge top, Glastonby." And there were Moore and Stonesifer and Coyne, out of B, dragging Bittendorfer with them. Shocked speechless. Bleeding. Obeying like whipped beasts. "Go on up, all of you, straight up the draw."

Cohill said that, because at that moment he saw the seventh man, still far below them. "And tell Sergeant Magee I'll be along in a few minutes . . . a few minutes behind you," and he scrambled on down the draw until he was crouched beside Owen Thursday.

"Cohill, sir."

Thursday turned and looked at him as if he had never seen him before in his life. The light was gone from his eyes and the pride was dead in him at last. All of his days the ghost of today had ridden with him, mocking his pride, pointing the finger of scorn at his personal ambition. General Thursday, of Clarke's Corps, of Cumberland Station, of Sudler's Mountain, with luck and the devil to help and a hero's crown for the snatching!

But today, the ghost was come alive at the cost of seventy-two men lying dead, through the ignorance that is pride's handmaiden, the stubbornness that is ambition's mistress.

"I am dug in on the ridge top," Cohill said, "with the wagon boxes loopholed, and rifle pits. I have thirty-seven men, one officer and one man wounded. I have water and ammunition—"

"Get ready to move out at once," Thursday said. "We must try to cut back into Fort Starke." But his voice broke.

Flint Cohill shook his head. "Stone Buffalo is already ringing the position. We cannot leave that ridge top. If we try, we'll be cut to ribbons before we've gone ten miles."

"Get ready to move out, Mr. Cohill!" The voice was a high and broken whine.

"I've sent a courier to Starke, sir. I believe he'll get through. I believe Captain Joplyn can get here in five days. I can hold until then. Besides, we've no other choice! General—" Cohill said it deliberately, but there was no defiance in it, no indictment. He was almost pleading. "General, there are two dead companies down there—all the friends I've had in the world for years." He snagged his hand gun from his holster, spun it until it was butt first toward Thursday, then he thrust it out and held it. "You don't have to tell me again, but A and B are all present or accounted for, and so am I! I'll move out to your order, but only under arrest, sir! Only under arrest!"

Thursday rose slowly to his feet, Cohill's gun in hand. "I've had all I can have," he said softly; "this is where the road stops at last." His eyes were completely empty as Flint looked into them. The light was gone forever. "Mr. Cohill, your ridge top. I'm going back down. Good luck."

"Mr. Sitterding can't talk, sir, nor can Shattuck nor Ershick nor Aiken, and you have my word of honor that I won't . . . ever . . . for the good of the service." Flint whispered it almost.

And that is how they found Owen Thursday when the flying column from Starke relieved Cohill's party on the fifth day.

He was dead with the little group that had defended the colors—dead beside Sitterding, Shattuck, Ershick and Aiken—shot in the right ear, with the gun held so close that the contract surgeon couldn't have missed knowing that the major had squeezed off the trigger himself. But Flintridge Cohill got there first, for there are ways of living that are finer than the men who try to live them, and a regiment has honor that no man may usurp as his personal property. Glory is a jade of the streets who can be bought for a price by anyone who wants her. Thursday wanted her but his pockets were empty, so Cohill lent him the two dollars for posterity. Cohill took his own gun from Thursday's dead hand. He threw out the cylinder and jerked the five ball cartridges and the one empty case into his left hand. He spun the gun far out into Crazy Man Creek.

The five ball cartridges, he dropped one by one as he moved away, but the empty cartridge case he always carried with him for the rest of his life, for fingering it in his pocket always gave him courage in moments when he needed it—when the way was dark and decisions not easy.

And it was Cohill, years later, who reconstructed the scene for Jonathan Redfield to paint. "Major Thursday," he said, "was a very gallant officer. We found him dead with the little group that defended the colors—with Lieutenant Sitterding and Sergeant Shattuck and Ershick and Private Aiken. No man could have wished for more."

But even when he was very old, Cohill always looked sharply at anyone who said, "for the good of the service," and he always said, "What exactly does that mean to you, sir?"

LUKE SHORT

FREDERICK DILLY GLIDDEN (1908–1975) was born in Kewanee, Illinois, and was graduated in 1930 with a bachelor's degree from the University of Missouri, where he had majored in journalism. Following graduation, Glidden worked for a number of newspapers, but no job lasted very long; the Depression years were not auspicious ones. He proceeded to wander throughout the Western regions of the United States and Canada. For a time he was an archaeologist's assistant; for two years he worked at trapping in northern Canada. In 1934 Glidden married Florence Elder of Grand Junction, Colorado, and they lived first in Santa Fe, New Mexico, settling finally in 1947 in Aspen, Colorado.

Glidden wrote in 1963:

Some twenty-nine years ago, newly married and lacking any kind of a job, let alone the newspaper job I wanted, I decided I'd write for the Western pulp magazines. Their contents seemed simple-minded to the point of idiocy; their stories appeared easy to write if you could complete a sentence. I studied them with a secret contempt since I'd graduated from Zane Grey at the age of twelve. Then I hacked out Western pulp stories that sold. I wasn't much of a slick-magazine reader either, but, since I was committed and aspiring, I thought I should study the work of my peers. [Alan] LeMay was admirable, [Eugene Manlove] Rhodes maddening but unique, and [James Warner] Bellah, then as now, inimitable. Reading them all, it was inevitable that I should come across a *Collier's* serial by a new-to-me writer named Ernest Haycox. It was the third installment, as I recall it. I hated to be suckered into the middle of a cliff-hanger, but I told myself this was work. Work? Before I'd read a dozen paragraphs, I knew I was into something special. When I was finished, I went up to my wife, took the book she was reading from her hands and ordered—not told—her to read the Haycox yarn. From that day on, we were hooked. . . . Why were his writings so special? . . . Pick up one of his best stories, and before you are ten pages into it, a mood has been established. There is menace here. . . . There is trouble ahead. Big trouble. . . . You are in a new and somehow fearsome country; in its harshness or darkness, there is a promise of cruelty. You have entered an unfriendly country with a man who has a grim past which he has conquered and who is heading into an even grimmer future.

Glidden's pseudonym was chosen for him by his agent and it was only later that he came to learn that Luke Short was the name of an actual Western gunman. By the time he wrote the second Luke Short novel, *The Branded Man* (Collins, 1939), the Haycox influence was discernible. I think eventually Glidden excelled Haycox at writing the kind of formulary fiction Haycox had pioneered. Glidden satisfied himself with polishing and enhancing his own variations of the formulary plot structures that appealed to him, and all of his novels, with one exception, have the same atmosphere he admired in Haycox' formulary fiction. The exception is *And the Wind Blows Free* (Macmillan, 1945), Glidden's one attempt at a romantic historical reconstruction; although he would never try one again, Glidden ranked this as his favorite among his own works. Soon the Luke Short name moved into the slick-magazine market right alongside that of Ernest Haycox and I think it is a good indication of how closely allied the slick magazines were in their editorial concept as to what constituted a Western story that when *Collier's* ceased publication in January 1957, partway through the serialization of Luke Short's *Doom Cliff* [alternate title: *The Whip* (Bantam, 1957)], *The Saturday Evening Post* took over and published the concluding installments of the novel.

Professor Robert L. Gale wrote an enthusiastic book titled *Luke Short* (Twayne Publishers, 1981). It has a fine bibliography, but I believe he overstated the case for historical accuracy in Short's fiction. I think the early Luke Short novels are the best. *Savage Range* from 1939 and *Sunset Graze* (Doubleday, 1942) are very tightly constructed and well plotted, with an economy of dialogue and suspenseful pacing. The short story "Court Day" dates from this same period, first appearing in *Collier's* in May 1939. A number of other writers have tried to imitate Glidden, Wayne D. Overholser and the early Louis L'Amour among them, but truly at his best he remains unsurpassed—provided we take that best to be a wholly imaginary West, a fearsome country with the promise of cruelty in its harshness or darkness, an unfriendly terrain peopled by men with a grim past heading into a grimmer future.

Court Day

The closing arguments were finished and, after instructing the jury and watching it file out, Judge Morehead recessed the court and went over to the Stockman's House for a beer.

The courtroom spilled its crowd onto the hard-packed adobe yard. A March wind that had been pelting sand against the courtroom windows and shaking them was a wild thing out in that thin sunlight, and the crowd of ragged nesters hugged the sheltered east face of the adobe building, as silent and patient in waiting as their teams that lined the tie rails.

Ernie Manners, his worn jumper gray and paper-thin over his thick shoulders, walked with a solid and deliberate step as far as the cast-iron watering trough by the tie rail and sat on its edge. Beyond him across the road and under a leafless cottonwood, the Socorro stage was waiting. It had been there since court convened this morning, and it would leave as soon as the jury returned a verdict and Joe Williams was either freed or put aboard it for the journey north to Santa Fe.

Trouble had ridden Ernie Manners and gentled him, so that his square weather-scoured face was almost impassive as he looked at the stage. To the other small ranchers it was a token of their and Joe Williams' defeat, soon to be made public.

Tim Bone came down the walk and stopped by Ernie and said, "Don't look like anyone ever doubted that jury, does it?"

"No."

"Are those Spade riders with the driver?"

"Yes, guards," Ernie murmured.

Tim Bone laughed shortly, without humor, and fisted his hands in his hip pockets. He was a middle-aged man and wifeless, his face shaped with a strange violence that danced wicked little lights in his eyes and made his speech aggressive. "Don't look like Bill Friend had any doubts either," he observed, quietly for him.

A bailiff left the courthouse door and walked over to the Stockman's House, the crowd's murmur following him. Almost immediately, Judge Morehead came out before the others and crossed the dusty road ahead of a team, waving at the driver. The others followed. To Ernie Manners and to all those small ranchers of the San Jon basin it was a roll call of their victors.

There was young John Comer, the deputy sheriff, who walked alongside the Spade foreman, Ferd Willis, as far as the near walk, and then stopped and waited for old Bill Friend, the Spade owner, and Martha Friend, his daughter.

Comer didn't need to stop, Ernie knew. Ferd Willis knew it too. Where it would have been easy for Ferd to walk past that clot of hostile men and women, ignoring them, it was not easy to stand and face them. But it was a concession he made to John Comer's arrogance, and Ferd stood there, idly scraping a circle in the dirt with the toe of his boot, looking down at the ground to avoid the stares.

Afterward, he fell in beside Bill Friend, while Martha Friend walked along with John Comer. Of those four, only Martha tried to greet the loose rank of nester men and women watching. Ernie saw her nod occasionally, saw the womenfolk nod in return and less often a man raise a hand to his worn hat. Bill Friend looked straight ahead, erect and unbending and implacable. John Comer whistled softly, his walk slow and unconcerned and somehow wary.

When they entered the door, Ernie looked down at his hand and then wiped it on his leg.

"Maybe we ain't ready yet," Tim Bone murmured. "Maybe we better wait and see what they do to Joe."

Ernie looked up quickly and Tim's glance slid away.

"Don't be a fool," Ernie said quietly. "This'll turn out short weight for us, but don't make the mistake of tryin' to fix it that way."

"Sure," Tim said, disbelief in his voice.

The crowd broke and filed back into the courthouse. Ernie was the last one in. What happened then was news to none of them. For the crime of killing and butchering out a Spade beef with which to feed his family, Joe Williams was found guilty by a jury of townsmen and sentenced to ten years in the Santa Fe penitentiary.

Out by the iron watering trough again, Ernie saw the arrangement of these waiting men was a little different this time. If trouble was coming, it would come now, and he hated the thought of it. It was patience that saved men, patience and waiting, and he wondered if these men would wait.

When the deputy came out the door with Joe Williams, it was Comer whom Ernie watched. The crowd stirred, gauging Comer's hand. It was a good one. Joe Williams, handcuffed, walked beside him. On Joe's other side was Ferd Willis, and on the stage top across the street were three Spade riders, rifles in hand.

Comer was so sure of himself that he paused to touch a match to his cigarette, a big man with thick shoulders and a proud way of carrying his young head.

In front of Ernie, Joe Williams said to Comer, "Can I talk to Ernie a minute?"

Comer liked the risk. He nodded and signaled Ferd Willis to step aside and then coolly surveyed the courthouse yard, knowing he and poverty had these silent men whipped.

Joe Williams said to Ernie, "She's goin' over with the Littlefields, Ernie."

"She'll be all right there, fine."

"She can raise a garden. Pay for her keep."

"Sure."

"Look," Joe's face was curiously attentive. "If she runs into any hard luck, you'll know it, won't you, Ernie?"

"I'll look out for her."

"That's what I mean. Thanks."

Ernie put out his hand and Joe took it wordlessly, a little of the bitterness and desperation in him mounting to his eyes.

Ernie said, "You find someone up there that can write, Joe. Keep the letters coming. We'll take care of her."

"So long," Joe said. Comer, seeing they were finished, threw his cigarette away and stepped up to Joe's side.

Tim Bone, from behind Ernie, drawled carefully, "Joe, you break out up there and I'll hide you."

Comer's gaze whipped to Tim. "Easy," he said.

"Mind now, Joe," Tim drawled.

Comer touched Joe's arm and they stepped into the street and crossed to the stage. Seconds later it rolled out and Ernie said to Tim, "Goin' upstreet?"

"In a minute," Tim murmured. He was watching Comer and Willis, who had turned and were coming back to the walk. Slowly the crowd was breaking up, drifting toward the stores.

Ernie sat down on the watering trough again, his sober and homely face watchful. Comer passed him and stopped in front of Tim.

"Your advice is likely to get him shot," Comer observed.

"I'd liefer get shot than spend ten years in Santa Fe. So would Joe," Tim drawled.

"If the rest of your friends feel that way about it, then tell them to leave the Spade stuff alone."

"You might tell 'em yourself."

"I'll do that," Comer said quietly. "Now move on."

Tim showed no intention of moving.

"Move on, I said."

"I heard you."

Ernie's quiet voice interrupted them. "I want to talk to Tim, John."

It was a graceful exit for Comer. He nodded and walked up into the courthouse, big and confident.

"Come on," Ernie said, and Tim joined him.

Court day always brought a crowd to Warms, but today there were horses at the tie rails whose brands hadn't been seen in town since last fall. They had come to see what Bill Friend would do to one of their own people, and they had found out.

Ernie stopped in front of the Emporium and Tim said, "See you down at the saloon?"

"Later, I guess," Ernie said.

Inside, he bought a sack of groceries and some dress goods with five of his last ten dollars and later, when nobody was looking, he left them in Littlefield's buckboard and went on downstreet.

Deputy Sheriff John Comer was talking to Martha Friend in front of the express office as Ernie hit the sidewalk, heading toward them. For a brief second, Ernie contemplated turning around, and then he gave it up. But he didn't want to see Martha after today's happenings.

Before Comer had come he had seen something of Martha, taken her to dances, and once he had taken her to the Fourth of July barbecue out on Tuesday Creek. But when old Bill Friend made it plain that Ernie was no different than any other range-stealing nester, Ernie quit seeing her.

Martha saw him first, and the surprise on her face was pleasant, Ernie saw. She smiled quickly, bent her arm at the elbow, raised her hand and wiggled her fingers in a wave to him. Ernie felt a flush of pleasure. He touched his hat, not intending to stop.

"Ernie," Comer called.

Ernie paused now, wheeled and walked over to them. Martha put out her hand and smiled again and said, "You're almost a stranger now, Ernie."

"It's a long ride from the San Jon, Martha. How've you been?"

She said fine and Ernie saw she was lying. Behind the welcome in her eyes lay a sadness that Ernie had seen once before, on the night when she listened to him and her father argue whose was the rightful side in the division of the San Jon basin range.

He wanted to say more, but there was nothing he could say without bringing in today's trial, so he looked up at Comer.

"I've got a favor to ask, Ernie." It was more like a command, and Ernie studied the man's face. It was not a kind face, not cruel either, only hard and lean and determined, almost humorless.

"I'd like to have you move your boys out of town before dark," Comer went on.

"My boys?" Ernie echoed.

"Yes. All the small outfits lined up against Spade."

Ernie watched him until he was finished and then looked at Martha. Her eyes avoided his, and he returned his attention to Comer. "Why me?"

"You're the only level head in the crowd," Comer said. "They'll listen to you."

"Not when I talk that kind of foolishness," Ernie said quietly.

Comer rubbed a finger along his lower lip and said just as quietly. "It's not foolishness, Ernie. I mean it. They've got to be out of town at sundown."

"Why?"

"Spade is here in town and there'll be trouble."

"Ever think of movin' Spade?" Ernie murmured.

Comer looked thoughtfully at him and then shrugged. "All right. Don't bother."

Ernie's temper was crowding him and he knew it and

didn't care. "How long you been here, Comer? Four months, isn't it?"

"Five."

"You aren't a Basin man," Ernie went on slowly. "When old Sheriff Baily died Bill Friend saw a chance to buy his own law. One way or another, every commissioner on that county board was in debt to Bill, so they voted with him. They voted to bring a man in from outside and they got you." He paused. "Begin to understand?"

"No."

"You were appointed, Comer, not elected. You're not our man. We'll take somethin' like happened today. It may take us five years to swallow it clean, but we will. Just don't crowd your luck until you know us, that's all."

He looked at Martha and touched his hat and left them.

The wind sent a rising sheet of grit against Budrow's saddle shop across the street. It caromed off the false front and raked the Spade ponies tied in front of Prince's Keno Parlor and Saloon.

Ernie walked past them and beyond Grant Avenue, toward Dick Mobely's Gem Saloon, his tramp deliberate as always. His anger had already dried up, and in its place was a deep knowledge of defeat. If he carried Comer's word to the men down there at the Gem, all his work, all those patient hours of reasoning with them, would be canceled. Men, even men ground to the ways of poverty, would take only so much. He had nursed their pride along with his own, had reasoned them into taking the long view in the face of the knowledge that Joe Williams would doubtless be convicted. They would be angry now, but he could swing them to his side again—but not if he carried the red flag of Comer's word to them.

They were all here, clotted at the bar or sitting in chairs hauled over from the poker tables. There was no drinking, for drinking took money and they had none.

The talk didn't stop as they made way for Ernie. He packed his pipe and then dragged up a chair to the edge of the circle. Ed Horstmann, from out on Tuesday Creek, was speculating on just how much nerve it took for Comer to bring Joe Williams out to the stage in front of the crowd. Miles Overbeck regretted that they hadn't made a try for Comer, and Tim Bone laughed.

"Hell, it takes just one bullet," he said quietly, looking at them. "Just one bullet." When he came to Ernie, his glance passed him quickly.

"Maybe that's what we ought to do," Ed said. "Draw straws, maybe, or cut cards for him. Anyway, have a try at him. Or somethin'."

Ernie said, "You do, Ed, and you'll see your kids carrying this fight."

Ed laughed. "The oldest is only six."

"That's what I mean."

Ed looked over at him and opened his mouth to speak. Tim Bone put a word in before him. "It's either that or pull stakes for most of us, Ernie. You too."

"There's an election coming," Ernie pointed out, as he had done before.

"Next fall," Miles Overbeck said. "Hell I ain't even got alfalfa to boil up for grub. Bill Friend sent a rider out last week while I was away, to stake my well for a homestead. The corner come right on the floor of my shack and damned if he didn't tip over my stove to drive his stake. I can't even drink."

"I know," Ernie said.

"You don't know," Tim said harshly. "If you did, Ernie, then why you arguin'?"

Ernie shifted in his chair. They were willing to listen to him; they always were. "You feel that way about it, pull up into the San Jon and live off the country till election time," he said. "Don't sell your places; don't give Bill Friend a claim; just pull out and wait."

"The other way's easier," Miles said.

"You know how it's comin' out," Ernie said slowly, repeating the old argument. "Why don't you wait? We'll vote Comer out next fall. After that, we'll give Bill Friend enough water and range for his needs and then it's done. But go at it with guns and he'll drive the lot of us over the mountains for good."

Tim Bone said, "Hell!" and walked out.

Max Troutman said, "Ernie, why you figure to play it that way? You was never afraid of a fight."

Ernie knocked his pipe out on his heel and pocketed it and then looked up at Max. He was back in the groove of the old argument, and he recited it as if it were new.

"We start pickin' and choosin' the laws we like and we ain't got any laws at all." He watched Ed Horstmann's face, which was eager to believe. "We got votes. We're Americans. And we elect our sheriffs by votes. If we can hang on this summer, we can vote Comer out—legal. And we'll vote in a fair man in his place. After that, Bill Friend will pull in his horns and leave us alone. But if we let Comer crowd us into gunplay, we're done." He looked at their faces. "What's the matter? Ain't you got the guts to starve a little for your places?"

Ed Horstmann said, "You're damn' right," and the argument started anew. Ernie knew how it would go. After an hour of talk Miles Overbeck would rise and say to Horstmann, "You goin' home, Ed?" and the meeting would break up. Safely, Ernie hoped, looking out under the swing doors to see how long the shadows were.

It worked out that way. Miles was on his feet, waiting only for a break in the talk to speak to Ed when Marty Beshears walked in. He came straight to the chairs and something in his face made Max Troutman cease talking. They all looked over at Marty.

"I just saw Comer," Marty announced, his eyes hot, his voice contained. "He's givin' us till sundown to clear out of town."

Nobody spoke for a minute. Ernie found them watching him, but he kept silent. There are times you can advise men, and there are times you can't.

"Well?" Marty said.

"Is that so?" Ed drawled. He tilted back his chair, turned his head and spat into the sawdust. Then he stood up. "I'm goin' up to Prince's and watch the games for a couple of hours."

A voice from the door, a cool commanding voice, said, "I don't think so."

It was Comer. He had both thumbs in the top of his wide leather gun belt. Ernie felt his stomach coil hotly. The fool! The whole sorry mess would blow up in their faces now. Comer would be killed and so would a couple of others and the war would come out in the open. Ernie opened his mouth and saw it was no use and shut it again.

Ed Horstmann said quietly, "Stand over, Marty, and let him open the ball."

Ernie slid off his chair toward the wall, his hand falling to his side.

It was then that Tim Bone shouldered through the batwing doors. He had a gun in his hand and he came to a full stop some five feet inside the door, gun leveled at Comer, and said, "Hold it!"

Comer watched Ed Horstmann for a full three seconds,

and then swung around to face Tim Bone. There was something in his face that told Ernie he knew he had made a mistake, and that he wasn't backing down.

"That's right," Tim drawled. "Turn around and take it in the belly."

"I said you're leavin' town by sundown," Comer said quietly. "Now get out of my way."

Tim Bone only said, "I don't reckon."

Comer didn't move. His iron bluff had failed, and a kind of panic crawled up into his face and was smothered. He shuttled his glance to Marty Beshears and got no help, and it was then he knew he might as well make his try for what it was worth, which was exactly nothing.

Ernie said sharply, "Tim, wait!"

Even as he spoke, he walked forward, knocking over a chair in his haste. He swung his body in between Comer and Tim and flipped both Comer's guns onto the floor. Then he reached up and took Comer's badge between his fingers and roughly ripped it off his shirt, taking a triangle of cloth with it. He grabbed Comer's upper arm and swung him roughly into a chair facing a table, and before Tim Bone could protest he turned to Dick Mobely behind the bar. "Paper and pen, Dick."

He got them and put them before Comer. Nobody else had moved. Ed Horstmann had his gun unlimbered now and was scowling.

"That's for your resignation," Ernie said swiftly, pointing to the paper. "Write it out to Bill Friend. When you're through with that, write another to him and tell him to move Spade out of town right now!"

Comer picked up the pen, twisted the wad of inky paper from the ink bottle, dipped his pen and wrote in quiet haste.

When Comer had signed his name, Ernie ripped the sheets off the tablet, wheeled, and said to Tim Bone on his way out, "Just wait a minute, Tim. Just one minute."

Bill Friend was in the Stockman's House lobby talking with Judge Morehead over in a corner. Ernie walked straight to him, tossed Comer's badge in his lap and shoved the papers at him.

Bill Friend's tired face was wary. He took out his spectacles; then, sensing the urgency in Ernie's manner, he forgot to put them on. Holding the papers at arm's length, he read the first one. Without comment he turned to the second.

His eyes were hard and speculative. "Where is Comer now?"

"Down at the Gem with a gun to his ear," Ernie said quickly. "All you got to do to get him murdered is sit there and ask me questions."

"Murdered?" Judge Morehead murmured.

Ernie didn't even look at him. He was watching Bill. He said, bitterly, "Ain't you rubbed it in enough for one day, Bill?"

Bill Friend didn't look at him. His glance roved the lobby, settled, and he called, "Ferd."

When Ferd Willis came over, Bill Friend said, "Get the boys together and go on out. Now."

Ferd looked at Ernie and grunted and went out. Ernie turned his back to Bill Friend and followed Willis as far as Prince's, where Ferd turned in. Dust was settling rapidly and the wind was dying.

At the Gem, Comer was still sitting in his chair. He had peeled a sheet of paper from the tablet and it lay torn in small pieces on the table top. Sweat runneled his cheekbones; he looked hard at the table.

Ernie stopped in front of him and he looked up.

"You're through," Ernie said mildly. "As soon as Spade gets moved out of town you better get your horse and ride out in the other direction."

He looked around for a chair and hauled it up to the table and sat down across from Comer, hearing the scrape of leather as Ed Horstmann holstered his gun.

"Damn you," Ernie said mildly, putting his elbows on the table, "I don't mind jumpin' on a man when he's down. Not on you anyway. If you don't clear this country by tonight you'll walk into a bushwhack inside another twenty-four hours."

He rose and walked to the door and stood in it a minute, his gaze directed upstreet. Tim Bone watched him, his gun sagging a little.

Ernie turned his head and said, "All right, get out."

Comer rose and walked past Tim without looking at him, his boot scuffing one of his own guns on the floor as he went. He passed Ernie and turned upstreet, his walk a little less hurried.

Ernie felt a little sick with the slackened tension. He let the door swing to and walked over to the hitch rail, placing both hands on it and hanging his head. The sudden explosion of voices from the inside welled out, and he turned away. There was a chance now. It had taken that threat of violence to crack Bill Friend. He had made a concession in moving Spade out of town, and if he could make one he would make more.

The court-day crowd had left town. Blank spaces gaped at the tie rails, and the street was quiet.

Ernie found himself walking toward the Stockman's House, and checked himself. He was ravenously hungry, but the meal at the hotel cost a half dollar. Too much. He fingered the coins in his pocket and then turned back and went into the Palace Café.

He was alone, and glad of it. Thinking back on this day, there was some order to it, some hope come out of it. If Comer would leave, if it was in the man to see wisdom, then there was something to work with and build on.

Finished, he stepped out of the Palace and paused on its step, reaching for his pipe. A rider passed, his face turned toward Ernie, the muffled clopping of his horse's hoofs in the thick dust the only sound. It was Ferd Willis, and he turned his head quickly, without speaking. Someone cursed a horse down the street.

Ernie stepped down onto the boardwalk. From across the street in the darkened doorway of the express office, someone called, "Ernie!"

Ernie stopped, half-turned. Ferd Willis pulled up his horse and looked over his shoulder, for something in this voice was urgent and angry.

John Comer swung under the hitch rack and stepped out into the street. "Make your brag again, Ernie," Comer taunted, walking forward.

Ernie didn't move. He watched Comer as he came to a stop in the middle of the street, and he wondered at the savage anger in the man's voice.

"You heard it," Ernie said quietly.

"I thought I did," Comer said. He reached down and pulled out his gun, and Ernie heard the distinct click of its cock. A wild haste seemed to be pushing Comer. He shot as the upswinging arc of his gun was only half completed, and the bullet smacked against the boardwalk, shaking it. His second shot was higher, and it slapped into the glass front of the store. The whole pane collapsed, jangling to the boardwalk.

Ernie reached down and brought out his gun, his breath held, and swung it up, moving smoothly. When the sight caught the light shirt of Comer, he fired. Comer shot once more, his slug rapping hollowly on the false front of the building, and in the same motion he sat down in the road. He put both hands to his chest and gagged, and then tried to get up and fell on his side, later rolling on his face.

Ernie walked over to him. Ferd Willis put his horse around and walked it back. Someone from Prince's ran up and then knelt by Comer, and by that time there were two more men there.

Ernie looked up at Ferd Willis. "What's your story, Ferd?" he asked quietly. Tim Bone, breathing hard, stepped over to Ernie's side.

"There's no question," Ferd Willis said quietly, without fear. "Comer tried to get you."

Ernie's glance shuttled to the low porch of the Stockman's House. A cluster of men stood on the steps, among them Bill Friend and Martha.

"Maybe you better tell Bill that right now," Ernie said. "Come along."

Ferd Willis put his horse in at the tie rail, and Ernie joined him. There were others now following.

Ernie stopped on the walk, and suddenly remembered he had his gun still in his hand. He holstered it, listening to Ferd Willis' steady voice. When Ferd was finished, Bill Friend said nothing, looking out at the people gathering in the road. Both he and Martha were facing Ernie, so that their faces were shadowed from the light behind them. It made a little golden halo around Martha's head as it touched her hair.

"Yes," Bill Friend murmured.

Tim Bone said quietly, "There's one of your deputies, Bill. How many more we got to fight?"

"None," Martha Friend said firmly. She put her hand on her father's arm and he looked at her in a tired way and did not speak.

Martha said to them, looking at Ernie. "This never would have worked and we all know it. It's an election you want, isn't it? For sheriff?"

"Yes, ma'am," Tim Bone answered.

"And the commissioners can set a date for it?"

"Any time," Max Troutman said.

"Then they will," Martha said. She looked up at her father. "Can you give them your word for that, Dad?"

Old Bill Friend never looked more weary. He watched Ferd Willis for several seconds, his eyes speculative, and then shifted his gaze to Ernie. "Yes, I can promise that." He turned and walked inside.

Those on the steps, all except Martha, walked out in the street to look at Comer, leaving Ernie to face her.

She stepped down to the walk, watching the men clot around the spot on the road, and her face was grave. Then she looked up at Ernie. "It's been a long wait, hasn't it?"

"Long enough," Ernie said.

Martha was silent a moment, and then she said, "Do you remember how it used to be, Ernie—before all this started?"

Ernie nodded, mute.

Martha put a hand on his arm, and smiled fleetingly. "It's been lonesome for me too, Ernie."

Ernie watched her closely. He parted his lips to ask, "But what about Comer?" and then remembered that figure out in the road. Martha shook her head slightly, as if she understood what he was about to ask and was forbidding him to ask it.

"Good night, Ernie," she said, and went quickly up the steps.

Ernie Manners thought he could see an end to patience, then. He put on his hat and went out into the road, steeling himself against the questions he would be asked. There would be an end to them, too, some day, because there was an end to everything a man hated to face but faced anyway. He had learned that again from her.

PART FOUR

THE WEST IN REVISION

ELMER KELTON

ELMER KELTON (1926–) was born on a ranch in Andrews County, Texas, and spent his youth and early manhood associating with cowboys and Western old-timers around the Midland-Odessa ranching country of West Texas. Kelton's great-grandfather, in his words, "came out into West Texas about 1875 with a wagon and a string of horses, started a big family and died young, leaving four boys to break broncs, punch cattle, and make a living the best way they could, supporting their mother and two baby sisters. I never was much of a cowboy myself, but the heritage stayed with me."

Following graduation from high school, Kelton enlisted in the U.S. army and served in the European theater. In 1948 he was graduated from the University of Texas at Austin with a bachelor's degree and proceeded to carve out for himself a promising career in journalism, as a ranch-and-livestock writer and editor. While thus employed, he continued writing Western fiction, having first appeared in *Ranch Romances*, a pulp publication, in 1947. His first novel was *Hot Iron* (Ballantine, 1955), a story set in Texas that deals with the cattle business—a subject in which Kelton was certainly well versed. His second novel, *Buffalo Wagons* (Ballantine, 1956), is about hide hunters in the Comanche territory in the early 1870s; it won for him the first of three Spur Awards from the Western Writers of America.

These first two novels and several that followed are more or less a combination of formulary and romantic ingredients. But as he matured as a novelist, Kelton increasingly became concerned with history and, commensurately, his fiction changed in tone and substance. "As a fiction writer," Kelton once said in an address to the Texas Folklore Society, "I have always tried to use fiction to illuminate history, to illuminate truth, at least as I see the history and truth. A fiction writer can often fire a reader's interest enough to make him want to dig into the true story and make him search out the real history to find out for himself what happened."

I believe that Kelton's formulary and romantic Western fiction is among the best of its kind; but his new course was truly heralded with the appearance of *The Day the Cowboys Quit* (Doubleday, 1971). Ever since, with each novel, he seems to me to be getting better and better. I believe that his book *The Time It Never Rained* (Doubleday, 1973) is one of the dozen or so best novels written by an American in this century. It is set in contemporary Texas during a seven-year drouth; Charlie Flagg, the protagonist, is an aged man possessed of the qualities most admired by Kelton in human beings: determination, integrity, and endurance. Moreover, Kelton's portrayal of Mexicans, their culture, and their relationships with whites is both insightful and humane.

Speaking with him about a selection for this anthology, I suggested an episode from *The Wolf and The Buffalo* (Doubleday, 1980). The humility of the man was such that he honestly wanted to know what I thought of that book, was it really good? I didn't tell him this at that time, but I will confide it to the reader. Many times when persons who have read one or another of my books have written me a letter, I have, in answering, recommended they read Elmer Kelton, preferably beginning with *The Time It Never Rained.* His fiction transcends literary debate and competitiveness; it is of the very essence of what I believe to be the American spirit, a spirit which defies pigmentation, chastened by the land, instilled by the Great Mystery with the deepest kind of reverence.

"Desert Command," as I have chosen to title this story, concerns a troop of buffalo soldiers lost in the wastes of the Southwestern desert. Among the books that Kelton recommended to the reader at the conclusion of *The Wolf and the Buffalo* were William H. Leckie's *The Buffalo Soldiers* (University of Oklahoma Press, 1967) and *The Comanches: Lords of the South Plains* (University of Oklahoma Press, 1952) by Ernest Wallace and E. Adamson Hoebel. I would second those recommendations, but first, and before all, I would recommend *The Wolf and the Buffalo* itself. The last line in that novel reads: "Old Rangers and old warriors would often smoke together and share memories of an open-plains era lost to them all." It has not been completely lost; Elmer Kelton has brought it to life again in his wondrous and beautiful fiction.

Desert Command

The captain went through the motions of setting up a guard mount, but it was a futile effort. Most of these suffering men could do little to defend themselves should the Indians choose this time to attack. Gideon's vision was so blurred that he could not have drawn a bead. Sergeant Nettles could no longer control his limp. He kept his eyes on the captain and contrived not to move more than necessary when the captain looked in his direction.

Gideon asked, "Sergeant, why don't you take your rest?"

Nettles' eyes flashed in anger. "You tryin' to tell me what to do, *Private* Ledbetter?"

"No, sir. Just come to me that you had a hard day."

"We all had a hard day. Mine ain't been worse than nobody else's."

"You've rode back and forth, walked back and forth, seein' after the men. You gone twice as far as most of us. You rest, why don't you? Tell me what you want done and I'll do it."

"I want you to leave me alone. Ain't nothin' wrong with me that ain't wrong with everybody here."

"The rest of them got no arrow wound that ain't ever healed up."

The anger in Nettles' eyes turned to sharp concern. "It's all right, and I don't want you talkin' about it." He glanced quickly toward the captain and showed relief to find Hollander's attention focused elsewhere.

Gideon said accusingly. "You been hidin' it from him."

He could not remember that he had ever seen Nettles show fear of anything. But the sergeant was fearful now. He gripped Gideon's arm. "Don't you be tellin' him. Don't be tellin' nobody. Without the army, what could I be? Where could I go?"

"Lots of things. Lots of places."

"You know better than that. In the army I'm a sergeant, a

top sergeant. I'm somebody, and I can *do* somethin'. Anywhere else, I'm just another nigger."

"Captain'll see for hisself sooner or later."

"Not as long as I can move. Now you git to your own business."

Sometime during the early part of the evening Gideon heard horses walking. He pushed up from the ground, listening, hoping it was Jimbo and the canteen carriers coming back. He was momentarily disoriented—dizzy—but he realized the sound was from the wrong direction to be Jimbo. It was coming from along the column's backtrail, to the west. He thought about Indians, but they wouldn't make that much noise. The clinking and clanking meant cavalry horses.

Captain Hollander figured it out ahead of Gideon. He walked to the edge of camp and did his best to shout. "Waters! Sergeant Waters! Up here!" His voice was weak and broke once.

The horses seemed to stop for a moment. The men—one of them, at least—had heard the captain. Hollander shouted again, his voice hoarser now. After a moment, the horses were moving again. The captain grunted in satisfaction. His good feeling was soon spoiled, for the horses kept walking, right on by the knoll.

"Waters!" Hollander tried again. Gideon took up the shout, and so did several others. The riders continued to move, passing the hill and going on eastward. The captain clenched his fists in anger.

Gideon volunteered, "I'll go, sir. I'll fetch them back." Hollander only grunted, but Gideon took that for approval. He started down the hill, his legs heavy. He shouted every so often for Waters, but he heard no reply. When he stopped to listen he could tell that the horses were getting farther from him. He tried to run but could not bring his legs to move that rapidly. He stumbled over the crown of some dried-up bunchgrass and sprawled on his belly. He invested a strong effort into getting on his feet.

Behind him Hollander called, "Come back, Ledbetter. Let them go."

He wavered on the point of insubordination but found he could barely hear the horses anymore. He had no chance to catch them. Wearily he turned and began the struggle back up the hill. It must have taken him an hour to reach the huddled company and fall to the ground.

Hollander stood over him, against the starlight. "You tried."

When he had the breath, Gideon said, "They just never did hear me."

"They heard you. Waters simply did not choose to stop. He's saving himself, or trying to."

A question burned in his mind, and he came near asking it aloud. *Are we going to save ourselves?* His throat was too dry to bring it out.

Nettles came over after a while to see if he was all right.

Gideon demanded, "What was the matter with Sergeant Waters? I *know* he heard me. I never figured *him* to panic out of his head."

"I seen him when the men commenced to groan. It was the groanin' done it. You ever wonder why he drank so much? It was to drive the groanin' sounds out of his mind."

"I don't understand."

"Old days, Waters was a slave catcher. It was him that kept the hounds, and him the white folks give the whip to when he caught a runaway. He didn't have no choice—they'd of took the whip to *him* if he hadn't done it. Now and again they made him keep whippin' a man till the life and the soul was beat out of him. I reckon them dead people been comin' after Waters ever since, in his mind."

The night breeze turned mercifully cool, but it held no hint of moisture. Gideon woodenly stood his guard duty, knowing he would be helpless if anything challenged him. He heard men groaning. The sound made his skin crawl. He could imagine how it had been with Waters. Across the camp someone babbled crazily, hallucinating. Gideon lapsed into sleep of sorts, or unconsciousness. When he awoke, color brightened the east. His head felt as if someone were pounding it with a hammer. His tongue was dry and swollen, his mouth like leather.

Sergeant Nettles lay on his blanket, his eyes open. Gideon crawled to him on hands and knees. He knew what he wanted to say, but his tongue betrayed him. He brought out only a jumble of sounds. He worked at it a long time before he summoned up a little saliva and forced his tongue to more or less his bidding. "You all right, sir?" he asked.

Nettles nodded and pushed himself slowly from the ground. At the edge of camp, Captain Hollander was moving about, the first man on his feet.

Little effort was made toward fixing breakfast. The men

could not eat. They could not swallow without water. The captain started trying to pack the mules. The regular packer had fallen behind yesterday with Waters. Gideon began to help. It was almost more than he could do to lift a pack to the level of a mule's back. Had the mules been fidgety, he could not have managed. But they were too miserable to move around.

He could see a little better this morning, for the rest, and his legs moved easier than last night, but the gain was of only minor degree. A stir among the buffalo hunters attracted his attention. He became conscious that many of their horses and pack mules were gone. They had strayed off during the night, or perhaps Indians had stolen into the edge of camp and quietly made away with them. The hunters staggered around uncertainly, accusing one another mostly by gesture, for they were as hard put as the troopers to convert gestures into understandable words. In a little while hunters and soldiers started a ragged march down the gentle slope and left the round hill behind them.

Grasping at hope wherever he could find it, Gideon told himself that perhaps Jimbo and the others had stopped at darkness for fear of losing the trail, and by now they were on the move again, coming to the rescue.

The morning sun was soon punishingly hot. Miles went by slowly and painfully, and Jimbo did not come. Far up into the morning, after a couple of troopers had slumped to the ground, Hollander called for a rest stop. They had moved into a sandy stretch of ground with low-growing stemmy mesquite trees and small oak growth shin- to knee-high. Many of the men draped blankets over these plants and crawled under them as far as they could go for partial protection against the punishing sun.

Gideon turned to look for Sergeant Nettles. He found him shakily trying to dismount from his black horse Napoleon. Gideon reached to help him. He spread a blanket across a bush and pulled the corner of it over Nettles' head.

Young Nash tried to dismount but fell and lay as he had landed. Little Finley sat hunched, crying but not making tears. He tried to talk, but the words were without form.

Hollander was somehow still able to articulate, though he spoke his words slowly and carefully. He said it was his judgment that José had become lost and was not coming back—not today, not ever. The men who had gone on after him with the canteens must be sharing whatever fate had overtaken José.

Thompson argued sternly that somewhere ahead lay Silver Lake, and that it was no doubt José's goal. It couldn't be more than a few more miles—fifteen or twenty at most, he declared.

Hollander shook his head violently, his face flushed. If water were that near, and José had found it, Jimbo and the others would be back by now. The captain pointed southeastward. He still had his compass. Water anywhere else was a guess, and evidently a bad one. But he *knew* there was water in the Double Lakes. It was time to stop gambling and go for the cinch.

Thompson was aghast. "You know how far it is to the Double Lakes? Those darkies of yours—they're almost dead now. They'll never live for another sixty-seventy miles."

"They'll live. They've *got* to live."

Thompson insisted that water lay much closer, to the northeast.

Hollander countered, "You said that yesterday. How far have we come? How many more men can we afford to lose?"

"Go that way," Thompson insisted, pointing his chin across the sandy hills toward Double Lakes, "and you'll lose them all."

"There is water at Double Lakes. There is only death out here in these sands. Will you go with us?"

Thompson turned and studied his hunters. "No, we're trying for Silver Lake. It's there. I know it's there. I beg you, Captain, come on with us."

But Hollander had made up his mind. "I've already gambled and lost. I'll gamble no more on water that may not exist. Best of luck to you, Thompson."

The buffalo hunter saw the futility of further argument. "God go with you, Frank."

Hollander nodded. "May He walk with us all." Anger stood like a wall between the men, but each managed to thrust a hand forward. The two groups parted, the hunters toward the hope of Silver Lake and a short trail, the soldiers toward the certainty of Double Lakes, a long and terrible distance away.

The last time Gideon glimpsed the hunters, fading out of sight far to his left, four were walking, the rest hunched on their horses. Though he had not become personally acquainted and could not have named any except Thompson, he felt an ache of regret, a sense of loss as they disappeared into the shimmering heat.

He had no feeling for time. His legs were deadweights that he dragged along, one step and another and another. His vision blurred again. He trudged with his head down, following the tracks of the men in front of him. He no longer thought ahead, or even thought much at all. He fell into a merciful state of half consciousness, moving his body by reflex and instinct. His tongue had swollen so that it almost filled his mouth, and at times he felt he would choke on it.

He was conscious of hunger but unable to act upon it. He put hardtack into his mouth but could not work up saliva to soften it. It was like dry gravel against his inflexible tongue. He had to dig the pieces out with his finger.

Rarely did the horses or mules urinate, but when they did, someone rushed with a cup. The thought was no longer revolting to Gideon. Captain Hollander passed out brown sugar for the men to stir into the urine and increase its palatability. Some was given back to the horses, which at first refused but later accepted it.

By midafternoon, when the heat was at full fury, a horse staggered and went down. Hollander cut its throat to put it out of its misery. Finley came with his cup and caught the gushing blood and drank it, and others took what they could catch before death overtook the animal and the flow stopped. Some of the men became violently ill; the blood was thick and bitter from the horse's dehydration.

Hollander was compelled to call a halt. Men were strung out for half a mile. Orders meant next to nothing. This was no longer a column of soldiers; it was a loose and straggling collection of half-delirious men struggling for individual survival. Gideon saw Nash fall and wanted to go to help him but for a long time could not move his legs. Only when he saw Sergeant Nettles collapse upon the sun-baked sand did he muster the strength to stagger twenty steps and throw blankets over the men's heads to shield them from the sun. He slumped then, too exhausted to do the same for himself. He lapsed into a dreamlike state and seemed to float away like some bodiless spirit, back to the plantation. He heard the happy voice of Big Ella and the others there, and he splashed barefoot into the cool, flowing river.

The heat abated with sundown, and night brought a coolness which broke Gideon's fever. He roused to the point that he could look about him and see the other men lying in grotesque positions, many groaning, half of them suffering from delirium.

He rallied enough to crawl to Sergeant Nettles. At first he could not tell that the man was breathing. He held his hand just above Nettles' mouth and felt that faint but steady warmth of breath. Probably the sergeant was unconscious. Gideon saw no point in trying to bring him out of it. The Lord was being merciful.

Sometime in the night Captain Hollander started trying to get the men on their feet to use the cooler hours for easier miles. Gideon watched him impassively at first, until the man's strong determination began to reach him. Sergeant Nettles arose and began limping from one man to another. Gideon pushed to his feet and helped.

He heard Hollander say thickly, "Good man, Ledbetter. Get them going."

In the moonlight it was apparent that several horses had wandered away. Judas was gone. Gideon could not bring himself to any emotion over that. Half the men were afoot now, their horses strayed or dead. Many of the pack mules were missing. Nettles asked Gideon to count the men, to be sure they left none behind. He found it difficult to hold the figures in his head. His mind kept drifting to other things, other times, other places far better than this one.

Many blankets and packs were left on the ground as the company moved out. A couple of men dropped their carbines, and Gideon forcibly put them back in their hands. A little later he looked back and saw that one of the men was empty-handed again.

He dreaded sunrise, but it came. He sensed that they had walked or ridden many miles in the cool darkness. The heat was blunted the first couple of hours by a thin cover of dry clouds that held no promise of rain. These burned away, after a time, and the men and horses trudged under the full punishment of an unforgiving July sun.

A transient thought flitted through Gideon's mind. He wondered where the Indians were. It struck him as strange that he had gone so long without the Indians intruding on his consciousness. It occurred to him that it had been most of two days since he had heard them mentioned. Odd, that the mission which had brought the soldiers into this blazing hell had been so completely forgotten in the face of a more elemental challenge, simple survival.

A staggering horse brought the procession to a halt. Without waiting for the captain to give an order, one of the troopers cut the animal's throat, and several fought over the gushing blood. Gideon saw Nettles start toward the men to break up the fight, then go to his knees. Gideon took it upon himself to part the fighters, throwing a couple to the ground with more strength than he had realized he still owned. Little Finley's own horse went down on its rump. Finley stared dumbly, making no effort to join the struggle to capture its blood. He lay down on the short, brittle grass and wept silently, his shoulders shuddering.

Through all of it, Nettles sat helplessly. The spirit was still strong in his black eyes, but the flesh had gone as far as it could. Gideon managed to get the men under some semblance of control, making gruff noises deep in his throat because he could not force his tongue to form clear words. He felt the eyes of Hollander and Nettles upon him. Without being formally bidden to do so, he took command upon himself and motioned and coaxed and bullied most of the men into movement. Lieutenant Judson, weaving a little, got on his droop-headed horse and took the lead.

Soon only five men were left, Gideon and Hollander on their feet, the sunstruck Nash and shattered little Finley lying on the ground, Sergeant Nettles sitting up but unable to keep his legs under him.

By signs more than by words, Nettles conveyed his intention of staying with Nash and Finley until they were able to move. Then he would bring them on, following the company's trail to water. Captain Hollander nodded his assent, though Gideon saw sadness in the man's blue eyes. Hollander took the big black hand in both of his own and squeezed it for a moment, silently saying good-bye to an old friend. Hollander turned away quickly, not looking back. Nettles raised his hand again, and Gideon took it.

The sergeant mumbled, but Gideon made out the words he was trying to say. "Take care of them, soldier."

Gideon tried to assure him he would be back as soon as they found water, but the words would not come. He turned back only once, a hundred yards away, and took a final look at the sergeant, still sitting up, holding the reins of big, black Napoleon. For a moment, in spite of the heat, Gideon felt cold.

The column moved until upwards of midday, when the heat brought more horses to their knees, and more of the men. By this time the company was out of control. Now and then a man in delirium struck out on a tangent of his own, away from the main body. At first Gideon tried to bring them back but soon had to give up, for the effort was a drain on whatever strength he still held in reserve. He stopped thinking ahead but concentrated on bringing one foot in front of the other.

When Lieutenant Judson went down, slipping from the saddle and landing limply in the dry grass, the column stopped. The lieutenant's horse braced its legs and stood trembling. It no longer sweated, though a crust of dried mud clung to its hide. Hollander tried to rouse Judson but could not. Hollander gave a little cry and slumped to the ground, covering his face with his hands. By instinct more than reason, Gideon helped him to a small mesquite and threw a blanket over it to shade him, and to shield the captain's emotions from view of the men. The lieutenant's horse, untethered, began wandering off southward, dragging the reins, drawn by instinct in the direction of Concho. Gideon knew he should make some effort to bring it back, but he lacked the willpower to move. He sat with his legs stretched out before him on the ground and watched the horse stumble away to a slow death somewhere out there on the parched prairie.

After a time, Gideon became aware that the captain was trying to call him. Hollander motioned with his hand. Gideon crawled to the officer on hands and knees.

Hollander extended his silver watch, despair in his sunken eyes. Very slowly, very deliberately, he managed a few clear words. "Wife. Give to my wife and baby."

Gideon reached for the watch until the import of the captain's words penetrated his fevered brain. Hollander was giving up. Gideon looked slowly around him at the men sprawled on the ground, covering their heads with blankets if they still had them, hats if they did not.

If Hollander died, these men would die. Hollander might be no better man than they, but his was the leadership. His was the example they had been conditioned to follow, as they had been conditioned all their lives to follow one white man or another. It came to Gideon that if he accepted the watch, that would release the captain to die in peace.

He felt a flare of deep anger. The captain had no right to die! He had brought these men here; he had to live and take them out. Gideon drew back his hand. Shaking his head, he tried to form words first in his mind, then get them out on his dry, swollen tongue.

"No! You'll live. *You* give it to her."

The captain reached out with both hands, the silver chain dangling. His eyes begged, though his cracked lips formed no discernible words.

Gideon almost gave in to pity, but the anger was still hot in his face. Stubbornly he pulled back. The words came clearly in his mind, though he could not get his tongue to speak them.

You got a baby now, more than likely. You owe that woman, and you owe that baby, and you owe us! You goin' to live if I got to kill you!

Only the anger came out, not the words. But the captain seemed to understand that Gideon refused to release him from his responsibilities. Hollander turned his head away, in the shadow beneath the blanket. He clutched the silver watch against his chest, his shoulders heaving.

In a while he was somehow on his feet again. He motioned for Gideon to help him lift the delirious lieutenant onto the captain's own horse. Gideon tied the young officer in the saddle. Hollander struck out again southeastward, his steps slow and deliberate. He was setting a pace, an example. His shoulders had a determined set. Gideon sensed that the captain would not give up again. He might die, but he would not surrender.

Gideon had trouble distinguishing reality from hallucination. His head roared from fever, and it ached with a steady rhythm like a drumbeat. He imagined he could hear the post band playing a parade-ground march, and he tried in vain to bring his feet into step with it. His vision was distorted, the men stretched out of shape, the prairie rolling in waves. Cajoling, threatening, he got the men to their feet one by one and set them to following the captain. Some moved willingly, some fought him, but by and by he had them all on the move.

Stumbling, bringing up the rear so no one could drop out without his knowledge, Gideon moved in a trance. It occurred to him that a couple of the pack mules had strayed off on their own. Only two were left.

Each time a horse staggered and fell, its throat was cut, and the men caught the blood and gagged it down. The captain's horse gave up after a long time, going to its knees. Gideon struggled to untie the lieutenant but could not bring his unresponsive fingers to the task. He cut the rope and tried to ease the officer to the ground. He lacked the strength to hold him. He and the lieutenant fell together in a heap. Gideon looked up at the horse, afraid it might roll over on them. He dragged himself and the lieutenant away before someone cut the animal's throat.

That was the last of the horses.

He lay struggling for breath; the exertion had been severe. The men were like gaunt scarecrow figures out of a nightmare, their uniforms a dusty gray instead of blue, many hanging in strips and ribbons. The faces were stubbled, the beards matted grotesquely with dust and horses' blood as well as some of their own, for their lips were swollen out of shape and had cracked and bled. They no longer looked like soldiers, they looked like madmen—and Gideon feared he was the maddest of them all.

The packs were untied from the mules, and Lieutenant Judson was lifted aboard one of the last two surviving animals. Again Gideon tried to tie him on, but he could not coordinate his hands and gave up the task. Delirious or not, Judson would have to retain instinct enough to hold himself on the mule.

The ragged column plodded and staggered and crawled until far into the afternoon. Hollander motioned for a rest stop in an open plain that lacked even the low-growing dune mesquites over which a blanket could be stretched for shade. Hardly a blanket was left anyway. The men had dropped them one by one, along with everything else they had carried. Troopers sprawled on the ground, faces down to shield them from the sun. Gideon fell into a state more stupor than sleep. After a time, he felt someone shaking his shoulder. Hollander was motioning for him to get up, and to get the other men up. Gideon went about the task woodenly. He helped Hollander and one of the other troopers lift the lieutenant back onto the mule.

Gideon saw that Hollander was studying the other mule, which had remained riderless. The wish was plain in the officer's eyes, but Gideon saw there a reluctance, too. They were no longer officers and men; they were simply men, all in a desperate situation together. Hollander was uncertain about using the advantage that might save his life.

Gideon felt a sudden temptation to take the mule himself. He had the strength to do it. At this moment, he was probably the strongest man in the column. Nobody—not even Hollander—could stop him if he made up his mind.

The thought became action to the point that he laid his hands on the reins, and on the mule's roached mane. He leaned against the mule, trying to summon strength to pull himself up. But he could not, and he realized slowly that it was more than simply a matter of strength. It was also a matter of will. Sergeant Esau Nettles forcibly pushed himself into Gideon's mind. In Nettles' eyes, such a thing would be a dishonor upon Gideon and upon the company.

Gideon cried out for Nettles to leave him alone, but in his mind he could see the sergeant's angry eyes burning like fire, and their heat seemed to touch him and force him back from the mule.

Gideon motioned for Hollander to take the mule. Somehow his tongue managed the words. "Ride him. Sir."

He had not been willing to give Hollander release to die, but now he offered him release to live. Hollander stared at him with remorseful eyes. With Gideon's help, he got onto the mule's back. He reached down and took up the reins to lead the mule on which the lieutenant had been placed.

A momentary wildness widened Hollander's eyes. The thought behind it was too clear to miss: with these mules the white men could leave the black soldiers behind and save themselves.

Reading that temptation, Gideon stared helplessly, his mouth hanging open. He knew he could not fairly blame Hollander, for he had almost yielded to the same temptation. One pleading word shaped itself into voice. "Captain . . ."

The wildness passed. Hollander had put aside the thought. He pointed with his chin and motioned for Gideon and the others to follow. They moved off into the dusk, toward a horizon as barren as the one behind them. But the waning of the day's heat brought a rebirth of strength. Gideon kept bringing his legs forward, one short step at a time.

Darkness came. He knew men had dropped out, but he could do nothing any more to help them. He followed the cloudiest notion of time, but somewhere, probably past midnight, he heard a cry from Hollander. Fear clutched at him—fear that Hollander was stricken. Gideon forced his legs to move faster, bringing him up to the mules. He stumbled over an unexpected rut in the prairie, and he went heavily to his hands and knees.

Hollander was making a strange sound—half laugh, half

cry. He pointed at the ground. "Trail," he managed. "Trail."

Gideon felt around with his hands in soft sand, trying to find solid ground to help him push back to his feet. Slowly he understood what Hollander was trying to say. He had stumbled into a trail—a rut cut by wagon wheels.

"Shafter," Hollander said plainly. "Shafter's trail."

Shafter. Of course. Colonel Shafter had been all over this country the year before, exploring it in a wetter, more amenable season. These ruts had been cut by his long train of supply wagons.

Lieutenant Judson seemed more dead than alive, responding not at all to Hollander's excitement, or to Gideon's.

Hollander pointed down the trail. "Double Lakes. Come on."

Gideon felt as if he were being stabbed by a thousand sharp needles. Strength pumped into his legs. He struggled to his feet and found voice. "Water, boys. Water, yonderway!"

The men quickened their steps, some laughing madly, some crying without tears. Gideon stood at the trail in the bold moonlight, pointing the troopers after the officers and the mules as they passed him, one by one. When the last had gone—the last one he could see—he turned and followed.

The mules moved out farther and farther ahead of the men afoot, and after a long time Gideon thought he heard them strike a trot. It was probably in his mind, for surely they no longer had that much strength. Unless they had smelled water . . .

That was it, the mules knew water lay ahead. His legs moved faster, easier, because now they were moving toward life, not death.

It might have been one mile or it might have been five. He had walked in a half-world much of the time and had little conception of anything except his revived hope. But suddenly there it was straight in front of him, the broad dust-covered expanse of the dry playa lake, and the moon shining on water that had seeped into the holes the men had dug in another time that seemed as long ago as slavery. The soldiers who had reached there ahead of him lay on their bellies, their heads half buried in the water. Captain Hollander was walking unsteadily around them, using all his strength to pull some men back lest they faint and drown themselves.

"Not too much," he kept saying thickly. "Drink slowly. Drink slowly."

Gideon had no time for reason. He flung himself onto his stomach and dropped his face into the water. The shock was unexpected. He felt his head spinning. He was strangling. Hands grabbed him and dragged him back.

"Easy now. Easy."

He tried to scramble to the water again, even as he choked and gagged, but the hands held him. "Slow, damn it. Slow." The voice was Hollander's.

He lapsed into unconsciousness. It might have lasted a minute, or it could have been much longer. When he came out of it, he was hardly able to raise his head. The terrible thirst returned to him, but this time he realized he had to keep his reason. He pulled himself to the edge of the water and scooped it up in his hands. He realized that if he fell unconscious again it must be on the dry ground, lest he drown before anyone could respond.

The water still had an alkali bite, but that was no longer a detriment. Gideon had never known water so sweet. He rationed himself, drinking a few sips, waiting, then drinking again, always from his cupped hand. He became aware that some men had slid into the water and were splashing around in it with all the joy of unleashed children. That this compromised sanitation never entered his mind; he kept drinking a few swallows at a time. Almost at once, it seemed, his tongue began to shrink. He thought of words, and they began to pass his lips in creditable fashion. "Praise Jesus! Bless the name of Jesus!"

Finally, when he came to a full realization that he would not die, he lay down and wept silently, no tears in his eyes.

There was no guard duty, unless Hollander stood it himself. Occasionally the thirst came upon Gideon with all its furious insistence, and he drank. When finally he came fully awake, the sun was shining warmly in his face. Gradually he heard stirrings, men going to the water or from it. He pushed to his knees, blinking in surprise at a bright sun an hour or more high.

His eyes focused on Captain Hollander, sitting up and staring back. Hollander's face was haggard, his eyes still sunken. But he was an officer again. "Ledbetter, let's see if you can walk."

It took Gideon a minute to get his legs unwound and properly set beneath him. But finally he was standing, swaying. He took a few steps.

"Ledbetter," Hollander said, "I need a noncom. I want you to regard yourself as a corporal."

"And give orders?" Gideon was stunned. "I ain't never led nobody. I been a slave for most of my life."

"So was Sergeant Nettles."

"I sure ain't no Nettles."

"Most of us would still be out there in that hell if it hadn't been for you. Perhaps all of us. Like it or not, you're a corporal." He dismissed further argument. "We left some men behind us. I want you to pick a couple or three of the strongest, fill what canteens we have left and go back. Take a mule." He pointed his chin at Lieutenant Judson. "The lieutenant will ride the other to the base camp and bring up wagons and supplies. I'll send a wagon on after you."

Gideon sought out three men he thought had regained strength enough to walk. Almost everything had been discarded along the way, so they had nothing to eat except a little hardtack. The men drank all the water they could comfortably absorb so they would not have to drain the canteens later. Those would be needed for whatever men they found along the trail. Looping the canteens over the mule, he set out walking, his step improving as he went along. His mind was reasonably clear, and he began mentally upbraiding himself for not counting the men at the lake before he left. He didn't know, really, how many were still out. His memory of yesterday's ordeal was hazy at best. Men had dropped by the wayside—he could remember that—but he could not remember who or how many.

The rescue party came in time to a Mississippian named Kersey, lying in yesterday's blown-out tracks. It took a while to revive him, and then he clutched desperately at the canteen, fighting when anyone tried to pull it away for his own good. Gideon asked if he knew who else might be behind him, but the man could only shake his head. He could not speak.

Gideon left one of his three men with Kersey and set out walking again, northwestward. Before long his legs began to tremble, and he knew he was approaching his limit. He and the other two looked at each other and reached silent agreement. They dropped to rest, the sun hot upon their backs.

By night they had found just one more man. Gideon had managed to shoot a couple of rabbits, and the men shared those, half cooked over a small fire before sundown. They smothered the fire and walked on for a time to get away from the glow, in case it might attract Indians.

All day he had watched the unstable horizon, hoping to see Esau Nettles and Nash and Finley riding toward them. Now and again a distant shape would arise, only to prove itself false as the heat waves shifted and the mirages changed. His hopes ebbed with his strength.

Night gave him time to brood about Jimbo. He could visualize Jimbo and the men who had gone with him, following the trail of the lost guide until one by one they fell. Jimbo would have been the last, Gideon fancied, and he probably had not given up hope until he had made the last step that his legs would take.

More men had dropped out than Gideon had found. The others had probably wandered off in one direction or another. Some might find the lakes for themselves. The others . . . He slept fitfully and dreamed a lot, reliving at times his own agony, seeing at others Jimbo or Esau Nettles, dying alone in that great waste of sand and burned short grass.

They moved again in the coolness of dawn, but the men had less of hope now to buoy them along. Though no one spoke his doubts, they were clear in every man's eyes.

The wagon came as Hollander had promised. The other men stayed behind to leave the load light. Gideon got aboard as guide. The driver and his helper had not been on the dry march. They could only follow the tracks, the trail of abandoned equipment, the swelling bodies of horses that had died one by one along the way. Riding silently on the spring seat as the wagon bounced roughly over dry bunchgrass and shinnery, Gideon drew into a shell, steeling himself for what he had become convinced he would find at the end of the trip.

It was as he had expected, almost. They found little Finley first. To Gideon's amazement, he was still alive. He fought like a wildcat for the canteen Gideon held to his ruined lips. Gideon was unable to keep him from drinking too much at first, and for a while he thought Finley might die from overfilling with the alkali-tainted water.

Like a candle flame flickering before it dies, Gideon's hopes revived briefly. Perhaps finding Finley alive was a good omen.

The hopes were soon crushed. They found black Napoleon, dead. As an act of mercy, Nettles had taken off the saddle and bridle and turned the horse loose on the chance it could save itself. The gesture came too late. Soon Gideon found Esau Nettles and the young trooper Nash lying beneath a blanket spread for shade over a patch of shin oak. Even before he lifted the blanket, Gideon knew with a shuddering certainty. They were dead. He dropped in the sand beside them, drew up his knees and covered his face in his arms.

In the wagon he could hear little Finley whimpering, out of his head. Anger struck at Gideon, sharp, painful and futile. For a moment the anger was against Finley, a liar, a sneak thief, a coward. Why should he live when a man like Esau Nettles had died? For a moment, Gideon's anger turned upon God. Then he realized with dismay that he was railing against the faith drilled into him since boyhood, a faith he had never questioned in his life.

The anger exhausted itself. Only the sorrow remained, deep and wounding.

The trip back to the Double Lakes was slow and silent. Little Finley regained mind enough to be afraid of the two bodies and to move as far from them as possible without climbing out of the wagon. "They're dead," he mumbled once. "Why don't we leave them?"

Gideon chose not to dignify the question by answering it. His contempt for Finley sank deeper into his soul. He made up his mind that he would do whatever he could to force the little man out of this outfit, if not out of the army. He wanted to blame Finley for Nettles' death, though he knew this was not totally valid. Perhaps Nettles had realized he would never make it to the Double Lakes on that bad hip. Perhaps he had stayed behind with Nash and Finley so someone else later would not have to stay behind with him. The more Gideon pondered that possibility, the more he wanted to believe it; it gave reason to Nettles' death, even nobility.

As the wagon went along, it picked up the men who had stayed behind. Most had walked some distance in the direction of the lakes rather than wait to be hauled all the way. All looked in brooding silence at the blanket-covered bodies. Those exhausted climbed into the wagon beside them. Those who could walk continued to do so. Gideon got down and joined them, for he was feeling stronger. The exertion of walking helped the black mood lift itself from him.

Captain Hollander met the wagon as it pulled up to the edge of the lake. Gideon stared, surprised. The captain had shaved and washed out his uniform. It was wrinkled but passably clean, within the limitations of the gyppy water. Army routine had again prevailed over the challenge of the elements.

Hollander counted the men who walked and who climbed out of the wagon. He asked no unnecessary questions. He seemed to read the answers in Gideon's face. He lifted the blanket and looked at the bodies, his face tightening with a sadness he did not try to put into words. "We had better bury them here. This weather . . ."

The digging was left to men who had come up from the supply camp, for they had the strength. Hollander had brought no Bible to read from, an oversight some might regard as indicative of the reasons for the company's travail. The captain improvised a long prayer asking God's blessings upon these men, these devoted servants of their country and their Lord, and upon any others like them who had met death alone on that hostile prairie, unseen except by God's own messengers come to lead them to a better land.

Three more men had wandered into camp during Gideon's absence, men who had lost the trail but somehow retained enough sense of direction to find the lakes. Toward dusk Gideon heard a stir and looked where some of the men were pointing, northward. He saw horsemen coming. His first thought was Indians. But soon he could tell these were soldiers. And the man in the lead was unmistakable.

Jimbo!

Jimbo spurred into a long trot, and Gideon strode forward to meet him. Jimbo jumped to the ground, and the two men hugged each other, laughing and crying at the same time.

In camp, when all the howdies were said and the reunions had lost their initial glow, Jimbo explained that the guide José had missed the Silver Lake he was trying to find and had come instead, somewhat later than he expected, to a set of springs just off Yellow House Canyon. Jimbo and the soldiers who followed had stayed at the springs long enough to recoup their own strength and that of their horses. Some had remained there with the buffalo hunters who straggled in, but Jimbo and three others had filled canteens and set out along their backtrail to carry water to the column they expected to find somewhere behind them. Hollander's decision to strike out for Double Lakes had thwarted them. They marched much farther than they intended and found no one. Fearing that the rest of the company had died, they had returned heavy-hearted to the springs, rested awhile, then set out to find Double Lakes and the base camp below.

Captain Hollander's face twisted in remorse as he listened. The hunters had been right; if he had followed them his troops would have reached water sooner than they did. Perhaps Esau Nettles and Private Nash would not be dead; perhaps others would not still be missing.

Lieutenant Judson tried to reassure him. "You used your best judgment based on the facts at hand, Frank. You knew this water was here. You couldn't know there was water where the hunters wanted to go. They were just guessing. What if they had been wrong? You had the responsibility for all these men. Those hunters could gamble. You could not."

Gideon knew Judson was right, as Hollander had been. But he could see the doubt settling into the captain's eyes. As long as Hollander lived, it would be there, the questions coming upon him suddenly in the darkness of a sleepless night, in the midst of his pondering upon other decisions he would be called upon to make in the future. To the end of his life, Hollander would be haunted by Esau Nettles and the others, and the unanswered question: did it have to be? Gideon looked at him. It was one of the few times in his life he had ever genuinely pitied a white man.

Gideon wrestled awhile with his doubts, then approached the captain hesitantly. "Sir . . ." He took off his hat and abused it fearfully in his nervous hands. "Sir, you done right. Old Sergeant, he'd of said so hisself, if he could. He'd of said you *always* done right."

Hollander stared at the ground a long time before he looked up at Gideon. "Thank you, Ledbetter. There's not a man I'd rather hear that from than you . . . and *him*."

Early on the fifth day, having sent out search parties and having given up hope that any stragglers still out would ever turn up alive, Hollander ordered the company to march southward to the supply camp. Water there was better, and timber along the creek would provide shade. The trip was slow and hot and dry, and Gideon found himself skirting along the edge of fear as terrible memories forced themselves upon him.

Late on the afternoon of the sixth day, a column of mounted men and two army ambulances broke through a veil of dust out of the south. A rider loped ahead of the column, pulling up in the edge of camp. He was the civilian scout Pat

Maloney, from the village of Ben Ficklin. He whooped in delight as he saw Captain Hollander and Lieutenant Judson standing beside a wagon.

"Frank Hollander! Dammit, man, we thought you were dead!"

He pumped Hollander's hand excitedly, but that was not enough. The ex-Confederate gripped the Union officer's arms and shook him in a violence of joy. "Tell you the God's truth, Frank, we come to hunt for your body. We thought every man jack of you had died."

His gaze swept the camp. Gideon felt the scout's eyes stop momentarily on him and Jimbo, lighting with pleasure at the sight of them.

Hollander replied gravely, "A few of us *are* dead. The best of us, perhaps."

Maloney looked around a second time, his face going grim as he missed Nettles. "The old sergeant?"

Hollander looked at the ground. "We buried him."

Maloney was silent a moment. "We thought from what we heard that we would have to bury you *all!*" He explained that Sergeant Waters had somehow made it back to Fort Concho, with two others. They had brought a report that Captain Hollander and all his men had been led astray by Indians on that great hostile plain, that they and all those buffalo hunters were dying from heat and thirst. They were certain, Waters reported, that no one except themselves had survived.

Maloney pointed to the approaching column. "You can imagine how that news tore up the post at Concho."

Apprehension struck Hollander. "My wife . . . Adeline. She heard that?"

"Everybody heard it."

"She must be half out of her mind. This, and the baby coming . . . We'll have to send word back right away."

Maloney smiled. "You know I got me a new baby boy, Frank?"

Hollander seemed not quite to hear him. "That's good, Pat. Glad to hear it." But his mind was clearly elsewhere.

Maloney said, "Who knows? He may grow up to marry that little girl *your* wife had. Join the North and South together again, so to speak."

Hollander's eyes widened. He had heard *that.* "A girl, you say? You've seen it?"

"Went by there last thing before I left the post. She looks

like her mother. Damn lucky thing, too, because her papa looks like hell."

The trip back to Fort Concho was made slowly and carefully, for more men were afoot than on horseback, and none had completely regained strength. At times even the civilian Maloney would step down from his horse and walk awhile, letting some tired black trooper ride.

Messengers had carried the news of their approach ahead of them, so that most of the people of Saint Angela were lined up to watch the arrival of men who had come back from the dead. An escort and fresh horses were sent out from the post. Hollander and Judson and Maloney rode at the head of the column. Gideon was behind them, urging the men to sit straight and look like soldiers that Esau Nettles would have wanted to claim.

Ordinarily they would not have ridden down the street, but this was an occasion, and the escort wanted to show them off. Lined along Concho Avenue were civilians of all ages, sizes and colors, white to brown to black. Most cheered the soldiers as they passed, though Gideon looked into some eyes and found there the same hostility he had always seen. Nothing, not even the ordeal the soldiers had been through, had changed that. Nothing ever would.

Two-thirds of the way down to Oakes Street, a seedy, bearded man leaned against a post that held up the narrow porch of a new but already-dingy little saloon. As Hollander came abreast of him the man shouted, "Say, Captain, why didn't you do us all a favor and leave the rest of them damned niggers out there?"

Hollander stiffened. He turned in the saddle, rage bursting into his face. He freed his right foot from the stirrup and started to dismount. Maloney caught his arm. "Frank, you ain't got your strength back."

Maloney swung slowly and casually to the ground, handed his reins to Gideon and walked up to the man with a dry and dangerous smile set like concrete. He crouched, and when his fist came up it was like a sledge. The man's head snapped back, then his whole body followed. He slid across the little porch, winding up half in and half out of the open front door.

Maloney looked first to one side, then the other, challenging one and all. Nobody took up his challenge. He reached down for the struggling man.

"Here, friend, let me help you up."

When the man was on his feet, Maloney hit him again, knocking him through the door and into the saloon. With a wink, he took his reins from Gideon's hand, swung back into the saddle and gave the silent Hollander a nod.

"You're welcome," he said.

WILL HENRY

HENRY WILSON ALLEN (1912–) was born in Kansas City, Missouri. After attending Kansas City Junior College, he drifted West, working at odd jobs until he ended up in Southern California. In 1935 he went to work for a company manufacturing animated films and in 1937 he was hired by M-G-M to work as a junior writer in that studio's short-subjects department. It was in midlife that Allen first decided to try his hand at writing Western fiction. *No Survivors* (Random House, 1950) was his first novel, published under the pseudonym Will Henry. It is a romantic historical reconstruction which addresses frontier issues seriously and, for the most part, accurately.

Allen's other pseudonym, Clay Fisher, came into existence when Harry E. Maule, then editor of Western fiction at Random House, rejected Allen's second novel, *Red Blizzard* (Simon & Schuster, 1951). *Red Blizzard* concerns the fate of a mixed-blood who finds himself ostracized by both the Indians and the whites. Because Maule didn't like the novel and felt it inferior to *No Survivors,* Allen's reaction—natural, perhaps, under the circumstances—was to believe that he was able to write two totally different kinds of Western fiction without knowing just how this was so, and that he ought to distinguish therefore between them by publishing those novels which Maule liked under the Will Henry name and those he didn't like under the Clay Fisher name.

I have known Henry Allen for some years now and he would be the first to admit that nothing is more misleading than this bifurcation of names, since he has written formulary Westerns as Will Henry and historical reconstructions as Clay Fisher, although his best historical fiction has been published preponderantly under the Will Henry pseudonym. *From*

Where the Sun Now Stands (Random House, 1959), *The Last Warpath* (Random House, 1966), *Maheo's Children* (Chilton, 1968 [now titled *The Squaw Killers*]), *Chiricahua* (Lippincott, 1972), and *The Bear Paw Horses* (Lippincott, 1973) are, when taken as a unit, to be ranked among the finer historical novels about the Indian Wars. To this group I would add *I, Tom Horn* (Lippincott, 1975) as one of Will Henry's more successful efforts to probe in fiction an actual frontier personality. Almost on a par with the latter are the Clay Fisher titles *Yellowstone Kelly* (Houghton Mifflin, 1958) and *Niño, The Legend of the Apache Kid* (Morrow, 1961), along with *Red Blizzard*, which, in *my* opinion, is a better novel than *No Survivors*.

The American West has at various times meant too many different things to Allen. He has written novels and stories set in the West in so many varied moods, has attempted so many literary experiments and has had such a personal and internal struggle with heroes and anti-heroes, that it is fundamentally impossible for anyone to give him a label. For critics, this has meant that he cannot be classified and therefore tends to be overlooked; for his various publishers, it has meant that they have never been certain whether to market him as a formulary writer or as a historical novelist. Those readers who admire him for his fine historical fiction find his formulary writing a source of dismay while those who prefer formulary writing are disturbed when they encounter the tragic vision which informs so many of the Will Henry books.

"Lapwai Winter" was excerpted and partially rewritten and reorganized by Allen himself for his book *Sons of the Western Frontier* (Chilton, 1966). Originally this material came from his novel *From Where the Sun Now Stands*, which I hold to be the masterpiece in what he has written so far. In addition to this novel, for the reader interested in the Nez Perce War of 1877 and Chief Joseph, I would recommend Helen Addison Howard's revised version of *Saga of Chief Joseph* (1965; reissued by the University of Nebraska Press, 1978) as a good place to begin. One last point: although they refer to themselves variously as Nimipu, Kamuinu, and Tsutpeli, their tradition tells them that their delegates to St. Louis in 1831 were called Nez Percé (pierced noses in French) and to accommodate white men they now permit themselves to be called this provided it is pronounced *nĕz pûrs* and provided it is accompanied by their *locus*, e.g., *Warm Springs* Nez Perce, or *Lapwai* Nez Perce, and so forth.

Lapwai Winter

I recall the day as though it were but one or two suns gone. It had been an early spring in the northeast Oregon country, the weather in mid-April being already clear and warm as late May. I was on the hillside above our village on the Wallowa River when Isiyiyi, Coyote, the friend of my heart in those boyhood times, came racing up from the lodges below.

Poor Coyote. His eyes were wild. His nostrils were standing wide with breath. His ragged black hair was tossing like the mane of a bay pony. I pitied the little fellow. He was always so alarmed by the least affair. Now I wondered calmly what small thing brought him dashing up from the village, and I awaited his news very superior in the advantage of my fourteen summers to his twelve.

But Coyote had the real news that morning.

Joseph, our chief, had decided to accept the invitation of White Bird and Toohoolhoolzote to go with them to Montana and hunt the buffalo. Since White Bird and Toohoolhoolzote were the chiefs of the fierce White Bird and Salmon River bands—what we called the "wild" or "fighting Indians" as against our own more peaceful Wallowa people—no news could possibly have been more exciting to a Nez Perce boy. With a cry as high-pitched as Coyote's, I dashed off down the hill to catch up my pony and get ready.

Within the hour, the entire village was packed and our horse herd strung out on the Imnaha Trail to Idaho and the Salmon River country, where the wild bands lived. There was no trouble crossing the Snake late that afternoon, and early the following sunrise we were off up the Salmon to see the famous warrior tribes.

The prospects sent my heart soaring higher than a hawk on hunting wing. Even though my mother, who was a Christian and had gone many years to the white man's missionary school at Lapwai, talked very strong against such "Indian nonsense" as going to the buffalo, and assured me with plenty of threats that I was going to spend that coming winter at Agent Monteiths' reservation school whether Joseph and my father agreed to it or not, I still could not restrain my joy at the adventure which lay ahead. I knew this was a time of times for any Nez Perce boy to remember, and I certainly was not going to let my mother's stern beliefs in her Lord Jesus, nor any of her threats about the white man's school, spoil it for me. I was an Indian, and this was a time for Indians.

It was spring. A fine shower during the night had washed the sky clean as a river stone. The sun was warm and sweet. Above us on the steepening hillsides the pine jays scolded with a good will. Below us along the rushing green water of the river the redwing reed-birds whistled cheerily. Tea Kettle, my dear mouse-colored pony, tried to bite me in the leg and buck me off. Yellow Wolf, my young uncle who was as fierce as any fighting Indian, jogged by on his traveling mare and gave me a friendly sign. Even Joseph, that strange, sad-eyed man who almost never smiled, brightened to nod and wave at me as I passed him where he sat his horse by the trail watching and counting to be sure all of his people were safe across the Snake and settled right upon the trail up the Salmon.

I looked all about me at the lovely pine-scented country and at those handsome, good-natured Nez Perce people riding up the sparkling river carefree and noisy-throated as the mountain birds around them and, doing that, I thought to myself that I might well take this moment to offer up some word of thanks to Hunyewat, our own Indian God. There was, too, good and real reason for the gratitude. Due to President Grant's good treaty of the year before, the trouble between our people and the white man was over for all time. The Wallowa, our beautiful Valley of the Winding Water, had been given back to us and, surely, as of that moment there among the Idaho hills there was nothing but blue sky and birdsongs in the Nez Perce world.

Bobbing along on my little gray pony, I bowed my head to the morning sun and said my humble word to Hunyewat.

Indians are supposed to be very brave, even the little boys. I was not such a good Indian, I fear. When we got to White Bird Canyon where the first village of wild bands was located, I am afraid I did great shame to my fourteen years. I certainly did not act like a boy but three summers away from his manhood.

White Bird—it was his village nestled there on the canyon floor—was not at home. Neither were his warriors. There were only the old men, the women, the children left in the silent village. Some of the old men rode out to tell us what had happened.

Word had come that the white settlers in Kamiah Valley had stopped our Nez Perce cattle herds at Kamiah Crossing of the Clearwater River. The white men had showed the Nez Perce herdsmen the rifle and told them they could not bring their cattle into the Kamiah any more from that time. It was white man's grass now. The Indian was going to have to stay off of it. White Bird had gone that same morning to gather up Toohoolhoolzote and the Salmon River warriors to ride to the crossing. Eeh-hahh! Bad, very bad. There was going to be real trouble now.

The moment I heard this I knew our trip to the buffalo country was ruined. It was then the tear came to my eye, the sniffle to my nose. Fortunately no one saw me. There were graver things to watch. Joseph's face had grown hard as the mountain rock above us.

It was a wrong thing, he told the old men, for the settlers to have closed the historic Indian Road to the Kamiah grass. The Nez Perce had used that trail and those pastures since the grayest chief could remember. But it would also be a wrong thing to let White Bird and Toohoolhoolzote come up to the river ready to fight. They were dangerous Indians.

"Ollikut, Elk Water, Horse Blanket, Yellow Wolf," said Joseph quickly, "you four come with me. Go get your best horses, pick your buffalo racers, we must go fast."

"Where are we going?" asked Ollikut, Joseph's tall young brother.

"To Kamiah Crossing. We must stop these angry men or there will be shooting. We have given our word against that. Do you agree?"

"Yes," said Ollikut. "We will get our horses."

In bare minutes they had mounted up and gone hammering down the trail around Buzzard Mountain to the Clearwater River. I sat there feeling my heart tear apart within me. Suddenly I saw Coyote motioning to me urgently. I guided Tea Kettle over toward him. He was on his scrubby brown colt and he had a pudgy White Bird boy with him. The boy had his own horse, a spavined paint with feet like snowshoes. I drew myself up, looking haughty.

"Well," I challenged Coyote, "what do you want?"

"This is Peopeo Hihhih," he replied, indicating his companion.

"Yes? What is so remarkable about that?"

"Not much. Only his father's name is Peopeo Hihhih, too."

"Coyote, what are you trying to say to me?"

"This much—this boy's father is Chief White Bird."

"No!"

I could not believe it. This small, ugly, little animal the true son of White Bird? Impossible.

"Boy," I said, "is my friend's tongue straight? Are you the blood son of Chief White Bird?"

"No. Only the near-son. My mother was his sister. But he raised me in his tepee and gave me his name. Everybody calls me Little Bird. You look like a nice boy, what's your name?"

"Heyets."

"Very fine name. It means Mountain Sheep."

"That's very smart of you, boy. And you only seven or eight summers. Imagine!"

"Seven summers," smiled the pudgy boy. "Ten more and I will be a warrior like you."

I watched him closely, but he was not bright enough to be flattering me. He actually thought I had seventeen summers. Clearly, although not clever, neither was he as stupid as I had believed. I began to feel better about my lot.

"Well," I said cheerfully, "what shall we do? Ride down the river and stone the potholes for mallard hens? Go for a swim in the Salmon? Hunt rabbits? Have a pony race?"

Instantly the fat White Bird boy was frowning at Coyote.

"I thought you said he would want to go over to the Clearwater and creep up on the fight at Kamiah Crossing," he said accusingly.

"I did! I did!" protested Coyote. "But with Heyets you can't tell. He changes his mind like a woman. You can't trust his mind. Neither can he."

I did not care to stand there listening to a simpleton like Coyote explaining the workings of my thoughts to a seven-year-old White Bird Indian. I grew angry.

"Be quiet!" I ordered. "Of course I would like to go to the Clearwater and see the fight. But what is the use of such talk? It will be all over before we could get these poor crowbaits of ours halfway around the mountain." I paused, getting madder. "Coyote," I said, "from here where I now say good-by to you, I will speak no more to you in this life. I warned you, now we are through Taz alago—!"

"Well, all right, good-by," shrugged Coyote. "Have it your way, Heyets. But I just thought you would like to beat Joseph and the men to Kamiah Crossing. That's why I wanted you to see Little Bird. He knows a way."

I spun Tea Kettle around.

"He knows what way?" I demanded.

"The secret way of his people over the mountain, instead of around it. It's a way he says we can get our poor horses to the crossing before any of them. Before Elk Water, your father. Before Horse Blanket, Yellow Wolf's father. Before Ollikut, Joseph's brother. Before—"

"Enough! Enough!" I cried. "Is this true, Little Bird?"

Little Bird lifted his three small chins. "I am the son of a war chief," he said. "Would I lie to a Wallowa?"

I made as though I did not understand the insult, and said, "Eeh-hahh, there has been too much talk. Let's go."

"Yes, that's right," spoke up Little Bird. "We have a tall mountain to get over. Follow me. And when we get up high, let your ponies have their heads. There are some places up there you will not want to look over. Eeh-hahh!"

Coyote and I understood that kind of instruction. We gave a happy laugh, hit our ponies with our buffalo-hide quirts, went charging off after Little Bird's splayfooted paint. We were gone as quickly as the men before us.

That was a wild track up over that mountain but it was a good one. We got to the Clearwater before Joseph and before even the White Bird and Salmon River warriors.

Little Bird led us off the mountain down a creek bed which had a cover of timber all the way to its joining with the river. This was below the crossing, up near which we could plainly see the white men sitting around their campfire making loud talk and boasting of the easy way they had run off the Indian herders that morning.

The day was well gone now. Whippoorwills were crying on the mountain. Dusk hawks were about their bug hunting. The sun was dropped from sight beyond the western hills. Only its last shafts were striking the face of the cliffs above us. North and east, heavy clouds were coming on to rain. The river was starting to drift a chilly mist.

I shivered and suggested to my companions that we circle the white camp and go on up the river to the village of Looking Glass, the Asotin Nez Perce chief. Up there we could get a warm sleep in a dry tepee, also some good hot beef to eat for our supper.

But Little Bird had not come over the mountain to visit the Asotin, who were even more settled than the Wallowa.

"No," said the fat rascal, "I won't go up there. My father says Looking Glass is strong but his people are weak. They take the white man's way. Kapsis itu, that's a bad thing."

"Well," I countered, "it's going to rain. We'll get soaked and lie here on the ground shaking all night. That's a bad thing, too."

"Eeh!" was all he would say to me. "I am a Nez Perce; you Wallowas are all women."

"Not this Wallowa!" cried Coyote. "I fear no rain. I fear no white man. I fear no fat White Bird boy. Ki-yi-yi-yi-yi!"

He threw back his head and burst into his yipping personal call before I could move to stop him. My stomach closed up within me like a bunching hand. Only one thing saved us from instant discovery. Coyote made such an excellent imitation of the little brush wolf for which he was named that the white men were fooled. One of them picked up his rifle and shied a shot our way. The bullet slapped through our cover at the same time my hand took Coyote across his yammering mouth. He gave a startled yelp and shut up. The white man laughed and put down his gun and said, "By damn, I must have clipped the leetle varmint. How's thet fer luck?"

We didn't answer him, letting him think what he wanted.

It got pretty quiet.

Presently Little Bird said respectfully to me, "What I suggest, Heyets, is that we creep up the river bed and listen to the white man's talk. Coyote said your mother has been to the school at Lapwai and has taught you their language. You can tell us what they are saying up there, eh?"

I started to give him some good reason why we should not attempt this riskful thing but was fortunately spared the need. Happening to glance up the river as he spoke, my eyes grew wide.

"Eeh!" I whispered excitedly. "It is too late. Look up there on the cliff!"

I flung out my arm, and my friends, following the point of my rigid finger to the mountainside above the white man's fire, became very still. Everything all around became very still. That was the kind of a sight it was.

On the crest of the last rise past the settler campfire, sitting their horses quiet as so many statues carved from the mountain granite, were two craggy-faced war chiefs and half a hundred unfriendly looking, eagle-feathered fighting Indians.

"Nanitsch!" hissed Little Bird, filling the silence with the fierce pride of his words. "Look, you Wallowas! See who it is yonder on the hillside. It is my father, White Bird and his friend Toohoolhoolzote, come to kill the Kamiah white man!"

The fighting Indians came down the hill. They came very slow, giving us time to slip up through the river brush to be close to it all when it happened. As they rode forward the white men left their fire and took up their rifles. They walked out on foot to meet the mounted Indians in the way such things were done. Both parties stopped about an arrow shot apart. For the Indians White Bird and Toohoolhoolzote rode out. For the white men it was a lanky fellow with no whiskers and a foxy eye, and a square-built man with blunt whiskers and a glinting eye like a rooting pig. We knew them both. They were Narrow Eye Chapman and Agent Monteith.

The talk began but did not go far.

Neither White Bird nor Toohoolhoolzote spoke a word of English. Monteith knew our tongue a little, yet had to wait for Chapman to explain many things for him. Chapman was a squaw man, living with a Umatilla woman up in White Bird Canyon. The Indians knew him from a long time and took him as their friend. Still the talk kept stopping because of Agent Monteith. Toohoolhoolzote, famous for his harsh temper, began to grow angry. He glared at the Lapwai agent and growled the one English saying he knew at Narrow Eye Chapman.

"Damn-to-hell," he said, "I will not stay here and listen to any more of this delaying. We know why we are here. You know why we are here. Why do we argue? I am going to ride back a ways and return with my gun cocked for shooting."

"No, no," the squaw man pleaded. "Wait now, old friend, don't do that. You haven't heard the whole story yet."

Toohoolhoolzote looked at him.

"Do you deny these men stopped our cattle?" he asked.

"No, I can't deny that. But—"

"Never mind, I only want to know if you stopped the cattle. Now I will ask it of you one more time. Can the cattle go over the river into the Kamiah grass?"

Chapman looked around like a rabbit caught by dogs in an open meadow. Then he spoke rapidly to Agent Monteith, telling him what Toohoolhoolzote had said. The agent got very dark in the face.

"You tell that Indian," he ordered, "to bring his cattle and come to live upon the reservation as the other Nez Perce have done. Tell him there is plenty of grass at Lapwai, and be done with him. Tell him I will send for the soldiers if he does not do as I say."

But Narrow Eye knew better than that. He shook his head.

"No," he said quickly, "we can't do that. I will ask him to wait until morning with his decision. That will give us time to send back for more men. We will need every gun in the Kamiah if we stay here. We wouldn't last five minutes if they started shooting now, and they're mortal close to doing it. Those Indians are mad."

Agent Monteith peered at the angry faces of the fighting Indian, and of a sudden his own stubborn face changed. Even from as far away as our river bushes we could see him get pale above his whiskers. At once he agreed to the squaw man's plan, and Chapman turned and told the big lie to the Indians.

Toohoolhoolzote was for war right then. But White Bird looked up at the sky and said "no." The light was already too far gone for good shooting. The morning would be time enough. There were only a dozen white men and by good daybreak light they could be more sure they got every one of them. For a moment I let out my listening breath, thinking everything was going to rest quiet at that agreement, giving Joseph time to get up and perhaps prevent the fight. I finished translating what had been said for my two friends, not thinking how they might take the white man's treachery. I had still much to learn about fighting Indians, even very small fat ones.

Little Bird, the moment he heard of Chapman's deceitful words to Monteith, burst from our cover like a stepped-on cottontail. Bounding through the twilight toward the Nez Perce, he kept shouting in our tongue for them to beware, to fight right then, that Narrow Eye Chapman was sending for more guns, maybe even for the horse soldiers, that all of them would be killed if they waited for the morning.

When Little Bird did that—jumped and ran—I didn't know what to do, but crazy Coyote he knew what to do. He jumped and ran after him yelling, "Wait for me! Wait for me! Wait for me—!"

One of the white men, a heavy one with yellow-stained red whiskers, cursed, using his God's name, and called out to the others, "Come on, boys, we had better beat through them willows. Might be a whole litter of them red whelps in thar!"

With the words he leaped on his horse and plunged him into the brush where I was running around in senseless circles trying to decide which way to go. He reached down and seized me by the back of my hunting shirt, rode back with me dangling in one great hand.

"Here, by cripes!" he bellowed. "Lookit here what I found. Damn me if it ain't a leetle red swamp rat!"

Well, it was no little red swamp rat but the fourteen-year-old son of Elk Water, the Wallowa Nez Perce. Still it was no time for false pride. Nor anything else for that matter. Before the red-whiskered man could bring me back to the campfire and before the startled Indians could form their line to charge upon the treacherous whites, a single shot rang out upon the mountainside.

The lone bullet splashed a whining mark of lead on a big rock which stood midway of the meadow between the settlers and our angry people, and a deep voice rolled down from above saying, "Do not fight. The first man on either side to ride beyond the rock will be shot."

We all fell still, looking upward toward the cliff down which winded the Clearwater trail.

There, fiery red in the reflected light of the disappeared sun, tall as giants on their beautiful buffalo horses, were Joseph and Ollikut, with my father and Yellow Wolf's father and Yellow Wolf himself. All save Joseph had their rifles pointed toward the midway rock, and there was still smoke curling from Ollikut's gun, showing it was he who had fired the lone shot. For himself, Joseph did not even have a gun. He was commanding the stillness with his upheld hand alone. It was a strange thing. All the Indians and all the white men likewise did his bidding. Not one man made to move himself, or his horse, or his loaded rifle in all the time it took our Wallowa chief to ride down from the cliff.

It was the first time I had seen the power of Joseph's hand. It was the first time I knew that he possessed this wyakin, this personal magic to command other men. I think that many of the Nez Perce had not seen it or felt it before this time either. It was as if they did not know this Joseph, like he was a stranger among them.

The stillness hurt the ears as he made his way across the meadow toward the white men from Kamiah.

Joseph talked straight with the white men. The other Indians came into the settler fire and stood at the edge of its outer light and listened without moving. But they did not talk, only Joseph talked.

In his patient way he went back to the beginning of the agreements on paper between our two peoples. He reminded Agent Monteith of the Walla Walla Peace Council of 1855 of which only the Nez Perce had stood faithful to the white man, and in which all the other tribes, the Yakimas, the Umatillas, the Palouse, Spokanes, Coeur d'Alenes—all of them save the Nez Perce—spoke against the paper and would not sign it.

Always, Joseph said, the Nez Perce had abided by that treaty. Only when the Thieves Treaty took away their lands in 1863, after gold was discovered at Oro Fino, had the Nez Perce faltered in their friendship. Even then they had made no war, only stayed apart from the white man, asking nothing but to be let alone. Now there was President Grant's good paper the Wallowa—returning country to the Nez Perce. Now all should be as it was in the old friendly days. But here was the white man trying to steal the Indian's grass again. The Kamiah was Indian country. There was no treaty keeping Nez Perce cattle away from it, yet here was the white man standing at Kamiah Crossing flourishing the rifle and saying hard things to Joseph, who was trying to keep the peace.

Was it not enough, cried Joseph, throwing wide his arms, that the white man had torn the gold from the Indian earth? That he had taken the best farmlands for himself? That he had built his whisky stores along the Indian trails? That he had lured the Indian children away from their parents into his Christian school? Had taught them to pray to Jesus Christ and to sneer at the old Indian gods? Had made them to forget the ways of their own fathers and mothers, and led them to think their own people were lower than dogs and the white man the lord of all on earth? That he had lied to, stolen from, cheated on the poor trusting Nez Perce for seventy snows and more? Were not all these things enough? Did he now also have to starve the Indian as well? To stomp in his water and stale in it, too? Must he not only take what grass he needs, alone, but also that small amount necessary to the Indian's poor few cattle?

What did such a situation leave Joseph to say to White Bird and Toohoolhoolzote? What could he tell his angry brothers to keep them from fighting in the morning? If any of the white men had the answer to that question, he had better give it to Joseph now.

There was a long silence then while Chapman translated and the white men talked it over. Then Agent Monteith showed his stumpy teeth and stood forth to talk unfriendly.

It was time, he said, for the Nez Perce to realize they could no longer move themselves and their cattle about the land as they pleased. They were going to have to keep themselves and their herds in one place from now on, even as the white man did. There was no choice. If they would not do it, the soldiers would come and make them do it. Was that perfectly clear to Joseph?

Joseph was a wise man. He did not say "yes" just to make a good feeling. He shook his head and said "no," he did not think he understood what Agent Monteith was saying. It seemed there was possibly more intended than was stated. Would the agent try again, Joseph asked Chapman, this time with his tongue uncurled?

Chapman winced and said to Joseph, "I hope you understand that my heart is with you. I think much of my wife's people. But I am white, what can I do?"

"Do nothing," answered Joseph, "that you do not think I would do."

"Thank you, my brother," said Chapman, and went back to Monteith. The latter proved quite ready to repeat his exact meaning. He did not like Joseph, because he could not fool him, so he took refuge in hard talk.

"All right," he scowled, "here is precisely what I mean: you and your people are not going to the buffalo any more; you are not leaving your lands to do anything. Such moving around makes the young men restless and wild. When you put your cattle out to grass and go to the buffalo, you are away six months. The children are kept out of school, they have no chance to learn the ways of the new life that will let them live side by side with the white man. This is a wrong thing, Joseph. We must start with the children. They must be put in school and kept there. It is the only way to real peace between our people. We must have a common God and common ways. Only through the children may this be done."

When Joseph heard this, he asked only what putting the children in school had to do with showing the rifle at Kamiah Crossing. Monteith answered him at once. Peaceful Indians, he said, were Indians who stayed in one place. Moving Indians were fighting Indians. And the day of the moving Indian was all done. From this time forward the Nez Perce must do as Indian Agent John Monteith said, not as White Bird said, not as Toohoolhoolzote said, not as any other fighting chief said. And what Agent Monteith said was that the Wallowas must now stay in the level valley, the White Birds in their deep canyon, the Salmon Rivers behind their big mountain. To guarantee this obedience there was but one sure way; put the children in the reservation school and raise them as white boys and girls. It was up to Joseph to make this clear to the other Nez Perce. Did Joseph understand?

Our chief nodded slowly. The hurt in his face would have made a stone weep. Yes, he said, for the very first time he did understand. Now it was revealed to him what the white man really wanted of the Indian. It was not to live in peace with him, as brother with brother. When the agent said that about not going to the buffalo, about the cattle not going into Kamiah, that was nothing. It was only an excuse. The white man knew that to shut up the Indian in a small place was to destroy his spirit, to break his heart, to kill him.

If that was what Agent Monteith now wanted Joseph to tell the other chiefs, he would do it. He would tell them that either they went home and stayed there or the horse soldiers would come and drive them upon the reservation. He would tell them that in any case their children must soon be sent into Lapwai School and made to live there. But he must warn the agent that he was asking a very dangerous thing.

With this low-voiced agreement, Joseph turned away from Monteith and told the fighting Indians what he had said.

I had a very good look at this last part of it. I was being held in the camp tent. The red-whiskered man was in there with me holding his bad-smelling hand across my mouth the whole time. But I could see between his fat fingers and through the slight parting of the tent flap. Of course none of the Nez Perce knew I was in there. They all thought I had gotten away down the river and would come into their camp when I had the chance.

When Joseph told the others about not going to the buffalo any more, about the horse soldiers putting them on the reservation if they moved around, about Agent Monteith demanding the surrender of the children as the earnest of their good faith, the Indians did a strange thing. Their faces grew not angry but very sad, and when Joseph had finished the last word, they turned and went back up on the mountain-side without a sound. Only old Toohoolhoolzote stayed behind with Joseph, and with our Wallowa chief he now went toward the white men.

Coming up to Monteith, Joseph said, "I have told my people what you said. Now Toohoolhoolzote will tell you what my people say in return." He stood back, giving over his place to the older man. Toohoolhoolzote stared at all the white men for a moment, then nodded.

"I will be brief," he said in Nez Perce to Chapman, but fixing his gaze upon the Lapwai agent. "Tomorrow, if you are still here, there will be shooting. We are going to the buffalo. We will graze our cattle where we wish. We will not bring our children into Lapwai. Joseph is a good man and he is your friend. Toohoolhoolzote is a bad man and he is not your friend. When the sun comes up, remember that. Taz alago, Agent Monteith. Sleep light."

For a time the old man stood there, the firelight making a black spiderweb of the seams and dry canyons in his face skin. His mouth was set in a line wide and ugly as a war-ax cut. His eyes burned like a wolf's eyes. His expression was unmoving. Suddenly I was as afraid of him as the white men. The sight of him braced there lean and dark and strong as a pine tree for all his sixty-eight winters, staring down all that bitter talk and all those menacing white rifles with nothing save his Nez Perce simiakia, his terrible Indian pride, put a chill along my spine from tail to neckbone. When he finally turned away to follow his warriors up onto the mountain it was even more quiet than when Joseph came down the cliff trail.

Now there was only my own chief left.

He told Chapman in Nez Perce that he was sad that Agent Monteith had done this dangerous thing to the spirit of the wild bands. He promised he would yet do what he could to prevent the shooting in the morning but begged Chapman to try and get the white settlers to leave the crossing when it was full dark, to be far, far from it when the sun came over Buzzard Mountain next day. Then he, too, turned to go. In the last breath, however, Agent Monteith requested him to wait a moment. Wearily Joseph did so, and Monteith wheeled toward the camp tent and said, "Bates, bring that boy up here."

Redbeard Bates grinned and spat and shoved me stumbling out of the tent. Outside, he pushed me forward into the fire's light to face my chief.

Joseph's tired face softened as he saw me.

But Agent Monteith's face grew hard.

"Joseph," he said, "tell your people over on the mountain

that I don't trust them. I will hold the boy with us until we see there is no shooting and no following us away from here. The boy will be perfectly all right. After a time you come into Lapwai and we will talk about him. I know this boy is of your own blood, and I have an idea for him you would do well to listen to. It may be that we can use him to lead in the others. Do you understand that?"

Joseph understood it.

But to Agent Monteith he merely nodded without words, while to me he spoke ever so gently in his deep voice.

"No harm will come to you, little Heyets," he said. "Go with the agent and do not fear. I shall come for you. As you wait, think well upon what you have seen here. Do you think you can remember it?"

I drew myself up.

"Yes, my chief, I will always remember it."

"Good. It is a lesson about the white man that you will never learn in his school at Lapwai." He smiled, touching me softly on the shoulder. "Taz alago, Heyets," he said, and turned for the last time away from that dark fire by the Clearwater.

"Taz alago, my chief," I called into the twilight after him, and was glad he did not look back to see the tears that stood in my eyes no matter that I was fourteen summers and would be a warrior soon.

I had never been to Lapwai longer than one day. Say, as on a Sunday to watch the tame Indians pray, or on a Saturday when they drew their agency beef and might favor a visiting "wild" relative with a bit of fat meat to take home at the white man's expense. Accordingly, as I now rode toward the mission school with the agent and the Kamiah settlers I began to recover from my fright and to wonder how it might be to live on the reservation over here in Idaho for a longer while, like perhaps two or three days, or even a whole week.

But I did not get to find out.

We had been riding most of the night, having slipped away from the crossing as Joseph advised. Now, as the sun came up, we stopped to boil water and make coffee. Before the water started to roll in the old black pot, five Nez Perce came out of a brushy draw nearby and rode up to our fire. We knew them all. They were Joseph, Ollikut, Horse Blanket, Yellow Wolf and Elk Water, my own father.

"Well, Joseph," demanded Agent Monteith at once, "what is this? Have you tricked me? What do you want here?"

Joseph looked at him steadily.

"It is not my way to play tricks," he said. "Last night I gave you the boy so there would be no trouble with those White Birds and Salmon Rivers. There was no trouble. Now I want the boy back, that is all."

"Give them the kid!" I heard Narrow Eye Chapman whisper to Monteith, but the agent set his stubborn jaw and said, no, he wouldn't do it.

Ollikut, great handsome Ollikut, pushed his roan buffalo racer forward. He cocked his gun. "Agent," he said, "we want the boy."

"For God's sake," said Chapman out of the side of his mouth to Monteith, "give them the kid and get shut of them. What are you trying to do, get us all killed? That damned Ollikut will tackle a buzzsaw barehanded. Smarten up, you hear? These ain't agency Indians you're fooling with."

Agent Monteith stuck out his stubby beard still farther and bared his many small teeth like a cornered cave bat, but he gave in.

"Joseph," he said, "I am charging you with this matter. I want this boy in school this winter. You know why. It is the only way he can learn the white man's way."

"Yes, but he should have his say what he will do."

"No, he should not. That is the trouble with you Indians. You let the children run over you. You never say 'no' to them and you never punish them for doing wrong. Children must be taught to do as they are told."

"We teach them. But what has that to do with striking them and saying no to everything they want? There are other ways to show them wisdom."

"Joseph, I won't argue with you. I leave it to your own mind. Whether this boy is going to grow up Indian or white is up to you. You and I are grown men, we will not change our ways. I have one God, you have another. My father taught from the Holy Book, your father tore up the Holy Book. We are as we are, you and I, but the boy can be anything which you say he can be. You are the head chief of the Wallowas, the most powerful band of the Nez Perce. If you send this boy of your own band and blood to go to school at Lapwai this winter, you will have said to all the other wild bands that you intend to take the white man's way, to obey your agent, to learn to live the new life. It will be a powerful thing for peace, an important thing for your people. What do you say? The decision is your own. You alone can make it."

It was a hard talk. I could see that Joseph was thinking much on it. I held my breath for I was frightened again now. Of a sudden I lost all my bravery about going to Lapwai for a few days. This was serious. They were talking about the whole winter, perhaps about several winters. This could be a sad thing. I had heard many stories of boys dying at the school of broken hearts and bad food and lonesomeness for tepee smoke and boiled cowish and dried salmon and roast elk and of horse sweat and saddle leather and gun oil and powder smell and all of the other grand things a wild Nez Perce lad grew up with around him in his parents' lodge, his home village, and his native hunting lands. Joseph, too, knew of these poor boys. The thought of them weighed heavy on him and made him take such a long time that Ollikut threw him a sharp glance and said, "Come on, brother, make up your mind. I feel foolish standing here with this gun cocked."

Joseph nodded to him and sighed very deep.

"All right," he said to Agent Monteith, "give us the boy now. When the grass grows brown and the smell of the first snow is like a knife in the wind, I shall bring him to you at Lapwai."

In May, in the land of the Nez Perce, the spring sun comes first to the southern slopes of the tumbling hills which guard the wide valleys and shadowed canyons. Here in the warm sandy soil the cowish plant breaks through the mountain loam even before the snows are all gone from the rock hollows and catch basins which hold it there to water this sturdy rootling of the upper hills. To these cowish patches in that month of May would come my people hungry and eager for the taste of fresh vegetables after the long winter of dried camass and smoked salmon.

The juicy roots of the cowish baked in the Nez Perce way had a breadlike, biscuity flavor, giving the plant its white man's name of biscuitroot. We called it kouse, and from that the settlers sometimes called us the Kouse Eaters. My people loved this fine food which was the gift of Hunyewat, and the time of its gathering was a festival time for us. All we children looked forward through the winter to the May travel to the cowish fields. Yet in that May of the year we did not go to the buffalo, I sang no gathering songs, danced no thankful dances, ate no kouse at the great feast held at that traditional Time of the First Eating. I sat apart and thought only of September and of that first smell of snow in the sharpening wind.

June was the time of going to the camass meadows. In that month my people took up the tepees and journeyed happily to the upland plateaus where, in the poorly drained places, large flats of snow-melt water would collect and stand. Up out of these meadow shallows, springing like green spears from the black soil beneath the water, would come the fabled blue camass plant—the lovely water hyacinth, Indian lily of the Northwest.

Even within a few days the surfaces of the water flats would be bright-grown as new meadow grass with its spreading leaves. Then, short weeks later, the brilliant bells of its blue blossoms would stalk out for their brief flowering. As the swift blooming passed, all the nourishment of Hunyewat's warm sky and cool snow water would go from the faded flower down into its underground bulb to store up strength and hardy life for its fortunate harvesters.

All this glad time of waiting for the camass root to come ripe and dry up for the digging, my band was camped with the other Nez Perce bands in the shady pines above the meadow. There was much gay chanting and dancing the whole while, but I did not take part in any of it. Instead, I stayed out on the mountain by myself thinking of September and the snow wind.

Under the mellow sun of July the shallow waters of the camass fields evaporated, the rich muck dried, the great Indian harvest began. Now while the men sat at their gambling games or raced their famous Appaloosa horses, and while the children played at stick-and-hoop, or fished and hunted the summer away, the women took out the digging tools with their stubby wooden handles and pronged elkhorn tips, and pried up the ripened bulbs of the blue lily.

After that came the cooking.

As many as thirty bushels of the bulbs were covered with wet meadow grass and steamed over heated stones. Then the bulbs were mashed, shaped into loaves, sun-baked into a nourishing Indian bread. This bread would keep easily six to eight moons. It was a good and valuable food, having a flavor much like a sweet yam. With the flesh of the salmon, the meat of the elk, the deer, and the antelope, it fed us through the severest winter. Thus, the July camass harvest was a time of tribal joy and gratitude for the Nez Perce. But I did not join in the Thankful Sing. I only wandered afar with Tea Kettle, my small gray pony, and looked with aching loneliness out across the blue peaks, hazy canyons, lapping waters, and lofty pines of the homeland I would see no more after the grass was brown beneath the autumn wind.

In late summer, in August, after the high spring floodwater had fallen and all the rivers were running low and clear, it was the Time of Silver Waters, of the great Columbia salmon run from the sea to the headwater creeks of Nez Perce country. This was the end of the Indian year, the very highest time of thanks for my people, and the very hardest time of work for them.

When the flashing salmon came at last, the men would strain from dawn to dusk with spear and net at every leaping falls from the mighty Celilo upward to the least spawning creeklets which fed the main forks of the Salmon, the Snake, the Clearwater, Grande Ronde, Wallowa, and Imnaha rivers. The sandy beaches would soon be heaped to a small child's waist with the great hump-backed fish. Then the women would work like packhorses to split, clean, rack, and smoke the bright-red slabs of that blessed flesh which provided nine of every ten Nez Perce meals around the year and which made my people immune to the famine which periodically visited the other Northwestern tribes.

Yes, August and the Time of Silver Waters was the real time to offer final thanks to Hunyewat. Yet even then I could think of no gratitude, no contentment, no happiness, but only of Joseph and Agent Monteith. And after them only of the brown grass and snow smell of September and of the log-walled prison waiting for me in the school at Lapwai.

At last the Moon of Smoky Sunshine, September, was but three suns away. In that brief space it would be Sapalwit, Sunday, and Joseph would ride up to the tepee of my father and call out in his soft deep voice, "Elk Water, where is the boy? Where is Heyets, our little Mountain Sheep? The grass is grown brown again, the skies have turned the color of gun steel. I smell snow in the wind. It is the time to keep our word to Agent Monteith."

I let two of those last three suns torture me. Then on the final night, late and when the chilling winds had blown out all the cook-fire embers and no one stirred in all that peaceful camp, I crept beneath the raised rear skins of my father's tepee.

Moving like a shadow I found my faithful friend Tea Kettle where I had tethered him in a dark spruce grove that same afternoon. He whickered and rubbed me with his soft nose and I cried a little and loved him with my arms about his bony neck. It was a bad time but I did not think of turning back. I only climbed on his back and guided him on into the deepening timber away from the camp of my father's people there beside the salmon falls of the Kahmuenem, the Snake River, nine miles below the entrance of the Imnaha.

I was bound for the land of our mortal foes, the Shoshoni. My reasoning was that if I could take an enemy scalp I would no longer be considered a boy. I would be a man, a warrior, fourteen summers or no, and they would no more think of sending me to school with Agent Monteith than they would my fierce uncle Yellow Wolf.

As for equipment I had Tea Kettle, who could barely come up to a lame buffalo at his best speed. I had a kopluts, or war club, which was no war club at all but a rabbit throwing stick cut off short to make it look like a kopluts. Also I had a rusted camp ax with the haft split and most of the blade broken off, a bow-and-arrow set given me by Joseph on my tenth birthday, a much-mended horse soldier blanket marked "U.S." in one corner and stolen for me by my father from the big fort at Walla Walla, three loaves of camass bread, a side of dried salmon, and my wyakin, my personal war charm, a smoked baby bear's foot, cured with the claws and hair left on. And, oh yes, I had my knife. Naturally. No Nez Perce would think of leaving his tepee without putting on his knife. He might not put on his pants but he would always put on his knife.

So there I was on my way to kill a Shoshoni, a Snake warrior far over across the Bitterroot Mountains in the Wind River country. I might, in addition, while I was over there and for good measure, steal a few horses. About that I had not entirely decided. It would depend on circumstances. Meanwhile, more immediate problems were developing.

I had left home in good spirit if weak flesh. Now, however, after a long time of riding through the dark forest, the balance was beginning to come even. It occurred to me, thinking about it, that I had ridden many miles. It might well be that I needed food to return my strength. Perhaps I had better stop, make a fire, roast some salmon, warm a slice of bread. When I had eaten I would feel my old power once more. Then, although I had already ridden a great distance that night, I would go on yet farther before lying down to sleep.

I got off Tea Kettle and gathered some moss and small sticks which I laid properly in the shelter of a windfallen old pine giant. With my flint I struck a tiny flame and fed it into a good little Nez Perce fire, say the size of a man's two hands spread together, and clear and clean in the manner of its burning as a pool of trout water in late autumn. I cut a green spitting stick and propped a piece of salmon and one of camass over the flames. Then I put the soldier blanket around my shoulders and leaned back against the big log to consider my journey plans. The next thing I knew a shaft of sunlight was prying at my eyes and two very familiar Indians were crouched at my fire eating my salmon and camass bread.

"Good morning," nodded Chief Joseph. "This is fine food, Heyets. You had better come and have some of it with us."

"Yes," said Elk Water, my father. "It is a long ride to Lapwai."

"What is the matter?" I mumbled, my mind bewildered, my eyes still spiderwebbed with sleep. "What day is this? What has happened to bring you here?"

"This is Sunday," answered Joseph in his easy way. "And what has happened to bring us here is that we have come to ride with you to Agent Monteith's school. You must have left very early, Heyets. That showed a good spirit. Probably you did not wish to bother us to rise so soon. Probably it was in your heart to let us have a good morning's sleep."

"Yes," agreed my father. "Surely that was it. Heyets is a fine boy. He wanted to let us sleep. He wanted also to ride into the white man's school alone so that we would be certain his heart was strong and he was not afraid. Is that not so, Heyets?"

My eyes had grown clearer, and it was in my mind to lie to them, to say, yes, that they were right about my thoughtful actions. Yet I could not bring myself to do it. To my father I might have lied, for he was a simple man and would not have guessed the difference, no, and would not have cared a great deal for it. But Joseph, ah, Joseph was completely another matter and another man. His great quiet face, soft deep voice, and sad brown eyes touched me with a faith and a feeling which would not let my tongue wander.

"No," I replied, low-worded. "That is not the way it was at all. I was running away. I was going to the Snake country to take a Shoshoni scalp so that you would think I was a man and would not send me to Agent Monteith's school. My heart was like a girl's. I was weak and sore afraid. I wanted only to stay with my people, with my father, and with my chief."

There was a silence then, and my father looked hard at Joseph. He turned his head away from both Joseph and me, but I could see the large swallowing bone in his throat moving up and down. Still, he did not say anything. He waited for Joseph to speak.

At last my chief raised his eyes to me and said gently:

"I beg your pardon, Heyets. The wind was making such a stir in the pine trees just now that I do not believe I heard what you said. Did you hear him, Elk Water?"

"No," answered my father, "I don't think I did. What was it you said, boy?"

I looked at Elk Water, my father, and at Joseph, my chief. Then I looked beyond them up into the pine boughs above us. There was no wind moving up there, no wind at all. I shook my head and got to my feet.

"Nothing," I said, untying Tea Kettle and kicking dirt upon my little fire. "Let us go to Lapwai and keep the word with Agent Monteith."

It will not take long, now, to tell of that Lapwai winter. It was not a good thing. The memory of it turns in me like a badly knitted bone. Yet, like a badly knitted bone, it will not let me forget.

I was sick much of the time, homesick all of the time. It was a hard winter, very cold, with a lot of wet-crust snow and heavy river ice the whole while. Some of my little Indian friends who sickened at the school did not grow well again. They were not watched over by Hunyewat as Heyets was. They lay down in the night and did not get up again in the morning. When we saw them the others of us wept, even we big boys. It hurt us very bad.

If they were Christian Indian children they were buried in the churchyard. Their mothers were there, their fathers were there. All their many friends of the reservation were there to stand and say good-by to them, and to sprinkle the handful of mother earth on them as was the old custom. Agent Monteith read from the Holy Book at the graveside, and the proper songs of Jesus were sung over them. They were treated like something.

But if they were wild Indian children, like myself, their little bodies were let to lie out overnight and freeze solid like dog salmon. Then they were stacked, like so many pieces of stovewood, in the open shed behind the schoolhouse. There they waited, all chill and white and alone, until such time as their parents could come in over the bad trails to claim them for the simple Nez Perce ceremony of The Putting to the Last Sleep.

It was not a happy nor a kind place for a boy raised in the old free Indian way. It made my heart sad and lonely to stay there. In consequence, and although I knew I was being watched closely because of my kinship with Joseph, both by my own and the agency people, I grew all the while more determined against the Lapwai, or white man's way.

Naturally I learned but little at the school.

I already knew how to speak the white tongue from my mother. But I did not let this help me. I would not learn to write, and in reading I was like a child of but six or seven. This blind pride was my father's blood, the old Nez Perce blood, the spirit, the simikia of my untamed ancestors, entering into me. I was not a wicked boy, but neither was I willing to work. I was like a young horse caught from out a wild herd. I knew nothing but the longing to escape. The only chance to teach me anything was to first gentle me down, and there was no chance at all to gentle me down. I thought, of course, and many times, about Joseph's faith in me. I wanted to do what was right for the sake of my chief's hope that I would serve as an example to the other wild bands that they might send their children in safety, and with profit, to the white man's school at Lapwai. But my own faith was no match for my chief's. Daily I grew more troublesome to Agent Monteith. Daily he grew less certain of my salvation.

When I had been with him five moons—through the time of Christmas and into that of the new year—it had at last become plain to Agent Monteith that I was not "settling down," as he put it, and Joseph was sent for. When my chief arrived, I was called in and stood by as interpreter while the talk was made about me. Joseph began it with his usual quiet direction, getting at once to the point.

"This boy's mother," he said, "reports to me that she has visited him here at the school and you have told her that her son is a bad boy, that he will not work, and that he is as bad for the other children as for himself." He paused, looking steadily at Agent Monteith. "Now I do not remember that Heyets is a bad boy. Perhaps my memory has failed me. Since I am also of his blood, you had better tell me what you told his mother."

Agent Monteith grew angry, his usual way.

"Now see here, Joseph," he blustered, "are you trying to intimidate me?"

"Excuse me. I do not understand what you mean."

"Are you trying to frighten me?"

"Never. What I want is the truth. Should that frighten you?"

"Of course not! This boy simply will not buckle down and study as he should. He will not work with the others. The class is told to draw a picture of our Lord Jesus humbly astride a lowly donkey and this boy draws a lurid picture of an armed warrior on an Appaloosa stallion. I ask him, 'What picture is that, Heyets?' and he says, 'Why, that is a picture of Yellow Wolf on Sun Eagle going to the buffalo.' Now I put it to you, Joseph, is that the right way for a boy to behave before the others? A boy upon whom we have all placed so much hope? A boy the other bands are watching to see how he fares at Lapwai? Answer me. Say what you think."

My chief frowned and pulled at his broad chin.

"I don't know," he said carefully. "Does he draw well?"

"He draws extremely well, easily the best in the class."

"He draws a good horse? a proper Indian?"

"Very good, very proper," scowled Agent Monteith. "Perfect likenesses, especially of the horse. He puts all the parts on the animal and when I reprimand him he offers to take me to the Wallowa and show me that Sun Eagle is, indeed, a horse among horses."

Agent Monteith blew out his fat cheeks, filling them like the gas-blown belly of a dead cow.

"Now you listen to me, Joseph! You promised to bring this boy here and to make him behave himself and work hard to learn the white man's way. This has since become a serious matter for the school. It can no longer be ignored. Heyets is creating a grave discipline problem for me. I mean among the other older boys. Some of them are beginning to draw pictures of spotted Nez Perce ponies in their study Bibles. I insist to you that this is no way for this boy of your blood to carry out our bargain."

Joseph shook his head in slow sympathy.

"You are right, Agent," he said, "if what you tell me is true. But before I make a decision I would like to have you tell me one special thing Heyets has done—show me some example of his evil ways that I may see with my own eyes—so that I shall know what it is you and I are talking about."

He hesitated a little, looking at the agent.

"Sometimes, you know," he said, "the white brother says

one thing and really means several others. It becomes difficult for an Indian to be sure."

Agent Monteith's blunt beard jutted out, but he kept his voice reasonable.

"Joseph, you are the most intelligent Indian I know. You are a shrewd man by any standards, red or white. You have been to this very school yourself in the old days. You were the best pupil they ever had here before your father, Old Joseph, tore up the Bible and took you away. You understand exactly what I mean and you do not have to ask me for any examples."

Joseph only nodded again and said, "Nevertheless, show me one special bad thing the boy has done."

The agent turned away quickly and picked up a study Bible from the desk of James Redwing, a Christian Wallowa boy of my own age and my best friend among the reservation Indians. He opened the book and handed it to Joseph.

"Very well," he snapped. "Look at that!"

Joseph took the book and studied it thoughtfully.

"Let us see here," he said. "Here is a picture of a young baby being carried in his mother's arms. She is riding a small mule led by her husband. They are leaving an old town of some sort in a strange land, and they are not going very fast with such a poor beast to take them. Nevertheless, they are in a great hurry. There is fear in their faces, and I believe the enemy must be pursuing them. Is there something else I have missed?"

Agent Monteith stamped his foot.

"You know very well that is the Christ Child fleeing Bethlehem with Mary and Joseph!"

"Oh yes, so it is. A fine picture of all of them, too. Better than in the book they had here before."

"You know equally well," Agent Monteith continued, very cold-eyed, "what else I am talking about, and what else it is you have missed. What is printed under the picture of the Christ Child?"

Joseph nodded and held the book up for me to tell him the words. I did so, and he turned back to Agent Monteith and said, "The words there are 'Jesus Fleeing the Holy City.' "

"Exactly. And what has some heathen pupil scrawled in by hand under that sacred title, with a Nez Perce arrow pointing to the donkey?"

My chief's face never changed. Again he held the book up to me, and again I whispered the words to him. Looking back at Agent Monteith, he shifted the Bible as though to get a better light on it and answered, "Oh yes, there is something else, sure enough. It says, 'If he had used an Appaloosa pony, his enemies never would have caught up to him.' Is that what you mean?"

"That is precisely what I mean, Joseph."

The agent took time to get a good breath and let some of it puff back out of his cheeks.

"That added writing was done by James Redwing, a Christian Indian of your own Wallowa band and a very fine boy who, until these past months, has been our star pupil. James is fifteen years old and I have worked with him a long time, Joseph. He had become a white boy in his thoughts and in his actions. I had saved him. He prayed on his knees every day and he had given over his life gladly to the service of his Saviour. Now he writes such things as you see there and the other boys all laugh."

"That is not right," said Joseph softly, "but they are only boys, all of them. Boys are full of tricks, Agent."

"Indeed they are!" cried Monteith, puffing up again. "And I will tell you about just one of those tricks!"

"Do that, my friend. My ears are uncovered."

"Well, this past Christmas we celebrated the birth of our Lord by making a little stable scene with the manger, and so forth, in Bethlehem. Of course there was the little packmule tied as the faithful ass beside the sleeping babe. And do you know what some monstrous boy had done to the innocent brute?"

Joseph shook his head wonderingly. "I could never imagine," he said. "Tell me."

"He had taken—he had stolen—some of the mission's whitewash and dappled the rear of that animal to imitate a Nez Perce Appaloosa horse, and had marked in red paint on the two halves of his rump the name 'Sun Eagle.' Now what do you think of that for your fine boy? He admitted it, you know. It was his work."

My chief put his chin down to his chest. He seemed to be having some trouble with his swallowing. It was as though he had caught a fishbone crosswise in his throat and were trying to be polite about choking on it. But after a bit he was able to raise his head and continue.

"I think it is very unfortunate," he answered the agent. "It is true my own father tore up the Bible and that I have followed his way, but I will not tolerate Wallowa boys making laughs about your God. What do you suggest we do?"

"Heyets must be punished severely."

"In what manner?"

"He should be flogged."

"Have you flogged him before, Agent?"

"No. Frankly, I've been afraid to try it. The rascal told me that if I touched him he would have his uncle Yellow Wolf come in and kill me."

"His uncle Yellow Wolf is but a boy himself, Agent."

"You do not need to tell me of Yellow Wolf. I know him very well. He has the eye of a mad dog. I wouldn't trust him ten feet away."

"I see. How else have you thought to punish Heyets?"

"He must be made to say the school prayers, on his knees, in front of the other boys."

"Alone?"

"Yes, alone."

"Has he prayed like this before, Agent?"

"Not once. He says he believes in Hunyewat. He says he did not come here to study Jesus Christ. He tells wild tales of the power of Hunyewat to the Christian boys and has them believing that anything Jesus of Nazareth did in 'ten moons' Hunyewat could do in 'two suns.' He asks them such sacrilegious questions as, 'Did you ever see a picture of Hunyewat riding a packmule?' and he has the entire class so disorganized they spend more time learning the Brave Songs, Scalp Chants, and Salmon Dances from him than they do the Sunday-school hymns from me. I will not tolerate it a day longer, Joseph. I simply cannot and will not do it. The matter is your entire responsibility and you must make the final decision on it right now."

Joseph moved his head in understanding and raised his hand for the agent to calm himself and wait while both of them thought a little while.

Presently he went on.

"Very well, Agent," he said. "Do you know what my father, Old Joseph, told me about this same school many snows ago when he came to take me away from it?"

"I can very well imagine what the old heathen might have said," agreed Agent Monteith. "But go ahead and tell it your way. You will anyway. That's the Indian of it."

"It is," replied Joseph, "and here is the way my father told it to me. He said, 'My son, always remember what I am about to say. A school is a good thing when it teaches school thoughts from schoolbooks. But the place for God and for His book is in the church. Pray in the church if you wish, and choose which God pleases you. But in the school do not pray. In the school work hard all the time at the printed thoughts of reading and writing and of the white man's way of figuring with numbers. Do that six days and on the seventh day go to church and pray all you want."

"Your father was a very wise man," admitted Agent Monteith, "until he left the church."

"He was a wise man after he left the church, too," said Joseph. "And here is the rest of his wisdom which you did not allow me to finish. The old chief finally said to me, 'But, my son, when the time comes that they will not let you learn your lessons except at the price of kneeling to their God, when they demand of you to become of their faith before they will give you a schoolbook, or feed you your food, or allow you your decent shelter from the snow and cold, then that is the time to tell them that they do not follow the way of their own Lord Jesus which He taught in the Holy Land two thousand snows before our little time here upon our mother earth. I once believed on Jesus Christ the Saviour,' said my father, 'and I know his words as well as any agent. It was not His way to ask for payment, neither before nor after He gave of Himself or of His goods!' "

"In heaven's name," fumed Agent Monteith, breaking in again, "what are you trying to say, Joseph?" And Joseph answered him very quietly, "I am only trying to say that it is not my way either," and after that both men stood a considerable time staring right at each other.

"Well," laughed Agent Monteith at last and somewhat nervously, "that is scarcely anything new. You have not been in church since your father tore up the Bible on this same spot eleven years ago."

"That is not what I mean, Agent."

"All right, all right, what is it that you do mean?"

"I mean about the boy."

"What about the boy?"

"I am doing with him as my father did with me when they would not teach me unless I prayed first."

"Joseph, I warn you!"

"It is too late for warning. All has been said. It is you and I who have failed, Agent, not this child. There is nothing he can do here. In his way he is wiser than either of us. He knows he is an Indian and cannot be a white man. I am taking him back to his own people, Agent. You will not see him in this place again. Taz alago."

I could not have been more stunned.

Since I knew the importance of my position at the school, I had been waiting to learn what kind of punishment would be agreed upon as the terms of my staying there. Yet, instead, here was my chief taking me proudly by the hand and leading me out of that log-walled schoolhouse there at Lapwai, Idaho, in the severe winter of 1875, without one more spoken word of parting, or rearward glance of consideration, for powerful Indian Agent John Monteith.

I will say that it was a strange and wonderful feeling.

Thrilling to it, I got behind Joseph on his broadbacked old brown traveling horse, and we set out through the falling snow toward the snug tepees along the Imnaha River where, since the most ancient among them could remember, our Nez Perce people had spent their winters.

In all the long way home Joseph and I said not a word to one another and that, too, was the Indian way. As he himself put it, all had been said back at Lapwai. Now was the time for riding in rich silence and, if a grateful Nez Perce boy remained of the old beliefs, for offering up a final humble word to Hunyewat.

So it was I bowed my small head behind Joseph's great shoulders and said my first prayer in five moons.

So it was I ended my Lapwai winter.

BENJAMIN CAPPS

BENJAMIN CAPPS (1922–) was born in Dundee, Texas. He grew up on the land, the son of a working cowboy, and rode horseback to a one-room schoolhouse for his elementary education. In 1938–39 he attended the Texas Technological College in Lubbock, Texas, quit, and worked for a time as a surveyor and truck driver, in Texas and in Colorado. During World War II, he was in the U.S. army air corps and served in the Pacific theater, attaining the rank of first lieutenant. After discharge, Capps returned to formal education, obtaining a bachelor's degree in 1948 and a master's degree in 1949 from the University of Texas. For the next few years he taught English and journalism at Northeastern State College, Tahlequah, Oklahoma, before changing his course entirely, entering industry as a tool-and-die maker, at which he worked for the next decade.

His first literary effort was *Hanging at Comanche Wells* (Ballantine, 1962). It is a formulary Western with a triad hero—an elderly judge, an elderly sheriff, and a young deputy. *The Trail to Ogallala* (Duell, Sloan, and Pearce, 1964) was his second Western novel, dealing with a cattle drive from Texas to Nebraska and reminiscent of Andy Adams' romantic historical reconstruction *Log of a Cowboy* (Houghton Mifflin, 1903). This novel won the Spur Award from the Western Writers of America in 1964, the Golden Saddleman Award, and was selected by the National Association of Independent Schools as one of the ten best books of 1964 for pre-college readers.

Capps also received a Spur Award for his next book, *Sam Chance* (Duell, Sloan, and Pearce, 1965), which like *The Brothers of Uterica* (Meredith Press, 1967) and like virtually all the novels he has written since depicts with ambivalence the struggle for survival on the Western frontier. I believe every book Capps has written bears reading. But the center of his historic vision is most ably found in *A Woman of the People* (Duell, Sloan, and Pearce, 1966), a captivity novel written with sensitivity and from an enlightened perspective, and *The White Man's Road* (Harper's, 1969), an unusually grim, albeit wholly realistic, view of reservation life among the Comanches.

"The qualities of a second-rate writer can easily be defined," Willa Cather once wrote, "but a first-rate writer can only be experienced. It is just the thing in him which escapes analysis that makes him first-rate." I know that that critic of critics, the late Stanley Edgar Hyman, would have come down hard on anyone who would so much as suggest that a writer can defy the literary critic. Yet this is very much the case with Capps. His fiction can, ideally, only be experienced.

When I told him that I wanted to include "The Slaughter" in this anthology—which is a chapter from *Sam Chance*—Capps urged to choose instead a chapter from *The True Memoirs of Charley Blankenship* (Lippincott, 1972). *Sam Chance,* after all, is the story of a man's struggle to become a cattle baron; Sam Chance, as he emerges throughout the novel, is a darkling, contradictory character. The American Indian lives by visions; the Anglo-American lives most often by dreams. These dreams seem to breed disillusionment. Sam Chance is both made and destroyed by his dream. As it turned out, however, I could find no episode brief enough in the picaresque adventures of Charley Blankenship which quite suited my purpose as well as "The Slaughter." When all is said and done, it shows us the implementation of an Anglo-American dream, a dream, which, unlike an Indian's vision, does not indicate to the dreamer his relationship with nature and his role in the natural order created by the Great Mystery. The dream of this Anglo-American requires that he participate in destruction: that he tear at, lay bare, and ravage the natural order. It is therefore fitting that at the end Sam Chance should find himself alone in the world, surrounded by the bones of those that had to die in order for him to fulfill his dream.

The Slaughter

During the first week in January Sam Chance set out west with a caravan, made of his own men and equipment, with the purpose of getting buffalo hides in large quantities. They took the old freight wagon, pulled by nine yokes of oxen, and three small wagons, pulled each by a span of mules. Fourteen men, including Chance, made up the party. They took only three saddle horses, these intended for scouting and for keeping the skinning crews in touch with each other.

The weather was clear and cool, with a light freeze each night. They could expect worse at any time, but it would not be much more difficult than what they were all used to. Picks, shovels, and axes were a part of the camping equipment in each of the smaller wagons; they would dig in and be ready for whatever bad weather came.

He had made a shorter hunt in December with only one wagon and three men, mainly for the purpose of finding where the concentrations of buffalo were and working out a reasonable plan. He had circled around to Fort Griffin and found a market there, though hide prices were low.

Now, it was his intention to hunt buffalo on a larger scale than had ever been done in this part of the country. He was paying the men of the outfit ten cents a hide on top of their regular wages. And the animals were there, by the hundreds of thousands, in the rough country below the Caprock.

The afternoon of the second day from home they met a small bunch of hunters who were headed east with about a hundred hides and the rest of their wagon loaded with meat. Chance, mounted on the dun horse Bullet, rode ahead to talk to them. Three of them, who seemed to be Tonkawa Indians, were walking. An old white man was on the wagon.

Chance greeted him. "I see you've got a load."

"Yeah, iffen I can just get out with my hair, I'd trade this load to be in Fort Griffin right now."

"You think there's danger from hostile Indians?"

"Danger! They's been a dozen hunters killed out here this

winter. Them Comanches are roused up. Ain't you Sam Chance that owns the Long-C Ranch?"

"That's right."

"Well, Mr. Chance, iffen you want some advice from an old hunter, you better turn around and go east. Them Comanches go to riding in the winter, they ain't out for a few horses. They want scalps."

"Have you seen any, or just heard rumors?"

"We seen a sight yestiddy morning that would turn your stomach; three hunters cut to pieces. By the signs they must of been twenty Injuns. Chico there says it was Comanches and Kiowas both. It don't matter to me; I seen what they done. We ain't stopped traveling since we seen it."

"Camp with us tonight if you want to," Chance said.

"You turning around?"

"Nope."

"Well, Mr. Chance, I just hope you know what you're doing. I ain't even got time to set here and talk to you." He swung his whip at the rumps of the two pinto steers he was driving and started them lumbering forward.

Chance led his men on as before. He had no doubt that the area was dangerous for a small party of white men, but it had always been so. It was a different matter for fourteen well-armed men who knew how to keep from being surprised.

Buffaloes were scattered all over the country, not in the great herds that they made up for migration, but in bunches of a dozen to a hundred that grazed together. Some few of these bunches were still on his own range, indeed even as far east as Briggs's Store, but Chance knew he had to find a concentration of the animals to make feasible the kind of hunting he planned. The fourth day, scouting out ahead of the wagons, he found what he wanted in a broad, broken valley. He could see bunches that must total five thousand animals within the ten miles of his view.

He guided the outfit in and found a campsite on the north rise of the valley, near water and good grass.

Just at sunrise he struck out on foot with his Sharps Big Fifty, his pockets swinging with forty heavy rounds of ammunition. There was a rim of ice around the water hole when he passed it. The dry grass was heavy with frost that sparkled like a fuzzy metal blanket in the morning light.

Lefors he had sent up to scout horseback along the ridge. The rest of the men were digging temporary quarters in the clay slopes of the camp area. He would divide them tomorrow into three groups with a shooter in charge of each. Now his purpose was to get off to a good start, demonstrate what could be done, so that no one would be satisfied with a dozen hides a day, or even a few dozen.

No more than thirty minutes from camp he had in sight two bunches. One was drifting, the other was stopped and nosing at the frosty grass, about thirty grown animals and a dozen calves. He chose the latter group. A light wind blew out of the east. He circled westward and came into a shallow gully in which he could hide himself as he approached them. He raised up cautiously several times as he moved forward, finally crawled to a point two hundred yards from them.

He studied the shaggy, hulking beasts. Steamy breath rose from them. They were more than half bulls, but the cows were more alert. The brown calves, six to eight months old, bounded about, tasted the grass, butted at each other. The adult animals were in heavy hair, shiny black. One big cow lifted her head regularly as if to scan the countryside.

He eased the Big Fifty into a comfortable rest on the bank, sighted in behind the point of the shoulder, just above the heart, and squeezed the trigger. The rifle butt slammed his shoulder back.

The boom seemed loud enough to split apart the cold quiet valley. The buffaloes all threw their heads up and stood frozen. They began to shift and turn, waiting alert. The cow suddenly collapsed to her knees. He could see red blood shining on her nose.

He quickly reloaded the single-shot Sharps and peered over the sights, studying their actions. One big bull seemed to be looking toward him, perhaps at the little flare of white smoke that was drifting away behind him. He sighted on the bull and fired again. The bull jumped forward violently, then slowed and drooped his head.

The bunch began milling. Some of them came up to the two that were down, sniffed, backed away. Another big cow began to walk away, a stream of animals following her. He carefully aimed and fired again, putting a slug into her lungs. She jumped and stopped, and her followers clustered about her. They began to bawl with uncertainty, blowing steam into the cold air.

By the sixth shot he had killed the leader and any that were inclined to be leaders. He began to pick them off deliberately, unhurriedly. The barrel of the Big Fifty became hot.

It felt good on his cold hands, but the heat would make his shots go wild and might cause leading of the barrel. He threw open the breech and, without showing any more of himself than necessary above the rim of the gully, rolled the big gun in the frosty grass. In a minute, he went back to the skillful, cruel business at hand. It took an hour, with a half dozen waits for the gun to cool. His right shoulder became sore. When he quit, the last adult of the bunch had sunk to the ground.

He carefully collected his scattered brass, then went along the gully the way he had come and walked to meet the wagon. It was Norton, one of the men who would act as shooters, and three others, one of them the boy Andy Prescott. They had started when they heard his shots, had seen his stand and waited. He climbed in the wagon, and they drove toward the downed buffaloes. The calves stampeded away.

The two mules snorted and shied as they were driven into the acre of shaggy heaps where spots of blood were clotting on the ground and in the coarse black hair.

"Stay in the wagon!" Chance cautioned the boy. "Wait till we see if anything's going to get up."

One of them said, "Look's like you've already got us a day's work here, Mr. Chance."

"For five men and a team? I count thirty-two. We ought to be through with these in an hour, if we don't mess around and let them get cold."

"Only thirty-two?" Norton said. "I thought I counted thirty-three shots, Chance. Ain't nobody else hunting around here, are they?"

Chance laughed. "When you get past thirty shots, you're allowed a miss or two. Well, let's get started."

They began the skinning. Each animal was slit down the inside of the legs and the center of the belly, also around the tail and around the neck behind the ears. The legs were skinned by hand and enough of the neck to make a wad around which a rope could be tied. The mules were unhooked from the wagon, singletrees, doubletrees and all, and used to peel the hides from under the buffaloes. The team did not like the work, particularly the appearance of the naked carcasses.

Chance, working alongside the others, but constantly thinking about ways to make their methods more efficient, decided that one man could handle the team if the knife men would stake down each buffalo's head so it could not move while its hide was being stripped. His plan to use crews of one shooter, two skinners, and one mule driver was about right.

They already had meat in camp. They hacked out the tongues and piled them on the flesh side of a hide in the wagon; it was the only part of the meat for which the market was good enough to pay for the hauling. In little more than an hour all the limp skins were piled in the wagon, the team was hitched, and they were headed back to camp. Behind them the great bare red and white carcasses were already drawing flies.

The following day a norther blew in. Sleet came with it and a drizzle that froze on the ground. They continued their work in the fierce wind, completing the dugouts, gathering buffalo chips for fuel, building a windbreak for the stock, cutting an entire wagon load of stakes and stretching pins from the willows that grew by the water hole.

Next day the wind had calmed but it was colder. The grass crackled with ice under their feet. They went about their business of slaughter and skinning. Chance spent part of the time scouting horseback out along high ground, the rest of the time shooting. It was cold on horseback, but not so bad as working with the Big Fifty. Lying prone he would become cramped and would shake. His numb hands were clumsy on the gun. The skinners did better keeping warm with their hard labor. They wore gloves, but these became damp with blood. When they got a big kill at one place, they would build a fire.

As days passed, the stretched, drying hides began to cover acres of ground in the flat below camp. They required daily care, first had to be sprinkled with arsenic water to prevent any kind of bug damage, then had to be turned from one side to the other to prevent spoilage. When they became hard enough to hold their shape without being pegged down, the hides were piled in loose stacks, through which air could circulate.

It was a dirty, smelly camp. The men became infested with vermin from the buffaloes. They worked hard and suffered constantly from the cold, endured long hours of guard duty at night. They made the life bearable with rowdy banter and coarse jokes. Chance kept them busy, took part in their kidding, but put a quick stop to any horseplay with knives or guns.

When they had five hundred hides flint dry, he had them

bound into tight bales and loaded on the big wagon. He picked out Winters, who was a good man with oxen, to take the load to Fort Griffin. It was about a five-day haul, one way.

Chance went over the route with the old man. "You know where Monday Creek is over yonder? Cross it and follow down. You've got to cross it, because the crossing on the Brazos is just above where the creek runs in. Right?"

"I won't have no trouble," Winters said.

"All right. If you don't find a crossing on the Clear Fork, just go on downstream on this side. How many men do you think you ought to have with you?"

"Hell, I don't need no help, Chance. We're getting a bonus on these hides, remember? I'd rather have the boys skinning buffalo than setting on their hind ends on the wagon, just getting in my way."

The boy Andy wanted badly to go see Fort Griffin. Chance decided to send him as one helper for the old man. The boy was almost grown, drawing full wages. They would bring back a receipt for the hides; food, including sorghum, dried fruit, and salt; twenty bushels of oats; and two more freight wagons with drivers, if such could be hired. They departed at dawn on a cold clear day, the boy walking, the old man on top of the load keeping warm by cursing and popping his long whip.

On the afternoon of the second day after Winters left, the buffalo camp was suddenly awakened to danger by three revolver shots from Lefors up on the ridge to the north.

Chance was in camp, just unsaddling the dun horse Bullet, meaning to go back out with the one skinning crew that had come in to unload. He called Norton to him as he swung the saddle back on the horse. "Tear the roofs off of those dugouts, Norton, and carry in everything we might need. I want the mules unharnessed and staked down there below the water hole. Hobble them and sideline them both. We can't afford to lose any stock."

He rode north uphill to meet Lefors. "What do you see?"

"The damnedest war party you ever saw! Must be a hundred. They don't know we're here yet, but the way they're heading they can't miss us."

"No, not with all those hides spread out. Could you see our other two wagons?"

"One's coming in. The one out on the creek didn't hear the shots, I guess."

"Go out and get them. Tell them to drop everything and really whip it up and come on in. We'll be in a position to cover you if you need it."

He had chosen the campsite as much for a defensive position as for any other reason. The dugouts were high enough to command the surrounding area, and no cover existed for several hundred yards around them. Below the dugouts the hill sloped away sharply to the place where the wagons were usually parked a hundred feet away, and more gently to the water hole. The stock would be in a low place, easily covered from the entrenchments in the red-clay hillside.

It was nearly half an hour from the time of the first warning shots until the mounted Indians began to appear on the ridge a mile to the north. The third wagon and its crew came bouncing into camp about the same time. The Indians were stopping, studying the valley.

The men talked back and forth in the dugouts. "God! Look at those Injuns! Look at those feathers and those horns!"

"And those dobbed-up horses! Those boogers are looking for a fight!"

"Hell, I've done counted forty and they keep coming!"

Awe showed in their voices. Chance called out, "Boys, I'll guarantee you I'd rather be right here than be one of those redskins. Norton, Lee, let's get these buffalo guns in the best positions. Bonham, let Lefors have your Sharps. We're going to introduce them to the Big Fifty, and I believe it will shake their confidence.

"See that yellow bank up there? About a thousand yards. I want you to fire at a spot in it a time or two, till you get your windage and elevation. Then when those fancy warriors come down right even with it, open up on them."

They zeroed in with the long-range rifles, Chance and three others. The Indians, numbering either seventy-eight or seventy-nine by the best count, poured down straight toward them in a leisurely trot, clearly confident that they were far out of range.

Chance waited them out, sighting carefully, and squeezed off a shot. The other three big guns pounded almost at the same time. An Indian pitched from his mount as if lassoed and jerked off, and two leading horses went down. The warriors milled a moment, drew back, and assembled as if in consultation.

Chance called, "Let's let them have another round. I think we can still reach them."

They fired the Big Fifties again, and another painted horse went down. The Indians scattered. They seemed to wave back and forth to one another a minute, then suddenly they charged forward in a broken line, hugging tight against their ponies. Their war cries drifted faintly down on the winter air, like the weak sounds of puppies before their eyes are open.

The buffalo guns began to take their toll again, and the Indians spread out more, guiding their mounts in zigzag patterns. They grew larger in the white men's vision and their cries louder.

"All right," Chance yelled. "Open up."

They began to fire the repeating Winchester carbines. Eight of these, with the four larger rifles, spouted a withering fire from the dugouts. Few marks showed except a naked leg on a horse's back, or a body that raised up only an instant, or a line of striped feathers or the horn of a headdress that peeped from behind a horse's mane. Here and there a horse tumbled and a savage form rolled on the ground trying to gain the protection of his dead mount while bullets spit dust around him.

The charge faltered. They whirled and dodged back in the direction from which they came, riding superbly, hugging the necks of their racing, plunging horses.

Bullets and a few high-trajectory arrows hit the dirt around the dugouts from a dozen Indians down behind dead horses. One wild and lucky shot struck a keg of powder in the end of one of the wagons. The result was a shattering explosion that blew the wagon box from its running gear and threw splinters of wood into the air. The Indians then concentrated their fire on the other two wagons, but the rest of the powder was safely in the dugouts.

Smoke from their own guns settled around the twelve white men. They swung at it with their hats and rubbed their eyes and squinted to pick out targets up the slope.

The howling melee of riders, some fifty of them still mounted, poured down the slope again. They were met with the same withering fire and this time would not face it long, but turned to the business of picking up their dead and wounded and horseless brothers, this without dismounting.

"I'll say one thing for them," someone said. "Them devils can ride."

The attackers seemed to have had their fill of it. They

withdrew well out of range, then part of them began to straggle back the way they had come, some of these walking, some riding double, some being carried limply across ponies' backs. The remaining Indians, some quarter of the original number, split into two groups, which headed in opposite directions, east and west, as if to go around the buffalo camp.

Chance had identified Comanches and Kiowas among the attackers and thought that there was at least one other tribe represented that he was not familiar with. The bunch of ten which was circling around to the east looked to be all Kiowas. Probably the original command and organization had broken down.

"What do you think, Mr. Chance?" someone asked. "Is it a trick, or what?"

"No, I don't think so. I think they've made a smart estimate of the military situation, you might say."

"How many Indians would it take to capture this place?"

"I guess that many could take it if they'd all come on at once. There might be a half dozen of them left alive to enjoy it. They've decided to look for some cheaper scalps."

Someone said, "There'll be some small bunches of hide hunters that won't ever get home."

"Let's get some supper cooking," Chance said.

Their only casualty was Ike, who had got dirt kicked into his eyes by a skipping bullet. Chance stood on the high ground above camp and kept in sight the two bunches of Indians, while the rest of the men built up the fire, mixed sourdough bread, put some thick slabs of liver on to fry, started a pile of marrow bones roasting.

It was just sunset and the ten Kiowas could be seen clearly three miles away to the southeast, going toward Monday Creek, where Chance called Lefors up to him. "What would you say those Indians are doing?"

"Going the other way, and it's fine with me."

"Just riding along?"

"They might be following a trail. My God, Chance! Are you thinking what I am?"

"I guess I am. They've cut Winters' wagon tracks."

"Well, they're two days old. We've got wagon tracks all over."

"Not with wide tires and loaded that heavy. Not pulled by oxen. Hell, they can read those tracks like a book. Probably guess right where he's going."

"Where would Winters be? He's away past the Brazos by now."

"But still got a long ways to go. Those devils will go clear in sight of the fort if they have a reason. There's a moon tonight. They could probably follow the tracks by moonlight and catch him tomorrow . . . if they don't stop. Why in the hell did I let Prescott's boy go with him?"

He went down and loosed the horse Bullet, saddled him, and led him up to the fire where the men were starting to eat. The early darkness of winter was closing in. "Lefors, have you got any liquor with you?"

"No, I ain't, Chance."

"I want the damned truth, Lefors. Have you got any liquor?"

"Hell, no! That's the truth!"

"All right, I'm putting you in charge of the defense of this place. You know what to do. I expect everybody to follow your orders about guard duty and such.

"Norton, you're in charge of the work. Get us some buffalo hides. If anybody has any spare time, put them to fixing that wagon. I'm going to catch Winters. Ought to be back in a week or less."

Ike broke in. "Let me go with you, Mr. Chance."

"No, you'll have just enough to hold this place. Don't any of you try to be a hero. Just do what Lefors tells you and try to get some work done."

He tied a carbine on the saddle, stuffed his coat pockets with bullets and a slab of hot bread, and set off toward Monday Creek in a lope.

The long-legged dun was a magnificent horse. Chance would urge him into a lope, let him pick his own footing, and feel him tiring at the end of two miles, then let him walk. When, after five minutes of walking, Chance would cluck and shake the reins along the dun's neck, the horse would jump back into his easy gallop as if he knew they had a long fast trip to make.

He followed the general course of the creek but on the other side from the course Winters had taken. Over there somewhere, three or four miles away, the Kiowas would be following the tracks. It was light enough. Or would they be so tired they would stop for the night? He wondered how closely they had guessed the age of the tracks. Probably pretty close. One thing, they had taken a beating today, would be frustrated, would be eager to overtake a lone wagon. The question came back to nag him: "Why did I let the Prescott kid go?"

Now and again in a fleeting moment he felt the loneliness of the clear winter night and his own puny size. The land was as big as the vast sky. The shadowed things and distant things on the earth were as mysterious as the empty spaces between heavenly bodies. Sky and land were one limitless enigma that he traveled in. But such occasional impression was always pushed back by the prodding of his purpose. He sensed the traveling of others in the loneliness, the Kiowas and their thoughts, their intentions, the cranky old man, the green boy. And constantly he felt the rapport with the horse that surged under him.

Bullet would slow as if asking "Which way here?" and a touch of the rein on the side of the neck would send him down a slope or along a ridge, guided, but finding his own way.

Sometime after midnight they came to the Brazos. They picked their way down to the water's edge, and Chance let him walk along the light-colored sand. The water gave no clew to a crossing; it was a dark movement with sparkles of moonlight, uncertain in depth. He could see only shadows across at the other shore. He nudged the horse toward it, then took the pressure off; repeated it. He spoke aloud to the horse. "We've got to get across, Bullet. What do you say?"

After fifteen minutes the horse suddenly turned back downstream a few yards and stepped into the water. The film of ice in the shallows crunched under his hoofs. He splashed forward.

Chance had concentrated his attention on finding a place where the horse would willingly take the river. Now he questioned himself for his trust in the horse. Had he been too hasty? The river was down, but he had no idea about this crossing. Maybe he should turn back and build a fire—wait till morning. But the Kiowas following Winters would have a shallow crossing. Probably he should have taken off his clothes, but that, too, would be a gamble. It was go ahead or turn back, and no good way to tell. Bullet seemed to have decided it could be done.

The water was no more than a few inches deep for two hundred feet, then the bottom sloped down. Bullet picked his way as if on rocks. The water rose. Chance felt it splashing up as high as his knees, and as it penetrated the layers of his clothing it was searing cold. Droplets that struck his face stung like blowing sleet.

For long minutes the horse pushed through the black liquid, slowing now and again to explore for footing. With relief, Chance felt them finally pulling up out of the channel. There was no swimming water. When Bullet struck sand footing, he burst into a run through the shallows.

Chance dismounted on the dry sand. His legs ached with the cold, but he was relieved to feel with his feet on the ground that his boots were not sloshing with water. He led the horse up the bank along a broken path. Evidently they had struck an old buffalo crossing. Bullet was stumbling, suddenly clumsy. Chance took off his coat and briskly rubbed the horse's legs. Chance shook so that he could hardly control himself enough to get the coat back on and buttoned.

He led the horse for an hour out through the river timber and into the open country. As he mounted, he said, "Bullet, old fellow, if those redskin devils are ahead of us, they've got the best horses on earth."

It was noon when he caught the freight wagon. Winters and Andy had enjoyed a peaceful journey. The boy became excited on hearing about the fight and disappointed that he had missed it.

"If you stick with this hide hunting, you'll see more Indians than you want to see," Chance told him.

He unsaddled the horse and, during the brief stop for lunch, fed him a half gallon of the oats Winters was carrying. He tied him behind the heavy wagon, then climbed inside to find a bed for himself. His position was cramped and the ride was rough, but he became warm for the first time since he had got wet and, feeling somewhat guilty that Bullet must keep walking, fell asleep.

That evening they watered the stock in a creek and filled their water keg, then pushed on out to open ground for night camp. They split the night into three guards, Chance taking the last. Since the moon would go down, leaving an hour of blackness before dawn, during which time a guard would be unable to see any distance, he planned to break camp early and be on the move in that dangerous time.

It was between three and four o'clock in the morning that he prodded the oxen from their bed ground and put them to the wagon. He unhobbled Bullet and tied him behind. By the light of the sinking moon, he and the other two ate a cold breakfast and prepared to move. When they pulled out, all landmarks had faded and they set their course by the stars.

Chance and the youngster walked, Winters perched atop the front bale of hides. The rattle of the yoke chains, the thump of wheels over bunch grass, and the creak of the wooden joints in the wagon hid any distant sounds. Chance, beside the team, became aware that Bullet was jerking at his lead rope. The horse neighed.

Chance yelled, "Hold up, Winters!" and ran to the lead oxen to stop them, so that he could hear.

Then close around them the air was rent with screams and rushing movements and the blast of guns. Out of nowhere they were attacked by a force that was attempting to appear overwhelming. Chance sprinted toward the rear of the wagon, toward the source of the biggest commotion, cocking his hand gun.

He threw himself on his belly, hunting a target against the night sky. He fired at a moving form, rolled from the tell-tale flash, and fired again.

The attackers had stopped firing. Evidently they had exhausted the loads in their single-shot rifles. Now, between their yells and the pound of their horses' hoofs, could be heard the swish of feathered arrows, some of which slammed into the wagon boards like thrown rocks.

Against the sky he saw a tall mounted form charging straight in. He fired up at point-blank range and saw the Indian topple.

Winters was shooting and cursing. Andy's hand gun was sounding from the other side of the wagon. Chance yelled, "Let 'em have it, boy!" His own gun snapped on an empty cylinder.

He rose and found the rear of the wagon with his hands, began to clamber up the tailgate to find the loaded Winchester he had stashed there. A blow like a swinging fist struck him in the center of the back. He caught himself and climbed on to get the rifle. An arrow had penetrated the layers of clothing on his back. It ground into his flesh as he moved.

As he went back to the ground, his hand brushed the rope that led from the rocking wagon to his saddle horse, and he realized that Bullet was down.

On his belly again, he searched for targets, fired at a dim movement, levered in another cartridge, fired again. The Indians were drawing back. Dawn was lighting the eastern sky faintly.

Winters called, "Chance, the bastards got my near wheeler! Are you all right?"

"Yeah. You all right, Andy?"

"Yes, sir, I think so."

A savage wailing song rose out in the darkness a hundred yards away, a kind of chant of guttural sounds, monotonous and sad. One of the Indians had crawled as far away as he could go and was making his peace with death. To this accompaniment the winter daylight crept over the landscape.

The first object that came clear to Chance was the horse Bullet sprawled motionless on his side, his neck twisted out over one front leg, four arrows embedded in him, any one of which might have been fatal. Chance stood over the horse. "The dirty devils! The filthy, dirty devils!" Unconscious of any human ears within hearing, he talked to himself and perhaps to the horse. "Best horse I ever had! Every great horse I get, they steal him or kill him! I ought to go on a few murdering raids myself!" He pitied the singing, dying Indian out there and understood him and hated him all at once.

He went forward to the ox team. Two were down.

"You want to give me a hand, Winters? I think we better move as soon as we can make up a team here."

"I can't move my God-damned leg, Chance."

"What? I thought you were all right."

"I ain't dead, but them bastards sure got me good."

"Bleeding much?"

"Not too much."

He could see the Indians now, seven mounted out there in the distance, holding a powwow, two motionless nearby, the other kneeling a hundred yards away, still moaning. Two Indian horses were dead and one free.

He got the boy to help him with the oxen. The youngster suddenly drew back, visibly shaken. "Mr. Chance, you got an arrow sticking out of your back!"

"I know it. It nicked me a little inside my clothes too. I wish you'd pull the thing out."

Andy took hold of it.

"Hey! Careful! Take hold easy and jerk straight out."

The thing was done and the boy held the shaft with a bare, bloody end. Chance said, "Feels like you left a tin can or something in there. Let's get these steers straightened out."

Winters' wound proved to be more serious. A jagged iron arrow head had sliced into the joint of his knee like a meat cleaver. His leg was bent at the joint and he could not stand for it to be straightened out or bent further. Chance split the leg of his trousers and underwear. The arrow head was buried, its shaft splintered off short. Chance used one of the old man's suspenders to make a tourniquet and shut off most of the bleeding.

He believed that he could reach the seven remaining Kiowas with the needle gun that Winters carried in the wagon, but decided against it. The thing to do was to move toward the fort. He sat as high on the load as possible in order to see a good distance and got the eight yokes of oxen moving. When he had come two miles, he could see the Indians back at the location of the fight. They were butchering one of the two dead oxen.

That day was a long tedious journey over the rolling plains. Winters groaned and cursed at every jolt of the wagon. Chance shouted at the patient, plodding oxen. His back became so sore that he could not swing the whip. He had the youngster cut a greasewood limb to flail at the slow beasts.

Late in the afternoon they came to the winding Clear Fork and could see miles ahead on a commanding hill the whitewashed stone buildings of Fort Griffin, an hour's ride on a fast horse, a long jolting ride in a freight wagon. To dump the load would not speed them enough to make any difference.

Chance turned east downstream. He would go around to the bridge on the Belknap-Fort Griffin road. Winters was becoming delirious; he moaned and cursed continuously. Nothing could be done to ease him. Chance pushed on through the moonlit night.

Some time in the small hours of the morning they crossed the bridge and came into the sprawling, dirty, wild town in the flats below Government Hill. The town's houses of recreation were booming even so late. Five minutes after they came in, Chance and Winters were being carried in a rancher's hack up the long ramped road to the fort hospital.

The back wound gave him little trouble after the piece of rusty steel was sliced out by the surgeon, and he never found it necessary to interrupt his own activity. When he went back to the buffalo camp, while it was still sore, Lefors and a few others who felt at liberty to joke with him would say, "Chance, you don't seem to put your back into your work like you used to," or, "Chance, why do you stand around at attention all the time? How come you don't bend over and help us?" Within three weeks he was bending over and working as hard as ever.

In March, he went back to the ranch to take Winters. The old man, on crutches, not yet able to get around on his new peg leg, fumed at his own clumsiness. Chance told him, "Be glad it was your right leg. You can still mount a horse."

"But how in the hell can I stay on the critter once I get him mounted?"

"You'll learn to. You've got a job working for me as long as you want it. You know that."

"Hell, it ain't that, Chance. I just hate for some of these young whippersnapper kids to get the idea they can do things I can't do."

Chance left him at the ranch to take up his old cooking duties.

He went back to the buffalo camp. The hide collecting was going well. The hauling was the problem. He made it a point to send two well-armed men in addition to the driver every time the freight wagon moved. To escape part of the hauling, he sold many hides out on the range to a dealer who did his own freighting and paid the poor price of a dollar a hide. The Fort Griffin price was a dollar and a half; even that was poor, a reflection of the general depression across the country.

The day before they were ready to go back to the ranch to start the spring roundup, he passed on horseback down through the valley where they had done most of their winter's hunting. The carcasses were scattered in groups everywhere, black against the gray grass and the new light-green grass. They lay in various stages of putrefaction, with darkened flesh drawn tight over skeletons, deflated by buzzards and coyotes and other carrion hunters. The massive heads with the thick black hair seemed grotesquely large on the hairless, shrunken, emaciated bodies. The air was heavy with the smell of rotten meat, the stench increasing now with warm weather coming on.

It struck him as a grim business, but these few months' work, his first extensive hunt, paid him just over nine thousand dollars—not a great amount considering the men he had on the payroll, but enough to keep the ranch going.

He had occasion later that year, in the late fall, to pass again through the same valley. The grim aspect of it was still there, the smell fainter, like a breath out of an ancient grave.

The carrion was no longer black; it was patches of bleaching bones with only strings of hair or dried flesh sticking on them. Where each buffalo had rotted, the grass grew taller, more lush, marking the spots, almost hiding the bones, thrusting up through the rib cages.

WALTER VAN TILBURG CLARK

WALTER VAN TILBURG CLARK (1909–1971) was born at East Orland, Maine, and in 1917 moved with his family to Nevada, the state which served as a setting for much of his subsequent fiction. Clark received a bachelor's degree from the University of Nevada in 1931 and went on for a master's degree in English, writing a thesis on the Tristram legend. In 1932 he published a volume of poetry and then assumed a teaching apprenticeship at the University of Vermont, this time earning a second master's degree, writing a thesis on Robinson Jeffers. Clark had personally met Jeffers at his Thor House on the California coast and was as impressed with the man himself and his way of life as with his poetry. Following his marriage, Clark took a position teaching and coaching basketball at a high school in Cazenovia, New York. According to Max Westbrook in his biographical and critical study, *Walter Van Tilburg Clark* (Twayne Publishers, 1969), the two most significant influences on Clark's creative writing were Jeffers and Swiss psychologist C. G. Jung. Clark's first novel was *The Ox-Bow Incident* (1940; New American Library, 1960); it won for him an immediate place in American letters. On the surface, this novel would seem to be concerned with the notion of frontier justice; it tells of three men encountered on the trail by a vigilante group and hanged as cattle rustlers only to have them ultimately proven innocent. Westbrook's analysis, however, went further. "The subject of *The Ox-Bow Incident*," he wrote, ". . . is not a plea for legal procedure. The subject is man's mutilation of himself, man's sometimes trivial, sometimes large failures to get beyond the narrow images of his own ego. The tragedy of *The Ox-Bow Incident* is that most of us, including the man of sensitivity and the man of reason, are alienated from the saving grace of archetypal reality. Our lives, then, though not without possibility, are often stories of a cruel and irrevocable mistake."

Certainly few authors prior to Clark had approached Western fiction with his profound erudition and mythic concerns. With the success of his first novel and the sale of motion-picture rights, Clark decided to concentrate exclusively on writing, publishing a number of short stories and working on his very long and not very successful *The City of Trembling Leaves* (Random House, 1945), an initiation novel in which setting or a sense of the land is negligible. In 1946, Clark went to live in Taos, New Mexico, returning to Nevada toward the end of the decade. He wrote *The Track of the Cat* (Random House, 1949), a novel which demonstrates why two hunters are killed pursuing a panther, symbolizing the principle of evil in the world, because they do not understand it, and why two hunters who do understand the principle are successful in killing the panther. This novel, too, was sold to motion pictures. Clark next published *The Watchful Gods and Other Stories* (Random House, 1950), a collection of his shorter fiction. The critics had become increasingly harsh on Clark with the appearance of each book after *The Ox-Bow Incident*.

In an essay titled "The Western Writer and the Eastern Establishment" (1966), the late Vardis Fisher observed, "I read recently a surmise that Walter [Van Tilburg] Clark, a fine artist, gave up writing because of the unfairness of some of his critics. If true, what a pity that he paid any attention to them!" I cannot say whether this rumor was true or not, but Clark did quit writing. He returned to teaching, at the university level, and left behind only the fragments of an unfinished novel when he died.

"The Wind and the Snow of Winter" is a short story which appeared for the first time in 1944 in *The Yale Review* and was later included in *The Watchful Gods and Other Stories*. I believe Clark's finest work—other than *The Track of the Cat*—is to be found in his shorter fiction. As in this story, he could often combine a vivid description of physical terrain and human personality with an eerie sense of metaphysical shadows and meanings less decipherable but somehow more potent.

The Wind and the Snow of Winter

It was near sunset when Mike Braneen came onto the last pitch of the old wagon road which had let into Gold Rock from the east since the Comstock days. The road was just two ruts in the hard earth, with sagebrush growing between them, and was full of steep pitches and sharp turns. From the summit it descended even more steeply into Gold Rock in a series of short switchbacks down the slope of the canyon. There was a paved highway on the other side of the pass now, but Mike never used that. Cars coming from behind made him uneasy, so that he couldn't follow his own thoughts long, but had to keep turning around every few minutes, to see that his burro, Annie, was staying out on the shoulder of the road, where she would be safe. Mike didn't like cars anyway, and on the old road he could forget about them, and feel more like himself. He could forget about Annie too, except when the light, quick tapping of her hoofs behind him stopped. Even then he didn't really break his thoughts. It was more as if the tapping were another sound from his own inner machinery, and when it stopped, he stopped too, and turned around to see what she was doing. When he began to walk ahead again at the same slow, unvarying pace, his arms scarcely swinging at all, his body bent a little forward from the waist, he would not be aware that there had been any interruption of the memory or the story that was going on in his head. Mike did not like to have his stories interrupted except by an idea of his own, something to do with prospecting, or the arrival of his story at an actual memory which warmed him to closer recollection or led into a new and more attractive story.

An intense, golden light, almost liquid, fanned out from the peaks above him and reached eastward under the gray sky, and the snow which occasionally swarmed across this light was fine and dry. Such little squalls had been going on all day, and still there was nothing like real snow down, but only a fine powder which the wind swept along until it caught under the brush, leaving the ground bare. Yet Mike Braneen was not deceived. This was not just a flurrying day; it was the beginning of winter. If not tonight, then tomorrow, or the next day, the snow would begin which shut off the mountains, so that a man might as well be on a great plain for all he could see, perhaps even the snow which blinded a man at once and blanketed the desert in an hour. Fifty-two years in this country had made Mike Braneen sure about such things, although he didn't give much thought to them, but only to what he had to do because of them. Three nights before, he had been awakened by a change in the wind. It was no longer a wind born in the near mountains, cold with night and altitude, but a wind from far places, full of a damp chill which got through his blankets and into his bones. The stars had still been clear and close above the dark humps of the mountains, and overhead the constellations had moved slowly in full panoply, unbroken by any invisible lower darkness; yet he had lain there half awake for a few minutes, hearing the new wind beat the brush around him, hearing Annie stirring restlessly and thumping in her hobble. He had thought drowsily. Smells like winter this time, and then, it's held off a long time this year, pretty near the end of December. Then he had gone back to sleep, mildly happy because the change meant he would be going back to Gold Rock. Gold Rock was the other half of Mike Braneen's life. When the smell of winter came, he always started back for Gold Rock. From March or April until the smell of winter, he wandered slowly about among the mountains, anywhere between the White Pines and the Virginias, with only his burro for company. Then there would come the change, and they would head back for Gold Rock.

Mike had traveled with a good many burros during that time, eighteen or twenty, he thought, although he was not sure. He could not remember them all, but only those he had had first, when he was a young man and always thought most about seeing women when he got back to Gold Rock, or those with something queer about them, like Baldy, who'd had a great, pale patch, like a bald spot, on one side of his belly, or those who'd had something queer happen to them, like Maria. He could remember just how it had been that night. He could remember it as if it were last night. It had been in Hamilton. He had felt unhappy, because he could remember Hamilton when the whole hollow was full of people and buildings, and everything was new and active. He had gone to sleep in the hollow shell of the Wells Fargo Building, hearing an old iron shutter banging against the wall in the wind. In the morning, Maria had been gone. He had followed the scuffing track she made on account of her loose hobble, and it had led far up the old snow-gullied road to Treasure Hill, and then ended at one of the black shafts that opened like mouths right at the edge of the road. A man remembered a thing like that. There weren't many burros that foolish. But burros with nothing particular about them were hard to remember—especially those he'd had in the last twenty years or so, when he had gradually stopped feeling so personal about them, and had begun to call all the jennies Annie and all the burros Jack.

The clicking of the little hoofs behind him stopped, and Mike stopped too, and turned around. Annie was pulling at a line of yellow grass along the edge of the road.

"Come on, Maria," Mike said patiently. The burro at once stopped pulling at the dead grass and came on up towards him, her small black nose working, the ends of the grass standing out on each side of it like whiskers. Mike began to climb again, ahead of her.

It was a long time since he had been caught by a winter, too. He could not remember how long. All the beginnings ran together in his mind, as if they were all the beginning of one winter so far back that he had almost forgotten it. He could still remember clearly, though, the winter he had stayed out on purpose, clear into January. He had been a young man then, thirty-five or forty or forty-five, somewhere in there. He would have to stop and try to bring back a whole string of memories about what had happened just before, in order to remember just how old he had been, and it wasn't worth the trouble. Besides, sometimes even that system didn't work. It would lead him into an old camp where he had been a number of times, and the dates would get mixed up. It was impossible to remember any other way; because all his comings and goings had been so much alike. He had been young, anyhow, and not much afraid of anything except running out of water in the wrong place; not even afraid of the winter. He had stayed out because he'd thought he had a good thing, and he had wanted to prove it. He could remember how it felt to be out in the clear winter weather on the mountains; the piñon trees and the junipers weighted down with feathery snow, and making sharp, blue shadows on the white slopes. The hills had made blue shadows on one another too, and in the still air his pick had made the beginning of a sound like a bell's. He knew he had been young, because he could remember taking a day off now and then, just to go tramping around those hills, up and down the white and through the blue shadows, on a kind of holiday. He had pretended to his common sense that he was seriously prospecting, and had carried his hammer, and even his drill along, but he had really just been gallivanting, playing colt. Maybe he had been even younger than thirty-five, though he could still be stirred a little, for that matter, by the memory of the kind of weather which had sent him gallivanting. High-blue weather, he called it. There were two kinds of high-blue weather, besides the winter kind, which didn't set him off very often, spring and fall. In the spring it would have a soft, puffy wind and soft, puffy white clouds which made separate shadows that traveled silently across hills that looked soft too. In the fall it would be still, and there would be no clouds at all in the blue, but there would be something in the golden air and the soft, steady sunlight on the mountains that made a man as uneasy as the spring blowing, though in a different way, more sad and not so excited. In the spring high-blue, a man had been likely to think about women he had slept with, or wanted to sleep with, or imaginary women made up with the help of newspaper pictures of actresses or young society matrons, or of the old oil paintings in the Lucky Boy Saloon, which showed pale, almost naked women against dark, sumptuous backgrounds—women with long hair or braided hair, calm, virtuous faces, small hands and feet, and ponderous limbs, breasts, and buttocks. In the fall high-blue, though it had been much longer since he had seen a woman, or heard a woman's voice, he was more likely to think about old friends, men, or places he had heard about, or places he hadn't seen for a long time. He himself thought most often about Goldfield the way he had last seen it in the summer in 1912. That was as far south as Mike had ever been in Nevada. Since then he had never been south of Tonopah. When the high-blue weather was past, though, and the season worked toward winter, he began to think about Gold Rock. There were only three or four winters out of the fifty-two when he hadn't gone home to Gold Rock, to his old room at Mrs. Wright's, up on Fourth Street, and to his meals in the dining room at the International House, and to the Lucky Boy, where he could talk to Tom Connover and his other friends, and play cards, or have a drink to hold in his hand while he sat and remembered.

This journey had seemed a little different from most,

though. It had started the same as usual, but as he had come across the two vast valleys, and through the pass in the low range between them, he hadn't felt quite the same. He'd felt younger and more awake, it seemed to him, and yet, in a way, older too, suddenly older. He had been sure that there was plenty of time, and yet he had been a little afraid of getting caught in the storm. He had kept looking ahead to see if the mountains on the horizon were still clearly outlined, or if they had been cut off by a lowering of the clouds. He had thought more than once, how bad it would be to get caught out there when the real snow began, and he had been disturbed by the first flakes. It had seemed hard to him to have to walk so far, too. He had kept thinking about distance. Also the snowy cold had searched out the regions of his body where old injuries had healed. He had taken off his left mitten a good many times, to blow on the fingers which had been frosted the year he was sixty-three, so that now it didn't take much cold to turn them white and stiffen them. The queer tingling, partly like an itch and partly like a pain, in the patch on his back that had been burned in that old powder blast, was sharper than he could remember its ever having been before. The rheumatism in his joints, which was so old a companion that it usually made him feel no more than tightknit and stiff, and the place where his leg had been broken and torn when that ladder broke in '97 ached, and had a pulse he could count. All this made him believe that he was walking more slowly than usual, although nothing, probably not even a deliberate attempt, could actually have changed his pace. Sometimes he even thought, with a moment of fear, that he was getting tired.

On the other hand, he felt unusually clear and strong in his mind. He remembered things with a clarity which was like living them again—nearly all of them events from many years back, from the time when he had been really active and fearless and every burro had had its own name. Some of these events, like the night he had spent in Eureka with the little, brown-haired whore, a night in the fall in 1888 or '89, somewhere in there, he had not once thought of for years. Now he could remember even her name. Armandy she had called herself: a funny name. They all picked names for their business, of course, romantic names like Cecily or Rosamunde or Belle or Claire, or hard names like Diamond Gert or Horseshoe Sal, or names that were pinned on them, like Indian Kate or Roman Mary, but Armandy was different.

He could remember Armandy as if he were with her now, not the way she had behaved in bed; he couldn't remember anything particular about that. In fact, he couldn't be sure that he remembered anything particular about that at all. There were others he could remember more clearly for the way they had behaved in bed, women he had been with more often. He had been with Armandy only that one night. He remembered little things about being with her, things that made it seem good to think of being with her again. Armandy had a room upstairs in a hotel. They could hear a piano playing in a club across the street. He could hear the tune, and it was one he knew, although he didn't know its name. It was a gay tune that went on and on the same, but still it sounded sad when you heard it through the hotel window, with the lights from the bars and hotels shining on the street, and the people coming and going through the lights, and then, beyond the lights, the darkness where the mountains were. Armandy wore a white silk dress with a high waist and a locket on a gold chain. The dress made her look very brown and like a young girl. She used a white powder on her face, that smelled like violets, but this could not hide her brownness. The locket was heart-shaped, and it opened to show a cameo of a man's hand holding a woman's hand very gently, just their fingers laid out long together, and the thumbs holding the way they were sometimes on tombstones. There were two little gold initials on each hand, but Armandy would never tell what they stood for, or even if the locket was really her own. He stood in the window, looking down at the club from which the piano music was coming, and Armandy stood beside him, with her shoulders against his arm, and a glass of wine in her hand. He could see the toe of her white satin slipper showing from under the edge of her skirt. Her big hat, loaded with black and white plumes, lay on the dresser behind him. His own leather coat, with the sheepskin lining, lay across the foot of the bed. It was a big bed, with a knobby brass foot and head. There was one oil lamp burning in the chandelier in the middle of the room. Armandy was soft-spoken, gentle, and a little fearful, always looking at him to see what he was thinking. He stood with his arms folded. His arms felt big and strong upon his heavily muscled chest. He stood there, pretending to be in no hurry, but really thinking eagerly about what he would do with Armandy, who had something about her which tempted him to be cruel. He stood there, with his chin down into his heavy dark beard, and watched a man come riding down the middle of the street from the west. The horse was a fine black, which lifted its head and feet with pride. The man sat very straight, with a high rein, and something about his clothes and hat made him appear to be in uniform, although it wasn't a uniform he was wearing. The man also saluted friends upon the sidewalks like an officer, bending his head just slightly, and touching his hat instead of lifting it. Mike Braneen asked Armandy who the man was, and then felt angry because she could tell him, and because he was an important man who owned a mine that was in bonanza. He mocked the airs with which the man rode, and his princely greetings. He mocked the man cleverly, and Armandy laughed and repeated what he said, and made him drink a little of her wine as a reward. Mike had been drinking whisky, and he did not like wine anyway, but this was not the moment in which to refuse such an invitation.

Old Mike remembered all this, which had been completely forgotten for years. He could not remember what he and Armandy had said, but he remembered everything else, and he felt very lonesome for Armandy, and for the room with the red, figured carpet and the brass chandelier with oil lamps in it, and the open window with the long tune coming up through it, and the young summer night outside on the mountains. This loneliness was so much more intense than his familiar loneliness that it made him feel very young. Memories like this had come up again and again during these three days. It was like beginning life over again. It had tricked him into thinking, more than once, next summer I'll make the strike, and this time I'll put it into something safe for the rest of my life, and stop this fool wandering around while I've still got some time left—a way of thinking which he had really stopped a long time before.

It was getting darker rapidly in the pass. When a gust of wind brought the snow against Mike's face so hard that he noticed the flakes felt larger, he looked up. The light was still there, although the fire was dying out of it, and the snow swarmed across it more thickly. Mike remembered God. He did not think anything exact. He did not think about his own relationship to God. He merely felt the idea as a comforting presence. He'd always had a feeling about God whenever he looked at a sunset, especially a sunset which came through under a stormy sky. It had been the strongest feeling left in him until these memories like the one about Armandy had begun. Even in this last pass, his strange fear of the storm had come on him again a couple of times, but now that he had looked at the light and thought of God, it was gone. In a few minutes he would come to the summit and look down into his lighted city. He felt happily hurried by this anticipation.

He would take the burro down and stable her in John Hammersmith's shed, where he always kept her. He would spread fresh straw for her, and see that the shed was tight against the wind and snow, and get a measure of grain for her from John. Then he would go up to Mrs. Wright's house at the top of Fourth Street, and leave his things in the same room he always had, the one in front, which looked down over the roofs and chimneys of his city, and across at the east wall of the canyon, from which the sun rose late. He would trim his beard with Mrs. Wright's shears, and shave the upper part of his cheeks. He would bathe out of the blue bowl and pitcher, and wipe himself with the towel with yellow flowers on it, and dress in the good dark suit and the good black shoes with the gleaming box toes, and the good black hat which he had left in the chest in his room. In this way he would perform the ceremony which ended the life of the desert and began the life of Gold Rock. Then he would go down to the International House, and greet Arthur Morris in the gleaming bar, and go into the dining room and eat the best supper they had, with fresh meat and vegetables, and new-made pie, and two cups of hot clear coffee. He would be served by the plump blond waitress who always joked with him, and gave him many little extra things with his first supper, including the drink which Arthur Morris always sent in from the bar.

At this point Mike Braneen stumbled in his mind, and his anticipation wavered. He could not be sure that the plump blond waitress would serve him. For a moment he saw her in a long skirt, and the dining room of the International House, behind her, had potted palms standing in the corners, and was full of the laughter and loud, manly talk of many customers who wore high vests and mustaches and beards. These men leaned back from tables covered with empty dishes. They patted their tight vests and lighted expensive cigars. He knew all their faces. If he were to walk down the aisle between the tables on his side, they would all speak to him. But he also seemed to remember the dining room with only a few tables, with oilcloth on them instead of linen, and with moody young men sitting at them in their work clothes—strangers who worked for the highway department, or were just passing through, or talked mining in terms which he did not understand or which made him angry.

No, it would not be the plump blond waitress. He did not know who it would be. It didn't matter. After supper he would go up Canyon Street under the arcade to the Lucky Boy Saloon, and there it would be the same as ever. There would be the laurel wreaths on the frosted glass panels of the doors, and the old sign upon the window, the sign that was older than Tom Connover, almost as old as Mike Braneen himself. He would open the door and see the bottles and the white women in the paintings, and the card table in the back corner and the big stove and the chairs along the wall. Tom would look around from his place behind the bar.

"Well, now," he would roar, "look who's here, boys."

"Now will you believe it's winter?" he would roar at them.

Some of them would be the younger men, of course, and there might even be a few strangers, but this would only add to the dignity of his reception, and there would also be his friends. There would be Henry Bray with the gray walrus mustache, and Mark Wilton and Pat Gallagher. They would all welcome him loudly.

"Mike, how are you anyway?" Tom would roar, leaning across the bar to shake hands with his big, heavy, soft hand with the diamond ring on it.

"And what'll it be, Mike? The same?" he'd ask, as if Mike had been in there no longer ago than the night before.

Mike would play that game too. "The same," he would say.

Then he would really be back in Gold Rock: never mind the plump blond waitress.

Mike came to the summit of the old road and stopped and looked down. For a moment he felt lost again, as he had when he'd thought about the plump blond waitress. He had expected Canyon Street to look much brighter. He had expected a lot of orange windows close together on the other side of the canyon. Instead there were only a few scattered lights across the darkness, and they were white. They made no communal glow upon the steep slope, but gave out only single, white needles of light, which pierced the darkness secretly and lonesomely, as if nothing could ever pass from one house to another over there. Canyon Street was very dark, too. There it went, the street he loved, steeply down into the bottom of the canyon, and down its length there were only the few street lights, more than a block apart, swinging in the wind and darting about that cold, small light. The snow whirled and swooped under the nearest street light below.

"You are getting to be an old fool," Mike Braneen said out loud to himself, and felt better. This was the way Gold Rock was now, of course, and he loved it all the better. It was a place that grew old with a man, that was going to die sometime, too. There could be an understanding with it.

He worked his way slowly down into Canyon Street, with Annie slipping and checking behind him. Slowly, with the blown snow behind them, they came to the first built-in block, and passed the first dim light showing through a smudged window under the arcade. They passed the dark places after it, and the second light. Then Mike Braneen stopped in the middle of the street, and Annie stopped beside him, pulling her rump in and turning her head away from the snow. A highway truck, coming down from the head of the canyon, had to get way over into the wrong side of the street to pass them. The driver leaned out as he went by, and yelled, "Pull over, Pop. You're in town now."

Mike Braneen didn't hear him. He was staring at the Lucky Boy. The Lucky Boy was dark, and there were boards nailed across the big window that had shown the sign. At last Mike went over onto the board walk to look more closely. Annie followed him, but stopped at the edge of the walk and scratched her neck against a post of the arcade. There was the other sign, hanging crossways under the arcade, and even in that gloom Mike could see that it said Lucky Boy and had a Jack of Diamonds painted on it. There was no mistake. The Lucky Boy sign, and others like it under the arcade, creaked and rattled in the wind.

There were footsteps coming along the boards. The boards sounded hollow, and sometimes one of them rattled. Mike Braneen looked down slowly from the sign and peered at the approaching figure. It was a man wearing a sheepskin coat with the collar turned up round his head. He was walking quickly, like a man who knew where he was going, and why, and where he had been. Mike almost let him pass. Then he spoke.

"Say, fella—"

He even reached out a hand as if to catch hold of the man's sleeve, though he didn't touch it. The man stopped, and asked impatiently, "Yeah?" and Mike let the hand down again slowly.

"Well, what is it?" the man asked.

"I don't want anything," Mike said. "I got plenty."

"O.K., O.K.," the man said. "What's the matter?"

Mike moved his hand towards the Lucky Boy. "It's closed," he said.

"I see it is, Dad," the man said. He laughed a little. He didn't seem to be in quite so much of a hurry now.

"How long has it been closed?" Mike asked.

"Since about June, I guess," the man said. "Old Tom Connover, the guy that ran it, died last June."

Mike waited for a moment. "Tom died?" he asked.

"Yup. I guess he'd just kept it open out of love of the place anyway. There hasn't been any real business for years. Nobody cared to keep it open after him."

The man started to move on, but then he waited, peering, trying to see Mike better.

"This June?" Mike asked finally.

"Yup. This last June."

"Oh," Mike said. Then he just stood there. He wasn't thinking anything. There didn't seem to be anything to think.

"You knew him?" the man asked.

"Thirty years," Mike said. "No, more'n that," he said, and started to figure out how long he had known Tom Connover but lost it, and said, as if it would do just as well, "He was a lot younger than I am, though."

"Hey," said the man, coming closer, and peering again. "You're Mike Braneen, aren't you?"

"Yes," Mike said.

"Gee, I didn't recognize you at first. I'm sorry."

"That's all right," Mike said. He didn't know who the man was, or what he was sorry about.

He turned his head slowly, and looked out into the street. The snow was coming down heavily now. The street was all white. He saw Annie with her head and shoulders in under the arcade, but the snow settling on her rump.

"Well, I guess I'd better get Molly under cover," he said. He moved toward the burro a step, but then halted.

"Say, fella—"

The man had started on, but he turned back. He had to wait for Mike to speak.

"I guess this about Tom's mixed me up."

"Sure," the man said. "It's tough, an old friend like that."

"Where do I turn to get to Mrs. Wright's place?"

"Mrs. Wright?"

"Mrs. William Wright," Mike said. "Her husband used to be a foreman in the Aztec. Got killed in the fire."

"Oh," the man said. He didn't say anything more, but just stood there, looking at the shadowy bulk of old Mike.

"She's not dead, too, is she?" Mike asked slowly.

"Yeah, I'm afraid she is, Mr. Braneen," the man said. "Look," he said more cheerfully. "It's Mrs. Branley's house you want right now, isn't it? Place where you stayed last winter?"

Finally Mike said, "Yeah, I guess it is."

"I'm going up that way. I'll walk up with you," the man said.

After they had started, Mike thought that he ought to take the burro down to John Hammersmith's first, but he was afraid to ask about it. They walked on down Canyon Street, with Annie walking along beside them in the gutter. At the first side street they turned right and began to climb the steep hill toward another of the little street lights dancing over a crossing. There was no sidewalk here, and Annie followed right at their heels. That one street light was the only light showing up ahead.

When they were halfway up to the light, Mike asked, "She die this summer, too?"

The man turned his body half around, so that he could hear inside his collar.

"What?"

"Did she die this summer, too?"

"Who?"

"Mrs. Wright," Mike said.

The man looked at him, trying to see his face as they came up towards the light. Then he turned back again, and his voice was muffled by the collar.

"No, she died quite a while ago, Mr. Braneen."

"Oh," Mike said finally.

They came up onto the crossing under the light, and the snow-laden wind whirled around them again. They passed under the light, and their three lengthening shadows before them were obscured by the innumerable tiny shadows of the flakes.

MAX EVANS

MAX EVANS (1925–) was born in Ropes, Texas, a town on the Texas/New Mexico border. At a very early age he went to work for a ranch near Santa Fe, where he first discovered translations of Honoré de Balzac in a set belonging to his employer. He read them by kerosene lamp in the bunkhouse at night and stopped reading only when the other men complained about the light. He went on to work as a hunter, trapper, a small-ranch owner, a miner, a calf-roper, and a salesman. A sufficiently talented artist, he made a living with his paintings at various times in his life. But from his earliest years, it seems, he most wanted to be a writer and it was to this craft that he repeatedly turned his attention. His most beautiful and sad books of contemporary range life were produced one after the other in the early sixties, *The Rounders* (1960; reissued by the Gregg Press, 1980), *The Hi Lo Country* (1961; reissued by the Gregg Press, 1980)—in my opinion his finest work—and *The One-Eyed Sky* (Houghton Mifflin, 1963). *The Rounders* (M-G-M, 1965) was adapted for the screen and directed by Burt Kennedy and it inspired a short-lived television series in 1966. Evans' protagonists in the *The Rounders,* Dusty Jones and Wrangler Lewis, returned in the short novel "The Great Wedding," included among the three short novels in *The One-Eyed Sky*. Evans has proven himself a worthy pupil of Balzac. Very much like Balzac, Evans can narrate the direst, most heartrending tragedy in such comic tones that you almost find yourself laughing.

In a PBS interview with John R. Milton of the University of South Dakota reprinted in *3 West* (Dakota Press, 1970), Milton made reference to a technique used by Paul Horgan in the latter's *The Common Heart* (Farrar, Straus, Cudahy, 1962). "He has a twentieth-century man, a physician," Milton told Evans, "become interested in history and find a journal and go outside Albuquerque to the place where the events in the journal actually occurred. Then the character simply looks at the place, sees the physical arena, and visualizes the action of the journal in his imagination. Horgan pulls in the historical action as a kind of extended flashback. . . ." Obviously Evans was intrigued by this technique and used it in "Candles in the Bottom of the Pool."

The story is an allegory. The first time I read it I could not help being reminded of an essay written in 1928 by C. G. Jung titled "Das Seelenproblem des modernen Menschen" ["The Spiritual Problem of Modern Humankind"]. Jung ended it with the sentiment that a new tempo had been introduced into the world, the American tempo, and that perhaps it is "a healthier or a more desperate attempt to escape from the dark laws of nature and to effect an even greater, even more heroic victory for the state of vigilance over the sleep of the ages." It is, he concluded, "a question which history will answer." And it was also in this same essay that he told this story.

> I have an Indian friend who is a Pueblo chieftain. We once spoke confidentially about the white man and he said: "We do not understand the white men. They always want something; they are always restless; they are always searching for something. What are they searching for? We don't know. We cannot understand them. They have such sharp noses, such thin, gruesome lips, such lines in their faces. We believe they are all crazy." My friend, without being able to find a name for him, had readily recognized the Aryan bird of prey and his insatiable eagerness for plunder which has led him into lands that otherwise would not concern him in the least and once there to foster our greatest delusion, that Christianity is the only truth, the white Christ the only redeemer.

Candles in the Bottom of the Pool

Joshua Stone, III, moved along the cool adobe corridor listening to the massive walls. They were over three feet thick; the mud and straw solidified hard as granite. He appeared the same.

The sounds came to him faintly at first, then stronger. He leaned against the smooth dirt plaster and heard the clanking of armor, the twanging of bows, the screams of falling men and horses. His chest rose as his lungs pumped the excited blood. His powerful hands were grabbing their own flesh at his sides. It was real. Then the struggles of the olive conquerors and the brown vanquished faded away like a weak wind.

He opened his eyes, relaxing slightly, and stepped back, staring intently at the wall. Where was she? Would she still come to him smiling, waiting, wanting? Maybe. There was silence now. Even the singing of the desert birds outside could not penetrate the mighty walls.

Then he heard the other song. The words were unintelligible, ancient, from forever back, back, back, but he felt and understood their meaning. She appeared from the unfathomable reaches of the wall, undulating like a black wisp ripped from a tornado cloud. She was whole now. Her black lace dress clung to her body, emphasizing the delicious smoothness of her face and hands. The comb of Spanish silver glistened like a halo in her hair. His blue eyes stared at her dark ones across the centuries. They knew. She smiled with much warmth, and more. One hand beckoned for him to come. He smiled back, whispering.

"Soon. Very soon."

"YES, YES, YES," she said and the words vibrated about, over, through, under and around everything. He stood, still staring, but there was only the dry mud now.

He turned, as yet entranced, then shook it off and entered through the heavily timbered archway into the main room. The light shafted in from the patio windows illuminating the big room not unlike a cathedral. In a way it was. Santos and bultos were all over. The darkly stained furniture was from another time, hand hewn and permanent like the house itself.

He absorbed the room for a moment, his eyes caressing the old Indian pots spotted about, the rich color of the paintings from Spain, the cochineal rugs dyed from kermes bugs. Yes, the house was old; older than America. He truly loved its feeling of history, glory and power.

Then his gaze stopped on the only discord in the room. It was a wildly colored, exaggerated painting of himself. He didn't like the idea of his portrait hanging there. He didn't need that. He allowed it only because his niece, Aleta, had done it. He was fond of her.

Juanita, the aged servant, entered with a tray. It held guacamole salad, tostados and the inevitable Bloody Marys. He asked her in perfect Spanish where his wife Carole was.

She answered in English, "On the patio, Señor. I have your drinks." She moved out ahead of him, bony, stiff, bent but with an almost girlish quickness about her. She'd been with them for decades. They'd expected her demise for years, then given up.

Carole lounged in the desert sun, dozing the liquor away. He couldn't remember when she started drinking so heavily. He had to admit that she had a tough constitution—almost as much as his own. It was usually around midnight before alcohol dulled her to retire. She removed the oversized sun glasses and sat up as Juanita placed the tray on a small table by her. The wrinkles showed around the eyes, but her figure was still as good as ever. She rubbed at the lotion on her golden legs and then reached for her drink. At her movement he had a fleeting desire to take her to bed. Was that what had brought them together? Was that what had held them until it was too late? Maybe. She pushed the burnt blonde hair back and placed the edge of the glass against her glistening lips. He thought the red drink was going down her throat like weak blood to give her strength for the day. He gazed out across the green mass of trees, grass, and bushes in the formal garden beyond the patio. He heard the little brook that coursed through it giving life to the oasis just as the Bloody Marys did his wife.

It was late morning and already the clouds puffed up beyond the parched mountains, promising much, seldom giving. It was as if the desert of cacti, lizards, scorpions and coyotes between the mountains and the hacienda was too forbidding to pass over. It took many clouds to give the necessary courage to one another. It rarely happened.

He picked up his drink, hypnotized by the rising heat waves of the harsh land.

"I've decided," he said.

"You've decided what?"

"It's time we held the gathering."

She took another sip, set it down and reached for a cigarette. "You've been talking about that for three years, Joshua."

"I know, but I've made up my mind."

"When?"

"Now."

"Now? Oh God, it'll take days to prepare." She took another swallow of the red drink. "I'm just not up to it. Besides, Lana and Joseph are in Bermuda. Sheila and Ralph are in Honolulu."

"They'll come."

"You can't just order people away from their vacations." She took another swallow, pulled the bra of her bikini up, walked over and sat down on the edge of the pool and dangled her feet in it. Resentment showed in her back. He still felt a little love for her, which surprised him. There was no question that his money and power had been part of her attraction to him. But at first it had been good. They'd gone just about everywhere in the world together. The fun, the laughs, the adventure had been there even though some part of his business empire was always intruding. What had happened? Hell, why didn't he admit it? Why didn't she? It had worn out. It was that simple. Just plain worn out from the heaviness of the burdens of empire like an old draft horse or a tired underground coal miner.

She splashed the water over her body, knowing from his silence there was no use. "Well, we might as well get on with it. When do you call?"

He finished the drink, stood up, and moved towards the house, saying, "As I said, now."

Joshua entered the study. His secretary for the past ten years looked up, sensing something in his determined movement.

"All right, Charlotte."

She picked up the pad without questioning. He paced across the Navaho rugs, giving her a long list of names. Occasionally he'd run his hands down a row of books, playing them like an accordion. He really didn't like organization, but when he decided, he could be almost magical at it. There was no hesitation, no lost thought or confusion. He was putting together the 'gathering' just as he'd expanded the small fortune his father had left him. It kept growing, moving.

When he finished dictating the names, he said, "We'll have food indigenous to the southwest. Tons of it. I want for entertainment the Russian dancer from Los Angeles, Alfredo and his guitar from Juarez, the belly dancer what's-her-name from San Francisco, the Mariachis from Mexico City, and the brass group from Denver."

His whole huge body was vibrating now. A force exuded from Joshua—the same force that had swayed decisions on many oil-field deals, land developments, cattle domains and on occasion even the stock market—but never had Charlotte seen him as he was now. There was something more, something she could not explain. Then he was done. He pushed at his slightly greying mass of hair and walked around the hand-carved desk to her. He pulled her head over to him and held it a moment against his side. They had once been lovers, but when she came to work for him that was over. There was still a tenderness between them. She was one of those women who just missed being beautiful all the way around, but she had a sensual appeal and a soft strength that was so much more. She had his respect, too, and that was very hard for him to give.

He broke the mood with, "Call Aleta and Rob first."

She took the book of numbers and swiftly dialed, asking, "Are you sure they're in El Paso?"

"Yes. Aleta's painting. She's getting ready for her show in Dallas." He took the phone, "Rob, is Aleta there?"

In El Paso, Rob gave an affirmative answer and put his hand over the phone: "Your Uncle *God* is on the horn."

Aleta wiped the paint from her hands and reached for the receiver. "Don't be so sarcastic, darling; he might leave you out of his will."

The vibrations were instantaneous down the wire between the man and the girl. She would be delighted to come.

When the conversation was over and Aleta informed her husband, he said, "The old bastard! He's a dictator. I'd just love to kill him!"

He finished with Lana and Joseph Helstrom in the Bahamas with, "No kids. Do you understand? This is not for children."

The husband turned to the wife, saying, "We're ordered to attend a gathering at Aqua Dulce."

"A gathering?"

"A party. You know how he is about labeling things."

"Oh Christ, two days on vacation and he orders us to a party."

"I could happily murder the son of a bitch and laugh for years," Joseph said, throwing a beach towel across the room against a bamboo curtain.

Finally Joshua was finished. Charlotte got up and mixed them a scotch on the rocks from the concealed bar behind the desk. They raised their glasses and both said at the same time,

"To the gathering." They laughed together as they worked together.

Suddenly Charlotte set her glass down and, not having heard the phone conversations, stated almost omnipotently, "Half of them would delight in doing away with you."

Joshua nodded, smiling lightly. "You're wrong, love, a good two thirds would gladly blow me apart and all but a few of the others would wish them well."

"Touché."

"They do have a tendency to forget how they arrived at their present positions. However, that's not what concerns me. All are free to leave whenever they wish, but most don't have the guts. They like cinches but never acknowledge that on this earth no such thing exists. Even the sun is slowly burning itself to death."

"Another drink?"

"Of course. This is a moment for great celebration."

She poured the drinks efficiently, enjoying this time with him. Sensing something very special happening. Thrilled to share with him again.

They touched glasses across the desk, and he said, almost jubilantly, "To the Gods, goddamn them!"

Carole instructed old Juanita in the cleaning and preparing of the house. She put old Martin, the head caretaker and yardman, and his two younger sons trimming the garden. This last was unnecessary because old Martin loved the leisure and independence of his job. He kept everything in shape anyway. It did, however, serve its purpose. Carole felt like she was doing *something*. In fact, an excitement she hadn't felt for a long time came upon her. She remembered the really first important entertaining she'd done for Joshua after their marriage. He was on a crucial middle east oil deal.

It was in their New York Townehouse in the days they were commuting around the world to various homes and apartments. She had really pulled a coup. Carole had worked closely with the shiek's male secretary and found what to her were some surprising facts. At first she'd intended to have food catered native to the guests' own country and utilize local belly dancers of the same origin. But after much consultation she served hamburgers and had three glowing, local-born blondes as dancing girls. The shieks raved over the Yankee food they'd heard so much about and were obviously taken with the yellow-topped, fair-skinned dancing girls. They were also highly captivated by Carole herself. The whole thing had been a rousing success. Joshua got his oil concessions and she had felt an enormous sense of accomplishment.

Today, as she moved about the vast hacienda she felt some of that old energy returning. There was something different though. Her excitement was mounting, but it was more like one must feel stalking a man-eating tiger and knowing that at the next parting of the bushes they would look into each other's eyes.

Joshua checked out the wine cellar. He loved the silence and the dank smell. He touched some of the ancient casks as he had the history books in the study. He was drawn to old things now, remembering, recalling, conjuring up the history of his land . . . the great southwest. He lingered long after he knew the supply of fine wines was more than sufficient. He moved the lantern back and forth, watching the shadows hide from the moving light. Carole had long wanted him to have electricity installed down here but he'd refused. Some things need to remain as they are, he felt. Many of the old ways were better. Many worse. He'd wondered uncounted times why men who could build computers and fly to distant planets were too blind, or stupid, to select the best of the old and the best of the new and weld them together. He knew that at least the moderate happiness of mankind was that simple. An idiot could see it if he opened up and looked. It would not happen during Joshua's brief encounter with this planet. He knew it and was disgusted by it.

He set the lantern on a shelf and stood gazing at the wall ending the cellar. It was a while before the visions would begin coming to him. He didn't mind. Time was both nothing and everything. Then he heard the hooves of many horses walking methodically forward. It was like the beat of countless drumsticks against the earth. A rhythm, a pattern, a definite purpose in the sound. Closer. Louder. The song came as a sigh at first, then a whisper, finally it was clear and hauntingly lovely. He felt thousands of years old, perhaps millions, perhaps ageless. Colors in circular and elongated patterns danced about in the wall. Slowly they took form as if just being born. Swiftly now they melded into shape and he saw Cortez majestically leading his men and horses in clothing of iron. From the left came Montezuma and his followers in dazzling costumes so wildly colored they appeared to be walking rainbows. They knelt and prostrated themselves to the Gods with four legs. Beauty had bent to force.

Joshua was witnessing the beginning of the Americas. The vision dissolved like a panoramic movie and the song seeped away.

Then Oñate appeared splashing his column across the Rio Grande at the Pueblo of Juarez and headed north up the river. The cellar suddenly reverberated with the swish of a sword into red flesh and there was a huge, moving collage of churning, charging horses, and arrows whistling into the cracks of armor, and many things fell to the earth and became still. Oñate sat astride his horse surveying the compound of a conquered pueblo.

The song came again suddenly, shatteringly, crescendoing as Joshua's Spanish princess stood on a hill looking down. She came towards him, appearing to walk just above the earth. As she neared, smiling, with both arms out, he moved to the wall. As they came closer he reached the wall with his arms outspread trying to physically feel into it, but she was gone. He stayed thusly for a while, his head turned sideways, pushing his whole body against the dirt. For a moment he sagged and took a breath into his body that released him. He turned, picked up the lantern, and zombied his way up to the other world. The one here.

All was ready. The tables were filled with every delicacy of the land from which Joshua, his father, and grandfathers twice back had sprouted. The hacienda shined from repeated dusting and polishing. A cantina holding many bottles from many other lands was set up in the main room and an even greater display was waiting for eager hands, dry throats, and tight emotions in the patio.

Carole moved about checking over and over that which was already done. Joshua had one chore left.

"Martin, drain the pool."

Martin looked at his master, puzzled. "But sir, the guests will . . ."

"Just drain the pool."

"Well . . . yes sir."

When Carole saw this she hurried to Martin and asked in agitated confusion what in hell madness possessed him to do such a thing.

"It was on orders of Mr. Joshua, madam."

"Then he's mad! We cleaned the pool only yesterday!"

She found Joshua in the study and burst in just as Charlotte finished rechecking her own list and was saying, "Everything has been done, Joshua. The doctors are even releasing Grebbs from the hospital so he can make it."

"Of course, I knew you'd take care of . . ."

"Joshua!"

He turned slowly to her.

"Have you lost all your sanity? Why did you have Martin drain the pool?"

"It's simple, my dear. Pools can become hypnotic and distracting. We have far greater forms of entertainment coming up."

She stood there unable to speak momentarily. She pushed at her hair and rubbed her perspiring palms on her hips, walking in a small circle around the room, finally giving utterance, "*I* know you're crazy, but do you want everyone else to know it?"

"It will give them much pleasure to finally find this flaw in my nature they have so desperately been seeking."

She turned and cascaded from the room, hurling back, "Oh, my God!"

Forty-eight hours later they came from all around the world. They arrived in jets, Rolls Royces, Cadillacs, Mercedes, and pickup trucks. They moved to the hacienda magnetized.

The greetings were both formal and friendly, fearful and cheerful. Carole was at her gracious best, only half drunk, expertly suppressing their initial dread with her trained talk. But there was a difference in the hands and arms and bodies that floated in the air towards Joshua. These appurtenances involved a massive movement of trepidation, hate and fatherhood.

Joshua took Aleta in his grand and strong arms and lifted her from the floor in teasing love and respect. Her husband, Rob, died a little bit right there. His impulse of murder to the being of this man was intensified and verified. Rob wanted *in* desperately. He craved to become part of the Stone domain; craved to be part of the prestige and power. Marrying the favorite niece had seemed the proper first step. It hadn't worked. Joshua had never asked him, and Aleta absolutely forbade Rob to even hint at it. His lean, handsome face had a pinched appearance about it from the hatred. He had dwelled on it so long now that it was an obsession—an obsession to destroy that which he felt had ignored and destroyed him. It was unjustified. Joshua simply didn't want to see Rob subservient to him—not the husband of his artiest niece. Aleta had never asked Joshua for anything but his best wishes. He felt that Rob must be as independent as she or else they wouldn't be married. He was wrong. Being a junior partner in a local stock brokerage firm didn't do it for Rob. And their being simply ordered here to Aleta's obvious joy had tilted his rage until he could hardly contain it.

Others—who were *in*—felt just as passionately about Joshua, but they all had their separate and different reasons.

Lana and Joseph Helstrom certainly had a different wish for Joshua. Joseph just hadn't moved as high in the organization as swiftly as he felt he should, and Lana had a hidden yen for Joshua. In fact, she often daydreamed of replacing Carole.

And there was the senior vice president, Grebbs, who wanted and believed that Joshua should step up to the position of chairman of the board and allow him his long overdue presidency. He had lately been entering hospitals for check-ups which repeatedly disclosed nothing wrong—but then x-rays do not show hatred or they would have been white with explosions all over his body.

None of these things bothered Joshua now. The gathering grew in momentum of sound, emotion, and color. The drinks consumed along with the food and talk was of many things. People split up into ever-changing groups. Those who had been to the hacienda before remarked about this alteration or that. Those who were new to its centuries made many, many comments about all the priceless objects of art and craft. Whether they hated or loved the master of the house they were somehow awed and honored to be in this museum of the spirit of man and Joshua himself.

Alfredo the guitarist from Juarez played. His dark head bent over his instrument, and the long delicate fingers stroked from the wood and steel the tenderness of love, the savagery of death. It seemed that these songs, too, came from the walls. Maybe somehow they did.

The music surged into the total system of Joshua. He felt stronger, truer than ever before. He was ready now to make his first move—the beginning of his final commitment. He looked about the room, observing with penetration his followers. His eyes settled on Charlotte. And then, as if knowing, unable to resist, she came to him. She handed him a new scotch and water, holding her own drink with practiced care. He turned and she followed at his side. They wandered to the outer confines of the house—to his childhood room. She did not question. He turned on a small lamp that still left many shadows.

"My darling," he said softly, touching the wall with one hand, "this is where it all started."

She looked at him puzzled, but with patience.

"I think I was five when I first heard the walls. It was gunfire and screams and I knew it had once happened here. You see, this, in the days of the vast Spanish land grants, was a roadhouse, a cantina, an oasis where the Dons and their ladies gathered to fight and fornicate. They are in the walls, you know, and I hear them. I even see them. I had just turned thirteen when I first *saw* into the walls."

Joshua's eyes gleamed like a coyote's in lantern light. His breath was growing and there was an electricity charging through all his being. Charlotte was hypnotized at his voice and what was under it. His hand moved down the walls as he told her of some of the things he'd seen and heard. Then he turned to her and raised his glass for a toast.

"To you, dear loyal, wonderful, Charlotte, my love and my thanks."

"It has all been a fine trip with you, Joshua. I could not have asked more from life than to have been a part of you and what you've done. Thank you, thank you."

He took the drink from her hand and set it on a dresser. Taking her gently by the arm he pulled her to the wall. "Now lean against it and listen and you, too, will hear." She did so, straining with all her worth. "Listen! Listen," he whispered, and his powerful hands went around her neck. She struggled very little, and in a few moments she went limp. He held her a brief second longer, bending to kiss her on the back of the neck he'd just broken. Then with much care he picked her up, carried her to the closet, and placed her out of sight behind some luggage. He quietly closed the door, standing there awhile looking at it. He moved, picked up his drink, and returned to his people.

In the patio, Misha, the Russian dancer from Kavkaz on Sunset Boulevard, was leaping wildly about, crouching, kicking. A circle formed around him and the bulk of Joshua Stone, III, dominated it all. He was enjoying himself to the fullest, clapping his hands and yelling encouragement. The dance had turned everyone on a few more kilocycles. They started drinking more, talking more and louder, even gaining a little courage.

The grey, fiftyish Grebbs tugged at Joshua, trying to get his true attention. He kept bringing up matters of far-flung business interests. He might remind one in attitude of a presidential campaign manager, just after a victory, wondering if he'd be needed now. He rubbed at his crew cut hair nervously, trying to figure an approach to Joshua. His grey eyes darted about slightly. His bone-edged nose presented certain signs of strength and character, but weakness around the mouth gave him away. He was clever and did everything that cleverness could give to keep all underlings out of touch with Joshua. He had hoped for a while that this gathering had been called to announce Joshua's chairmanship, and the fulfillment of his own desperate dream.

Joshua motioned to Lotus Flower, the belly dancer, and she moved gracefully out into the patio ahead of the music. Then the music caught up with her. The Oriental lady undulated and performed the moves that have always pleased men.

As Grebbs tugged at Joshua again, he said, without taking his eyes from the dancer, "Grebbs, go talk business to your dictaphone." Just that. Now Grebbs knew. He moved away, hurting.

Lana stood with Carole. They were both watching Joshua with far different emotions.

Lana spoke first, about their mutual interest. "Has Joshua put on some weight?"

"No, it's the same old stomach."

"He's always amazed everyone with his athletic abilities."

"Really?" This last had a flint edge to it.

"Well, for a man who appears so awkward it is rather surprising to find how swiftly and strongly he can move when he decides to. Carole, you do remember the time he leaped into Spring Lake and swam all the way across it, and then just turned around and swam all the way back. You must remember that, darling. We all had such a good time."

"Oh, I remember many things, *darling*."

Rob was saying to Joseph Helstrom, "There's something wrong here. I feel it. Here it's only September, and he's already drained the pool."

Joseph touched his heavy rimmed glasses and let the hand slowly slide down his round face, "Yeah, he demanded we all come here on instant notice and he's not really with us."

"The selfish bastard." Rob exhaled this like ridding himself of morning sputum.

The dancer swirled ever closer to Joshua, her head back, long black hair swishing across her shoulders. He smiled, absorbed in the movement of flesh as little beams of hatred were cast across the patio from Grebbs, Rob, Joseph—and others. Joshua didn't care—didn't even feel it. As the dance finished, Rob walked out into the garden and removed a small automatic pistol from the back of his belt under his jacket. He checked the breech and replaced the gun.

Joshua worked his way through the crowd, spoken to and speaking back in a distracted manner. His people looked puzzled after his broad back. He made his way slowly down the stairs towards the wine cellar, one hand caressing the wall. He stopped and waited. The song came from eternities away, soft, soothing, amidst the whispers of men planning daring moves.

The whole wall now spun with colors slowly forming into warriors. Then there before Joshua's eyes was Estaban the black man, standing amidst the pueblo Indians. Joshua had always felt that Estaban was one of the most exciting and mysterious—even neglected—figures in the history of America. It has never been settled for sure how or why he arrived in the southwest. However, his influence would always be there. He had started the legend of The Seven Golden Cities of Cibolo, which Coronado and many others searched for in vain. He was a major factor in the pueblo rebellion, afterwards becoming the chief of several of these communities. He became a famous medicine man and was looked on as a God. But, like all earthly Gods, he fell. A seven-year drouth came upon the land of the Tewas, and when he could not dissipate it, he was blamed for it. They killed him and the superstitious Zunis skinned him like a deer to see if he was black all the way through.

Now, at last, Joshua was looking upon this man of dark skin and searing soul as he spoke in the Indian tongue to his worshipers. He talked to them of survival without the rule of iron. They mumbled low in agreement. Maybe Joshua would learn some of the dark secrets before this apparition dissolved back to dried mud.

Joshua watched as up and down the river the Indians threw rock and wood at steel in savage dedication. Men died screaming in agony, sobbing their way painfully to the silence of death. The river flowed peacefully before him now, covering the entire wall and beyond. Then the feet splashed into his view and he saw the remnants of the defeated Spanish straggle across the river back into Mexico.

Joshua's Spanish lady in black lace sat on a smooth, round rock staring across a valley dripping with the gold of autumn. She was in a land he'd never seen. She turned her heel toward him, and gave a smile that said so much he couldn't stand it. He reached towards the wall and she nodded her head up and down and faded away with the music. Silence. More silence. Then,

"Joshua."

He turned. It was Lana. She moved to him, putting her hands on his chest. "Joshua, what is it? You're acting so strangely."

"Did you see? Did you hear?" he asked, looking out over her head.

"I . . . I . . . don't know what you mean, darling. See what?"

"Nothing. Nothing," he sighed.

"Can I help? Is there *anything* I can do?"

He pulled her against him and kissed her with purpose. She was at first surprised and then gave back to him. He picked her up and shoved her violently against the wooden frame between two wine barrels.

"No, no, not here."

"There is no other time," he said. "No other place." As he reached under her, one elbow struck a spigot on a barrel. He loved her standing there while a thin stream of red wine poured out on the cellar floor forming an immediate pool not unlike blood.

She uttered only one word, "Joshua," and the wine sound continued.

Both he and Lana were back among the people now. Carole came to him.

"Where've you been? Where is Charlotte? The phone is ringing constantly. Where is she?"

"She's on vacation."

"Today? I can't believe you, Joshua. You always bragged about how she was there when you needed her."

"We don't need her now."

"You really are mad. Mad! Today of all days we need her to answer the phone."

"Take the damned phone off the hook. No one ever calls good news on a phone, anyway. If they have anything good to say, they come and see you personally." He walked away and left her standing there looking after him in much confusion.

All afternoon he had been waiting to visit his old friend, Chalo Gonzales, from the Apache reservation. They met when they were kids. Chalo's father had worked the nearby orchards and alfalfa fields for Joshua's father. He and Chalo hunted, fished, adventured together off and on for years. He'd gone with him to the reservation many times, and learned much of nature and the Redman's ways. Chalo had given him as much as anyone—things of real value. He found him dressed in a regular business suit and tie, but he wore a band around his coarse, dark hair.

"Ah, amigo, let's walk in the garden away from this . . ." and he made a gesture with his arm to the scattered crowd. "How does it go with you and your people?"

"Slow, Joshua, but better. As always, there's conflict with the old and the young. The old want to stay with their own ways. The young want to rush into the outside world."

"It's the nature of youth to be impatient. It can't be helped."

"Oh, sure, that is the truth. But our young want to take the best of the old and good ways with them. They want both sides now. Now."

"That's good, Chalo. They're right."

"But nothing happens that fast. It has been too many centuries one way. You can't change it in a few years."

"It's a big problem I admit, but you will survive and finally win. You always have, you know."

"You've always given me encouragement. I feel better already."

They talked of hunts, and later adventures when they both came home for the summer from school. Chalo had been one of few to make it from his land to Bacone, the Indian college.

Joshua felt Chalo was his equal. He was comfortable with him. They stood together and talked in a far recess of the secluded garden where they could see the mountains they'd so often explored. Joshua felt a surge of love for his old friend. He knew what he must do. He'd spotted the root a few minutes back. He didn't dare risk it with his hands. Chalo was almost as strong as he was in both will and muscle.

He picked up the root and began drawing designs with it in a spot of loose ground, as men will do who are from the earth. Then, as his friend glanced away, Joshua swung it with much force, striking him just back of the ear. He heard the bone crunch and was greatly relieved to know he wouldn't have to do more. Without any wasted time he dragged and pushed him into a thick clump of brush. He checked to see that the body was totally hidden, tossed the root in after it, walked to the wall and looked out across the desert to the mountains again. He was very still; then he turned, smiling ineluctably, and proceeded to the party.

Dusk came swiftly and hung awhile, giving the party a sudden subdued quality. It was the time of day that Joshua liked best. He finally escaped the clutchers and went to his study, locking the door and grinning at the phone Carole had taken off the hook and deliberately dangled across the lamp.

He drew the shades back and sat there absorbed in the hiding sun, and watched the glowing oranges and reds turn to violet and then a soft blue above the desert to the west. He knew that life started stirring there with the death of the sun. The coyotes and bobcats were already moving, sniffing the ground and the air for other living creatures. Many mice, rabbits, and birds would die this night so they could live. The great owl would soon be swooping above them in direct competition. The next day the sun would be reborn and the vultures would dine on any remains, keeping the desert clean and in balance.

Someone knocked on the door. It was Carole.

"Joshua, are you in there?" Then louder, "Joshua, I know you're there because the door is locked from the inside. What are you doing with the door locked anyway?" Silence. "At least you could come and mix with your guests. You did *in-*

vite them, you know." She pounded on the door now. "My God, at least speak to me. I am your wife, you know." Silence. She turned in frustration and stamped off down the hall, mumbling about his madness.

Joshua turned his lounge chair away from the window and stared at the wall across the room. There were things he had to see before he made the final move. Pieces of the past that he must reconstruct properly in his mind before he took the last step.

It did come. As always he heard it first, then saw it form, whirling like pieces of an abstract world—a new world, an old world, being broken and born, falling together again. The Spanish returned. They came now with fresh men, armour horses, and cannon. They marched and rode up the Rio Grande setting up the artillery, blasting the adobe walls to dust. Then they charged with sabers drawn and whittled the shell-shocked Indians into slavery. They mined the gold from the virgin mountains with the Indians as their tools. And then it all vanished inwardly.

There was quiet and darkness now until he heard his name. "Joshua, Joshua, Joshua." It came floating from afar as if elongated, closer, closer. She was there. He leaned forward in the chair, his body tense, anxious. She stood by a river of emerald green. It was so clear that he could see the separate grains of white sand on its bottom. The trees, trunks thicker than the hacienda, rose into the sky. They went up, up past his ability to see. The leaves were as thick as watermelons and fifty people could stand in the shade of a single leaf. The air danced with the light of four suns shafting great golden beams down through the trees.

She moved towards him through one of the beams and for a moment vanished with its brilliance. Now she was whole again, standing there before him. He ached to touch her. He hurt. An endless string of silver fish swam up the river now. The four suns penetrated the pure water and made them appear to be parts of a metallic lava flow from a far off volcano. But they were fish, moving relentlessly, with no hesitation whatsoever, knowing their destination and fate without doubt.

Again the word came from her as she turned and walked down the river, vanishing behind a tree. "Joshua."

For a fleeting moment he heard the song. He closed his eyes. When he opened them there was just the darkness of the room. He didn't know how long he sat there before returning to the party.

He moved directly to the bar in the patio and ordered a double scotch and water. His people were scattered out now, having dined, and were back into the drinking and talking. The volume was beginning to rise again. It was second-wind time. As the bartender served the drink he felt something touch his hand. It was Maria Windsor.

She smiled like champagne pouring, her red lips pulling back over almost startling white teeth. She smiled with her blue eyes, too.

"It has been such a long time," she said.

"Maria, goddamn, it's good to see you." And he hugged her, picking her off the floor without intending to. She was very small and at first appeared to be delicate. But this was a strong little lady. She was a barmaid in his favorite place in El Paso when he first met her. He'd always deeply admired the polite and friendly smoothness with which she did her job. One never had to wait for a drink, the ash tray was emptied at the proper moment, and she knew when to leave or when to stand and chat. Joshua had introduced her to John Windsor, one of his junior vice presidents, and now they were married.

"I love the portrait Aleta did of you."

"Well, I feel embarrassed hanging it there, but what could I do after she worked so hard on it. How are you and John getting along?" he asked.

"How do you mean? Personally or otherwise?"

"Oh, all around I suppose."

"Good," she said. "Like all wives I think he works too hard sometimes, but I suppose that's natural. Here he comes now."

John shook hands and greeted his boss without showing any apparent fear and revealing a genuine liking for him. He once told Maria that he'd love Joshua to death just for introducing her to him. He was about five eleven, straight and well-muscled, and had thick brown hair which he wore longer than anyone in the whole international organization. He, too, had a nice, white smile.

Joshua ordered a round for the three of them. He raised his glass: "My friends, you'll be receiving a memo in the next few days that I think you will enjoy. Here's to it." Several days before the party Joshua had made out a paper giving

John Windsor control of the company. It had not been delivered yet.

He left them glowing in anticipation and went to find his favorite kin, Aleta. As he moved, the eyes of hatred moved with him . . . drunker now, braver. He walked into the garden, bowing, speaking here and there, but not stopping. The moon hung in place by galactic gravity beamed back the sun in a blue softness. The insects and night birds hummed a song in the caressing desert breeze. The leaves on the trees moved just enough to make love. There was a combination of warmth and coolness that only the desert can give.

Aleta had seen her uncle and somehow knew he was looking for her. She came to him from where she'd been sitting on a tree that was alive but bent to the ground. She'd been studying the light patterns throughout the garden for a painting she had in mind.

"Uncle Joshua, it's time we had a visit."

He took both her hands and stood back looking at her. "Yes, it's time, my dear. You are even more beautiful than the best of your paintings."

"Well, Uncle, that's not saying so much," she said, being pleasingly flattered just the same.

He led her to an archway and opened the iron gate. They walked up a tiny rutted wagon road into the desert. The sounds of the gathering subdued. The yucca bushes and Joshua trees—that he'd been named after—speared the sky like frozen battalions of soldiers on guard duty forever.

"Remember when we used to ride up this trail?" she asked.

"Yes, it seems like yesterday."

"It seems like a hundred years ago to me."

He laughed. "Time has a way of telescoping in and out according to your own time. That's the way it should be. You were a tough little shit," he added with fondness. "You were the only one that could ride with me all day."

"That was simple bullheadedness. I knew I was going to be an artist someday and you have to have a skull made of granite to be an artist."

He was amused at her even now. "But you also had a bottom made of rawhide."

They talked of some of her childhood adventures they'd shared. Then the coyotes howled off in a little draw. The strollers stood like the cacti, listening, absorbing the oldest cry left.

When the howls stopped, he spoke: "I love to hear them. I

always have. I even get lonely to hear them. They're the only true survivors."

"That somehow frightens me," she said with a little shudder.

"It shouldn't. You should be encouraged. As long as they howl, people have a chance here on earth. No longer, no less. It is the final cry for freedom. It's hope."

They walked on silently for a spell. "You really are a romantic, Uncle. When I hear people say how cold you are I laugh to myself."

"You know, Aleta darling, you're the only person that never asked me for anything?"

"I didn't have to. You've always given me love and confidence. What more could you give?"

"I don't know. I wish I did."

"No, Uncle, there's no greater gift than that."

"Aleta, the world is strange. Mankind has forgotten what was always true—that a clean breath is worth more than the most elegant bank building. A new flower opening is more beautiful than a marble palace. All things rot. Michelangelo's sculpture is even now slowly breaking apart. All empires vanish. The largest buildings in the world will turn back to sand. The great paintings are cracking, the negatives of the best films ever made are right now losing their color and becoming brittle. The tallest mountains are coming down a rock at a time. Only thoughts live. You are only what you think."

"That's good," she said; "then I'm a painting, even if I am already beginning to crack."

He liked her words and added some of his own: "You know, honey, the worms favor the rich."

"Why?"

He rubbed his great belly. "Because they're usually fatter and more easily digestible."

"Do you speak of yourself?"

"Of course," he smiled. The coyotes howled again, and he said, "I love you, my dear Aleta."

"And I love you."

He stroked her hair and moved his hand downward. It had to be swift, clean. With all his strength, even more than he'd ever had before. He grabbed her long, graceful neck and twisted her head. He heard the bones rip apart. She gasped only once and then a long sigh of her last breath exuded from her. He gathered her carefully in his arms and walked out through the brush to the little draw where the coyotes had so recently hunted. Then he stretched her out on the ground with her hands at her side and gently brushed her hair back. She slept in the moonlight.

He walked swiftly back to the hacienda. As he left the garden for the patio, Rob stepped in front of him.

"Joshua, have you seen Aleta?"

"Of course, my boy, of course."

"Well, where is she?"

"Look, I don't follow your wife around. She's certainly more capable than most of taking care of herself." Joshua moved on. Rob followed him a few steps, looking at his back with glazed eyes.

Grebbs grabbed at him in one last desperate hope that Joshua was saving the announcement to the last.

"Joshua, I have to talk with you. Please."

Joshua stopped and looked at the man. He was drunk, and that was something Grebbs rarely allowed himself to be in public. He looked as if pieces of flesh were about to start dropping down into his clothing. His mouth was open, slack and watery.

Joshua said, with a certainty in his voice that settled Grebbs' question, "Grebbs, you're a bad drinker. I have no respect for bad drinkers." And he moved on.

Grebbs stared at the same back the same way Rob had. He muttered, actually having trouble keeping from openly crying, "The bastard. The dirty bastard. I'll kill you! You son of a bitch!"

The thing some of these people had been uttering about Joshua now possessed them. A madness hovered about, waiting for the right moment, and then swiftly moved into them. Now all the people of music started playing at once. The Russian was dancing even more wildly, if not so expertly. The belly dancer swished about from man to man, teasing. The Mariachis walked about in dominance for a while, then the brass group would break through. It was a cacophony of sound that entered the heads of all there . . . throbbing like blood poison.

Carole started sobbing uncontrollably. Lana began cursing her husband Joseph in vile terms—bitterly, with total malice. Joseph just reached out and slapped her down across the chaise longue, and a little blood oozed from the corner of her mouth. He could only think of a weapon, any weapon to use on the man who he felt was totally responsible for the matrix of doom echoing all around. We always must have something to hate for our own failures and smallness. But this did not occur to Joseph, or Lana, or Carole, or the others. Only Alfredo the guitarist sat alone on the same old bent tree that Aleta had cherished, touching his guitar with love.

Maria took John aside and told him they were leaving, that something terrible was happening. She was not—and could not be—a part of it. He hesitated but listened. They did finally drive away, confused, but feeling they were right.

Grebbs dazedly shuffled to the kitchen looking for a knife, but old Juanita and her two sisters were there. He then remembered an East Indian dagger that lay on the mantel in the library as a paperweight. In his few trips to the hacienda he'd often studied it, thinking what a pleasure it would be to drive it into the jerking heart of Joshua Stone, III.

He picked it up and pulled the arched blade from the jeweled sheath. He touched the sharp unused point with shaking fingers. At that precise instant Rob felt in the back of his belt and touched the automatic. He removed it and put it in his jacket pocket. Joseph Helstrom looked about the patio for an instrument to satisfy his own destructive instincts.

Joshua entered the door to the cellar, shut it, and shoved the heavy iron bolt into place. He called on all his resources now in another direction. An implosion to the very core of time struck Joshua. Now, right now, he must visualize all the rest of the history of his land that occurred before his first childish awareness. Then, and only then, could he make his last destined move. It began to form. The long lines of Conestoga wagons tape-wormed across the prairies and struggled through the mountain passes bringing goods and people from all over the world to settle this awesome land. They came in spite of flood, drouths, blizzards, Indian attacks and disease. They were drawn here by the golden talk of dreamers, and promising facts.

The ruts of the Santa Fe Trail were cut so deep they would last a century. The mountain men took the last of the beaver from the sweet, churning waters of the mountains above Taos and came down to trade, to dance the wild fandangos, to drink and pursue the dark-eyed lovelies of that village of many flags.

A troop of cavalry charged over the horizon into a camp of Indians and the battle splashed across the adobe valleys in crimson. Thousands of cattle and sheep were driven there and finally settled into their own territories. Cowboys strained to stay aboard bucking horses, and these same men roped and jerked steers, thumping them hard against the earth. They gambled and fought and raised hell in the villages of deserts and mountains, creating written and filmed legends that covered the world more thoroughly than Shakespeare.

The prospectors walked over the mountains searching for—and some finding—large deposits of gold, silver and copper. And, as always, men of money took away the rewards of their labors and built themselves great palaces.

And Joshua saw the Italians, Chinese, and many other nationalities driving the spikes into the rail ties. The trains came like the covered wagons before them—faster, more powerful—hauling more people and goods than ever before. The double-bitted axes and two-man saws cut the majestic pines of the high places, taking away the shelter of the deer, lion and bear.

Now Joshua closed his eyes, for he knew all the rest. When he opened them he heard the song begin again. It was both older and newer each time he heard it. There was a massive adobe church and his lady walked right through the walls and into the one he sat staring at. Now as she spoke his name, he knew his final move was near. For the first time he turned away from her and headed for the door. She smiled, somehow exactly like the song.

As he opened the door and pulled it shut, he felt a presence come at him. He was so keyed up, so full of his feelings, that he just stepped aside and let it hurtle past. It was Grebbs. He'd driven the dagger so deep into the door that he couldn't pull it out to strike again. Grebbs had missed all the way. Joshua gathered him up around the neck with one hand, jerked the dagger from the door with the other, and smashed him against the wall. He shoved the point of the dagger just barely under the skin of Grebbs' guts. Grebbs' eyes bulged and he almost died of fright right there, but the hand of his master cut any words off. It was quite a long moment for the corporate vice president.

"What I should do, Grebbs, is cut your filthy entrails out and shove them down your dead throat. But that's far too easy for you."

Joshua dropped him to the floor and drove the knife to the hilt in the door. He then strode up the stairs three at a time, hearing only a low broken sob below him.

As he entered the world of people again, Carole grabbed at him, visibly drunk and more. She said, "God! God! What are you doing?" He moved on from her as she shrieked, "You don't love me!" He ignored this too, and when she raked her painted claws into the back of his neck he ignored that as well. She stood looking at her fingers and the bits of bloody flesh clinging to her nails.

Rob blocked his way, again demanding attention. "I'm asking you for the last time! Do you hear me? Where is Aleta?"

He pushed the young man aside, saying as he went, "I'll tell you in a few minutes." This surprised and stopped Rob right where he stood.

Then Joshua raised his arms and shouted, "Music, you fools! Play and dance!" The drunken musicians all started up again, jerky, horrendously out of synchronization.

Joshua went to the kitchen and very tenderly lifted an exhausted and sleeping Juanita from her chair. He explained to her two sisters that he would take Juanita to her room on the other side of the hacienda. They were glad and went on cleaning up. He led her slowly out a side door. On the other side of many walls could be heard the so-called music sailing up, dissipating itself in the peaceful desert air.

As he walked the bent old woman along he spoke to her softly, "It's time for you to rest, Juanita. You've been faithful all these decades. Your sisters can do the labors. You will have time of your own now. A long, long time that will belong just to you. You've served many people who did not even deserve your presence."

There was an old well near the working shed where her little house stood. They stopped here.

"Juanita, you are like this—this dried-up well. It gave so much for so long it now has no water left."

He pulled the plank top off. Juanita was weary and still partially in the world of sleep. Joshua steadied the bony old shoulders with both his hands. He looked at her in the moonlight and said, "Juanita, you are a beautiful woman."

She twitched the tiniest of smiles across her worn face and tilted her head just a little in an almost girlish move.

Then he said, "Juanita, I love you." He slipped a handkerchief from his pocket, crammed it into her mouth, jerked her upside down and hurled her head first into the well. There was just a crumpled thud. No more.

In the patio the music was beginning to die. A dullness had come over the area. A deadly dullness. But heads started turning, one, two, three at a time towards the hacienda door. Their center of attention, Joshua, strode amongst them. There were only whispers now. Joshua saw a movement and stopped. The heavy earthen vase smashed to bits in front of him. He looked up and there on a low wall stood Helstrom like a clown without makeup. He, too, had missed.

Joshua grabbed him by both legs and jerked him down against the bricks of the patio floor. He hit and his head bounced. Joshua gripped him by the neck and the side of one leg and tossed him over and beyond the wall.

He turned slowly around, his eyes covering all the crowd. No one moved. Not at all. He walked back through them to the house and in a few moments returned. He carried a huge silver candelabra, from the first Spanish days, with twenty lighted candles. He walked with it held high. None moved except to get out of his way. Alfredo sat on the edge of the empty pool. His feet dangled down into its empty space. He tilted his head the way only he could do and softly, so very softly, strummed an old Spanish love song—a song older than the hacienda. Joshua walked to the steps of the pool and with absolute certainty of purpose stepped carefully down into it. It seemed a long time, but it was not. He placed the candelabra in the deepest part of the pool, stepped back, and looked into the flames. Then he raised his head and stared upwards at all the faces that now circled the pool to stare down at him. He turned in a complete circle so that he looked into the soft reflections in each of their eyes. He saw all things in that small turn. None of them knew what *they* were seeing. He walked back up the steps and there stood Rob.

Joshua said, "Come now, Rob, and I'll tell you what you really want to know."

Alfredo went on singing in Spanish as if he was making quiet love. The circle still looked downwards at the glowing candles.

Near the largest expanse of wall on the whole of the hacienda, Joshua said quietly to Rob, "I killed her. I took her into the desert and killed sweet Aleta."

Rob was momentarily paralyzed. Then a terrible cry and sound of murder burst from him as he ripped the edge of his pocket pulling out the gun. He fired right into the chest of Joshua, knocking him against the wall. He pulled at the trigger until there was nothing left. Joshua stayed upright for a moment, full of holes, and then fell forward, rolling over face up. The crowd from the pool moved towards Rob, hesitantly, fearfully. They made a half circle around the body.

Rob spoke, not looking away from Joshua's dead, smiling face as if afraid he'd rise up again, "He killed Aleta."

Grebbs, saying things unintelligible like a slavering idiot, pushed his way through the mass, stopping with his face above Joshua's. Then he vented a little stuttering laugh. It broke forth louder and louder, and haltingly the others were caught up with him. They laughed and cried at the same time, not knowing really which they were doing. None thought to look at the wall above the body. It didn't matter, though, for all those who might have seen were already there. On a thin-edged hill stood Charlotte the dedicated, Aleta the beloved, Chalo the companion, and old Juanita the faithful. They were in a row, smiling with contentment. Just below them the lady in black lace walked forward to meet Joshua.

As he moved into the wall there came from his throat another form of laughter that far, far transcended the hysterical cackling in the patio. He glanced back just once and the song overcame his mirth. He took her into his arms and held her. They had waited so very long. It was over. They walked, holding hands, up the hill to join those he loved, and they all disappeared into a new world.

The wall turned back to dirt.

None could stay at the hacienda that night. Just before the sun announced the dawn, the last candle in the bottom of the pool flickered out. The light was gone.

Suggested Further Reading

As a matter of convenience, I have included a brief, annotated guide to a few of the principal reference books that have recently appeared and are in print at the time of writing. The interested reader may wish to consult them for further biographical and bibliographical information about authors of Western fiction. Although recommendations for books by the authors included in this anthology can be found in the prefaces to the stories, a number of authors are not represented and recommendations for novels by some of these follow. I have tried to confine myself to only one book per author and only in a few cases have I had to abuse this self-imposed limitation. Since a number of these books have been in and out of print several times, the publication information is that of first publisher and first year of publication.

General

Dobie, J. Frank. *Guide to Life and Literature of the Southwest* (Southern Methodist University Press, 1952).

This is the oldest of the books listed. Fortunately, it is still in print. Less fortunately, many of the books cited in its pages are now out of print and difficult to find. Dobie's book, however, remains an instructive source about numerous authors of Western fiction whose focus was the Southwest.

Tuska, Jon, and Vicki Piekarski (eds.). *Encyclopedia of Frontier and Western Fiction* (McGraw-Hill, 1983).

Consisting of several hundred entries for the principal authors of frontier fiction both in the last century and this, our one-volume encyclopedia also lists in chronological order all the books written by each author according to their American titles, including motion-picture adaptations (where such existed) and a guide to any criticism that has appeared in book form about an entry's work.

Tuska, Jon, and Vicki Piekarski (eds.). *The Frontier Experience: A Reader's Guide to the Life and Literature of the American West* (McFarland and Company, 1984).

We were originally inspired to do this book by Dobie's monumental effort. Our subject area, however, was broader than his had been. There is a major section devoted to the history and growth of Western fiction and an annotated critical listing of most of the books devoted to literary criticism of Western fiction.

Vinson, James (ed.). *Twentieth-Century Western Writers* (Macmillan Publishers, 1982).

Although a number of Americans served as advisers and contributors to this book, the bibliographies for the entries often contain references only to novels under their British titles without mention of alternative American titles. However, the bibliographies are rather more complete than in our *Encyclopedia,* with reference where possible to all short stories, verse, and nonfiction by the various authors.

Western Fiction

1. FORMULARY WESTERNS

Adams, Clifton. *The Last Days of Wolf Garnett* (Doubleday, 1970).
Ahlswede, Ann. *Hunting Wolf* (Ballantine, 1960).
Arthur, Burt and Budd. *The Stranger* (Avon, 1966).
Athanas, Verne. *Maverick* (Dell, 1956).
Ballard, Todhunter. *Plunder Canyon* (Avon, 1967).
Bonham, Frank. *Lost Stage Valley* (Simon and Schuster, 1948).
———. *Last Stage West* (Dell, 1959).
Bower, B. M. *Chip of the Flying U* (Dillingham, 1906).
———. *Lonesome Land* (Little, Brown, 1912).
———. *The Whoop-Up Trail* (Little, Brown, 1933).
Cook, Will. *The Drifter* (Bantam, 1969).
———. *Bandit's Trail* (Doubleday, 1974.
Coolidge, Dane. *Gun-Smoke* (Dutton, 1928).
———. *The Fighting Danites* (Dutton, 1934).
Cunningham, Eugene. *Texas Triggers* (Houghton Mifflin, 1938).
———. *Riding Gun* (Houghton Mifflin, 1956).
Curwood, James Oliver. *Steele of the Royal Mounted* (Cosmopolitan, 1911).
Daniels, John S. (pseud. Wayne D. Overholser). *Smoke of the Gun* (Signet, 1958).
Dawson, Peter (pseud. Jonathan Glidden). *The Stagline Feud* (Dodd, Mead, 1942).

———. *Trail Boss* (Dodd, Mead, 1943).
Elston, Allan Vaughan. *Roundup on the Picketwire* (Lippincott, 1952).
Ermine, Will (pseud. Harry Sinclair Drago). *Rider of the Midnight Range* (Morrow, 1940).
Evarts, Hal, Sr. *Tumbleweeds* (Little, Brown, 1923).
Flynn, T. T. *The Man from Laramie* ((Dell, 1954).
———. *Riding High* (Dell, 1961).
Foreman, L. L. *The Road to San Jacinto* (Dutton, 1943).
Foster, Bennett. *Seven Slash Range* (Morrow, 1936).
Fox, Norman A. *Night Passage* (Dodd, Mead, 1956).
———. *Reckoning at Rimbow* (Dodd, Mead, 1958).
Gregory, Jackson. *Guardians of the Trail* (Dodd, Mead, 1941).
Gruber, Frank. *Fort Starvation* (Rinehart, 1953).
Halleran, E. E. *Double Cross Trail* (Macrae-Smith, 1946).
Hamilton, Donald. *The Big Country* (Dell, 1954).
Holmes, L. P. *Water, Grass, and Gunsmoke* (Doubleday, 1949).
Ketchum, Philip. *Gun Code* (Signet, 1959).
Leonard, Elmore. *The Law at Randado* (Houghton Mifflin, 1954).
———. *Hombre* (Ballantine, 1961).
Lomax, Bliss (pseud. Harry Sinclair Drago). *The Leatherburners* (Doubleday, 1939).
Lutz, Giles A. *The Honyocker* (Doubleday, 1961).
McCarthy, Gary. *The Derby Man* (Doubleday, 1976).
MacDonald, William Colt. *The Mad Marshal* (Pyramid Books, 1958).
Mann, E. B. *The Valley of Wanted Men* (Morrow, 1932).
Newton, Dwight Bennett (first published under the name Dwight Bennett). *The Big Land* (Doubleday, 1972).
Nye, Nelson C. *Riders by Night* (Dodd, Mead, 1950).
Ogden, George Washington. *The Guard of the Timberline* (Dodd, Mead, 1934).
Olsen, Theodore V. *Bitter Grass* (Doubleday, 1967).
O'Rourke, Frank. *The Last Chance* (Dell, 1956).
Overholser, Wayne D. *Tough Hand* (Macmillan, 1954).
Patten, Lewis B. *Death of a Gunfighter* (Doubleday, 1968).
Raine, William MacLeod. *Ridgway of Montana* (Dillingham, 1909).
———. *The Big-Town Round-Up* (Houghton Mifflin, 1920).
Roderus, Frank. *Journey to Utah* (Doubleday, 1976).
Savage, Les, Jr. *Return to Warbow* (Dell, 1955).
Schaefer, Jack. *Shane* (Houghton Mifflin, 1949).
Seltzer, Charles Alden. *The Boss of the Lazy Y* (A. C. McClurg, 1915).
Shirreffs, Gordon D. *The Border Guidon* (Signet, 1963).
Stuart, Matt (pseudo. L. P. Holmes) *Dusty Wagons* (Lippincott, 1949).
Thompson, Thomas. *Brand of a Man* (Doubleday, 1958).
Tuttle, W. C. *Thicker Than Water* (Houghton Mifflin, 1927).

2. ROMANTIC HISTORICAL RECONSTRUCTIONS

Adams, Andy. *The Log of a Cowboy* (Houghton Mifflin, 1903).
Arnold, Elliott. *Blood Brother* (Duell, Sloan, 1947).
Barry, Jane. *A Time in the Sun* (Doubleday, 1962).
Beach, Rex. *The Spoilers* (Harper's, 1905).
Berger, Thomas. *Little Big Man* (Dial, 1964).
Bristow, Gwen. *Jubilee Trail* (Crowell, 1950).
Brown, Dee. *Creek Mary's Blood* (Holt, Rinehart, and Winston, 1980).
Burnett, W. R. *Saint Johnson* (Dial, 1930).
Burroughs, Edgar Rice. *The War Chief* (A. C. McClurg, 1927).
Carter, Forrest. *The Vengeance Trail of Josey Wales* (Delacorte, 1976).
Cook, Will. *Comanche Captives* (Bantam, 1960).
Coolidge, Dane. *Wun-Post* (Dutton, 1920).
Cooper, James Fenimore. *The Last of the Mohicans* (1826).
Davis, H. L. *Honey in the Horn* (Harper's, 1935).
———. *Winds of Morning* (Morrow, 1952).
Everett, Wade (pseud. Will Cook). *Fort Starke* (Ballantine, 1959).
Ferber, Edna. *Cimarron* (Doubleday, 1930).
Fergusson, Harvey. *Wolf Song* (Knopf, 1927).
———. *The Conquest of Don Pedro* (Morrow, 1954).
Fisher, Vardis. *Mountain Man* (Morrow, 1965).
Garfield, Brian. *Bugle & Spur* (Ballantine, 1966).
Giles, Janice Holt. *The Plum Thicket* (Houghton Mifflin, 1954).
Gulick, Bill. *Treasure in Hell's Canyon* (Doubleday, 1979).
Henry, O. (pseud. William Sydney Porter) *Heart of the West* (Doubleday, 1904).
Hillerman, Tony. *The Blessing Way* (Harper's, 1970).
Horgan, Paul. *A Distant Trumpet* (Farrar, Straus, 1960).
Hough, Emerson. *The Covered Wagon* (Appleton, 1922).
James, Will (pseudo. Joseph Ernest Nephtali Dufault). *The Lone Cowboy* (Scribner's, 1930) [a fictional autobiography].
King, General Charles. *Two Soldiers* and *Dunraven Ranch* (Lippincott, 1900) [short novels published together].
Knibbs, Henry Herbert. *The Ridin' Kid from Powder River* (Houghton Mifflin, 1919).
LaFarge, Oliver. *All the Young Men* (Houghton Mifflin, 1935).
Lea, Tom. *The Wonderful Country* (Little, Brown, 1952).
LeMay, Alan. *The Unforgiven* (Harper's, 1957).
McMurtry, Larry. *Horseman, Pass By* (Harper's, 1961).
Pattullo, George. *The Untamed* (Fitzgerald, 1911).
Phillips, Henry Wallace. *Red Saunders* (McClure's, 1902).
Richter, Conrad. *The Sea of Grass* (Knopf, 1937).
Schaefer, Jack. *The Canyon* (Houghton Mifflin, 1953).
———. *Monte Walsh* (Houghton Mifflin, 1963).

Sorenson, Virginia. *The Proper Gods* (Harcourt, Brace, 1951).
Stegner, Wallace. *The Big Rock Candy Mountain* (Duell, Sloan, 1943).
Steinbeck, John. *The Grapes of Wrath* (Covici, Friede, 1939).
West, Jessamyn. *The Friendly Persuasion* (Harcourt, Brace, 1945).
White, Stewart Edward. *Arizona Nights* (McClure's, 1907).

3. HISTORICAL RECONSTRUCTIONS

Abbey, Edward. *Fire on the Mountain* (Dial, 1962).
Ahlswede, Ann. *The Savage Land* (Ballantine, 1962).
Berry, Don. *Trask* (Viking, 1960).
Braun, Matthew. *Black Fox* (Fawcett, 1972).
Comfort, Will Levington. *Apache* (Dutton, 1931).
Easton, Robert. *The Happy Man* (Viking, 1943).
Fisher, Vardis. *Children of God: An American Epic* (Harper's, 1939).
———. *City of Illusion* (Harper's, 1941).
Garland, Hamlin. *Main-Travelled Roads* (1891).
Guthrie, A. B. Jr. *The Big Sky* (Sloane, 1947).
———. *The Way West* (Sloane, 1949).
Hoffman, Lee. *The Valdez Horses* (Doubleday, 1967).
Kesey, Ken. *One Flew over the Cuckoo's Nest* (Viking, 1962).
LaFarge, Oliver. *The Enemy Gods* (Houghton Mifflin, 1937).
McNickle, D'Arcy. *The Surrounded* (Dodd, Mead, 1936).
———. *Wind from an Enemy Sky* (Harper's, 1978).
Manfred, Frederick. *Conquering Horse* (McDowell-Obolensky, 1959).
———. *Riders of Judgment* (Random House, 1957).
Mathews, John Joseph. *Sundown* (University of Oklahoma Press, 1934).
Momaday, N. Scott. *House Made of Dawn* (Harper's, 1968).
Richter, Conrad. *The Lady* (Knopf, 1957).
Rölvaag, O. E. *Giants in the Earth* (Harper's, 1927).
Sandoz, Mari. *Miss Morissa: Doctor of the Gold Trail* (McGraw-Hill, 1955).
Scarborough, Dorothy. *The Wind* (Harper's, 1925).
Silko, Leslie. *Ceremony* (Viking, 1977).
Waters, Frank. *The Man Who Killed the Deer* (Farrar and Rinehart, 1942).
———. *Pike's Peak: A Family Saga* (Swallow, 1974).